THE EUROPEAN COUNCIL

The European Council

by

Jan Werts

JOHN HARPER PUBLISHING

The European Council

Published by John Harper Publishing
27 Palace Gates Road
London N22 7BW, United Kingdom.

www.johnharperpublishing.co.uk

ISBN 978-0-9556202-1-8

© John Harper Publishing 2008

Printed and Bound in Great Britain by Cromwell Press Ltd.

Dedicated to Professor Dr Jan Rood, Director of European Studies at the 'Clingendael' Netherlands Institute of International Relations, who initiated this book and supported the project with his excellent advice.

TABLE OF CONTENTS

Annexes

List of boxes

Acknowledgements

The author is indebted to many people. I found inspiration and a lot of information by way of a series of extensive interviews. A list of those persons is given on page xiv. I would like to take this opportunity to thank them for their cooperation in sharing their expertise and insights. Important for me also was the advice and the encouragement of my thoughtful publisher John Harper whom I met thanks to Martin Westlake.

As an author with Dutch as his mother tongue, I enjoyed the indispensable, highly qualified, unremitting and careful help and advice of my colleague and friend the journalist Willem Kootstra in Madrid, and of the lawyer Mary Macken in Dublin and the jurist-linguist Giles Swannell of the Council of the EU in Brussels.

This study is based on exhaustive research of literature and archives with tedious work in ploughing through mountains of documents, reports and publications. I am enormously grateful for the excellent collaboration and continuous assistance provided by the officials of the Library of the European Commission in Brussels. My appreciation goes to the many members of staff, in particular Margreet Doorlag, Catherine Benoît and Stephanie Bevilacqua who assisted me in my research, as also to Riitta Tingander, Head Librarian at the Council of the EU.

The day in 1975 on which I was appointed as European Affairs Correspondent for *Haagsche Courant - Sythoff Press*, was a major event in my life. I thank the General Editor in Chief and later Publisher of this group of newspapers, Hans A.M. Hoefnagels, for the trust he put in me. I am also grateful to Professor Bart De Schutter and Professor Marc Maresceau who encouraged me in 1982 to write my doctoral dissertation on the European Council and to Professor Tony Joris and Professor Bernard Schloh for their excellent advice.

Finally I would like to emphasise that the writing of this book has given me a great deal of intellectual satisfaction. The achievement of such a large project as a purely private activity, absorbing a good part of my thinking and writing for over four years, in combination with a burdensome job as foreign correspondent would have been absolutely impossible without the support of Margriet M.C. Berkulin and our daughters Godelieve and Denise. My most heartfelt appreciation, for having (again!) patiently endured the whole process of this project, goes therefore to them.

Jan Werts

Brussels, January 2008

Foreword

Last year we celebrated the 50th anniversary of European integration, five decades in which peace has gone hand in hand with increasing prosperity and economic progress, and in which the divisions between North and South and East and West have largely disappeared. The Treaty of Lisbon, signed by the members of the European Council on 13 December 2007, constitutes a further advance in the ongoing process of European integration, for it ensures that the voice of Europe's citizens will be heard more clearly and that the Union's institutions will function more effectively.

Anyone interested in learning more about how Europe functions should read Jan Werts' fascinating book on the European Council. It is now impossible to imagine European cooperation, in all its complexity, without the involvement of the European Council. Twenty years ago, however, things were very different. Werts addresses a number of highly relevant questions with great clarity. Who is in charge in Europe? What powers do the various institutions have, and how are they divided? Now that the European Council has reached maturity, what are the consequences for the institutional balance of the European Union?

An EU journalist par excellence, no-one is better qualified to write on this subject than Werts. No-one else has been as close to quite so many European Council meetings. The questions he poses, and the articles he writes, are testimony to his special understanding of the subject, and are all the more impressive given the necessarily closed character of the European Council summits. Many outsiders are tempted to focus on atmospherics, rumours or irrelevant comments, instead of on policy for Europe and the influential conclusions of the European Council. Jan Werts has chosen his own course. His sharp intellect, as keen now as when he began his career, ensures that his focus is always on the issues of substance, often with remarkable results.

This book is a completely revised and updated edition of Werts' 1992 *summa cum laude* dissertation. It was consulted regularly at the Binnenhof in The Hague, the political heart of the Netherlands, in preparation for European Council meetings, parliamentary debates and speeches. This new edition will undoubtedly stimulate new discussion, not only among academics but also among anyone involved with the European Union and the European Council on a daily basis.

Dr Jan Peter Balkenende,
Prime Minister of the Kingdom of the Netherlands

List of Interviewees

1. Jan Willem Beaujean, Press Councillor, Netherlands Permanent Representation to the EU.
2. Professor Dr Sven Biscop, the Royal Institute for International Relations Brussels.
3. Frans Boogaard, European Correspondent, *Algemeen Dagblad* (Rotterdam).
4. Dr Bernard R. Bot, Minister for Foreign Affairs of the Netherlands.
5. Hans Brunmayr, Director General, Chef Protocol, Council of the EU.
6. Catherine Day, Secretary General of the European Commission.
7. Ambassador Tom J.A.M. de Bruijn, Permanent Representative of the Netherlands at the EU.
8. Professor Dr Jaap de Zwaan, Director of the Netherlands Institute of International Relations 'Clingendael'.
9. Frederic Eggermont, Faculty of Law, VUB Brussels, preparing a PhD. on 'the changing role of the European Council in the institutional framework of the EU'.
10. Dr Alexander Italianer, Deputy Secretary General of the European Commission.
11. Professor Dr Jean Paul Jacqué, Director of the Legal Service of the Council of the EU.
12. Jean-Claude Juncker, Prime Minister of Luxembourg.
13. Tony Joris, Jean Monnet professor, Director of the Centre for European Law, Faculty of Law, Vrije Universiteit Brussels.
14. Marc Jorna, Councillor Legal and Institutional Affairs, Netherlands Permanent Representation to the EU.
15. Jacques Keller-Noëllet, Deputy Director-General Council of the EU, with particular responsibility for European Council meetings.
16. Frits Kemperman, Press Councillor, Netherlands Permanent Representation to the EU.
17. Johannes Laitenberger, Head of the Spokesperson's Service of the European Commission.
18. Dominique-Georges Marro, Head of the Press Office, Council of the EU.
19. Atzo Nicolaï, Minister of European Affairs of the Netherlands.
20. Dr Leo Tindemans, former Prime Minister of Belgium.
21. René van der Linden, member of the European Convention - President of the Assembly of the Council of Europe.
22. Jan Versteeg, Advisor for European Affairs of the Prime Minister, The Hague.

List of Abbreviations

AE	Agence Europe Bulletin
AFSJ	Area of Freedom, Security and Justice
ALDE	Alliance of Liberals and Democrats for Europe
BEPGs	Broad Economic Policy Guidelines
Bull	Originally Bulletin of the EEC, from 1968-1993 of the European Community, since 1994 of the European Union
CAP	Common Agricultural Policy of the EU
CDE	Cahiers de Droit Européen
CEPS	Centre for European Policy Studies, Brussels
CFP	Common Fisheries Policy
CFSP	Common Foreign and Security Policy
CMLRev	Common Market Law Review
Coreper	The Permanent Representatives' Committee (CPR or Coreper in the French abbreviation): the body for preparing and co-ordinating the Council decisions
CRP	Council's Rules of Procedure
EAEC	European Atomic Energy Community
EC	European Community
ECB	European Central Bank
ECHR	European Convention on Human Rights
ECJ	European Court of Justice
ECLR	European Constitutional Law Review
EcoFin	Regular meeting of the Ministers of Finance (and sometimes Economic Affairs) with an important role regarding EMU
ECSC	European Coal and Steel Community
ECU/ecu	European Currency Unit, forerunner of the euro
ELR	European Law Review
EMU	Economic and Monetary Union
EP or PE	European Parliament
EPC (1)	European Political Cooperation, the forerunner of the CFSP
EPC (2)	European Policy Centre, think tank, Brussels
EPP	Group of the European People's Party
EPP/ED	European People's Party - European (Conservative) Democrats
ESCB	The national central banks of the European System of Central Banks (ESCB)
ESDP	European Security and Defence Policy
FD	Het Financieele Dagblad
GAC	General Affairs Council
GAERC	General Affairs and External Relations Council
General Report or Gen Rep	General (Yearly) Report on the Activities of the European Union
HSG Council	Council of the EU in the composition of the Heads of State or Government

IGC	Inter Governmental Conference of the representatives of the Member States
IHT	The International Herald Tribune
JCMS	Journal of Common Market Studies
JHA	Justice and Home Affairs
LGDJ	Librairie Général de Droit et de Jurisprudence
MEP	Member of European Parliament
OJ	Official Journal of the European Union
Off. Off. Publ.	Office for Official Publications of the European Communities
PES	Group of the Party of European Socialists
PM	Prime Minister
Presidency	Presidency of the Council of Ministers of the EU
PR/EU	Permanent Representation of a Member State at the EU
PSC	Political and Security Committee
Rebate	Repayment made to compensate the UK for its high net contribution to the Union
QMV	Qualified Majority Voting in the Council of Ministers on the basis of Article 205 TEC
RMC	Revue du Marché Commun
SG/HR	Secretary General of the Council of Ministers/High Representative for the Common Foreign and Security Policy (CFSP) of the Union
TENs	Trans-European (transport) Networks
TFEU	Treaty on the Functioning of the EU
The Six	The founding members of the EC (France, FRG/Germany, Italy, Belgium, the Netherlands, Luxembourg)
TEC	Treaty Establishing the European Community
TEU	Treaty on European Union

Note on Sources

- Save as otherwise indicated, reference to the *General Report* and the *Bulletin of the European Union* is always made to the numbered points, not to the pages.

- All page numbers referring to sources are marked with a 'p'. For all references to a paragraph however only the number is given without further specification.

- For the *Bulletin* the English edition is used from 1973. For earlier years the French or the Dutch edition is used and reference is in that case made to the page numbers.

Introduction

After half a century of European integration, a big question remains unanswered: who leads the European Union? At the heart of this question stands the role of the European Council in determining both the broad strategy and (often) the detailed policy of the Union. Is it the case that the larger Member States prevail in the European Council, as is commonly presumed by the governments of the smaller Member States? How does the European Council operate in practice? How does it exert its authority in respect of the formal EU institutions and how do they respond to and implement its wishes? What have been its greatest successes and biggest failures – and has its strategic leadership overall been a positive factor in the development of the Union? The European Council has come to symbolise the European Union. Therefore its study is an essential part of any attempt to understand the direction in which Europe has been travelling.

This book is a product of my incessant fascination with European integration since 1967. In that year I arrived in Brussels for the first interviews. Since the 1970s I have followed EU developments in the Brussels Schumann conference centres on a daily basis as a European affairs media correspondent. It can be difficult to grasp what precisely happens behind the scenes of the European Council and what its political significance may be in legal and political science terms given the closed character of the meetings. As a consequence, every meeting attracts a great deal of attention from the media but researchers take far less notice. That is why I consider myself lucky to have covered as a reporter the majority of the some 130 meetings since 1974. In 1991 my work resulted in the first legal Ph.D. thesis ever devoted to this issue. It was published in 1992 by the T.M.C. Asser Institute - Elsevier Science Publishers as 'The European Council'.

That early publication has now been completely revised, rewritten and updated right up to the beginning of 2008 to produce the present volume. The research on which it is based includes (a) my close personal observation of the course of the European Council over a period of 35 years; (b) my doctoral dissertation; (c) countless press conferences over the years given by the Heads of State or Government as members of the European Council and by other participants in these meetings; (d) an extensive documentary analysis which includes the literature cited in the Bibliography; (e) interviews with participants in the European Council and officials from the EU institutions.

In this volume I seek to explore the basic questions behind the European Council. Firstly I try to outline the unstoppable march of the European Council to become the Union's supreme political organ. Secondly, I analyse the background of this important development. In addition I describe how the European Council worked its way into the Union's decision-making process. An important question is to what extent the European Council undermines the power balance in the European Union: the position of the European Commission, the European Parliament and the Council of Ministers. To the extent it does so, what are the consequences for the Community Method? Another important issue is how the European Council will function in an enlarged Union in the future with more than 27 Heads of Government. Underpinning all is the basic question 'Who leads the European Union?'

Jan Werts

Brussels, January 2008

The European Council meeting in Rome in 1975.

Photo courtesy of the Council of the European Union

A contemporary meeting of the European Council, in Brussels.

Photo courtesy of the Council of the European Union

1   The origins of the European Council

Introduction

The brave demand 'I want my money back' by British Prime Minister Margaret Thatcher in Dublin in 1979 is etched in my memory; next to the 'tummy ache Summit' of 1981 in Maastricht, from which many returned sick because the buffet was contaminated with salmonella; the sultry sleepless night in June 1985 in Milan where Italian Prime Minister Bettino Craxi challenged Thatcher; the unimportant meeting on Rhodes (1988) where Greek Prime Minister Andreas Papandreou brazenly introduced his latest flame, the former stewardess Dimitri Leani, who was scantily dressed in yellow; the thick layer of snow through which I shuffled on my way to the Vienna Winter Summit in 1998; the darkness in Helsinki one year later where the Heads of Government 'wrapped up' the Twentieth Century with a joint declaration; the gorgeous first Spring of this century in Lisbon and the sweltering heat (40°C+) some months later in Seville; the stormy weekend in Biarritz which preceded the exhausting record-length December 2000 meeting which resulted in the Treaty of Nice. What exactly does this continuous 'Summitry' mean to us in Europe?

This chapter is based on the thesis that intergovernmental Summit conferences played an important role in the European Community, not only from the creation of the European Council in 1974, but also from the start of the EEC and Euratom in 1957. The chapter seeks to examine the factors which led to the emergence of the European Council in 1974.1 It is moreover assumed that the legal structure of the Community is strongly determined by its historical context. For this reason, the chapter sketches the historical context in terms both of the phenomenon of Summit meetings and of the birth of the European Council. The creation of a European Council is here seen as the result of a series of changes in the domestic, international and economic environment of the European Community in the early 1970s. In addition, there were political and institutional developments which led to the creation of the European Council. In this chapter I attempt to trace, describe and evaluate the different aspects of these changes and developments.

I will seek to show that from the beginning of the integration process there was a need for a body which, within a framework of relations with the Union's Institutions, would be capable of taking and implementing crucial political decisions. After the achievement of the Customs Union in 1968, the phenomenon of the European Council, as described here, became a necessity due to *a series of events*.

Box 1

A confusing terminology

For readers not versed in this matter, we should explain the confusing terminology:
–   European Council,
–   HSG Council,
–   Council of the European Union (widely referred to as the Council of Ministers or simply as Council),
–   Council of Europe.

   The European Council is composed of the Heads of State or Government of the Member States and the President of the Commission of the European Union, being the Union's supreme political authority and meeting mostly in Brussels. The **HSG Council** is the Council (of Ministers) in the composition of the Heads of State or Government, so without the President of the Commission. This book employs the term European Council except were the specificity of the reference legally needs to be the HSG Council. The **Council of the European Union (Council of Ministers)** is the Institution of the European Union composed of the Ministers of the Member States. Council meetings are held weekly in Brussels or Luxembourg. The **Council of Europe** is an entirely separate body from the EU; it is based in Strasbourg, has as its members all the States of Europe, including the Russian Federation, and is particularly active in the fields of human rights and culture.

A.   TOWARDS THE FIRST MEETINGS OF THE HEADS OF STATE OR GOVERMENT

A.1.   The roots of the European Council

   The European Council had its origins some fifty years ago, although it was only officially launched in 1974. It was in 1953 that the French Gaullist Michel Debré, in the Constitutional Commission of the Assembly of the European Coal and Steel Community (ECSC), unsuccessfully proposed the idea of a purely intergovernmental Political Union, with a Conference of the Heads of State or Government. The French never abandoned this idea. At their initiative the leaders of the Member States of the European Economic Community (EEC) and Euratom met from 1957, whenever the need arose.

By 1974 they had clocked up eight Summit meetings, all initiated by the French and moreover all provoked by a crisis in the EEC.

In January 1953, the Assembly of the ECSC discussed a report from its Constitutional Commission. It rejected a draft resolution from Michel Debré, proposing a 'Pact for the Union of European States'. Debré followed the approach of the future French President, General Charles de Gaulle, who from the beginning in 1950 had condemned the Schuman Plan in all its aspects. Six years later, in 1959, new French Prime Minister Michel Debré declared it to be France's policy to have regular consultations among Heads of State or Government of the Member States, outside the framework of the Community.[2]

In the meantime an interesting report was presented in March 1953 by the Working Committee of the Ad Hoc Assembly (the forerunner of the European Parliament). It had been requested by the Ministers for Foreign Affairs of the six Member States and it was intergovernmental in character. It proposed a Council of Ministers composed of the Heads of State or Government, the Ministers for Foreign Affairs or other members of national governments. Furthermore the Committee proposed a reduction of the powers of the European Executive in favour of the Council of Ministers. The phenomenon of intergovernmental cooperation, eliminating the original supranational character of the European treaties, was later to reappear time and again. France's political leaders were not the only ones who preferred a Council composed of the Heads of State or Government at the apex of the institutional framework. Later in this chapter it will become evident that other leading politicians in Western Europe also had this formula in mind as long ago as the early 1950s. In other words, the creation of a European Council of Heads of State or Government was an idea which existed from the start of the European integration process.

In 1956 and 1957 long preparatory talks had taken place in Brussels between the Ministers for Foreign Affairs of 'the Six', focusing on the drafting of treaties establishing a European Economic Community (EEC) and a European Atomic Energy Community (Euratom or EAEC). Already in that early stage of European integration, the Heads of Government were occasionally consulted (Dinan, p. 72-76). Between 18 and 20 February 1957, Heads of Government of the Six and their Ministers for Foreign Affairs met in Paris. It was their first meeting within the European Community in *statu nascendi*.

A.2.   The Summits of the 1960s

The five Summit meetings held in the 1960s – 1961 Paris (twice) and Bonn, 1967 Rome and 1969 The Hague – were part of a general effort towards institutionalised political cooperation which had not been provided for in the Treaties of Rome. It was hoped that foundations would be laid for 'a Union' based upon a Common Market and also upon political cooperation. The initiative for these meetings lay with France and, to a smaller extent, with the Federal Republic of Germany (FRG) (European Parliament, Battista). After his emergence as the political leader of the French Republic, de Gaulle's priority became the achievement of a position whereby the inde-

pendence of France within the Community would be assured. His Prime
Minister, Debré (1959-1962), as remarked earlier, perceived the fight against
the Community's supranationality as one of his most important tasks. Soon
Debré's ideas again became a topic for discussion. The President attached
credence to intergovernmental cooperation and insisted that the EEC should
accept moreover French protectionist traditions. France wanted a Political
Union based on intergovernmental cooperation, with a Conference of the
Heads of State or Government that should determine the course of action of
the 'Union'. The French never abandoned that idea. The incubation period
of the phenomenon of Summits started with this direction in French foreign
policy. At a press conference on 5 September 1960 the President stated that
the foundations of Europe would only be built upon the Member States
acting jointly. He stressed the need 'to proceed, not on the basis of dreams,
but in accordance with reality' (De Gaulle, p. 5-6 and p. 169-171). Brushing
aside the roles of the High Authority of the European Coal and Steel
Community and of the European Commission, de Gaulle said that they
'have their technical value but do not, and cannot, exert authority or effective political influence'. De Gaulle was anxious to avoid a situation in which
foreign technocrats (the Commission) and European parliamentarians were
empowered to take decisions in the name of the French people. He believed
that only the Member States could take binding decisions.

The Paris Summit of 10-11 February 1961, held at the invitation of
President de Gaulle, focused on how to organise closer cooperation which
would lead in the future to a Union based upon a confederation which
would develop progressively. It instructed a Committee of Representatives
of the six governments to submit 'concrete proposals' for future meetings of
Heads of State or Government and the Ministers for Foreign Affairs (*Bull* 3-
1961, p. 13-23). On 9 February 1961, the day before the Summit in Paris, de
Gaulle and Adenauer at their own 'mini-summit' had already decided to
hold another Summit meeting of the Six later in the year. Owing to this
Franco-German collaboration it proved very difficult to organise opposition
to the holding of Summit meetings and the introduction of political cooperation outside the strict Community framework (Jansen, p. 53-54).

The Paris Summit brought about a remarkable result: its work went
beyond the framework of the European Community, so returning to the
intergovernmental approach. In 1952-1953 the Member States had referred
the task of submitting a draft for a European Political Community to the
European Consultative Assembly. This draft received no follow up. But
now this task, a decisive one for the future of European construction, went
to the national governmental elite: the Heads of State or Government. This
change marked an important departure. The Community Method of supranational decision-making (see Box 2) had been to a degree replaced by more
traditional methods of collective bargaining, in accordance with the ideas of
the Gaullists (Alting von Geusau, p. 24). During the Summer of 1961, influential representatives of Germany and France recommended that regular
meetings of the Heads of State or Government be held. The prominent
Gaullist Alain Peyrefitte stated at that time that they should – in line with
the old proposal of Michel Debré – meet regularly, to formulate European
policy. They would decide upon technical and economic measures of integration. Furthermore, they would consult on foreign and defence policies.

It was, in short, a perfect foreshadowing of the European Council which emerged 14 years later (Peyrefitte).

The second Summit of 1961, on 18 July in Bonn, took place in a critical international climate. Once more there was the growing threat of the Soviet Union against Berlin. It was only under that threat, in the interest of internal western cohesion, that the Dutch Government agreed to participate. The Dutch delegation felt unable to agree to a series of proposals made by the Fouchet Committee. Named after its chairman, the French ambassador to Denmark Christian Fouchet, the Committee had suggested that the Heads of State or Government should meet about once every four months and that no restriction should be placed on the subjects discussed. The Dutch and also the Belgians were however of the opinion that those issues of international policy which in principle came under the jurisdiction of NATO, should be excluded from the consultations (*Bull* 7/8-1961, p. 35-39; De Gaulle, p. 196-197).

Box 2

The Community Method: centrepiece of decision-making

The Community Method characterises the original system of decision-making in the EU. It is based on an initiative of the European Commission, followed by a decision on the basis of a qualified majority vote (QMV) in accordance with Article 205 TEC, or on the basis of unanimity in the Council of Ministers, representing the Member States. The European Parliament acts as co-legislator or is at least consulted. An important element is the interplay between the autonomous Institutions: the Commission, the Parliament and the Council. According to the critics the emergence of the European Council has over time changed the Community Method. The increased involvement of the regular meetings of the Heads of State or Government which decide on specific matters damages in their eyes the quality of the interplay in the so-called 'institutional triangle' of the Commission, the Parliament and the Council of Ministers. (Regarding the crucial importance of the Community Method, see also Rood, in Michalsky, (ed.), p. 71-84.)

A compromise was eventually reached. Chancellor Konrad Adenauer, backing President de Gaulle, played the role of mediator between the French and the opposing Italians and Benelux countries. It was decided to hold meetings at regular intervals, the aim of which would be to compare views, to develop joint policies and to reach common positions 'in order to further the political union of Europe, thereby strengthening the Alliance'. After the meeting in Bonn, the creation of a 'European Council' became a regular point for discussion. Although the Dutch here blocked the creation of a Political Secretariat, the European Council was from now on in *statu nascendi*.[3]

A.3.   The Fouchet Plan

By means of the Fouchet Plan President de Gaulle tried, after the Summits of 1961, to secure a leading role for his country within a European political framework. On 2 November 1961 the Fouchet Committee received a purely French 'Draft Treaty for the establishment of a political Union'. It was unilaterally and without previous consultation submitted by chairman Fouchet, an old ally of the President. Fouchet proposed an intergovernmental political 'Union of States'. This was not in line with the more supranational approach, the 'Union of Peoples', which emerged from Bonn, which the five other partners felt to be possible, particularly through the direct election of the European Parliament. Further, Fouchet proposed a Council with unlimited powers including over economic and defence matters, consisting of two levels. It would be formed by the Heads of State or Government, meeting every four months, and by the Ministers for Foreign Affairs, meeting at least once in the intervening period. No representation by the Commission was foreseen by Fouchet. Thus President de Gaulle, through this draft, revived the ideas he had earlier unsuccessfully proposed. Decisions in the Council were to be taken unanimously, so national sovereignty would be safeguarded. Moreover, Member States which did not take part in the decisive meeting (for instance because they did not agree with a proposal) were not to be bound.

In an abruptly presented second French draft of 18 January 1962[4] de Gaulle hardened his position by including economic policy – the core of the EEC – in the intergovernmental Political Union which would stand above the European Community and had to be based in Paris. De Gaulle's Council of Heads of State or Government would meet quarterly, exercising unlimited powers, political, economic and also military. On the basis of this French draft, a complicated watered down compromise was agreed between Paris and Bonn.

The negotiations between the Six ended, however, in failure at a meeting of the Ministers for Foreign Affairs on 17 April 1962, after several unsuccessful attempts to make a breakthrough.[5] Joseph Luns and Paul-Henri Spaak, Ministers for Foreign Affairs of the Netherlands and Belgium respectively, jointly stated that the Six could sign a treaty as proposed by France only after the entry of the United Kingdom, which had in the meantime applied for membership of the Community. The Dutch government in particular was afraid of remaining 'locked up' in a European satellite state under French and/or German hegemony with uncertain democratic principles. Therefore it wanted British and Scandinavian accession as a guarantee 'for maintaining democracy in Europe' (Dutch PM Piet de Jong, quoted by Harryvan, p. 189).

It may be concluded that the idea of a future Political Union, including a Council of Heads of State or Government, proposed by France with the backing of the Federal Republic of Germany, came to grief at this point because such a Union would have weakened the existing European Economic Community. An attempt by France to integrate outside the economic area by the creation of a 'European Council' had failed. 'Summitry' (Chapter I.B.1) had, for the time being, been rejected as a tool for the unification of Western Europe.

Since France had in vain proposed a Political Union of the Six, France and the FRG signed on 22 January 1963 a treaty for mutual cooperation (Treaty of Friendship and Reconciliation, or Élysée Treaty). The treaty laid down that both governments would consult each other before taking decisions in matters relating to, among other things, the European Community, political cooperation and strategic issues. The regular Franco-German Summit meetings held from 1963 may be characterised as a form of successful pre-negotiation which would – as will be outlined in Chapter 3 – have very important consequences for the subsequent regular meetings of the European Council.[6]

President de Gaulle was undoubtedly the most important initiator of periodical Summit meetings. His underlying thought was that there would be a United Europe, based on the Nation States. Today, more then half a century after 1953, the European Council has assumed the importance and the powers which its real father, Charles de Gaulle, had in mind. This fact of life means that de Gaulle may be accorded the status of co-founder of the European Council.

A.4.   Preamble to the European Council

At the end of the prosperous 1960s there was no evidence anywhere of a European spirit. There seemed to be no end to political disagreements between Member States concerning vital issues, such as enlargement and the necessary strengthening of the Community. Time and again the Council of Ministers required one or several night sessions in order to hammer out every compromise, however unimportant. Given such a situation, the Commission lost all the dynamism that it ought to demonstrate as initiator of legislative policies. Moreover, since the signing of the Rome Treaty in 1957, nothing had been done except to develop a Common Market. It was commonly held that 'Political Europe has made no advance whatever' (Spaak, 1965, p. 202) and this was, as Spaak rightly underlined, in spite of the fact that the authors of the treaty had conceived the European Economic Community as only a stage on the road to a politically more integrated Europe.

An important development was the replacement as French President of the intransigent de Gaulle by Georges Pompidou in the Spring of 1969. At a meeting of the Council on 22 and 23 July 1969 France, following agreement with the FRG, proposed a new conference of Heads of State or Government. Many saw the upcoming Summit in The Hague (since the Netherlands was at that time President of the Council of Ministers) as a response to the despair felt throughout Europe. On the Sunday before the meeting, the Dutch Gereformeerde Synode, the highest organ of the Calvinistic churches, held a national prayer-meeting for this purpose.

The Summit (details in Van der Harst) opened with a cautious statement by Pompidou on British entry. He stated his three main issues: completion, especially a permanent funding of the CAP (l'achèvement); deepening, in other words embracing new politics (l'approfondissement); and enlargement (l'élargissement). During the night, there was a breakthrough on the basis of a Franco-German understanding when President Pompidou in a personal talk with Chancellor Willy Brandt gave his approval for enlargement with the United Kingdom, Ireland, Denmark and Norway (Brandt, 1976, p. 245-247). On the stuttering political scene, the Communiqué stated that, with the expiry of the transitional period, the irreversible nature of the Community was confirmed. The Heads of State or Government instructed the Ministers for Foreign Affairs 'to study the best way of achieving progress in the matter of political unification'.[7] Finally, a plan for the creation, in stages, of an Economic and Monetary Union was to be worked out. In a comment on the meeting, Commission President Jean Rey regretted that a strengthening of the Institutions was not even discussed.[8] Nevertheless, the Hague Conference resolved the old conflicts of the 1960s on the CAP and British entry. It created 'the spirit of The Hague' and marked – for the first time by way of a successful Summit meeting – the beginning of a new era in European integration.

The Summit of Paris of 1972 was the first one of 'the Ten' (the Six 'founding fathers', plus the candidate Member States – the United Kingdom, Denmark, Ireland and Norway which later by referendum rejected membership). During the preparation France asked again in vain that in the framework of regular Summit meetings a Political Secretariat – as proposed by the FRG – separate from the Community, should be established and based in Paris. The Heads of State or Government agreed in Paris on a timetable for launching the Economic and Monetary Union (EMU). It was decided to set up a European Monetary Cooperation Fund. The Institutions of the Community were requested to draw up a report along broad lines for the establishment of a *'European Union'*, a new term in the dictionary of the Community. It would later reappear at every meeting of the European Council. 'European Union' had to be realised before the end of the decade (meaning 1980 at the latest).[9] Although 'environment' as such was not specifically mentioned in the Treaty of Rome, the meeting decided 'to establish, before July 31, 1973 a programme of action'. In Paris, again, the old conflict of the Community, namely the question whether regular meetings of the Heads of State or Government should plot its political course, remained unresolved.

The Copenhagen Summit on 14 and 15 December 1973 was to tackle economic problems arising in the Community, such as oil supply, after the disrupting and dangerous conflict of October 1973 in the Middle East, as well as the battle against inflation.[10] Inflation was to delay any further moves to introduce EMU. The Middle East conflict was followed by a series of failed attempts to launch a Community energy policy. There were, moreover, major internal problems concerning another promise of the Paris Summit of 1972: the Community's Regional Fund. The meeting itself was held in a chaotic atmosphere. It turned out to be, moreover, grossly under-prepared. The Summit ended with the publication of lengthy and wordy statements and three results: a decision to meet more frequently; a mandate to the Commission to submit proposals 'aimed at resolving in a concrete manner the problems raised by the developing energy crisis' and a unique and interesting effort to formulate a 'Declaration on European Identity'. The statement on energy fell short of an open commitment to a sharing of oil, which some Member States, especially the Netherlands, had urged.

In Copenhagen President Pompidou, who would die shortly afterwards, was already ill, Chancellor Brandt was caught up in the Guillaume spy affair which would later topple him and British Prime Minister Edward Heath was in severe problems on the home front. The flimsy result of Copenhagen shows that as soon as the Heads of State or Government of the larger Member States are in political trouble at home, their room for manoeuvre in the EU is restricted. This is still the case today.

With the benefit of hindsight one may conclude that the Summit meetings in The Hague in 1969, in Paris in 1972, and in Copenhagen in 1973 focused minds on the creation of a European Council and upon the activities which it would take upon itself from 1975.

B.   THE GENESIS OF THE EUROPEAN COUNCIL

B.1.   France as the initiator of the European Council

Summitry[11] is the art of dealing at the top level. Heads of State or Government meet at Summits through bilateral, multilateral and institutional meetings. A Summit meeting is based on the notion that diplomacy can best be practiced by face-to-face meetings of national political leaders. In many cases Summit meetings manage, on the basis of good understanding between the very limited number of participants, to break through a blockade put up at a lower level of bureaucracy. An important aspect of summitry is that an important 'package-deal' which settles a number of separate items simultaneously will only emerge where a political link is achievable between different sectors in the involved States, for instance trade, energy policy and fiscal policy. The possibility of arranging 'cross sector agreements' (much in use in the EU) is an important basis for summitry. Such arrangements are mostly only to be accomplished through the commitment of the Heads of Government (or State). Since 1945, most international organisations, for instance the Arab League, NATO and the Organisation for African Unity (OAU, now the African Union), had had regular Summit meetings and as such preceded the European Council.

The initiative for organising Summit meetings was always taken by France: by Prime Minister Guy Mollet in 1957, by President de Gaulle in the early 1960s and by his successor President Pompidou in 1969 and 1973. The rhythm of the series of Summits usually coincided with the occurrence of a crisis in the Community. The initiative for the creation of a 'European Council' came from Jean Monnet who in the early 1970s made several *démarches* at the French, German and British political leaders. According to Emile Noël, first and famous Secretary-General of the European Commission from 1968-1987, Giscard d'Estaing dictated the whole process of the birth (Noël).

During September and October 1973, President Pompidou proposed, in line with the old Fouchet Plan of 1961, periodical *tête-à-têtes* of the Heads of State or Government, without the attendance of the Ministers for Foreign Affairs. The objective was to discuss political cooperation with the purpose of harmonisation and a confrontation of the different attitudes. Two weeks after Pompidou's initiative the Prime Minister of the UK, Edward Heath, stated that he favored such informal meetings. But in contrast to Pompidou, Heath would have liked the President of the Commission to be present when matters which concerned that Institution were discussed. In a speech to the Parliament, Chancellor Willy Brandt also called for more frequent meetings of the Heads of Government. Brandt saw regular Summit meetings in the context of a future European government.[12]

The real process of the birth of the European Council began with a speech by President Giscard d'Estaing on French television on 27 August 1974. 'In the next few months, France will take initiatives regarding the political organisation of Europe', the President announced (*AE*, 29 August 1974, p. 2). Early in 1974 a crisis had developed in the Community. Economic and political difficulties had arisen in many areas, 'and the Community was not sufficiently equipped to cope with these properly'. 'There emerged a trend towards inter-state cooperation based on the achievement of national interests' (*Gen Rep*, 1974, p. 1). Even the enduring cooperation between France and the FRG that guided the Community in many cases, was to stumble in those days. In 1974 there had been no progress on the edicts issuing from the Summit meetings of Paris 1972 and Copenhagen 1973. On 16 September 1974 the French President invited to Paris the Heads of Government and the President of the Commission.

The question of possible Summit meetings was broached at this so-called 'Summit picnic' (a working lunch). President Giscard d'Estaing had earlier already agreed with Chancellor Helmut Schmidt to create a European Council which would meet regularly. That afternoon Giscard had deliberately arranged the easy chairs in the Grand Salon of the Élysée to create the atmosphere of a non-committal, informal talk for the Heads of Government. 'In such an atmosphere people are easy-going', was the underlying thought of the tactician Giscard d'Estaing. Civil service personnel were not admitted. There was not even an agenda (Giscard d'Estaing, p. 119-120). The President asked his guests to come up with ideas. The Dutch Prime Minister Joop den Uyl was the only one to stress the need for a strengthening of the role of the Commission. Each Head of Government declared himself personally prepared to take a larger responsibility for European issues. The Heads of Government and the President of the Commission agreed with the French President to meet regularly (Dondelinger, 1977, p. 15-19). There remained unresolved the question of the 'lightweight secretariat' proposed by France to prepare for these meetings. The majority of the Member States did not see any need to set up such a body. Giscard d'Estaing would get his way thirty years later in 2004 in the Constitutional Treaty later replaced by the Reform Treaty/Treaty of Lisbon (not yet in force).

B.2.   The Paris Summit of 1974

At the Paris Summit of 9-10 December 1974[13] the Heads of State or Government worked towards achieving a package-deal based on a system of give and take, with some concessions for the hesitant smaller Member States but at the same time retention of the framework earlier laid down by President Giscard d'Estaing and Chancellor Schmidt. According to the Communiqué (Annex 4 to this publication):

(a)   the Heads of Government would meet, together with the Ministers for Foreign Affairs, at least three times a year. A detail worth remarking: the President of the Commission is not mentioned in this 'birth certificate' of the European Council;

(b)   the arrangement for such institutionalised regular meetings would not in any way affect the rules and the procedures laid down in the treaties nor in the provisions on European Political Cooperation (EPC);

(c)   the Nine reaffirmed their determination to adopt common positions and to coordinate their diplomatic actions in all international affairs which affect the interests of the Community;

(d)   an end should be put to the Council's practice of making agreement even on the less important questions conditional upon the unanimous consent of the Ministers;

(e)   agreement in principle was reached on the direct election of the European Parliament by universal suffrage. The competence of the Parliament would be extended;

(f)   the Belgian Prime Minister Leo Tindemans would prepare a report on what form the 'European Union' might assume.

The outcome of this Summit meeting proved to be satisfactory. At the conclusion, a satisfied President Giscard d'Estaing exclaimed: *'Les sommets sont morts, vive le Conseil Européen'* (The Summits are dead, long live the European Council!) (*AE*, 12 December 1974, p. 4). That was moment the term 'European Council' was born. Nevertheless this newly defined creation of the European Council – which today would be seen as the most important achievement of this Summit in Paris – was not mentioned in the Communiqué since the hesitant smaller Member States did not like such emphasis. According to the European Parliament its old ambition 'that the transformation of the present political cooperation procedure into a Community procedure be speeded up' (Resolution OJ C. 5/10, 8.1.75) had been fulfilled. After years of strict separation between Community matters and European Political Cooperation, a Community in the political sense had finally emerged. The Paris (1972) and Copenhagen (1973) Summits had discussed the setting up of a European Regional Development Fund. This was especially urged by the UK, Italy and Ireland. Their request now finally bore fruit and work for a Regional Policy was to start on 1 January 1975. On the basis of a compromise an agreement would be worked out for the details of a correcting mechanism (a rebate) to be applied to the UK's budgetary contribution.[14]

The agreement on the creation of the European Council was generally seen as a compromise. It was regarded as a triumph for advocates of intergovernmental cooperation but went hand in hand with the promise of a democratically elected Parliament with legal powers, a Federalist countermove. It was due to the opposition of the Benelux governments that the Council was deprived of any legal basis in the institutional framework. In general, the new departure was seen as a sort of institutional relaunch – through the vague idea of 'European Union' – of a more institutionalised intergovernmental system. After this meeting the Community took on a healthier appearance. In its 1975 General Report, the Commission a few weeks later noted 'a resurgent spirit of Community solidarity' (*Gen Rep*, 1975, p. 1).

C.   BACKGROUND TO, AND REASONS FOR, THE CREATION OF THE EUROPEAN COUNCIL

C.1.   A Series of changes and influences

The creation of a European Council may be seen as the result of a series of changes in the domestic, international, economic and Community environments. In addition, there were political and institutional developments which led to the creation of the European Council. Finally, the two fundamentally differing concepts of the European Community (supranationalism and intergovernmentalism) played a role. Let us now attempt to trace, describe and evaluate the different elements.

The domestic background

First, the domestic background. In general it is acknowledged that the pattern of negotiations in the Union is determined by the domestic situation and the interests of the Member States. In the Spring of 1974, 'a turning-point in relations among Western European countries' (Morgan, p. 16) there were important governmental changes in three major Member States. In the UK in March, Harold Wilson (Labour) replaced Edward Heath (Conservative) as Prime Minister. After the death of Georges Pompidou, Valéry Giscard d'Estaing was elected in May to the presidency of the French Republic. In the same month Helmut Schmidt became Chancellor of the Federal Republic of Germany (FRG). The very good relationship between the former Ministers for Finance, Giscard d'Estaing and Schmidt, was important. Both men were sceptical about the capacity of the European Commission, let alone the European Parliament, to develop wide-ranging policies. They saw the *leitmotiv* of their European policy not in the writing of idealistic programmes, but in a 'politicisation' of integration under member governments' control (Lodge, 1979, p. 167; Dinan, p. 157-161).

There remains the question of why at this time the Heads of State or Government deemed it necessary to involve themselves intensively and regularly with the activities of the European Communities and the work on European Political Cooperation.

On the eve of the emergence of the European Council, there was a growing tendency for Heads of State or Government to take more initiatives on international and economic questions. In the new climate of cooperation between the three larger Member States, a better harmonisation of national policies was being sought, with the Community operating not as an actor but more as a *facilitator* (Dondelinger, 1975, p. 9). Moreover, on many occasions in the early 1970s the Council of Ministers faced very complex problems, interrelated with different aspects of domestic policy, which were politically too 'hot' and too complicated to be handled by the Ministers for Foreign Affairs alone. In tackling such issues, only national political leaders had the coordinating power to seek to resolve conflict.

Heads of Government moreover could use the European Council as a means to secure popularity in the arena of foreign (European) policy. There came about a growing personalisation of national politics, especially through the medium of television. The European Council phenomenon afforded all its members as 'European Statesmen' the possibility, on a regular basis, of elevating their status vis-à-vis their national public audience (Ferretti, p. 137-148). And so there evolved a means of negotiation in situations where a Member State's vital interests were at stake. Within that framework, *domestic politics* could have an influence on Community policy-making. From a purely domestic point of view, the emergence of a European Council dominated by the political leaders was, therefore, not illogical.

The economic and international scene

Then there were events on the international scene and in the economic environment. The Community had in 1973 been disrupted by successive monetary crises with the threat of currency devaluations, rises of commodity prices, risks of restrictive trade measures, the problem of enormous and destructive inflation and, last but not least, a series of political developments in the Middle East resulting in an almost 30% increase in energy costs. With this economic slowdown, the Western European welfare state which had been the most important achievement of the post-war era, became more vulnerable (*Gen Rep*, 1973, p. XV-XXVI). All those developments together blew the Community off course in 1974 and created the necessity of a guiding body.

The Member States had, moreover, to find a common strategy or at least some coordinated approach vis-à-vis the Soviet Union, NATO, the emerging Conference on Security and Cooperation in Europe (CSCE)[15] and the USA, which had attempted after the collapse of the dollar and the failure in Vietnam, to re-establish its influence over Western Europe through the so-called 'European Year'. The latter was proposed in 1973 by US Secretary of State Henry Kissinger (Kissinger, 1979, p. 1273-1275). The institutional structure of the Community was not ready for these tasks. Regular meetings of a European Council composed of the Heads of State or Government and the President of the Commission were expected to play an important role in this regard.

The emergence of the phenomenon of the European Council coincided with the creation of regular Western Economic Summit Meetings (later the G7/G8). According to German Chancellor Helmut Schmidt these meetings represented 'a very private, informal meeting of those who really matter in the world' (Putnam). The first of those meetings was held in Rambouillet (near Paris) on 15-17 November 1975. The invitation came from President Giscard d'Estaing. Behind the initiative to launch both the European Council and the Western Economic Summit lay the sensitivities of the French political leaders to the fact that they played a chief role neither in the framework of the Western hemisphere nor within the Community. Through these regular Summit meetings President Giscard d'Estaing was able to play, if not a leading, then certainly a coordinating role within the Community and even on the Western stage. Those invited were the top political leaders of the USA, Japan, West Germany, France, the United Kingdom and Italy, together with their Ministers for Foreign Affairs and Finance. The invited countries at the time accounted for 70 percent of world trade. Canada joined the Summit in 1976 (San Juan, Puerto Rico) and the

European Community in 1977 (London), being represented by the President of the European Council, the President of the Commission and the Commissioner responsible for external relations or for economic affairs. The group was referred to as the Group of Seven (G7). The subjects on the agenda were, according to Henry Kissinger, in many cases used as a smoke-screen for secret political consultation in order 'to set common goals for common policies'.[16] All meetings closed with a non-binding Final Communiqué. Through these yearly Economic Summits the leaders of France, the FRG, the UK and Italy together with their regular European Council meetings were able to play a coordinating role within the Community and on the Western stage.

The Community background

Finally the Community background. In 1974 when Chancellor Schmidt, President Giscard d'Estaing and Prime Minister Wilson first assumed their roles as national governmental leaders, the Community system as it had been developed was no longer able to achieve its domestically related core objectives, for instance a common management of economic policy, a common agricultural policy, regional development and other central tasks of the Community. The European Commission recognised that 'on the real issues Europe stumbles and slips downhill because our institutions are fail-ing in important areas' (*Gen Rep*, 1974, Introduction, p. X).

For most of the 1970s the Community as such had at least three weaknesses: an inefficiently working Council where the majority rule of the treaties was not adhered to; a Commission which lacked a strong President and moreover lacked fundamental political room to formulate ideas which satisfied the national governments (Delors, 2004, p. 178); and a Parliament that did not have the authority to become deeply involved in the decision-making process. Signs of disunity and crisis led observers at that time to speculate on a disintegration of the Community given that the Institutions were in a state of near-collapse.[17] The 'political element', a supreme political organ, was the missing component in the Community as it had developed during the 1960s.

Chancellor Schmidt and President Giscard d'Estaing in 1974 sought the set-ting up of a European Council. This was a necessity 'because otherwise a con-glomerate of specialised Councils of Ministers decide in Brussels, in Luxembourg, in Strasbourg on a large number of issues, leaving us [the top political leaders] there without any influence' (quoted by Weinachter, 2005, 209). Both the German and French political leaders were of the opinion that the Commission should not develop into a European government. According to Belgian Prime Minister Leo Tindemans, in his earlier prescient visionary report, the need for a body like the intergovernmental European Council arose because the Institutions 'have shown themselves in practice to be too weak to give the continuing political momentum needed for the construction of Europe'.[18] Therefore the Community required the more active and regular par-ticipation of the top political players from the Member States.

After the smooth achievement of the Customs Union in 1968, the Community now arrived at the really difficult problem of creating an economic, and hence also a political Union. This development coincided, as earlier mentioned, with the oil crisis and the economic depression of the early 1970s. It resulted in a tendency within governments to seek national solutions. After the transitional period in the creation of the EEC, sensitive areas involving national sovereignty of Member States became a matter for debate. From the mid-1970s, the Member States and the Institutions had to find a solution through the creation of a package deal. It fell, moreover, to the Community and its Member States, during this period, to tackle two difficult questions: firstly, that of a possible *further enlargement* to include three former dictatorial regimes in the Mediterranean area (Spain, Portugal and Greece); and secondly, a necessary strengthening or restructuring of its *institutional framework*. Only the European Council had the necessary coordinating and political powers to negotiate and finalise such complicated agreements.

The European Council was, as has been said, a re-invention of the earlier disregarded Fouchet Plan: a forum for political consultation at the very highest level. This, surprisingly, was accomplished by Jean Monnet, who earlier had taken the very ambitious first step in the direction of a European federation which resulted in the ECSC. Monnet now took a decisive step in the direction of intergovernmental cooperation. In August 1973 he had written a draft for a 'Provisional European Government', which was, with the benefit of hindsight, the forerunner of the European Council. 'Countless signals tell us that the Institutions of the Community are incapable of carrying out the tasks allotted to them', he concluded in 1973 (Monnet, p. 758, my translation from his French text). He apportioned some of the blame to the lack of cooperation from national governments. The Heads of State or Government of the Six therefore had to form a 'Provisional European Government' (Monnet, p. 760-762). This genuine *'autorité européenne'* should meet at least every trimester in closed session, and give precise instructions to the Council of Ministers to bring about the achievement of the promised European Union (Fontaine). The intervention of Monnet was crucial. It was to provide the political leaders with the stimulus necessary to make the progress that was needed towards the construction of Europe. In his first effort, Monnet won over PM Heath, Chancellor Brandt and President Pompidou. In 1974, Monnet, then 86, succeeded in influencing the three new national political leaders: Giscard d'Estaing, Schmidt and Wilson. Monnet's intervention was purely based on the Paris-Bonn-London triangle.[19]

The intergovernmental and supranational concepts

Now we focus again on the intergovernmental and the supranational aspects as factors to be taken in consideration. Many authors saw at the time the European Council as an example of intergovernmentalism, (Werts, 1992, footnote 624) replacing or diminishing the original supranationalism of the Institutions. The Communiqué of the 1972 Summit in Paris spoke of 'the Member States of the Community: the driving wheels of European construction' (*Bull* 10-1972, p. 16). The eight Summits earlier described which were held between 1957 and 1974 represent a systematically applied intergovernmental formula, fitting into the framework that President de Gaulle's disciple Michel Debré had proposed unsuccessfully in 1955: 'a periodic and organic Council of the Heads of Government, rendering common service to prepare their decisions in the areas of politics, economics, culture and defence' (Bodenheimer, p. 54). Perhaps it is telling that at the official signing of the treaties in Rome in 1957 the larger Member States sent their Heads of Government, whereas the opponents of the direct involvement of the Heads of Government in European matters by way of a European Council, the Netherlands and Belgium, were represented at a lower level by their Minister for Foreign Affairs.[20] The Tindemans Report of 1975, unanimously approved in the European Council, confirmed 'the role of the European Council as a driving force'; a force 'to build European union by strengthening the practical solidarity of the nine member states'.

Box 3

Intergovernmental organisation versus supranationality

Intergovernmental organisation has three characteristics: (a) decision-making by unanimity, (b) in bodies composed of government representatives, (c) followed by implementation by the States themselves. If you abandon these three characteristics in a process in which States are interwoven, the word 'supranational' may be used. The essence of supranationality is a real and autonomous power placed at the service of objectives common to several states. The supranationality of the European Community is moreover characterised by a direct relation between the legislative power and the citizens of the Member States by way of the European Parliament, and by agreements concluded between the Commission and non-member States.[21]

The Luxembourg Compromise: a setback for supranational integration

Two other important factors contributed to the creation of the European Council. Firstly, supranational integration was not extended after the crisis in the Community of 1965-1966. In the course of 1965 the ambitious first President of the Commission, the German Dr. Walter Hallstein, became *persona non grata* in Paris. A key element in President de Gaulle's position was his conviction that the supranational principle of majority voting for decision-making in the Council of Ministers, which according to the EEC Treaty was to be applied in certain sectors from 1 January 1966, was not acceptable to France. Hallstein blundered in presenting very important proposals (regarding the CAP and own financial resources for the Community) without any consultation of the Member States. After the withdrawal of all his negotiators in Brussels in 1965, creating the famous *'empty chair'*, de Gaulle secured in 1966 the so called 'Luxembourg Compromise'. A mutual pledge was made that, as a political guideline, decisions taken by majority voting in the Council of Ministers could be postponed indefinitely upon request by a Member State, when it invoked its (national) 'very important interests'. The decision elevated the national veto to a sacrosanct principle. It foreshadowed the need to create, in the Community, a body for decision-making at the highest political level, in other words a European Council composed of the Heads of State or Government. After 1966 qualified majority voting on politically sensitive issues, as opposed to decision-making by consensus, became exceptional in the Council of Ministers.

Secondly, the hope of the functionalists – that there would be a shift in public sentiment resulting from a 'spill-over' from national to supranational government and from the economic EEC to the general political arena – had not been realised.

Linthorst Homan, one of the Dutch co-founders of the European Community, has spoken of his remarkable personal experiences concerning the gradual dismantling of the Community's supranational characteristics. First there came with the ECSC a request by the Netherlands for the creation of an intergovernmental Council of Ministers. This was followed by a further development of this Council, concentrating upon its intergovernmental structure. From the 1960s on there was a trend towards thinking in terms of the famous 'juste retour', a balance between national concessions and national gains. In 1965-1966 the French idée fixe against majority voting arose. Finally in 1974, there was the 'tragedy when the European Council began to play its role as cuckoo in the Community nest' (Linthorst Homan) by putting its inter-governmental level above that of the Commission and the Parliament.

Nevertheless, it is generally accepted that legally the Community through the Commission, its directly elected Parliament and, not least, the Court of Justice, has authority vis-à-vis the Member States. Soldatos (p. 191-197) underlined the important aspect of the 'supranationalité normative' (norma-tive supranationalism) of the European Community. He summarised a series of six major aspects of this, including the direct effect of Community law, laying down individual rights which must be upheld by the national courts and the precedence of Community law over a national provision con-flicting with it. Via a long series of judgments of the Court of Justice, the important process of normative supranationalism has been strengthened. This took place to such an extent that 'the relationship between the (legal) order of the Community and that of the Member States has come to resem-ble increasingly a fully fledged (USA type) federal system' (Weiler, p. 273).

It became evident to leading national politicians, after the Community had been functioning for some years, that the Court of Justice was creating this 'normative supranationality', whereas the Commission became known as the 'Brussels bureaucracy'. I would refer here to the remarks of Chancel-lor Schmidt and of President Giscard d'Estaing cited earlier in this chapter. It was against this background one may assume that the intergovernmental phenomenon, the European Council, was especially directed.

To summarise: the emergence of the European Council may be looked upon as the result of a long process. It resulted in a strengthening of inter-governmental working in the Community system and a decline of supranationalism. Initiatives are now taken by the Heads of State or Government as well as by the Institutions. Because of this new division of power the functioning of the European Council as the Union's supreme political organ is somewhat controversial in almost all smaller Member States and also in the Institutions (Council of Ministers, Commission, Parliament) – as will be discussed in subsequent chapters.

The approach of the Heads of State or Government to the process of creating a European Council is worth a final mention. Neither the Parliament nor the Commission, nor any pressure group or national parliament, nor the academic world, let alone public opinion or the press, gave any impetus to its creation. This is admittedly in line with the 'Neofunctionalist' approach stressing the psychology of leaders and elites, those who know, control and decide, in the whole European integration process. That is an interesting conclusion. Chapter 4 shows that this purely leadership approach was repeated exactly in 2004. Then, Giscard d'Estaing as President of the Convention and with the support of the big Member States, took exactly the same approach to the upgrading of the European Council to an official Institution.

D.   CONCLUSION

D.1.   The European Council: a necessity

From the very beginning of the integration process there was a need for a body which, working together with the other Union Institutions, would be capable of taking and implementing decisions. Until then there had been no Community institutional system that was able to take an overall view and supply answers for the central major issues. The European Council's coming into being brought about such a single common decision-making body.

After the smooth achievement of the Customs Union in 1968, the phenomenon that would become the European Council became a necessity due to a series of events. The stagnation of the integration process at the end of the 1960s was followed by international financial and economic turmoil which led to a growing unmanageability of the Community. As described earlier, there was the search for an organ for intergovernmental consultation at the highest level by France, the FRG and the UK, who were unwilling to accept the supranational aspects of the Community. In the early 1970s there was moreover a crisis in decision-making. In general there was the incapacity of the Community's Institutions (especially the Council of Ministers) to give the needed momentum to overcome this crisis. The Heads of State or Government had to seek some way to reconcile the different domestic interests.

Summit meetings have a series of functions. The exchange of information and opinions is important. Another element is the fostering of personal understanding between the top political leaders. As a participant said: 'The main point is to learn how others see the problems'. The meetings energise the policy process by seeking to overcome resistance from domestic bureaucrats or from national public opinion, take an overview of what is desirable internationally and endeavour to accommodate divergent national policies. In many cases an important side-effect of Summits has been to make not only Heads of State or Government but also their domestic constituencies aware of the complexity of the problems and the limitations which it imposes upon national sovereignty.

In the early 1970s, moreover, a certain resistance to integration on the part of Member States – especially the executive departments of the governments – blocked the Community.[22] It was not widely accepted that the Commission should be the driving force for integration. Another phenomenon was the general recognition of a growing interdependence especially in the economic area between Member States, and a growing internationalisation of the production process and its connected employment.

In 1973 the UK, Denmark and Ireland joined the Community. After the mid-1970s, Greece, Spain and Portugal applied for membership. Internally the Community faced problems associated with this continuing process of enlargement. The UK's accession brought problems regarding the internal financial structure of the Community. There were also growing domestic political problems in the Member States, which demanded a solution at the Community level. The creation of the European Council can be seen as an attempt to reinforce the powers, overall consistency and decision-making of the Community through a strengthening of the role of the Member States' governments. There evolved also a more personalised role for the Heads of State or Government, with the Community as their common framework.

Finally, externally there was a search for a political role for the Community which, since the Summit of 1972 via EPC, 'must be capable of making her voice heard in world affairs' (Declaration 1972 Paris Summit, *Bull* 10-1972).

Why did the integration process, which had started at the beginning of the 1950s, not give birth to the European Council earlier than 1974? Our whole analysis shows that the European Council was in *statu nascendi* from 1953 to 1974. As a compromise between, on the one hand, France and the FRG and, on the other, the hesitant smaller Member States especially the Netherlands and Belgium, it was developed as 'a systematic rapprochement' and 'a concert of European States which in developing all sorts of ties between them would increase their interdependence and solidarity' (quotes from President de Gaulle, p. 171). The fundamental difference as compared with the efforts of 1960-1961 was, as we will see in Chapter 2, that the European Council developed within the legal limits of the treaties. At the creation of the European Council in 1974 it was laid down in its 'birth certificate' (Annex 4 to this publication) that 'these arrangements do not in any way affect the rules of the Treaties' and that 'the Commission will exercise the powers vested in it'. Such a structure, always insisted upon by the Netherlands and Belgium, had been absolutely unacceptable to President de Gaulle. Another founder, the French 'father of Europe', Jean Monnet, saw the European Council as a collegial 'Provisional European Government'. It had in his opinion, besides its strategic and political guiding role (as later laid down in the TEU[23]), a function as the Union's highest political decision-maker. How amazing it is that we have to wait thirteen years, until 1987, before the European Council became by the Single European Act (SEA, in force since 1987) part of the treaty law of the European Community.

In summary, during the mid-1970s a European Council composed of the

Heads of State or Government and the President of the Commission became indispensable, because (a) the basic structure of the Community from the beginning lacked an overall political leadership; (b) European integration in those years touched ever more on important sensitive matters of internal politics, which resulted in the necessity of the highest national political leaders involving themselves personally with the Community; (c) the integration process faltered and required new leadership; (d) crucial matters developed on the international scene, forcing the Heads of Government to join forces (G-7, economic crisis, oil crisis/Middle East).

Endnotes

1   For a more exhaustive description and analysis of the birth and further evolution of the European Council I refer to my earlier publication: Werts, Jan, *The European Council*, Amsterdam, T.M.C. Asser Instituut - Elsevier Science Publishers, 1992, 377 pp.

2   Monnet, p. 540; Lacouture, 1985, p. 645; Debré, 1979, together with notes by the author taken at an interview with Mr. Debré at that time.

3   The Bonn Summit instructed the Fouchet Committee to work out its decisions and to submit to it proposals on the means 'which will as soon as possible enable a statutory character to be given to the Union of their peoples' - see *Bull* 7/8-1961, p. 35-36; Silj, p. 8; Jouve (ed.), Tome I, p. 290.

4   For the Fouchet Plan see Parliament, 1964, p. 11-24; Silj; Bodenheimer.

5   Jansen, p. 70-73; Council, 1979, p. 2; Bloes, p. 358-364; Spaak, 1971, p. 443-444.

6   A quarter of a century later, German Chancellor Schmidt regretted the fact that at the time he had not understood President de Gaulle. According to Schmidt, de Gaulle rightly saw this treaty as the core of European self-awareness. 'We Germans need the close alliance with France if an independent Europe is to develop' (my translation from the German text), see Schmidt, farewell speech in Deutscher Bundestag, 228 Sitzung, Bonn, 10 September 1986, p. 17674. After the signing of this treaty, the construction of a united Europe was no longer of prime concern to de Gaulle; Jouve, Tome II, p. 58-66.

7   A committee under the chairmanship of the Belgian diplomat Etienne Davignon on 20 July 1970 presented its report. It was accepted by the Ministers for Foreign Affairs on 27 October 1970. This project was to become known as European Political Cooperation (EPC), the forerunner of the Common Foreign and Security Policy (CFSP).

8   JO Annex, Débats du PE, 11 décembre 1969, No. 120/168.

9   Regarding the Paris Summit see *Gen Rep*, 1972, p. 5; Leigh, p. 168; Brandt, 1976, p. 258-259; Everling, p. 796-797; Kobbert, p. 722.

10   See *Bull* 12-1973, 1106, plus the Annex and 2501. Final Communiqué. Copenhagen saw the unexpected arrival of the Ministers for Foreign Affairs of Algeria, Egypt, Sudan and the United Emirates, to general surprise and consternation. They came as emissaries of the Arab Summit, held in November 1973 in Algiers, to work on cooperation in the Mediterranean and the Middle East. The Arabs were not received by the Heads of State or Government but they met the Ministers for Foreign Affairs and Prime Minister Anker Jörgensen, the President of the Summit.

11   See Melissen, in Van Staden, et seq., p.160-183; Merlini; Iklé, p. 222-223; Pambou Tchivounda, 452 pp.

12   *Bull* 11-1973, 1401-1402; *Bulletin d'Information Franzözische Botschaft*, 2 November 1973; Brandt, Willy, Address to Parliament, OJ Annex, Debates of the EP, 168/20, 13.11.73.

13   The French President announced his invitation to meet as late as November 29. The reason was reservations on the part of at least one delegation – the Netherlands - about the appropriateness of holding a Summit. In addition there were low expectations in other circles.

14   At its first meeting as European Council, in March 1975 in Dublin the Heads of Government struck a deal on a 'correcting mechanism' to provide a rebate. On the basis of this deal the UK decided by way of a referendum in 1975 to stay in the EC, see *Bull* 3-1975, 1502 and 1106.

15   The CSCE brought the NATO Member States and the Warsaw Pact countries around one negotiating table for the first time.

16   Kissinger, 1975, p. 758. On G-7/G8 see further Hellmann; also Lamy.

17   Lodge, p. 626-651; see also Address Commission President Ortoli, François Xavier, at the presentation of the General Report, OJ Annex, Debates of the EP, 186/43, 18.2.75.

18   Tindemans, 1976 p. 30. The EU as it developed later in the 1990s contained many other elements from Tindemans' report : a two-speed Europe, the EMU, the CFSP, regional and social policy, more powers for Parliament and qualified majority voting (QMV) in the Council of Ministers.

19   See Monnet, p. 653-659 and p. 762-771. Earlier already, surprisingly, the creation of a European Council was advised by the European Parliament in the VEDEL, 'Report of the Working Party examining the problem of the enlargement of the powers of the European Parliament', *Bull Suppl.* 4/72, 89 pp.

20   The treaties were signed by German Chancellor Konrad Adenauer, by the PMs of France, Edgar Faure, and of Italy, Antonio Segni, by the FMs of Belgium, Paul-Henri Spaak, and the Netherlands, Joseph Luns, and by Joseph Bech, PM and FM of Luxembourg.

21   Sources: Aron, p. 744, Kapteyn and VerLoren van Themaat, 1989, p. 1-2; Pescatore, p. 51.

22   Jean Rey, President of the European Commission 1967-1970, in Dehousse, p. 69.

23   The Treaty on European Union, agreed at Maastricht in December 1991. It came into force on 2 November 1993.

2 The functioning of the European Council in the institutional framework of the Union

Introduction

In a political as well as legal sense there are enormous differences between the first Summit meeting in 1957 in Paris and the meetings of the European Council of today. In 1957 the Heads of Government met as representatives of fully sovereign States, bound only by the ECSC Treaty of 1951. Today, with a European Council legally based on Articles 4, 13, 17 and 40 of the TEU, they are bound also by the whole range of the TEC and EAEC Treaties[1], the aforementioned TEU (with some rules regarding European Council meetings), the so-called *acquis communautaire* (a recognition of the rights and obligations acquired under the Community's treaties and laws) and, in the future, in the proposed Treaty of Lisbon (Reform Treaty), being the follow up to the defunct Constitutional Treaty. The first part of this chapter, Section A, traces this development from a legal perspective. Then follows an analysis of the decision-making process in the European Council. Finally we try to give an overview of its differing functions and tasks.

In Section B, I present an analysis of the European Council/HSG Council in the institutional framework of the Union. The relationship between the European Council and the European Commission, the European Parliament and the Council of Ministers is described. The line of approach is the promise made by the 1974 Paris Summit that the agreements and arrangements concerning the European Council 'do not in any way affect the rules and procedures laid down in the Treaties or the provisions on political cooperation' (Annex 4 to this publication, point 3). That was an important promise. The starting point of this chapter is a comparison of this sacrosanct promise with the real evolution of the European Council. It will reveal to what extent the Heads of State or Government in nearly every meeting reneged on their promises of 1974. The matter is important, because the Convention on the Future of Europe and the subsequent Intergovernmental Conferences (IGCs) of 2002-2004 and 2007 contain comparable promises regarding the future development of the European Council.

Finally, Section C of this chapter deals with the organisation and working procedures of the European Council.

Note to the reader

In this publication, in line with the approach taken by the 1974 Paris Summit meeting where the European Council was created, whenever we henceforth mention, with reference to the European Council, *'Heads of Government'*, this stands for the *whole membership of the European Council*: the Heads of State or Government of the Member States of the Union plus the President of the Commission; *'Commission'* stands for the Commission of the European Union; *'Council'* stands for the Council of Ministers of the European Union; *'Parliament'* stands for the European Parliament. The term 'Heads of Government' also includes the Presidents if they are a member of the delegation of a Member State in the European Council, such as the Presidents of France, Poland, Cyprus and Romania. In some cases Bulgaria, the Czech Republic and Lithuania are also represented by their President.

A. THE LEGISLATIVE MECHANISMS

A.1.   The legal nature and form of the European Council

The legal position of the European Council and its decision-making have not been regular topics for discussion.[2] The listing of its functions and tasks in this chapter clearly reflects a gradual development. At its creation in 1974 it was foreseen that the European Council would also act as a decision-making body in the framework of the Council of Ministers. Since the President of the Commission is never a member of the Council of Ministers, his participation in the meetings of the European Council was not expressly laid down in the 'birth-certificate' (Annex 4 to this publication). Three years later, in the 'Organizational Rules for European Council meetings' (*Bull* 6-1977, 2.3.1) it was confirmed that the European Council can 'produce decisions'. Although the legal nature of those decisions in some cases remained unclear, they were nevertheless politically binding. In its Stuttgart Solemn Declaration on European Union in 1983 (*Bull* 6-1983, 1.6.1 under 2.1.3) the European Council stated that when it acts in matters within the scope of the European Communities it does so in its capacity as the Council of Ministers. However, the European Council has never acted in the manner of the Council of Ministers by agreeing a legally binding Regulation or Directive on the basis of a proposal by the Commission.

After a further four years, in 1987, the European Council became by the SEA part of the treaty law of the Community. That was a particularly important moment in the development of the European Council. Article 2 of the SEA legally formalised its institutionalisation by laying down its composition and the minimum number of its meetings. The membership of the President of the European Commission was also officially acknowledged in the SEA.

Even in 1987, however, the European Council did not obtain the status of an Institution of the European Communities. That important step was not attempted until 2004 when the Council became an Institution under the terms of the the subsequently-abandoned Constitutional Treaty, a provision also included in the the Lisbon Treaty (not yet in force) which replaced it. This is described in detail in Chapter 4.

In 1991 in Maastricht, with the Treaty on European Union (TEU), a 'pillar' structure was introduced. The First Pillar covers the activities of the EC, the ECSC and EURATOM which are based on the so called Community Method (see Box 2). The Second Pillar comprises the Common Foreign and Security Policy (CFSP) and the Third Pillar the field of Justice and Home Affairs (JHA). The Second and the Third Pillars have a different institutional and legal structure, with the European Council and the Council of Ministers (in other words the political leaders of the Member States) in the predominant role. Spanning the three pillars is the European Union, with the European Council as the leading body

It is a remarkable fact that in 1993, with the coming into force of the TEU, various articles of the treaty afforded the European Council, as decision-making body, the possibility 'to meet in the composition of the Heads of State or of Government' (HSG Council), without the President of the Commission. Since then the European Council as such has no longer been able to operate as decision-making body in the framework of the Council of Ministers.

The TEU distinguished between:

a.   the 'European Council' as such. Its task is: to provide the Union with the necessary impetus for its development; to define the general political guidelines plus the principles of, and general guidelines for, the CFSP[3];

b.   the Council, meeting in the composition of the Heads of State or Government, in this work 'the HSG Council'. See for instance Articles 121.2 – 122. 4 TEC (Ex 109j(2) – 4) dealing with the transition to the EMU and 122.2 TEC (Ex 109K2) dealing with Member States with a derogation. For more details see Chapter 3.B.2;

c.   decisions of the Governments of the Member States as a diplomatic conference meeting at the level of the Heads of State or Government, for instance as an Intergovernmental Conference (IGC). In this setting, the rules of the treaties concerning decision-making in the Union, their implementation and judicial review do not apply. More details regarding these three aspects are given later in this chapter.

The activities of the Heads of State or Government and the President of the Commission had over the years taken on a particular shape in practice. That took place under the influence of the problems and the challenges (such as the continual enlargement) which confronted the Union. As the analysis in Chapter 3 shows, the European Council became involved with every main issue and, where it wished, with each detail of European integration, including forms of intergovernmental cooperation. It has been noticed that such a political institution can be considered legitimate only if the citizens of the Union accept its right to make vital decisions affecting their lives, as is undoubtedly the case here. After every meeting each Head of Government involved usually reports to their national Parliament. It seems that a Head of Government has never been censured by means of a vote of no confidence in their actions in the European Council and forced to resign.

Article 4 of the TEU, extends the rule as from the 1974 Paris Summit: 'The European Council shall provide the Union with the necessary impetus for its development and shall define the general political guidelines thereof'. In the Lisbon Treaty this task is widened to define the Union's 'general political directions and priorities' (see Chapter 4). Given these very limited definitions of its powers, the European Council is largely free to operate as it wishes. Its radius of action is not limited so as to 'exercise their powers under the conditions and for the purposes provided for' by the various treaties, as in the case according to Article 5 TEU with the Council of Ministers, the Commission and Parliament. Its role deliberately having been left vague, the European Council's evolution has been shaped above all by the political needs and wishes of the Heads of Government.

In Maastricht with the TEU, the European Council received express authority for the Common Foreign and Security Policy (CFSP), via Article J(3) TEU (Article 13 TEU). Another important innovation was the clauses where the Council 'meeting in the composition of Heads of State or Government' (the HSG Council) was given the task of shaping the Economic and Monetary Union (EMU). A third new task resulting from Maastricht is Article 99.(2) where the European Council yearly discusses the 'broad guidelines' of the economic policies of the Member States.

The creation of a European Council in 1974 could not be seen as the creation of an Institution, in accordance with Article 4 EEC, because that required amendment of the treaty in accordance with Article 236 EEC. From a legal standpoint, therefore, the European Council remained outside the institutional framework of the Community until the SEA came into force in 1987. The Council itself indicated that 'when discussing matters within the scope of the Treaties, (…) the European Council may, in accordance with the said Treaties, act in the capacity of Council within the meaning of Article 2 of the Merger Treaty'.[4] The European Commission described the meetings as being just like those of the Council, 'respecting both the letter and the spirit of the treaties' (*Bull* 3-1975, 1504). In its 'Resolution on the role of the European Parliament in its relation with the European Council' Parliament came to a similar conclusión (OJ C. 11/192, 18.1.82).

It can be argued that the success of the European Council depends to a great extent upon the manner in which it is able to fit itself in the institutional machinery of the Union. That has been largely achieved over the course of the years. But although the European Council has been seen since 1974 as the top-level policy-making body, its decisions have always been of a *political nature* only. The difference is important because '*certaines pratiques ont une valeur politique, d'autres ont une valeur juridique*'. The European Council's decisions have therefore 'a legal status in *statu nascendi*'. On the other hand it is a fact that the Institutions and especially the Council of Ministers and the Commission usually stick closely and thus literally to the suggestions, directions and decisions of the European Council. Today the decisions of the European Council are, even in the absence of a legal basis, treated by the Union's Institutions effectively as binding in a political sense.

It was agreed in the Stuttgart Solemn Declaration in 1983 that 'when the European Council acts in matters within the scope of the European

---

Box 4

The European Council: producer of requests and orders

Take as a random example the meeting in Brussels in December 2004. It can be deduced from the Conclusions that the Heads of Government and the President of the Commission here took 19 decisions. In no less than 48 cases they 'welcomed' (sometimes 'with satisfaction') or 'noted' a political development. In five cases 'intentions' were voiced. In 14 clearly described cases the Commission was 'invited' or 'urged' to take action. Six times the Council was 'called upon' or 'requested' (sometimes with a deadline) to undertake action. Six times the European Council asked for action without specifying the Institution(s) concerned. The Council Secretary General-High Representative for the CFSP received 8 orders. The Member States or Candidate Member States received 10. The Council and the Commission received another 7 assignments. The Presidency received 5.

Community, it does so in its capacity of the Council within the meaning of the treaties'. The TEU clarified this situation in 1993. It elevated the European Council to the sole body of the Union as a whole, in other words a body that covers in full all three pillars. Another consequence of the clarification of the legal position of the European Council is that since the coming into force of the Single European Act (1987) it has been unable to operate in the guise of a meeting of the Council of Ministers, wielding the legislative authority of the latter, if only because the President of the Commission is included in its membership. For the future it looks as if this will continue, since according to Article 9b TEU as amended by the Lisbon Treaty, the European Council 'shall not exercise legislative functions. . .'.

As mentioned, the sphere of action of the European Council (see Chapter 3) is very wide. The vastly extended remit of the EU since the mid-1970s is an important cause. A second element of the explanation is that from the mid-1970s onwards the issues became more complicated. Let us take the Common Agricultural Policy (CAP) as an example. The Agriculture Ministers covered this area. In later years the budgetary burden became too heavy for the Union, while the CAP gave rise to international trade and environmental policy objections. As a consequence, Finance, Trade and Environment Ministers also became involved in CAP matters. More than once the Heads of Government have been forced to separate these bickering Ministers via the European Council and cut through stalemates regarding crucial decisions. Another important element is that the European Council operates in such a wide legal framework that whatever interpretation it gives to its role, it cannot be challenged by the Court of Justice. The ever increasing sphere of action and the factors just mentioned have upgraded the authority of the European Council enormously.

Since its first meeting in Dublin in 1975 the European Council asks, calls upon, demands, requests, directs, orders, urges and instructs the Institutions and even related bodies like the European Investment Bank. It requests, for instance, that the Institutions or bodies 'should provide' or 'should attest', 'should take full account of' or 'underline the importance or the need of' (see Chapter 3). Of course, being independent Institutions, the Commission and the Parliament are not obliged to accept such instructions. None of the Institutions has ever refused to follow up a demand of the European Council.

Although there was no legal basis for the European Council before the SEA came into force, it nevertheless acted for years in many cases as a political decision-making body for the European Community. In the long period until 1987, with the coming into force of the SEA, key decisions and orientations were even taken outside the institutional framework of the Community. As early as 1984, President Mitterrand stated that 'the European Council is becoming a permanent court of appeal, or even a local court, in the running of our every-day affairs' (OJ Annex, Debates of the EP, 1-314/258-262). In short: in this way, the European Council puts itself in the place of the Union's Institutions as soon as the really important or difficult political decisions come up for discussion.

In Paris in 1974, the Heads of Government created the European Council by way of a political decision. They also raised the question of the legal nature of their creation and concluded that the new arrangement did 'not in any way affect the rules and procedures laid down in the Treaties' (*Gen Rep*, 1974, p. 297). From a legal point of view this is a very important conclusion. The appearance of the European Council within the framework of the Community's institutional system could subsequently not fail to attract the attention of lawyers. Their differences of opinion ranged from what some saw as 'nothing new' to what others looked upon as an innovation within the terms of the treaty, 'which distorts the balance between the Institutions'.[5]

The European Council has at times approached the essential boundary between decision-making in a *political* sense and *de jure*. In many cases, very detailed decisions made on the basis of a Commission Communication have touched on crucial issues. In a subsequent meeting of the Council, on the basis of a proposal by the Commission and after consultation of the Parliament, they were transformed into Community law within the meaning of Article 249 TEC. This occurred sometimes even without inserting a comma – see the examples described under Chapter 4. The boundary between a detailed decision or orientation by the European Council and a decision by the Council of Ministers is in conclusion often wafer-thin.

Until Maastricht in 1991, it was a valid proposition that 'all decisions of the European Council, insofar as they lead to legislation, must be incorporated in Community legislation through the action of the Institutions involved' (Werts, 1992, p. 125). Today, however, the Heads of Government meeting as HSG Council take legally binding decisions. In other situations the legal status and the enforceability of the decisions of the European Council as such remain unclear. Parts of the Conclusions include texts with the nature of 'hard law', whereas other parts of these declarations, statements which set a certain direction or understanding but are not a legally binding statutory act, are to be categorised as 'soft law'. The latter phenomenon is, according to the European Parliament 'a widely tried and tested alternative to, or preparation for, legislation in the European Union' (Report by Manuel Medina Ortega, 28. 6. 2007, p. 19). It is from this viewpoint that one may start the analysis.

Box 5

The Lisbon Treaty and the European Council

The draft Reform Treaty/Treaty of Lisbon was negotiated in 2007 after the negative referenda on the Constitutional Treaty in France and the Netherlands. The upgrading of the European Council in the Constitutional Treaty and then the Lisbon Treaty (for instance the installation of a permanent President) came as a result of strong pressure from the governments of the Union's six largest Member States in the Convention of 2003/2004. Their politics indicate that they will not relinquish their hold on the upgrading even should the Lisbon Treaty be rejected somewhere in a national referendum. The relevant articles of the Lisbon Treaty are referred to below. It should be emphasised, however, that at the time of publication of this book it was not known if and when the Lisbon Treaty would come into force.

According to Article 9b TEU of the Lisbon Treaty, the European Council 'shall not exercise legislative functions'. This is obviously an important statement. But is it correct? The European Council has, for instance, in accordance with Article 13(2) TEU, to 'decide on common strategies to be implemented by the Union' for the CFSP. Such common strategies are a category of formal legal instruments created for the CFSP and represent an example of the European Council's power 'to take decisions' in accordance with Article 202 EC, second indent. This mechanism of Article 13 is 'a particular egregious example of conferment on the European Council of a power to take decisions (…) since it authorizes the adoption of measures having direct consequences in law' (Dashwood, p. 85 who gives on the basis of the TEU some more examples). It is in other words questionable if the future room for the European Council to exercise legislative functions by way of the Lisbon Treaty really will be limited. Article 33(3) TEU of the Lisbon Treaty grants it the possibility to switch in some cases a legal basis from unanimity to qualified majority or from a special legislative course of action to the ordinary legislative procedure. Does the involvement of the European Council in such a 'small revision' of the treaty, contrary to Article 9b TEU of the Lisbon Treaty, not exercise a legislative function? Another example: Articles 69e to 69f TFEU (Treaty on the Functioning of the European Union, the amended TEC) give the European Council the possibility, on the basis of an appeal by a Member State, to examine a draft piece of legislation and to decide whether the normal legislative procedure regarding adoption should be resumed or whether, instead, it should be considered as not having been adopted. 'It should be noted that this gives the European Council a decision-making power over the outcome of a current legislative process, a power which it had never had before'.[6] The European Parliament shares this opinion. It stated that even if the European Council 'does not directly perform legislative functions (...) it may at least interfere in a virtually decisive manner in a legislative procedure'.[7]

A.2.   Decision-making in the European Council

The treaties do not in general dictate rules for decision-making in the European Council. Generally speaking also the European Council follows the well-known pattern of the six-stage cycle: preparation, agenda setting, negotiation of formulas, negotiation of details, agreement and implementation. European Council meetings make politically binding decisions (and in the composition of HSG Council legally binding decisions). Although political decisions have no legally binding effect, they nonetheless have a legal status in *statu nascendi*. They are in many cases aimed at the creation of Community law through the action of the Institutions involved, with the Council of Ministers to the fore. As a result, the difference between these two categories, politically binding and legally binding, is not very great, in practical terms, for the Union.

Box 6

The 'mumbling auctioneer tactic'

Part of the European Council's decision-making process is sometimes the so called 'mumbling auctioneer' tactic. The President mutters something, but his audience is not quite sure it has understood it. Later it turns out that on a not very important, but for some Heads of Government sensitive point, a decision was actually taken at that moment. An example is the 'unanimous agreement' in Nice in 2000 to meet in the future in Brussels instead of in one of the Member States (as described in Chapter 3.A.6). Another example – see *Bull* 7/8-1976, 2434 – occurred under the Presidency of Dutch Prime Minister Joop den Uyl, at Brussels in 1976. Den Uyl said afterwards that it had been decided to consult the smaller Member States before the annual Western Economic Summit (G7) meeting took place. But British Prime Minister James Callaghan told the press he had not heard of any such agreement. Therefore, he and President Giscard d'Estaing, who did not like such a settlement, were able to play it down, whereas den Uyl told the press emphatically there was now a common position on this issue, which was so important for the smaller Member States (based on author's notes at the meeting).

The European Council does not take votes. The decisions are taken by *consensus*, even where the TEU provides otherwise. In other words, the European Council does not apply the rule of qualified majority voting, as does the HSG

Council. The threat of using the veto is rather exceptional. In very extreme cases a roll-call vote takes place. In 1987 in Brussels Belgian PM Wilfried Martens as President manipulated the vote regarding the setting up of a Cohesion Fund in such a way that PM Thatcher was the last one to vote, although the rules allowed her to be the first one. She was the only one to vote against. 'Yet the Summit had failed. Because unanimity was required agreement could not be reached', Martens recalls in his Memoirs (p. 606). Only five years later in Edinburgh (1992) did the Cohesion Fund see the light of day, notably under the guidance of Thatcher's successor, John Major. Decision-making by consensus, instead of voting with the requirement of unanimity, has an advantage because in some cases Member States who are only half satisfied with a text or an evaluation are only willing to acquiesce in it.[8] Consensus is, moreover, a typical phenomenon of the European Council because consultations, negotiations, compromise and decision-making are strongly interrelated here. Declarations or resolutions are often adopted in the area of the CFSP, to show the wishes, analyses and intentions of the European Union. Such decisions require unanimity (Article 23 TEU).

Since the European Council is not a Community Institution, it cannot adopt legally binding acts. In 1985 in Milan it disguised itself, in accordance with Article 236 EEC, as the Council of Ministers and called for an IGC by way of Article 148(1) EEC (currently Article 48 TEU). In order to respect the latter article, this decision was formally taken in the Council of Ministers of 22 July 1985, after both the European Commission and the Parliament had had their say in the matter (details in Chapter 3.A.2). Half a year later in Luxembourg, during the final part of the negotiations on this first institutional renewal in the history of European integration, the Heads of Government ran out of time. They solved that problem by unexpectedly passing on to the Council of Ministers a crucial point: the naming of the new treaty. Whatever the opinion of legal experts, the conclusion is that in any case the Heads of Government regard their European Council as a 'Special Community Institution' which is interchangeable with the legally binding decision-making Council of Ministers.

Another example is the decision taken in the meeting in 1992 in Edinburgh regarding the distribution of its seats between the Member States. This decision by the European Council was confirmed formally in the Council of Ministers of 1 February 1993. The European Council's decisions, in conclusion, insofar as they lead to legislation, must be incorporated in the Union's legislation through the action of the Institutions involved, with the Council to the fore. Declarations or resolutions are often adopted in the area of the CFSP, to show the wishes, analyses and intentions of the European Union.

In most cases, decision-making in the Union has a highly technocratic and sectoral character (financial services, agriculture, transport, banking, etc.). The Heads of Government in the European Council mostly look for a compromise for each problem. In some cases the way to a solution lies in a broad 'package deal', via the interplay between the Specialised Councils, the European Parliament and of course the Commission. It happens rather often that the experts and the specialised Ministers reach a deadlock. In the last resort the European Council intervenes. In such cases (see Chapter 3) the national political leaders, by offering mutual concessions, manage to show a pragmatic way out of the impasse thanks to their more global view on the matter whilst not being burdened by the technicalities.

The meetings of the European Council, in other words, have to be seen as a very essential part of the process of decision-making in the Union. This decision-making takes place by means of 'upgrading the common interest' in which benefits and costs are carefully weighted, shared out and agreed. This often succeeds because the process (with a degree of group pressure) satifies the requirements of the Member States and therefore results in a positive-sum game. Each Head of Government can finally agree because the accord dovetails with his national interest in the short or medium term. The European Council's very authoritative but legally non-binding decisions form a determining, although in most cases not a final, step in that process. This peculiarity of the decisions of the European Council characterises its position as the *mediator* in the institutional framework. This is a most important characteristic of the European Council. 'The European Union is the only large international organisation of which can be said that each problem will be solved whatever it is that must be solved. In many other international organisations (UN, Council of Europe, WTO, etc.) the deliberations frequently fail to deliver consensus. In the EU however, when the need arises, things happen, often thanks to the European Council. That is quite an achievement', according to the experienced Dutch former Minister for Foreign Affairs, Bernard Bot.

Most Heads of Government are (sometimes directly) elected politicians. Without exception they have a bond with the citizenry of their country. As the highest elected representatives of the Member States' peoples, they take their own collective initiatives, sometimes preparing decisions, making decisions and they come together as the European Council, as executive body. At the conclusion of every meeting each Head of Government gives an account in his parliament. Often there is also preparatory consultation in the national parliament before the meeting.

Ever since the coming into being of the European Council each six-monthly rotating President strives for draft conclusions, which have been agreed to as much as is possible before the start of the meeting. Therefore a European Council meeting is pre-programmed as far as possible. The need for this has grown because of the increasing number of Member States represented. As a result, the real preparatory negotiations have become more difficult. Coreper (the 27 Permanent Representatives meeting usually each week), the General Affairs Council, the EcoFin and other specialised Councils and, for CFSP/ESDP matters, the Political and Security Committee (COPS), negotiate beforehand on various levels in order to eliminate as many difficult details as possible. They do so in close cooperation with the Council's General Secretariat and the Commission under the leadership of the Presidency. During this process and also during the European Council itself, the Permanent Representatives of the Member States play a key role in the defence of national positions on special issues on the agenda. Each of them advises his own Head of State or Government on which strategy to adopt in the meeting, in order to achieve their national objectives.

In some cases the European Council asks a special preparatory committee or High Level Group composed of their national representatives to prepare a detailed report on a particular important issue. Sometimes a highly esteemed person, for example the former Dutch PM Wim Kok, who in 2004 advised the European Council on a new strategy regarding the Lisbon Strategy, chairs such a group.

Little is divulged about the exact way in which decisions under the requirement of consensus are reached in these strictly private meetings. An important element of the decision-making in such meetings is of course the national interest of the Heads of Government. In the European Council (as in the Council) we see a pattern of 'serial exceptionalism', according to which individual Heads of Government signal that a given issue is indeed a 'very important interest' to be accommodated (Hayes-Renshaw and Wallace, p. 312). Examples are agriculture for the French and the Irish, monetary policy for the British, fisheries for the Spanish and so on. It goes without saying that the President of the meeting in particular has to keep this in mind. As mentioned earlier, the President plays a key role in the process of decision-making. Informal rules and understandings also determine the outcome. There are no minutes which, after the passing of the years, may be opened for scientific research. Of importance sometimes is the power game by the political leaders of the largest Member States plus the attitude of those smaller Members States whose agreement in this case for decision-making is vital.

The negotiating process tends not to follow the lines of the political divisions/parties in Europe. Neither in my research nor in 35 years' coverage of the meetings has any trace of ideological conflict (or harmony) been ascertained initially. The purely national interests of Member States and of their governmental leaders have rather been the main force. However, this appears to be changing. Political preferences do sometimes emerge, albeit by way of exception. In 1998 in Pörtschach (Austria) I noticed for the first time how the result of a meeting was decided completely through prior consultation by eleven (of the fifteen) Heads of Government belonging to the Group of European Socialists (PES).

Another phenomenon is the influence of the large political factions in the European Parliament. Nowadays, particularly the European People's Party Group (EPP/ED), the strongest political group, followed by the PES, try from within the European Parliament to pre-cook the decision-making in the European Council, since their size gives them strength. That struggle has led to the calling of preparatory Summits of the Heads of Government of these groups as well as from the smaller Alliance of Liberals and Democrats for Europe (ALDE), several hours before the start of the European Council. There is the example of the 'EPP national political leaders Summit meeting' of 16 December 2004 in Meise/Brussels. Shortly before the crucial decision to start membership negotiations with Turkey, the internally divided EPP-national political leaders cut the knot during their own 'Mini-Summit'. That considerably facilitated decision-taking several hours later in the European Council. It is worth noting that the (supposedly politically independent) President José M. Barroso of the Commission (with an EPP affiliation) also took part in this meeting in Meise.

The European Council differs clearly, both in operational approach and in composition, from the Council of Ministers, the 'regular' decision-making body, and from the Commission in its role as the official initiator. The Heads of Government cleverly sidestep their handicap of not being in fact a decision-making body. They present their agreement concerning an issue in many cases as a political accord. Shortly after their meeting such an accord is put on a legal footing by the Council of Ministers and the other Institutions, often without changing the text one iota. 'Because texts are approved by Heads of Government, it is in practice impossible after the event to alter language which has received their blessing', according to the advisor of the Secretary-General of the Council David Galloway (2001, p. 25). In this way, the European Council created two-phase decision-making: politically in the European Council and legally in the Council of Ministers – see the examples described in Chapter 3.

Another important aspect of decision-making in the European Council is that here the Heads of Government, in contrast to decision-making in the Council with a differing number of votes for every Member State (Article 205(2) TEC), represent their State on an equal basis. In the European Council every Head of Government has one vote. Our analysis of the long series of activities of the European Council in Chapter 3 shows, however, that the Heads of Government, because the States they represent are very unequal in political importance for the Union, are unequal also in the European Council in the process of decision-making. The larger Member States have, as will be outlined in more detail in Chapters 3 and 4, no small influence on decision-making.

Coalition building, bilateral and trilateral meetings

Cooperation between France and Germany constituted the driving force behind the creation of the European Council. I have attempted to show, especially in Chapters 3 and 4, that Franco-German cooperation may be seen as pivotal. It is hard to find an area in which the shared approach of the French President and the German Chancellor in preparation and decision-making in the European Council did not prove decisive. The Franco-German Treaty of 1963 introduced regular Summits (at least bi-annual) of the leaders of those two Member States, at which it became the practice to prepare the European Council's agenda point by point.

The expansion of the number of Member States has resulted in a prolifer-ation of other preparatory Summit meetings (Rittelmeyer, p. 73-107). In 1991 the Visegrad Group, comprising Poland, the Czech Republic, Hungary and Slovakia, saw the light of day. Soon afterwards the 'Weimar Triangle' came into being, a regular Summit of Germany, France and Poland. In some cases Italy and Spain also take part in these Summits. Other examples are the Paris-Berlin-Madrid or Paris-Warsaw Summits. Nowadays there are joint Summits of the Benelux and the Visegrad countries. In addition the northern Member States (Denmark, Finland and Sweden) and the Baltic States (Estonia, Latvia and Lithuania) hold joint meetings. At the beginning of this century the trilat-eral Summit of Germany, France and the UK appeared on the horizon. It pro-voked protest, however, from other Member States and from the Commission. They feared the creation of a 'Directorate' that would take decisions which the other Member States in the European Council would have no option but to swallow (though I know no example of such a decision).

In reality the influence of most of these various Summits on the course of European Council meetings has been limited. Only the regular Franco-German Summit has put a stamp on the course of the European Council. In many cases, at their preparatory meetings, France and Germany anticipate the decisions of the European Council (perhaps during a breakfast or supper meeting of the French President and the German Chancellor in the margin of the European Council) – as was the case at the important 2003 Brussels Council, to give only one example of many (details in Chapter 3.C.3). Mitterrand and Kohl had no less than eighty official bilateral Summits between 1982 and 1995. They clocked up a total of 150 meetings, plus more than sixty conversations by telephone (Saunier, p. 240).

Take as an example of the process of decision-making in the European Council the intended introduction of co-decision for the entire asylum and migration policy (apart from legal migration) simultaneously with decision-making on the basis of QMV. The European Council was able to agree on the matter on 4 November 2004. Next the JHA Council, together with the European Parliament, had formally to adopt and develop the agreement in detail. On 21-22 December 2004 the Council of Ministers' meeting officially accepted this decision as an A-item. Here we see how the European Council operates ideally. The Heads of Government and the President of the Commission take a political decision. The specialised Councils then convert this political decision into a legal text (*Gen Rep*, 2004, 13).

Changing the classic Community Method

The classic triangular Community Method for the development of legislation involves a proposal by the independent European (minded) Commission, co-decision or an opinion by the supranational Parliament, and a final decision in the Council of Ministers. The creation of the European Council has changed this method for a number of important decisions to a system based on negotiations between the Member States. The Heads of Government have created their own channels for preparation and command, which are essentially intergovernmental in nature. In the European Council approach the Commission 'has found itself excluded from these procedures and has lost its power to make proposals' (European Parliament, Poos, p. 12). Although this quotation exaggerates, it is true that, due to the emergence of the European Council, the role of the European Commission as the exclusive initiator and honest broker in the negotiating process between the Member States has been weakened. Over the years, as outlined in Chapter 3, the European Council has taken the initiative on a number of key issues (as in the founding treaties was to be done by the Commission). The European Council itself sometimes even prepared the whole process of decision-making[9], originally done by the Commission and the Council, and subsequently took the crucial political decisions which, according to the treaties, should be taken by the Council and the Commission.

Implementation of the European Council's decisions

Regarding the implementation of the European Council's decisions it is in most cases for the Presidency, through the General Affairs Council

(GAERC), to take the necessary steps. The different Institutions concerned then receive the mandate to give effect to its results in legally binding decisions. In their first meeting after the European Council, the Ambassadors of the Member States (Coreper) add their individual comments to the Conclusions and try to hammer out differences over the text where they arise. Coreper and COPS report to the General Affairs Council, and the Article 36 Committee to the JHA Council (via Coreper). It sometimes happens that the Commission or lower-level working parties of the Council use the Conclusions to reopen deliberations about a checkmated dossier, in order to reach an agreement after all. So the first aspect of implementation of European Council decisions is that it takes place outside the European Council *stricto senso*.

Chapter 3 describes how and when an agreement or decision of the European Council is finally implemented, in many cases in a legal act. Sometimes the moment of implementation is difficult to determine. It can take many years before even a decision made more than once is realised. In some cases implementation has never taken place. An example is the decision of the Lisbon European Council in 2000 to create a single EU patent (see Chapter 4.A.1). In other situations it has remained unclear what exactly was decided, since the European Council refused to reveal the correct interpretation when the disputed matter was politically too 'hot'. The latter was the case after the debate on the seat of the Institutions (question by MEP Damseaux, OJ C. 210/14, 19.08.81). Sometimes the 'agreement' in the European Council was in reality an illusion.[10] In other cases an erroneous or incomplete solution was found. In some cases, the European Council tries to frame the implementation of its agreements, mandates and demands by including in the Conclusions a timetable for their completion or implementation. In conclusion, a second aspect of implementation is that it is at times hard to discern exactly how many of the European Council's Conclusions finally become law.

There is one important exception: the CFSP. Once a Statement is agreed in the area of the Union's foreign policy, it is also the *final opinion* of the Member States as a whole and, as such, the Union's authoritative position on the international scene. The follow-up might, in such cases, usually be described as a diplomatic declaratory action by the Presidency and the High Representative for the CFSP. In exceptional cases when the Union as such is involved, for instance in the deployment of its Battlegroups or by way of its trade policy (see Chapter 3.E.2), the Council of Ministers does play a role.

Thirdly, as will be described in Chapter 3, the European Council has, since 2000, in some cases taken over the Commission's task of being the neutral supervisor regarding the implementation of important parts of the *acquis communautaire* as decided by it.

Has the President of the Commission veto power?

Of interest is the question regarding the legal position of the President of the Commission in the process of decision-making in the European Council. Let us assume that the Heads of State and Government have reached consensus regarding a certain decision in the European Council, but that the President of the Commission is against it. Has the President in such a case the right of veto in order to block decision-making?

Article 4 TEU provides that the President of the Commission is a fully-fledged member of the European Council; one may therefore assume that his agreement is required. On the other hand, arguments exist to question the above-mentioned conclusion. Is the President of the Commission really a fully-fledged member? In 1965 the President of the Commission, Walter Hallstein, became *persona non grata* in Paris because he began to behave like a Head of Government. The French government did not accept that. Furthermore, it is remarkable that the President of the Commission had to wait from 1961 until the coming into force of the Single European Act in 1988 to be officially endorsed as a member of the European Council. The position of the President in the meetings was, in other words, unclear for a long time. The Commission President is, moreover, the only member of the European Council without a legitimate mandate as a Head of State or Government. In addition his political room for manoeuvre is restricted by the requirement of collegiality in the Commission (Article 217(1) TEC). Authoritative legal experts concluded in 1985 that the collaboration of the President of the Commission is not needed for the formation of a common accord in the European Council (European Parliament, Capotorti, Art. 31). The European Council has an intergovernmental character. By virtue of the rules and customary law, the Heads of State and Government there take decisions by way of consensus. But the President of the Commission is not a Head of State or Government. Therefore the question arises whether he is fully and legally entitled to block decision-making in the European Council by acting against it. A third important point is that in the Lisbon Treaty ex Article 201(a) (although not yet applicable), the President of the Commission is explicitly denied the right 'to take part in the vote'.

Finally there is the important political aspect. As far as is known, never during the more than thirty years of existence of the European Council has a President of the Commission attempted to block decision-making. On the contrary: the course of the discussions has shown that the Commission is always very sensitive to the activities and the decisions of the Heads of Government in the European Council. In these meetings the Commission President strives constantly for consensus. Finally, it is difficult to imagine that a President of the Commission is politically capable of showing convincingly that a unanimous decision of the Heads of State and Government should be blocked. To conclude, the right of the President of the Commission to block decision-making is doubtful.

An insider notes, however, that in the meetings the weight of the Commission President is greater than that of many a Head of Government. Take for instance the important meeting in June 2007 with the agreement for a precise mandate for the IGC after the collapse of the Constitutional Treaty. During this meeting the deliberations lasted sixteen hours. With 28 participants, each of them would have had the floor for an average of half an hour. President José M. Barroso however secured everyone's attention longer. That was partly due to the fact that Heads of Government bickered about the French demand to scrap 'free and undistorted competition' as an objective of the Union. The President of the Commission is neither a member of the HSG Council nor of the Council in the composition of the Highest Representatives of the Member States. Yet the President always takes part, takes the floor and makes proposals, proficient in forging a political deal. In the face of this threatened conflict over an amendment of the treaty regarding competition policy, President Barroso immediately took on the role of broker and achieved success. The course of this meeting shows that the distinction made by legal experts between the European Council with the President of the Commission as a member and the meeting without his membership in (a) the composition of the Heads of State or Government (HSG Council) or (b) in the context of Conferences of the Highest Representatives of the Governments (IGC) does not exist in the conduct of the meeting. In all three types of meeting the President of the Commission takes an active role.

A.3.   Functions and tasks of the European Council

The European Council is today the highest political and leading body of the EU. Its meetings have, according to the Council's 'founding father' Valéry Giscard d'Estaing (AE, Europe Documents, 1977, Nr. 931), a broad range of tasks, functions and roles. It is difficult to create order in its activities. The reason is that they range across a dual capacity: on the one hand tasks expressly laid down in the treaties (in particular the TEU) and on the other hand the tasks with a more political character which the Heads of Government have either taken upon themselves over the years or with which they were faced as the result of political developments in the Union. The European Council's tasks may be conceptually divided into two categories: giving political direction to the Union and resolving problems that have proved intractable at Council of Ministers' level. However, such a neat division into a package of A tasks (the TEU) and B tasks (the remainder) turns out to be impracticable. One immediately encounters the problem that the main task of the European Council in Article 4 TEU was formulated very widely and broadly: *'To provide the Union with the necessary impetus for its development'* and to *'define the general political guidelines thereof'*. These terms of reference resulted in the European Council now operating as agenda-setter for the Union. However, it should not be concluded that setting the agenda of intended activities is a task of the European Council, laid down in the treaties. The nature of the European Council's activities, in other words, frequently makes it difficult to say in which kind of mode it is working.

In the overview, we include the functions, tasks and roles as laid down in the treaties plus those which the Heads of Government have taken upon themselves. Since Heads of Government structure their meetings in accordance with their changing national and personal interests, the following outline of tasks and functions is wide-ranging and emphasises change dependent upon the various Heads of Government.[11] Given the many hats worn by the Heads of Government, it pays first to mention briefly the tasks arising from the treaties.

1.   *The European Council as an organ of the Union.* By virtue of Article 4 TEU, its task is to 'provide the Union with the necessary impetus for its development' and to 'define the general political guidelines thereof'. On the

basis of this broadly formulated and general task, the European Council has grown into the Union's helmsman or the 'political dynamo' of the Union (Commission, Relations between the Institutions of the Community, COM (81) 581 final, p. 7). The European Council takes, in its role as agenda-setter, the major political initiatives and determines the position of the Union on major issues. In many cases it has taken the task of 'deliberating upon matters concerning European Union in its different aspects' in order to issue 'general political guidelines' (Solemn Declaration on European Union, *Bull* 6-1983, 1.6.1). These measures are likely to produce legal effects for the Institutions in so far as they translate them into Union policy and legislation.

In a certain sense this task as *agenda-setter* logically includes a very substantial part of the vast range of activities. For this reason it is impossible to give a complete account in this brief summary. We restrict ourselves to some typical examples and refer for the remainder to Chapter 3. A typical example of 'defining the general political guidelines' was the laying down of the 'Copenhagen Criteria' in 1993 for the admittance of the applicant countries from Central and Eastern Europe and later in that year the adoption, as an action plan, of the detailed White Paper 'Growth, Competitiveness, Employment' in the fight against unemployment (*Bull* 6-1993, I.13 and *Bull* 12-1993, I.2-I.6). The latter was presented by the Commission following a request from the European Council. The paper referred to some treaty articles new at that time: 103 TEC, 'economic policy as a matter of common concern' and 129 B TEC, 'Trans-European networks in the areas of transport, telecommunications and energy infrastructures'. In the same category is the task of 'improving Community procedures' (see Annex 4 to this publication, point 5). As another example, the Edinburgh 1992 meeting decided upon an 'overall approach to the application by the Council of the subsidiarity principle: the Union will be given responsibility only for those matters which the Member States are no longer capable of dealing with efficiently' (*Bull* 12-1992, I.15-I.22).

2.   The European Council in its 'quasi constitutional function' (Piris, 92) acts as *implementer* of a series of articles and provisions laid down in the treaties since the coming into force of the Treaty of Maastricht (1993). In other words here the European Council acts as a policy and decision-making body. The proposed Lisbon Treaty makes the European Council an official Institution with specific decision-making tasks in such politically highly important matters as the CFSP and JHA.

Foreign policy has been part of the agenda of every meeting for as long as the European Council has existed. In accordance with Title V TEU, the CFSP belongs to the European Council's prerogatives. The European Council sets out the principles and the general guidelines of this policy. They include the common strategies of the Union in areas where the Member States have important common interests (e.g. vis-à-vis Russia or the Mediterranean region).

The Treaty of Amsterdam (1999) affirmed the competence of the European Council to decide on common defence policy-making on the CFSP (Article 17 TEU) and gave it the last word regarding decision-making on the CFSP in the Council of Ministers.[12] The Heads of State or Government have via the European Council taken upon themselves the responsibility for important parts of their national foreign policy. In the field of the European foreign policy the Ministers for Foreign Affairs have had to make a step back.

In cases where the rule of decision-making by qualified majority applies, any Member State has the right to oppose the taking of a decision on this basis 'for important and stated reasons of national policy'. The Council of Ministers may then decide by QMV to request that the matter be referred, for decision-making by consensus, to the European Council. With regard to Article 40(2)TEU and 11(2) TEC this approach has not the same effect as the famous Luxembourg Compromise (see Chapter 1.C.1) since after the matter in question has been 'raised before the European Council', the Council of Ministers has the option to cut the knot on the basis of QMV. We see here the European Council in its specific role as an *'instance d'arbitrage'*.

Other examples are the decisions referred to in Articles 109a(2) and 109f(1) TEC in Maastricht regarding important appointments. According to Article 112 TEC, the governments of the Member States at the level of the Heads of State or Government, and 214 TEC the HSG Council, decide on the most important appointments in the Union: the President of the Commission; the President, the Vice-Presidents and the other members of the Executive Board of the European Central Bank (ECB); the High Representative on the Common Foreign and Security Policy (CFSP) (Article 207(2); and, moreover, determine the seat of the Institutions according to 289 TEC.[13] Most legal experts agree that the Institutions of the EU can decide on the designation of seats of agencies or other EU offices and bodies. Therefore we see here an example of a regular activity of the Heads of Government, which they together took away from the Institutions. Another example is Article 99(2) TEC where the European Council discusses the 'broad guide-lines' of the economic policies of the Member States.

Finally, for more examples of the European Council in its 'quasi constitu-tional role' one may refer to the Treaty of Amsterdam, which brought the task of authorising closer or enhanced cooperation initiatives between the Member States in the Third Pillar, and to the Treaty of Nice, which allowed the same in the Second Pillar (Article 27C TEU). At the time, this innovation was seen as a breakthrough. However, during the years since then, enhanced cooperation has never been put into practice.

In 1997 in Amsterdam it was agreed under pressure, especially from France, that the European Council should 'each year consider the employ-ment situation (…) and adopt conclusions thereon' (Article 128 TEC). These conclusions are the basis for guidelines, set out by the Council of Ministers, which the Member States are required to take into consideration. At an extraordinary meeting on employment in November 1997 the European Council decided on an early implementation of this task in 1998. More is said regarding its effects in Chapter 3.F.1.

3.   *Meeting as Council of Ministers in the composition of the Heads of State or Government – the HSG Council – in the framework of the European Council.* The TEU stipulates that the meeting in this composition exercises several functions. In 1993 new developments were to be seen in the clauses ex Article 109 J (2), (3) and (4) and 109 K (2) TEU, where the Heads of State or Government shape the EMU. (For a description and an evaluation of 'the long march by the Council towards a European currency', see Chapter 3.B.1- B.2.)

A second example is the important process of enlargement of the Union. Before each enlargement, the Heads of State or Government will have, in accordance with Article 49 TEU, laid down the conditions of admission. The subject was on the agenda of every meeting between 1983 and 1985 and moreover has been since the early 1990s. (For a description and an evaluation of these activities, see Chapter 3 C.1- C.3.)

A third example is the Treaty of Amsterdam where it introduced Article 7 TEU. The HSG Council can identify a 'serious and persistent breach' by a Member State of the fundamental rights, as stipulated in Article 6(1)TEU. In such a case, the Council of Ministers can, on the basis of QMV, 'suspend certain of the rights deriving from the application of this Treaty' (e.g. the voting right) attached to Union membership. It goes without saying that the votes by the Member State in question are here not taken into account (Article 309.(4) TEC).

Worth mentioning here is how in 2000 the Heads of State or Government were unprepared and took a rash decision on which they had to renege. They took the remarkable decision to downgrade 'to the lowest possible level'[14] the ministerial relations between the Member States and Austria for an indefinite period, starting 1 February 2000. The action stemmed from the expected agreement in Vienna to form a coalition between the People's Party (ÖVP) and the far-right Freedom Party (FPÖ), headed by Jörg Haider. The decision had no legal basis. The sanctions therefore had no legally binding result, but were nevertheless of politically binding significance. The decision had been taken without any discussion with Vienna. The ÖVP and FPÖ had clearly won the democratic elections in Austria. There was no evidence at all of human rights or democratic rights abuses. What is incredible is the fact that in the Spring of 2000 Portuguese PM Guterres as European Council President, under pressure from the Member States with a large extreme right-wing voting population (such as France and Belgium) skipped Vienna during the usual tour of the capitals. At the subsequent Lisbon European Council, President Chirac, his PM Jospin and Belgian PM Verhofstadt, initially refused to appear in the traditional 'family portrait' if Austrian Chancellor Schüssel was included. In the end, the sanctions had no effect whatsoever. The ÖVP and FPÖ formed their envisaged coalition. The German Christian Democratic leader Wolfgang Schäuble remarked later in an interview with the Belgium daily *De Tijd* (2 July 2005, p. 4) that none of the large Member States would have been treated like Austria.

4.   *Meeting as an Intergovernmental Conference* (IGC). The Heads of State or Government decide in accordance with Article 48 TEU on all changes regarding the institutional structure of the Union. In this composition, as what is called the 'constitutional architect' of the Union, they have to conduct direct negotiations on complex legal texts affecting the Union's basic structure. Since 1985 the Heads of State or Government have been occupied with institutional reforms almost constantly. (For a broad view and an evaluation of these activities see, Chapter 3.A.)

In what now follows as the second category there are various tasks with a more political character which the Heads of Government have taken upon themselves in the course of the years.

5.   An originally (at least officially) unforeseen, but nevertheless very characteristic and important task, is that of acting in controversial issues in the last resort as *supreme arbitrator*, or *instance d'appel*. In other words the settling of issues after deadlock in the Council of Ministers, or to settle issues outstanding from discussions at a lower level. (For more on this issue of arbitration, see Chapter 3.)

6.   The consensual adoption of the multi-annual seven yearly financial framework or *Financial Perspectives* of the Union, which is later implemented by an 'Own Resources Decision' of the Council of Ministers. Initiated in 1988 in Brussels, it was repeated in Edinburgh 1992, in Berlin in 1999 and Brussels in December 2005. The agreed spending limits often go side by side with important policy changes at the Structural Funds and Common Agricultural Policy level, by far the biggest budget items of the Union. At the same time the problem of the disputed burden-sharing among the individual Member States is addressed. (For a broad view and an appraisal of these negotiations see Chapter 3.D.1-D.2.)

7.   The regular *confirmation and coordination* of the most important projects and decisions taken by the General Affairs Council (GAERC), by the different Specialised Council meetings and by the Commission. With this action, which results from the earlier mentioned tasks, the European Council underscores the political importance thereof and the need for precise implementation. Here the European Council functions as a 'well oiled stamping machine' (Eijsbouts, 2000, p. 76) for pre-cooked decisions of the Council of Ministers, the Coreper or the Commission. In other words in the spotlight of publicity the Heads of Government pocket the honour for decisions taken at a hierarchically lower level. This role of the European Council confirms once more who really rules Europe. In some cases (see Chapter 3.F.2) the Council has taken on the task of controlling the implementation of its own agreements and decisions. In November 2004 the Heads of Government even assumed the original task of devoting a meeting to two important partly-failed projects: the Lisbon Strategy of 2000 and the Tampere Programme of 1999 for the creation of an area of freedom, security and justice (see Chapter 3).

8.   *'Informal exchanges of view* of a wide-ranging nature held in the greatest privacy and not designed to lead to formal decisions or public statements'. (Organisational Rules for European Council Meetings, *Bull* 6-1977, 2.3.1) This has always been an important aspect of the meetings. It was originally even the *raison d'être* for the creation of the European Council (Werts, 1992).

9.   Meeting as a *high political conference*. The Heads of State or Government as political leaders of independent states then take binding decisions regarding international public law, if required on the basis of the rules of the Vienna Convention on Treaties. In this setting they are able to take on any subject without restrictions, except for their constitution. In so doing they discuss and settle issues both inside and outside the jurisdiction of the European treaties. This means that the meeting in this case and this composition is not bound by the 'single institutional framework' ex Article 3 TEU, of the Union.[15]

.

Previously we have (a) described and analysed all the functions of the European Council *resulting from the treaty*. That showed moreover that the European Council (b) has a number of tasks which result *only partly* from the treaty. In sum this means that the European Council has to provide the Union with the necessary impetus for its development; to define the general political guidelines plus the principles of, and general guidelines for, the CFSP. Chapter 3 shows that in practice the European Council carries out its mostly vaguely and verbosely formulated tasks in great detail. What is characteristic, moreover, is the task of acting as *'instance d'appel'* – settling issues after deadlock in the Council. Finally, observation of the meetings reveals (c) the existence of a third and final category of activities that are related to various fields and sometimes even lie outside the European Council's responsibility. The following examples show that the Heads of Government – individually or jointly – have granted the European Council separate activities and even functions and tasks. Later on we also mention these activities because they serve as examples of the European Council's functioning. In particular the following specific activities come to the fore.

10.   Being 'the European Union's main *point of contact with the mass media*, with the six-monthly [June and December] European Council meeting attracting 2000 to 3000 journalists (...) it also provides an opportunity to take stock of the state of the Union and discuss the issues of the day' (Council, Trumpf Piris Report, 1999, p. 14).

11.   From the beginning these meetings have been used by Heads of Government to find international approval for their (sometimes controversial) domestic social, economic and monetary policies (examples in Chapter 3). In many cases an important side-effect of such meetings has been to make their domestic constituencies aware of the complexity of the Member States' interdependence in the EU and the limitations which it imposes upon national sovereignty.

An interesting phenomenon is that of the Council (exceptionally) acting as an instrument of urgent national domestic government policy. German Chancellor Kohl at the Dublin 1990 Summit meeting insisted on the urgent necessity of appropriations for the Soviet Union which were seen as the *'quid pro quo'* for Soviet acceptance of NATO membership for a united Germany. Also in this category is the European Council acting as a forum for the discussion of undesirable conditions and situations in Member States in order to enforce changes. In Maastricht in 1981 a discussion was held about the inflationary linking of wages and salaries to price index movements in Belgium, at the time the only Member State to do this. Belgian PM Wilfried Martens had been lumbered with this policy. Upon his return to Brussels he used the criticism to kill off this Belgian 'holy cow'. Another example is President Chirac's fierce criticism in Cannes and Madrid (both in 1995) of the liberal Dutch drugs policy. A third example is of the European Council being used as an instrument to turn a national political preference into a priority for Europe. A case in point here is the Lisbon Strategy of 2000 aiming to turn the EU into the world's most dynamic economy. The driving forces behind this were Prime Ministers Tony Blair and António Guterres. They themselves were at that moment in the process of launching economic revivals in the UK and in Portugal respectively. The decisions in the European Council in Lisbon served to help them obtain public acceptance at home for their national priorities (see PMs Blair and Guterres, IHT, March 23, 2000 p. 10). These examples are of course activities of the European Council, rather than tasks.

12.   Sometimes the European Council, instead of giving the necessary impetus, does the opposite: it intentionally (under pressure from its most influential members) *puts the brakes on European integration*. It does so by watering down the plans, ambitions and expectations of the European Commission, the European Parliament and some governments. As outlined in Chapter 3, the meetings of Dublin (October 1996) and Biarritz (2000) made clear that the envisaged Treaty of Amsterdam (1997) and later the Nice Treaty (2001) would present few innovations. The time was not yet right. The winding down of over-ambitious expectations also took place at the November 1997 Employment Summit in Luxembourg. Commission proposals for the creation of twelve million jobs were swept off the table.

Box 7

Cash down

Heads of Government regard the European Council as their doormat for everything. In 2003 after seven years of tug of war the European Council finally agreed on an EU-wide savings tax. The measure was intended to root out massive tax evasion by people placing their deposits in non-reported or secret accounts abroad. At the very last moment however, Italy demanded a higher national milk quota. This demand bore no relationship whatsoever to the savings tax. Reduction of milk production in Italy was a hot potato in national politics because Italy traditionally has a shortage of milk. This event demonstrates the extent to which the European Council is sometimes used in the pursuit of purely national interest.

We further mention the remarkable request at the Spring 2005 meeting by President Chirac, with the backing of Chancellor Gerhard Schröder and the Heads of Government of some small Member States, to rewrite the proposal for the Directive on Services in the Internal Market. The move was a reaction to the proposal for a general throwing open of services, from architects to plumbers, to cross-border competition on the basis of, in some cases, lower social standards. An important bone of contention was the use of the 'country of origin principle' which meant that a service provider was only subject to the (in most cases less stringent) social laws of his own country. Opinion polls suggested the majority of voters in France would react to it by voting against the proposed Constitutional Treaty in the upcoming referendum. Unexpectedly, President Chirac brought this subject up in the meeting. The upshot was a chaotic discussion without any clear conclusion. The

European Council discussed the Directive for 2½ hours. The Commission, which had done its utmost in this respect, was distressed that only five minutes remained for the mid term evaluation of the Lisbon Strategy, 'the main topic of the meeting', as a participant said afterwards. At their press conferences in Brussels Chirac and his allies said that the Services Directive would be rewritten. The directive, however, was at that moment before the European Parliament and the Council of Ministers for approval. This is an example of how influential Heads of State or Government sometimes use the European Council to push aside the decision-making laid down in the treaties, in order to achieve their national political priorities.

Box 8

The tip of the iceberg that is the European Council

Another classification of the functions of the European Council, which we summarise here, is to be found in Dashwood and also in Jacqué. They deduced a series of functions expressly attributed to the European Council or the HSG Council in the process of decision-making.[16]

The first function is that of the *definition of principles and guidelines* appropriate for decisions in a given area of the Union's activities. An example is Article 13(1) TEU. That article gives the European Council the power to define the principles of, and general guidelines for, the CFSP. Such a task is in line with its role envisaged in Article 4 TEU.

The second function is that of *holding only a discussion*, as a step in the procedure leading to the adoption of a formal instrument. In such case the Heads of Government fulfil a condition in order to enable the procedure in question to run its course. The European Council, or the HSG Council, offer here political guidelines in a question which is the subject of the procedure. Examples are Article 99(2) TEC regarding the broad economic policy guidelines (European Council) and Article 122(2) TEC on the lifting of a Member State's derogation from participation in the single currency (Council meeting in the composition of the Heads of State or Government).

The third variety of functions is the *adoption of a conclusion*, as a step in a procedure leading to the adoption of a formal instrument. Here the European Council or the HSG Council has to take a common position on the matter in question as a pre-condition of the adoption of an instrument at a lower decision-making level. An example is Article 128 TEC. Here the drafting of employment policy guidelines by the Council of Ministers is dependent on the prior adoption of conclusions regarding the employment situation in the Union by the European Council.

Finally there is the – very exceptionally employed – function of *adopting a definitive measure* having immediate legal consequences. In the TEU three cases can be traced of the attribution of such a task to the European Council: Article 13(2) on common strategies for the CFSP; Article 17(1) regarding the transition to a Common Defence Policy; and Article 23(2) on breaking the deadlock resulting from an objection to a CFSP measure by QMV. Examples of this function of decision-making by the HSG Council are Article 121 TEC on the procedures for the transition to the third stage of EMU and the introduction of the euro; Article 7(2) TEU to determine the existence of a serious and persistent breach of the principles of liberty, democracy, respect for human rights and fundamental freedoms (a provision which has never been applied); the provision under Article 214(2) EC to nominate the President of the Commission and the power under Article 10(6) of the ESCB Statute to amend the voting rules of the ECB's Governing Council.

Dashwood rightly concluded that the foregoing represents the proverbial *'tip of the iceberg'*. By far the greatest part of the involvement of the European Council, or the HSG Council, in decision-making and other activities takes place *without being prescribed or authorised by, or even alluded to, in the treaties*, as will be amply shown in our Chapter 3.

Another special role the European Council sometimes takes on is trying to roll back unpopular measures, taken earlier by the Institutions. Around the turn of the century, the Prime Ministers of the three larger Member States (the Big Three), Tony Blair, Lionel Jospin and Gerhard Schröder in chorus demanded a reprieve for duty-free shopping (or, in German the popular tax free *'Butterfahrten'*). In doing so they tried to overturn a decision which had been taken unanimously in the EcoFin in 1991. The three came up against a *'njet'* of the smaller Member States.

In this overview of tasks, roles and functions we should, finally, not overlook the European Council's role as an important centre where the Heads of Government continuously work on their personal mutual political relationships. Many problems of the cumbersome decision-making in the Union are the result of a weak foundation of trust between the national capitals.

What finally remains is a number of diverging functions and tasks, including for instance discussing purely internal affairs – for example, about the number of places available in day nurseries, discussed in Seville in 2002.

B.   THE RELATIONSHIP BETWEEN THE EUROPEAN COUNCIL AND THE INSTITUTIONS

B.1.   The subservient position of the Commission

According to the treaties, the Commission (Articles 211-219 TEC), the most supranational Institution, is the initiating body. The Commission acts in 'the general interest of the Community' (Article 213(2) TEC) independently of the Member States. It is 'the strategic authority (...) that would guarantee the continuity of the project despite the political or geopolitical hazards', as Commission President Jacques Delors, stated at the 30th anniversary of the signing of the Treaties of Rome (*Bull* Suppl. 2/87, p. 10). The Commission has the right of legislative initiative and therefore also of political initiative. Besides, the Commission is the guardian of the treaties and the executive with the competence to take decisions in order to implement decisions of the Council of Ministers and/or Parliament.

So much for the theory. In practice, things are different. The Commission has never developed as a political body (let alone as a European Government). In the course of the years indeed 'a practice of transferring the right of initiative in important questions to the European Council is settled' (Kapteyn & VerLoren van Themaat, 1998, p. 412). This development started with the rules of conduct emanating from the 'Luxembourg Compromise' outlined earlier. This agreement sets out rules governing collaboration between the Council and the Commission, whereby, before adopting any important proposal, the latter 'should establish the appropriate contacts with the Governments of the Member States' (*Gen Rep*, 1966, 12-16 and *Bull* 3-1966). Since then, Member States have had (although the Commission remains fully responsible for the final drafting of its proposals) the power to try to shape an initiative of the Commission at the earliest stage. The continuing increase in the importance and power of the Presidency as a broker in the negotiating process and the growing activities and importance over the years of Coreper and the General Secretariat of the Council also diminished the Commission's role.

Already in 1972 the President of the Commission, Sicco Mansholt, had stated that the Heads of Government should 'define the priorities' (*Bull* 8-1972, p. 25). In 1974 the emergence of the European Council was welcomed by the Commission as a 'major innovation'. The Commission acknowledged that it would have to adapt its *modus operandi* 'to the new system in which ideas will come from the top' (*Gen Rep*, 1974, p. XII). Later the Commission foresaw that the creation of the European Council had resulted in 'a shift in the balance of powers from the Commission to the Council', with the result that its 'political function has been heavily compromised, as regards both its involvement in the legislative process and its executive and management functions' (*Bull* Suppl. 3/82, p. 9), with the Member States via the European Council as dominant legislators. The European Council has in some cases indeed forced the Commission to take important measures to which it had great political objections. An example is the blunt refusal by the Heads of Government in 1982 to reform the CAP as proposed by the Commission in order to fight the growing agricultural surpluses. The European Council adopted instead a further 5 percent rise in CAP prices paid to farmers without any reform (Werts, 1992, p. 229).

The Commission agrees that only some ten percent of its proposals relate to proper initiative (AE, 14 September 2002, p. 5, see also Peterson, p. 59). Nowadays, as will be outlined in Chapters 3 and 4, it is the European Council which initiates. In every meeting, the European Council asks the European Commission to present proposals or develop certain issues and projects. This undermines the independent position of the Commission laid down in Article 213(2) TEC stating that the members of the Commission 'shall neither seek nor take instructions from any government or from any other body'. The numerous demands and instructions coming from the Heads of Government put the seal on a practice whereby the right to make the propopals in important matters of policy moved to the European Council. Take for instance the Lisbon 2000 Strategy. This project comes from the European Council. Or take the negotiations for a Constitutional Treaty and the subsequent Lisbon Treaty. Here, indeed, the major task falls to the HSG Council. According to Article 48 TEU the Commission has the right here to table proposals. But during the lengthy deliberations from 2001 to 2007 in the framework of the meetings of the Heads of Government, Commission President Romano Prodi in particular was left on the sideline (details in Chapter 3). As outlined more extensively in Chapter 4, in the Constitutional Treaty and the subsequent Lisbon Treaty the European Council has preserved and strengthened its predominant position.

This development in which the European Council asks the Commission to take certain initiatives or present proposals also has its down side. In the Third Pillar (Justice and Home Affairs) the Member States initially took such initiatives. But especially as the result of the European Council launching a stream of requests, the Commission was handed the opportunity (and the honour) of submitting its proposals.

The European Council encompasses the qualities which enable it to be the highest authority of the Union. In the first place it takes political decisions regarding all principal matters which immediately bind in a political sense all the Member States' Governments. The Commission cannot do that. Moreover the European Council is, as has been said, in charge of the most important appointments in the Union. The European Council is, thirdly, in a position to mobilise the national politics in all 27 Member States. Again the Commission cannot do this.

The European Council cannot exclusively be credited or blamed for this development. It fits into the process of the weakening of the European Commission in the institutional framework, which has been going on for years. This is partly also the result of the larger Member States' attempts to minimise the Commission's political position. Due to the enlargements of 2004 and 2007, moreover, the Commission, with the now 27 EU members, is more fragmented and has, according to some of my interviewees in Brussels, been further weakened. All these changes together have, in summary, weakened the position of the Commission vis-à-vis the European Council.

Since the meeting in Maastricht (1991) the Commission has issued many of its reports, communications and sometimes its proposals regarding important projects, directly to the European Council. In so doing the Commission seeks endorsement by the Heads of Government. Examples are the important Agenda 2000 (*Bull* 7/8-1997, I.1), enlargement, the Lisbon Strategy and the creation of a European citizenship (COM(2006) 211final). To what extent the Commission channels its initiatives via the European Council, instead of the Council of Ministers and/or the European Parliament, is clearly shown, for instance, in a letter from President Prodi on 19 November 2002. Six months before the Spring meeting of 2003 in

Brussels, the Commission President urged the Heads of Government to take 'six concrete steps' and start the preparations thereof at once (AE, 21 November 2002, 13). It regularly happens moreover that the acting President asks the Commission to report directly to the European Council on an important political subject. Since 1997 the Commission has referred in some cases to the Conclusions of the European Council in the citation 'having regard to' of an enforceable proposal for a law. In this introduction 'having regard to' the lawmaker refers to the legal base, here the European Council, for the Regulation, Directive or Decision.

Moreover, since the European Council meets every quarter nowadays, it interferes with the permanent dialogue between the Commission and the Council of Ministers. Anyone who studies the relationship between the European Council and the Commission over the years will reach the conclusion that the Commission is in fact clearly subservient. In Vienna (1998), to take just one of many examples, the European Council saddled the Commission with eighteen varying tasks, as President Jacques Santer observed at the conclusion. After the European Council in June 2006 a proud Commission President, Barroso, remarked that at the meeting 'ten of the twelve' of his proposals had been approved (AE, 17 June, 2006, p. 3). A few moths later Barroso stated that he would not make legislative proposals until after the European Council had given a positive response on his draft. 'Otherwise the chances of our plans being adopted are almost zero' (interview by Simon Taylor in *European Voice*, 11 January 2007, p. 1). Barroso received a quick response. The Conclusions of the subsequent meeting in March 2007 contained 22 tasks and invitations to the European Commission to take action. A day after the meeting, the Commission distributed in its Press Room a list which counted as many as 49 tasks. The refrain is similar at every meeting, as the Conclusions show.

As early as the first meeting in 1975 the Commission warned that the European Council could shake the institutional structure set up by the treaties (*Bull* 3-1975, 1503). The European Council, it warned, 'may be tempted to choose the low road of inter-governmental cooperation when we should be taking the high road of integration' (*Gen Rep*, 1974, p. XIV). The Commission, once 'a European government in the making', has, over the past years, even had to endure attacks from within the European Council on parts of its executive powers, as will be discussed further later in this chapter.

It is remarkable that the European Council (and the Council) as a central collective entity in the framework of the Institutional machinery has paid so little attention to the case for improving the efficiency and effectiveness of the Commission. It has been argued that this demonstrates the Council's collective determination to keep the Commission in its place. Both the European Council and the Heads of Government individually keep the Commission at arms' length. Take for instance the fierce and unprecedented conflict in 1999 in which the Parliament accused the Commission of irregularities and nepotism. It led to the stepping down of the Santer Commission. Nothing like this had ever happened before. The European Parliament used the conflict to deflect attention from its own functional deficiencies and its peripatetic functioning. Remarkable therefore was the total absence of any

Box 9

How Commission President Jacques Delors dominated at the Summits

Experience shows that the role of the Commission in Council meetings depends to a large extent on the input of its President. Commission President Jacques Delors (1985-1995) dominated the meetings. The relations Delors went on to sustain with Heads of State and Government, individually and collectively, and his 'apparent politisation of the Commission presidency' were the keys to his success (Drake, p. 261-263). Delors even developed the earlier unknown and rather undiplomatic habit of giving in plain terms his opinion on the behaviour of the different Heads of Government at European Council meetings and splitting them into 'good and bad guys' (FT, 18 December 1990; *The Independent* 17 December 1990; AE, 12 December 1991). For years, Delors personally introduced the subjects to the Heads of Government. The Heads of Government took their most important decisions on the basis of the Delors I (Brussels, 1988) and Delors II (Edinburgh, 1992) packages. In the margin of the Milan 1985 meeting, to take another example, Delors went as far as personally scuppering intrusive Franco-German proposals. On the table was a proposal from Chancellor Kohl and President Mitterrand for a system of intergovernmental political cooperation, led by the European Council, flanked by a Secretary-General for European Union (AE, 29 June 1985, p. 3-7; Delors, 2004, p. 208-210). Before the start of the meeting, Delors personally torpedoed these proposals. This example proves the firm grip of this 'presidential' head of the Commission on both the preparation and the course of the meetings in those days. Delors' name is associated with what must be the 10 most successful years of European unification. He was famous for his ability to forge a good working relationship with the Heads of Government. In narrow collaboration with Chancellor Kohl and President Mitterrand, as Delors himself later confirmed (Delors, 2001, p. 41-48), he was the chief actor in completing the big projects of his era: the Single European Act (1986), the Single Market (1993), the EMU and enlargement. Delors never criticised the European Council phenomenon. On the contrary: he saw it as an instrument to realise his political ideas. Since 1995, with the appointments of Jacques Santer (1995-1999) and later Romano Prodi (1999-2004), both 'low profile' and not really relevant in the meetings, and José Manuel Barroso (although today more influential) the influence of the Commission President has clearly waned (Tallberg, p. 26; Trojan, former Secretary General of the Commission, p. 26).

comment from the European Council or from Heads of Government individually, let alone support, for the beleaguered Santer Commission. From a
formal point of view this was a conflict between Parliament and the
Commission. Nevertheless the total silence for weeks on end from the 15
Heads of Government is noteworthy since these Heads of Government had
earlier appointed their own colleague Prime Minister Jacques Santer (after
ten years of membership of the European Council) as Commission
President. Santer, although operating without the 'grandeur' of his forerunner Delors, did a good job as President with the two major projects of that
era: EMU and enlargement. Even though it was 'their' Jacques Santer who
was butchered politically on partly dubious grounds, neither the Heads of
Government individually nor as HSG Council (for instance by way of the
Presidency) made any effort to lessen the conflict. It may be logical to
deduce from the foregoing that these Heads of Government do not involve
themselves with the internal functioning of the Commission.

In thirty years of covering the European Council I only remember two
criticisms of the functioning of the Commission. In the 1995 Madrid meeting, Chancellor Kohl was quite critical of the way the Commission was run.
Kohl repeated his critical remarks in 1998 in the meeting in Cardiff.
However, he uttered his criticism behind closed doors.

My general conclusion that the European Council rarely if ever involves
itself with the internal functioning of the European Commission as a whole
is not applicable to all the individual Heads of Government. For example:
Chancellor Helmut Kohl quickly put his belief in the political independence
of the European Commission to one side as soon as German interests were
involved. For details of Kohl's interventions in Brussels see for example the
memoirs of former Commissioner Karel Van Miert. In 2008 Van Miert said
that 'Heads of State and Government are increasingly speaking to the
President of the Commission to get him to become involved in others' areas
of responsibility', AE 15 February 2008.

The less fecund role of the Commission in the European Council is by
now structural and thus no longer particularly dependent on its President.
One of the reasons is that the European Council nowadays concerns itself
with different items from those on the table during the era of Delors.
Nowadays many issues concern the so-called Third Pillar, in other words
the increasingly important Justice and Home Affairs (JHA) as laid down in
Title IV TEC, and further CFSP-related questions and other questions that
require unanimity at decision-making in the Council. Examples are EMU,
enlargement, the Lisbon process and the Union's financial framework.

These projects, and also those emanating from the Second Pillar with the
CFSP and the ESDP, fall largely outside the scope of the Community
Method with its strong role for the Commission. The most important core
projects created since Maastricht (1991), EMU, CFSP and JHA, were tackled
by the European Council with the Commission in a more subservient role.
The coming into force of the Comstitutional Treaty might entail new
changes with a negative character for the Commission. Article 12 TEU as
amended by the Lisbon Treaty formalises the decision-making process in
the CFSP area. The European Council will decide on the basis of a recommendation from the Council. Although this advice in so far as it covers areas
to which the Community Method applies, will have to be based on a pro-

posal of the Commission such a 'formalization of the European Council decision-making procedure might hamper the direct access of the Commission to the European Council' (Timmermans, p. 347).

Box 10

Embarrassing climb-down by President Barroso

José M. Barroso as President of the Commission failed miserably in organising an informal mini-European Council in 2007. The UK, Germany, Portugal, Poland, the Czech Republic, Sweden, Italy and the Netherlands were invited. It was a novel initiative. According to Barroso's spokesman the aim was a 'very informal brainstorming' to try and break the deadlock over the Constitutional Treaty. But according to many commentators the project was also aimed at improving Barroso's political image and the standing of the Commission. Immediately following the despatch of the invitations a storm of protest came from the governments that had not been invited. The President was forced into an embarrassing climb-down. The meeting was cancelled. 'The fiasco illustrates the nature of a union with 27 member states. On the one hand it faces complaints that it cannot make decisions quickly enough with all the national governments involved. On the other hand, any moves for a select group to discuss policies relevant to all cause concern, particularly among smaller EU states', *EUobserver* concluded on 26 April 2007. This event shows that the President of the Commision lacks the authority and the leadership of the other members of the European Council: the Heads of Government. They regularly organise bilateral, trilateral and even multilateral Summit meetings in preparation for an upcoming meeting of the European Council.

Under the now-defunct Constitutional Treaty and the subsequent Lisbon Treaty – not yet in force – the European Council would get a full-time President (see also Chapter 4) instead of the current part-timer. To summarise: for the various reasons mentioned above, it seems hardly conceivable that either Commission President José Manuel Barroso (2004-) or his successor will ever be capable of reconquering the position once held by Delors. To do his job well today, every Commission President needs, more than ever, broad support in the European Council for his programme. The current President Barroso is fully aware of that and operates accordingly.

Why the Commission never protested against the emergence of the European Council

Why did the Commission never protest against the emergence of the European Council, 'the new system in which ideas will come from the top?' (*Gen Rep*, 1974, XII). Its attitude can be explained.

There is an important other side to the weakening of the Commission as a result of the emergence of the European Council. The Commission President is a fully fledged Member of the European Council. That is important for the position of the Commission. Through its President, the Commission is involved in the discussions and the decisions. In a legal sense the President holds a remarkable position. He deliberates and takes part in the decision-making of this intergovernmental body and is the one and only person who has to consider all matters from the viewpoint of the interest of the Union as a whole. Even where the meeting is formed of only the Heads of State or Government (HSG Council), the President of the Commission and the vice-presidents participating in the European Council remain at the table and take the floor. The President of the Commission is, due to the emergence of the European Council, the one and only political personality who as a fully fledged participant joins both the meetings of the European Council, the Intergovernmental Conferences (IGC), the meetings of the Council of Ministers, the informal half-yearly meetings of the Ministers for Foreign Affairs (Council GAERC) as well as the yearly G8 (Western Economic Summit). This accumulation of activities and functions has *strengthened* the Commission's position.

The underlying (but seldom expressed) motivation of the Commission to deal with the European Council in this way is that while its initiating task may be undermined in the legal sense, its proposals once adopted in the European Council enjoy the support of the highest political leaders of the Member States. During the 1970s, before the arrival of the European Council, the Commission often ran aground with proposals and projects which the national governments subsequently ignored. This changed with the arrival of the European Council. Thanks to the emergence of the European Council, the Heads of Government delved into the 'nitty gritty', the complicated technical details. The fact that the Heads of Government command the Council of Ministers, each quarter, to settle certain Commission proposals, reinforces the Commission.

One may conclude that although the European Council has eroded the *initiative-taking powers* of the Commission, it has simultaneously upgraded the latter's *political* position. All presidents of the Commission since Roy Jenkins have understood that very well. They have used the European Council as an instrument in order to realise their own programme, even though this remained rather invisible to the outside world. Take for instance Jacques Santer (1995-1999). Shortly after taking office, Santer presented the European Council with the full programme of his term. He did so behind closed doors at the informal meeting in September 1995 in Mallorca. Santer there received the backing of the European Council for his strategy: to complete the IGC (agreed in Amsterdam in 1997) as a first priority, then launch far-reaching reforms called Agenda 2000 (agreed in Berlin in 1999) and at the same time publish the advice of the Commission regarding enlargement with ten applicant countries. On the basis of the last-mentioned recommendation, the European Council of Luxembourg in December 1997 formulated its enlargement strategy. With his appearance at Mallorca, which was never publicised, Santer as President set out the path for his entire term of office until 1999. Thanks to the European Council, President Santer's programme was fully realised on schedule.

Nowadays the Commission even goes so far as to use the European Council as an effective vehicle to present its own priorities. A well placed source in the Commission has said: 'Nine times out of ten we are asking them (the Heads of Government) to ask us to bring up a paper or a proposal. For instance, in cases where we see we are stuck in the lower level Specialised Council, we try to go over their heads by getting the agreement of the "Big Boys and Girls" in the European Council and in doing so kill the lower level opposition.'

As earlier mentioned, in 2007 the Commission President stated that he would not make legislative proposals until after the European Council had given a positive response. That is why the Commission sees to it that its priority projects and proposals receive mention in the Conclusions. Catherine Day, Secretary General of the European Commission, claims that the role of the Commission has been strengthened by the arrival of President J.M. Barroso for two reasons. One is that Barroso is a strong communicator 'which is terribly important in such meetings, where messages need to be clear and understandable'. Secondly, the enlargement of the Union from 15 to 27 Member States has nearly doubled the number of participants and has changed the dynamics. 'We see the role of the Commission enhanced by the enlargement. If the Commission succeeds in bringing forward high quality, well-thought-through proposals, it is easier for the Member States to find common ground – so the potential extra hurdle of more Member States around the table can be overcome.'

Sometimes the Commission manipulates in such a way that some of its most cherished subjects which did not even get a mention in the meeting of the European Council, do appear in the Conclusions. Next the Commission regularly casts these sacrosanct Conclusions in the teeth of the Council of Ministers and the EP. 'Should you not come to decisions, then the Heads of State will have to solve this priority', it suggests threateningly. Thus is seen the paradoxical sight of the Commission carrying out its initiating role not by means of its formal rights, but via the back door of the European Council.

In contrast, the Heads of Government use the European Council to speed up their priority projects. At the 1978 Bremen meeting for example, a very hesitant UK tried to prevent the publication of the 'Annex' on the Conclusions, which revealed the basic structure of EMS. This action shows that the publication of an agreed text constitutes a kind of fundamental commitment of the Member States. When requesting initiatives and action, the Heads of Government sometimes go so far as to enlist the Commission in fields outside the scope of the Community, namely the Third Pillar (Justice and Home Affairs).

In *The European Council: Gatekeeper of the European Community*, an American researcher, summarised the process thus: 'While the Commission became more politically competent, the European Council became more technocraticallly competent' (Johnston, p. 132-133). In conclusion: the Heads of Government with their far-reaching 'meddling' have in the end reinforced the role of the Commission in the entirety of the Union's activities. Seen from the outside, it looks as if the two today form a *tandem*!

Summarised, the above analysis contains a paradox. On the one hand, there is the subservient position of the Commission. On the other hand, we reach the conclusion that the arrival of the European Council has to a certain extent reinforced the position of the Commission in the Institutional Triangle, or Community Method. The Commission in other words made a good assessment of the positive influence of the European Council on the progress of the integration process. That conclusion applies all the more because, thanks to the European Council, the Commission was also allocated strategic tasks in the Third Pillar where the Community Method does not really lend itself to a leading role for the Commission. Therefore, once again, it seems today as if the European Council and the Commission form a tandem, albeit a tandem driven and governed by the former.

B.2.   The shallow relationship with Parliament

The European Council and the Parliament are antipodeans. The one represents the Member States of the Union; the other the citizens. It is the Member States that, by way of the European Council, have the final word in the Union, not the European Parliament. In the European Council the Heads of Government represent their own State. Parliament claims to be the only Institution with direct democratic legitimacy and the legitimate representative of all citizens of the EU Member States. However, the European Council's activities are not controlled by Parliament. In other words, for its strategic political leadership the former is *not answerable* to the latter.

Although approximately forty former members of the European Council have become members of the European Parliament[17], the latter has a certain mistrust vis-à-vis the European Council. It perceives it as an influential intergovernmental organ that could undermine the institutional balance to the detriment of Parliament. According to Jacqué, this concern is exaggerated (Jacqué, 2006, p. 347). When the European Council arbitrates, the issue under discussion has in most cases reached a sufficiently advanced point for Parliament's position to be known. Should, moreover, the European Council arbitration result in substantial changes, the Council of Ministers has the obligation to comply with the jurisprudence of the Court of Justice to reconsult Parliament. Where the Parliament has a right of co-decision, arbitration by the European Council cannot deprive it of this right. In general, for that matter, virtually all decisions and conclusions of the European Council later appear on the agenda of Parliament for discussion. In this respect the good functioning of Parliament is not hindered.

Parliament remains the only one of the three Institutions which, though involved in the legislative procedure, does not attend the European Council. Since Parliament has no input in the European Council's agenda it is not well informed on what exactly happens in the meetings. In its Reports, Parliament refers regularly to the European Council. 'Strasbourg', in other words, takes note of the Council, but the opposite rarely happens. There has not been much progress beyond the verbal report by the President of the European Council to the plenary after every meeting in Strasbourg (since 1981) and the speech by the President of the Parliament at the start of the Council meeting (since 1987). In this speech the President of the Parliament gives the opinion of Parliament regarding the most important items on the agenda and often also regarding other subjects. After delivering his text, which is sometimes followed by a brief discussion, the President leaves the meeting.

Vis-à-vis the Parliament, the European Council operates entirely on its own conditions. That leaves the Parliament in a weak position.

The only obligation towards the European Parliament is laid down in Article 4 TEU. The European Council has to submit to Parliament a report after each of its meetings and a yearly written report on the progress achieved by the Union.

In 1993 the TEU introduced the obligation for the European Council (Article D) to submit the aforementioned report to the European Parliament after each of its meetings. This report contains only a short, hollow, formal summary of little informative value. After the verbal report of every meeting by the President of the European Council, Parliament always has a debate resulting in a resolution. However, the content, in other words the opinion of 'Strasbourg' about the European Council, is open-ended. Exceptionally the EP uses the debate as an opportunity to criticise members of the European Council. For instance, after the Cardiff meeting (1998), Chancellor Kohl and President Chirac were clobbered. 'They shove dissatisfaction in their own country on to the European Commission and the Court of Justice in Luxembourg', according to the parlamentarians (AE, 20 June 1998, p. 4-5). The reactions often show that Parliament had unrealistic expectations. Sometimes the reactions are based on party-political grounds, which is not really fair. It so happens that 'Strasbourg' dismisses the results of a meeting as 'disappointing', even when there is no reason to do so. In its comment in 2001 after the Stockholm Summit, to give one example, Parliament evaluated the disappointing results of the Lisbon Strategy along the line of its own national sentiments and (political party) interests. The Social Democrats in Strasbourg, then amply represented in the European Council, accepted the results of the Stockholm meeting. The Christian Democrats, thinly represented in Stockholm, gave vent to biting criticism in the Parliament. We often witnessed such national or party political interests in Strasbourg.

An interesting obligation of the European Council vis-à-vis the Parliament is contained in Article 197 TFEU as amended by the Lisbon Treaty. It says that the European Council is to be heard by the Parliament. This, however, happens on conditions unilaterally formulated in its Rules of Procedure. The European Council can in fact on this basis decide to inform the Parliament only scantily.

The customary debate regarding the course of a recent or upcoming European Council meeting is sometimes marked by widespread absenteeism in the Parliament. For instance, when the Luxembourg Presidency presented its programme on 17 January 2005 less than ten percent of the MEPs showed up. Such a meagre turnout is not unusual at this event in Strasbourg. In other words, the Parliament's interest in the European Council's activities is rather minimal.

Before each European Council meeting, the European Parliament tries to develop specific proposals by way of a Resolution wherein it underlines its most important priorities regarding the upcoming meeting.

Just a few hours before the start of a European Council meeting the larger political groups (such as the EPP, PES, or ALDE) hold 'Summits' involving Heads of Government, party leaders, the chair of the political group in the EP and members of the Commission. Good personal contacts between politically like-minded Heads of Government of course play a role here. These events have in some exceptional cases been influential in pre-arranging the outcome of a European Council meeting (see the example of the meeting in Pörtschach, earlier in this chapter).

In the following paragraphs we mention a series of episodes which indicate that the European Council and European Parliament have a laboured relationship.
– In 1999 Parliament welcomed the German Presidency's initiative of setting up a 'European Employment Pact' at the Cologne meeting. In Cologne, however, the President of the Parliament, José Maria Gil-Robles, declared it 'both inexplicable and frankly deplorable' that the Parliament would continue to be excluded from the preparatory work on this pact and its future assessment. 'I trust that you will come to your political senses sooner rather than later, and put an end to this exclusion in the near future'. (Address by J.M. Gil-Robles, distributed in Cologne by Press Service EP.)
– In Tampere (1999), the President of the Parliament, Nicole Fontaine, tried to enter into a debate with the Heads of State or Government. She asked in vain for an 'exchange of minds'. She wanted the wishes and expectations of the Parliament to be included in the deliberations.[18]
– After the important Lisbon Summit (2000) launching the plan for a decade-long strategy for economic reform, Strasbourg, paralysed by internal divisions, was incapable of delivering the usual resolution regarding the results.
– At the next meeting in Feira, the French Fontaine, allowed her 'room for manoeuvre' to be dictated by her capital. During the discussion on an EU-wide savings tax system Fontaine suddenly yielded to the position of France, instead of that of the Parliament.
– Worth mentioning is that President José-Maria Aznar, after reading out his optimistic report of the meeting in Barcelona in 2002 and not realising that the microphone was still left open, audibly uttered 'what a shit story!'
– In 2006 several political groups in the Parliament started an action to move the monthly plenary session from Strasbourg to Brussels, where the Commission and the Council of Ministers are seated. That would end the money-guzzling 'travelling circus' with plenary meetings mostly in Strasbourg, Commission meetings in Brussels and the Parliament secretariat in Luxembourg. Approximately 600,000 Europeans signed a petition to that effect. Also, several Heads of Government were in favour of seating the Parliament permanently in Brussels. In spite of all this support, the President of Parliament Josep Borrell did not dare table the matter in the European Council meeting in June 2006, for fear of a negative response from the French President. This timid stance was considered as proof of the Parliament's weak position in the Union's institutional framework.[19]
– According to Parliament, the European Council curtailed its role as the budget authority (European Parliament, Final A-6-0150/2006, p. 37). As described in Chapter 3, the Council fixes the financing of the Union (the so called Financial Perspectives), every seven years. This working method interferes with the authority of the Parliament, which, according to Article 272 EC, makes up the budget authority, together with the Council of Ministers. In Petersberg (1999) and Brussels (December 2004), the President of the Parliament warned the European Council bluntly that the EP, which has to approve details, would refuse the Financial Perspectives if it disagreed with

the results. Yet in both cases the Parliament agreed after relatively small amendments. The Copenhagen 2002 meeting decided a Financial Perspectives which included the costs of enlargement. The figures were then included in the Accession Treaties. This meant that the Parliament was sidelined.

– An interesting development was the decision by President-designate José Manuel Barroso to delay the presentation of his newly formed European Commission for approval before Parliament on 27 October 2004. Here we saw a novel conflict between the Parliament and some members of the European Council, on the issue of the composition of the new Commission. For the first time ever, the European Parliament tried to influence the composition of the European Commission.[20] Under Parliament's pressure, the Italian and Latvian governments had to replace their original nominees, Rocco Buttiglione and Ingrida Udre, and Barroso also had to reshuffle two portfolios. It was remarkable that the Netherlands, Denmark and Hungary ignored the strong Parliamentary criticism of their designated commissioners. In doing so The Hague, Copenhagen and Budapest forced their will on Strasbourg (AE, 28 October p. 3 and 5 November p. 4).

– In the vast field of the Single Market, with co-decision for the Parliament, the European Council acts as the body which in some cases dictates the policy. It is the European Council which in this area regularly asks the Council of Ministers and the Parliament for implementation, often imposing timetables. In other words the Heads of Government control the politically important precursor of that law-making.

– Next we address the 'hard nut': Economic and Monetary Union policy. There *not one single area* is subject to the co-decision procedure with its strong influence of the European Parliament. The Council of Ministers takes the decisions after having received the green light from the European Council. The Parliament is simply informed and not even consulted.

To sum up, the relationship between the Parliament and the European Council is shallow, with a very formal character. The European Council and European Parliament 'don't gel'. But is there any other way? The European Parliament is (as it should be at any rate) supranational through and through, whereas the European Council has an intergovernmental character with the different national interests to the fore. In short, the Parliament and the Council remain in different spheres.

Finally, it should be acknowledged that the European Parliament is indebted to the European Council for important boosts to its authority over three decades. In 1974 the Heads of Government decided on an important upgrade of the Parliament through its direct election. In the SEA of 1987 Parliament received the right of cooperation, followed in 1993 in the TEU by the very important right of co-decision. In the proposed Lisbon Treaty Parliament obtains the right of co-decision (with the Council) over almost all legislation.

B.3.   The lost key role of the Council of Ministers

Decision-making in the Union comes primarily from the Member States, meeting in the Council of Ministers, this being both a political and a legislative Institution. The EC Treaty states that the Council of Ministers has decision-making authority (Article 202 TEC). Besides its legislative function, exercised more and more jointly with the European Parliament, the Council of Ministers has an important policy-making role. Among other things, it must ensure the coordination of the general economic policies of the Member States.

The Council has been divided into sections, the earlier mentioned 'Specialised Councils'. It is in session at ministerial level more than 100 days per year. Coreper, the ambassadors who prepare the Council meetings, also meets for at least 100 days. At the level of the working groups and committees, around 4300 meetings per year are held. In total there are more than 4500 meetings yearly (Council, 1999, p. 98; Westlake and Galloway, p. 220). Given the availability of 200 workings days per year, it is no exaggeration to claim that the Council of Ministers in varying formations is permanently in session.

In 1974 when the European Council was created, the Heads of Government gave the Ministers for Foreign Affairs the role 'to act as *initiators and coordinators*', 'in order to ensure consistency in Community activities and continuity of work' (see Annex 4 to this publication). It is curious that those Ministers went on to neglect that task. Generally speaking, the Council's methods of operation have been a source of poor coordination. As described also in Chapter 3, both the Seville reforms and the provisions of the Constitutional Treaty and the subsequent Lisbon Treaty were intended to redress these problems by an enhanced role for the European Council; by streamlining the work of the Council of Ministers in its different configurations, with a more pronounced task for the General Affairs Council; and by the introduction of more coordination across successive Council presidencies.

As a result of Maastricht and the negotiations for Economic and Monetary Union (EMU), EcoFin has partly taken over the coordinating role from the Ministers for Foreign Affairs in the financial, economic, social and budget area. As a result, the EcoFin Ministers – also due to their reluctance to report to the European Council through the General Affairs Council – now act as 'initiators and coordinators'. They exercise the task of processing and selecting the material from their important portfolio for the meetings of the European Council.

The main aspects of the General Affairs Council's problems, sketched by the 'Three Wise Men' in 1979[21], have not changed much since. Firstly, an unmanageable burden of major and minor business. Secondly, as a result of its own and the European Council's acts, an eroded position as the main seat of authority in the Union's vertical hierarchy. Thirdly, a loss of collegial sense arising from irregular attendance. Fourthly, the fact that the General Affairs Council has ceased to be general, both in the sense of directing the work of the separate Specialised Councils, and in that of providing a forum for the discussion of all new major issues. As a result of all these developments, the General Affairs Council's task to avoid gridlock in the decision-making by reconciling in the Specialised Councils the sometimes conflicting sectoral interests, has shifted to the European Council.

The European Council regularly commands – sometimes even imposing a deadline or a draft summary – the completion of a given Regulation, Directive or other agreement. The Council (e.g. of Agriculture, EcoFin, or

Transport) duly obeys. Nowadays even national governments, as said, get their orders. An example is the meeting in Essen (1994). There the Member States were asked to 'translate into their national policy' the fairly detailed recommendations for the improvement of the employment situation. The Social Affairs Council together with the Commission had to monitor these activities and report them to the European Council annually.

The conclusion is that through the arrival of the European Council, the 'ordinary' Council of Ministers has lost its key *political* role. The real political debates no longer take place there. The Council of Ministers, although it remains the ultimate legal and therefore official decision-making body, has been downgraded. This happened because the shadow of the Heads of Government seems to be too long for the General Affairs Council to recover lost ground. To sum up: the Council has been greatly affected by the emergence of the European Council.

B.4.   The limited role of the Court of Justice

The Court of Justice and the Court of First Instance ensure under Article 220 TEC the observance of law in the interpretation and application of the treaties and their implementing rules. The Court decides on disputes between the European Community and its Member States (Article 226 and 228 TEC), between EC organs and Institutions (Article 230 and 232 TEC) and between Member States (Article 227 TEC). Another important role of the Court is to give, at the request of national courts of the Member States, preliminary rulings regarding the interpretation of the TEC, the validity and interpretation of acts of the Institutions and of the European Central Bank and the interpretation of the statutes of bodies established by an act of the Council, where those statutes so provide (Article 234 TEC). In practice the Court has 'often acted as the motor of integration' (Kapteyn and VerLoren van Themaat, 1989, p. 173) in order to ensure that Institutions as well as Member States fulfill their obligations.

The jurisdiction of the Court of Justice over the provisions of the Treaty on European Union is rather limited (Article 46 TEU). According to that article, the provisions of the European Council in Article 4 of that treaty are not subject to the jurisdiction of the Court of Justice. Apart from Article 46 TEU, neither the 1974 Paris Communiqué nor the SEA, the two basic founding acts of the European Council, refers to any role for the Court of Justice in relation to the European Council. The European Council operates largely outside the framework of the treaties and its decisions are of a political rather than a legal nature. The Council operates in other words in such a wide legal framework that whatever interpretation it gives to its role, it cannot be challenged by the Court. The latter confirmed this in its judgment of 13 January 1995. In Bonnamy C 264/94P it concluded that 'neither the declaration of the European Council nor the Treaty on European Union is an act whose legality is subject to review under Article 173 of the Treaty' (as in effect in 1995).

The Court of Justice has made references to the activities of the European Council since 1983. It began with the Case *Luxembourg v European Parliament.* In its Decision, the Court refers briefly to the Maastricht 1981 European Council, where it was 'unanimously decided to confirm the status quo in regard to the provisional places of work of the European institutions'.

The question remains to what extent decisions of the European Council have influenced decision-making by the Court of Justice. In the cases we found, the Court limited itself to referring the matter to the European Council in brief terms, thus avoiding questioning in any way the European Council's motivation or procedures. Nonetheless, the facts of the Court's considerations suggest that the European Council's decision in all the instances cited was of importance to the decision-making of the Court of Justice. The decisions of the European Council, in other words, clearly contributed to the motivation of the Court. One, and a not unimportant, conclusion, therefore, is that the activities of, and the decision-making in, the European Council, although not an Institution of the Community, nonetheless are relevant to the Court in its analysis.

Article 365 of the Constitutional Treaty, to be replaced by Article 230 TFEU as amended by the Lisbon Treaty, introduces a review option by the Court of Justice of the legality of the acts of the European Council as far as they are intended to produce legal effects vis-à-vis third parties.

Should the European Council encroach upon the competence of one of the Institutions, such an act would not have any legal effect within the Community because the position of the Institutions changes only in accordance with the rules laid down in the treaties. Where an Institution – as experience with the Commission (as detailed under Chapter 3) has shown – regularly accepts such practices, decisions or acts of the European Council, however, one could question whether such conduct nevertheless becomes a legal part of the Community by precedent.

Where the Council meets in the composition of the Heads of Government (HSG Council) it obviously has to respect the judicial authority of the Courts of the Union in order to operate in accordance with the regime of the treaties. This evidently means that the meeting has to respect all procedural requirements, for example a proposal by the Commission, the required role of Parliament, etc.

C. ORGANISATIONAL RULES AND FUNCTIONING OF THE EUROPEAN COUNCIL

C.1.   The crucial preparation of meetings and the drafting of the Conclusions

Although this is often overlooked, the preparation is as important as the course of the meetings. According to our experience, for every meeting to be successful there is the '*necessité d'un enjeu*' (the necessity to have something at stake) (Pambou Tchivounda, p. 53). The process of preparation allows countless players from both the Member States and the Union's Institutions to contribute to the course of the meeting. All the participants are therefore aware of the ins and outs of the order of the day. Concentration of the discussions on a limited number of precisely defined points is a prerequisite for success. As regards the preparation, moreover, there is a fundamental difference between the European Council as conceived in 1974, with as its guiding principle of Chancellor Helmut Schmidt's '*Keine Papiere*' ('No papers'), and today's meetings, which are prepared in detail.

Box 11

The agenda of a typical European Council meeting

The Presidency confirms that the next meeting of the European Council will take place in Brussels, on Thursday 14 and Friday 15 December 2006

1   PROGRAMME

Thursday 14 December 2006

Members of the European Council arrive at the Justus Lipsius building (not in protocol order) and are received by the Presidency

Meeting with the President of the European Parliament

First working session of the European Council

Family photograph

Separate working dinners

Dinner for delegates, at the Justus Lipsius building

Presidency press conference

National press briefings

Friday 15 December 2006

Arrival of members of the European Council and delegations at the Justus Lipsius (not in protocol order)

Second working session of the European Council

Concluding Presidency press conference

National press briefings

The distinctive honour of being the President

In 1991 the Luxembourg PM, Jacques Santer, as President of the European Council met US President George Bush for the first in a series of twice-yearly presidential visits established in 1990. Being the President and the official spokesman of the largest political union in the world is not only a very distinctive honour for the Prime Minister of a small country such as

Luxembourg but also for the President of the French Republic or the German Chancellor. Success in the role is generally seen as having an important influence on the President's domestic public opinion (and therefore on their political prospects). The President of the European Council meeting has a prestigious key role in the preparation and the direction of it. They are the centre of gravity and the pivot of the European Council. The President is at one and the same time:

–   the manager of that meeting with a vital and delicate political role in diplomatically steering its way towards a compromise,
–   the promoter of political initatives,
–   the representative to and of the other Member States and to the Union's Institutions participating in the meeting,
–   the spokesman for the European Council and for the Union,
–   and finally, an important actor on the international scene regarding the CFSP.

The Conclusions: guidance for the EU's Institutions

The decisions and guidelines issued by the European Council are included in the Conclusions or Statements prepared by the Presidency with the assistance of the Council Secretariat. Although it was agreed in Helsinki in 1999 that 15 pages should be the maximum for Conclusions, these Conclusions nowadays amount to some 25 to 40 pages. The pursuit of concise Conclusions is still being ignored. Both the Commission and sometimes the Council or the Presidency seize the opportunity to highlight their political wishes and priorities in the Conclusions. They are nonetheless an extremely useful resource for the Institutions and the Member States when they come to follow up the guidelines of the European Council.

A distinction must be made between:

(a)   *Conclusions of the Presidency* generally covering questions regarding the Union. These Conclusions are discussed in depth in the meeting, are politically binding, and adopted in all the official languages of the Union;

(b)   *decisions of the Council* in its composition of the Heads of State or Government (HSG Council);

(c)   *common Declarations/Statements/Resolutions* of the Union as such, in all the official languages. To this category belongs the 'Resolution of the European Council of 5 December 1978 on the establishment of the European Monetary System (EMS) and related matters' (*Bull* 12-1978. 1.1.11) binding all the Member States;

(d)   common Declarations/Statements/Resolutions *related to the CFSP* giving the concerted opinion of the EU on a subject of international interest;

(e)   *speaking notes* of the President or the Presidency[22];

(f)   conclusions in the form of *unwritten and not to be published* 'common understandings'. These politically sometimes very sensitive issues, excluded from the official Conclusions, are according to the then Secretary General Emile Noël of the Commission (1979, p.56) in some cases the most important result of a meeting because of their decisive influence on the future political course of Member States.

We describe this assortment here in order to give a view of the way in which the Presidents of the European Council suit themselves and, so doing, enjoy a certain freedom of interpretation in giving concrete form to the results by using 'the power of the pen'. With a very few exceptions, these texts are distributed at the final press conference by the Presidency. Surprisingly, none of these Conclusions is published in the Official Journal; not even in the annual 'General Report on the Activities of the European Union', but in the monthly 'Bulletin of the European Union', the only official reference publication covering all the Union's spheres of activities. Decisions, however, taken by the Council in the composition of the Heads of State or Government are published in the Official Journal. In very exceptional cases there are no Conclusions at all. This was for instance the case at the collapsed 1983 Athens and the 1984 Brussels meetings.

The Seville (2002) Rules of Procedure: a breakthrough

The Seville European Council in June 2002 agreed, as has been said, on a number of important operational measures (none of them requiring treaty change) designed to improve the effectiveness of the European Council (see Annex 5 to this publication). In principle, the proceedings of the European Council last according to these rules for two days. The first day the meeting starts nowadays in the late afternoon with a plenary session which is followed by separate working dinners for the Heads of State or Government and the President of the Commission and the Ministers of Foreign Affairs together with the High Representative for the CFSP/Secretary General of the Council. The European Council meeting continues the next day until the end of the afternoon. Since Seville, the agenda is prepared in great detail. It is, some days before the meeting of the European Council, formally adopted by the General Affairs Council (GAERC). Practical arrangements for meetings have also been streamlined, with tighter programming over a shorter period, and smaller delegations of officially at most 20 people. Many delegations, however, dodge the limitation of their official delegation to 20 people maximum by adding a number of other officials usually described as non-official or technical delegation members.

Since the introduction of the Seville Rules in 2002, the role of Coreper in the preparations has increased. Previously no one knew what would happen in the European Council. The President always kept the draft Conclusions close to his chest. On the first day of the meeting he avoided discussing them. Not until the early morning of the second day would all the delegations find the draft Conclusions of the Presidency slipped under the door of their hotel rooms. During the morning hours the meeting would then as a collective editorial board compose the final text. 'The final result was really a lottery with surprises. It was simply not professional', an insider claims. Since the coming into force of the Seville Rules, the Presidency puts the items on the agenda well in advance. Nowadays, as long as three months before the meeting, the General Secretariat of the

Council of Ministers and the Presidency prepare the concept of an agenda in cooperation with the Commission. Then the Secretariat starts, in close cooperation with the Presidency (which obviously has the last word), drafting the concept Conclusions. Next, both the concept agenda and draft Conclusions go to Coreper. The method used is usually an annotated agenda, e.g. enlargement, with a short description of the concrete issue for deliberation. The preparation of the meeting held in June 2006 may be taken as an example. On 11 May Coreper held a long, difficult and detailed discussion on the first version of the annotated agenda and of the concept of the Conclusions. The Permanent Representatives explained their differing priorities and brought some doubts regarding each other's priorities. 'The deliberation made clear that it is the Coreper that today prepares the European Council meeting', according to a top official with insight into the negotiations.

The latter conclusion, however, deserves a note. Technological developments have changed the way things are done. The role of Coreper has in some respects been overtaken by the fact that Prime Ministers now in crucial cases negotiate directly with each other, by mobile phone or email instead of via their Permanent Representative in Brussels. The members of Coreper do not always know when the Prime Ministers are talking to each other or with the President of the Commission.

For CFSP and ESDP issues, the preparation is in the hands of the Political and Security Committee (COPS, after the French acronym). A few days before the European Council meeting, the Ministers for Foreign Affairs confirm or modify these agenda items in the General Affairs Council (GAERC).

As a result of this approach, each Head of Government can well in advance react, propose modifications or make suggestions by way of the Council of Ministers or Coreper. Each delegation is now able to prepare properly, well in advance. In between, the European Commission frequently drafts reports and documents, the so-called Communications, for the European Council meeting. At least four weeks before the European Council, the General Affairs Council, acting on the Presidency's proposals, draws up the annotated agenda and in so doing acts as the 'gatekeeper' of the European Council.

The largest Member States have sometimes a tendency to keep the preparation of the meetings more in their own hands. That was for instance the case in 1984, at a time when the Community itself appeared in grave crisis, especially over the budget contribution of the UK. French President François Mitterrand's approach consisted on that occasion of having no fewer than 30 preparatory meetings with other members of the European Council (Cole, 1994, p. 122-123). It resulted in the very successful Fontainebleau Summit (of which more details in Chapter 4). A more recent example was the preparation in December 2005 of the important Financial Perspectives for the period 2007-2013. British PM Tony Blair at that time had strained relations with his own Chancellor of the Exchequer, Gordon Brown. This was an extra reason for Blair to work intensively through the General Secretariat of the Council plus the Commission, thereby keeping the preparation of this important meeting largely in his own hands. Blair gambled (successfully) that he himself as President of the meeting would be in a better position to hammer out this politically significant but complex agreement on the Union's financial system.

Meanwhile, the acting President makes a `tour of the capitals'. In the early years he went to visit all colleagues. Nowadays, with 27 capitals, the visit is restricted to the larger Member States and those Heads of Government who might stir up trouble over the subjects on the agenda. By the time of the meeting the President will have had personal contact with all other Heads of Government and of course the President of the Commission, in order to prepare the meeting in the most detailed way possible. A few days before the European Council, the General Affairs Council holds a final preparatory session and adopts the definitive agenda. Meanwhile the draft Conclusions of the meeting drawn up by the Presidency will have been in circulation for some time. The General Affairs Council and Coreper negotiate the details of those Conclusions in the run-up to the European Council, except for the most important (or most contentious) political decisions which are to be taken by the Heads of Government.

The agendas of the meetings in June and December (so-called end-of-Presidency meetings) tend to be particularly packed. Some subjects are invariably listed because of their importance. There is always a discussion of the general economic situation in the Union with EMU and employment as topics. Furthermore, the CFSP is always an agenda item. Constitutional and institutional matters, new accessions and difficult to handle decisions about personalities (like the five-yearly nomination of the Commission President) are also in many cases heard. The Presidency and the Commission may wish, moreover, to use the meeting for a political initiative. The presentation of such an item is a third example of an almost invariable part of the meeting. Fourthly comes a discussion on matters that have come to be accepted as needing acceptance, approval or sometimes quite detailed decision-making by way of the Conclusions of the meeting. This occurs on the basis of reports usually from either the Commission or the Council or presentations by the President.

Preparing a meeting is a mammoth task that falls directly on the Member State holding the Presidency of the Council of the Union. Therefore, on most occasions the preparation is taken extremely seriously by the Presidency. Since the outcome of the 'Summit' will enhance (or harm) the reputation of the Member State in the chair and its political leader, as many political difficulties as possible are removed from the agenda before the meeting starts. The acting President has the power of the pen and can rely on the help and experience of Coreper, the General Secretariat of the Council of Ministers (here acting as also the secretariat of the European Council, the HSG Council, IGCs and the Conventions), with its rich knowledge of procedures and objectivity in drafting the compromise solutions and the Conclusions of the meeting, and, of course, of the European Commission. They also make suggestions for the composition of the agenda. Both the Commission (by its Communications) and the General Secretariat of the Council (by its 'Notes to the President' with some tactical negotiation advice) send their reports. However, every six months each new President clearly has a personal approach and priorities which are particularly dependent on main issues of the day. A lesser-known part of the preparations is that Heads of Government with special problems make phone calls to – besides the President of the meeting – those colleagues whose support they may require in the meeting. They are not only the leaders of the Big Three, but also the Heads of Government of the countries with a similar problem.

A few days before the European Council meets, the Head of State or Government holding the Presidency sends a short letter to his counterparts and the Commission President inviting them to the meeting. This letter generally contains a list of subjects to be discussed and the organisation of the discussion. Sometimes Presidencies operate too much on the basis of their own priorities or overload the agenda in their zeal to achieve a result.[23] Moreover, it has happened that meetings were surprised by one or more Heads of Government ambushing their colleagues with a proposal or a pressing problem which required taking an immediate stance.[24]

The decisions by the European Council, although they have mostly no legal status, carry considerable political weight. The Rules of Procedure state that the Conclusions are to be 'as concise as possible' and moreover 'set out policy guidelines and decisions (…) placing them briefly in their context and indicating the stages of the procedure to follow on from them'. These quotations confirm the extent to which the Heads of Government regard their Conclusions, in particular for the Commission and for the Council of Ministers, as a manual for their political, initiating and executive tasks.

It is fitting to note that these Conclusions are often open to more than one interpretation. Member States who agree with the text declare it sacrosanct whereas those who do not like to stress that they are not bound. Therefore the Conclusions provide an escape route for Member States to have freedom of interpretation and even have a chance to refuse to follow certain guidelines or limit their effectiveness. Taulègne (p. 137) pointed out another four elusive elements in addition to the fact that the legal position of the Conclusions is difficult to pin down. In the first place it happens that the Conclusions do mention the points agreed by the European Council, but suppress the elements of disagreement regarding the same issue. A second technique consists of not putting on the agenda hot items, which might give rise to disagreement. A third option involves wrapping up the disagreement in such general terms that it becomes undetectable. A variant is that the members of the European Council each give their own interpretation of a contentious part of the Conclusions, after the meeting. Finally it is possible that Heads of Government who do not agree with a certain part of the Conclusions reserve their agreement (and therefore keep their hands free). In 1985 for instance Denmark, Greece and Italy kept a reserve on the total agreement by the other Heads of Government regarding the creation of the Single European Act. It is remarkable, given the required consensus for the renewal of the treaties, that the representatives of the other nine Member States nevertheless solemnly signed the SEA. The obstructors signed later. Last but not least regarding the Conclusions, it can happen that Heads of Government and the President of the Commission take advantage of the media spotlight on the Summit meeting to air their pet subjects.

Finding agreement on the Conclusions has for many years now been the final job on the morning of the second day of the meeting. The remaining differences concerning details are resolved so that a final text can be produced. It is then (afterwards) interesting to examine which modifications the Presidency, at the insistence of some Heads of Government, had to introduce in the Conclusions. Those modifications indicate where the political tensions existed in the meeting. The meeting is then concluded with a working lunch with the Heads of State or Government of the Candidate Member States.

Sometimes the agenda is modified by unexpected events. In Feira (2000) for example the Council had to express 'its shock at the tragic deaths of 58 foreign nationals arriving in the United Kingdom' found in a Dutch lorry on the day of the meeting. The grizzly death of these Chinese refugees provoked the instant decision of 'intensified cooperation to defeat such cross-border crime, which has caused so many other deaths across Europe'. The incoming French Presidency and the Commission were asked 'to take forward urgently the Tampere Conclusions in this area (...) in detecting and dismantling the criminal networks involved'. Here one sees how (as the result of media pressure) the meeting is overtaken by the topic of the day.[25]

The importance of the Conclusions is also shown by the fact that sometimes in the aftermath of a meeting great confusion ensues (and henceforth political problems) about the exact nature of the agreement. Nowadays it often takes some time until, after the meeting, each Member State and the Commission put all the pieces of the puzzle together. 'Only then does everybody know exactly what has happened during the meeting', says an insider. Confusion occurred for instance with the results of the IGC of Nice 2000 concerning the threshold of votes for decisions under QMV, a very important element, further in Brussels December 2003, and again in December 2004 with the accession of Turkey. (More details about the Conclusions are given in Chapter 4.B.1.)

C.2. The participants and the conduct of a European Council meeting

The European Council is composed of the Heads of State or Government of the Member States and the President of the European Commission. They are 'accompanied' by their Ministers of Foreign Affairs (Article 4 TEU), another member of the Commission and the High Representative for the CFSP/Secretary-General of the Council of Ministers. In addition the member of the Commission responsible for External Relations is in some cases present as is the Commissioner for Economic and Monetary Affairs. The SG of the Commission, the deputy SG of the Council, the Head of the Legal Service of the Council as well as a small group of important advisers, which includes the Permanent Representative of the Member State of the President, also attend the meetings although they do not take part in the discussions. These officials assist in working out the terms of the compromises, in respect of both drafting and content. The Permanent Representatives of the Member States in Brussels although they 'are involved in all stages of the European decision-making process' (De Zwaan, 41), do not take part in the meetings. Obviously these influential officials are always a member of their national delegation. The 'double' representation of the governments (President or PM and Foreign Minister) has the advantage that constitutional problems regarding the position of the Head of Government or of the President are avoided. Moreover, having two participants offers the advantage that Member States with traditional coalition governments based on different political parties are better represented in such a setting.[26]

A number of decisions taken during the Summit meetings do not, as mentioned earlier, fall under the jurisdiction of the European Council, but under that of the Council of Ministers in the composition of the Heads of State or Government (HSG Council), or as a meeting of the Governments of the Member States as a diplomatic conference, or as an Intergovernmental Conference (IGC). In a legal sense these are distinguishable entities. The difference is that the President of the Commission is officially only a member of the European Council, not of the meeting in any other composition. Yet as President of the Commission he always participates in these meetings, takes the floor and acts as a fully fledged participant who is aware of the differing positions of the Member States and the Institutions' proposals and suggestions.[27] The only difference is that in the meetings with a composition other than that of the European Council the President of the Commission may not take part in the voting (which in theory is allowed, but very rarely happens in practice). The non-membership of the President of the Commission of a Summit with a composition other than that of the European Council therefore involves only a subtle distinction which does not manifest itself in the course of the meeting.

Box 12

A whispering participant ....

During the important negotiations about a new treaty in Maastricht (1991) UK PM John Major apparently felt insecure. The UK Permanent Representative at the time, John Kerr, who was of modest height, then decided to secrete himself under the meeting table. From that position he whispered his advice to the PM. Whenever the Dutch President of the meeting took the floor Kerr got into trouble, since there was no simultaneous translation available under the table. According to a story which may have been exaggerated over time, Kerr is said to have flipped a coin in despair when Major requested a speedy yea or nay (Ludlow, 2002, p. 18; Oldag and Tillack, p. 136).

Initially a European Council consisted of only 13 participants (twelve Heads of State or Government plus the President of the Commision) plus the twelve Ministers for Foreign Affairs and one member of the Commission, making a total of 26. Nowadays the number of participants, including the Foreign and EcoFin Ministers, and, also the political leaders of the candidate Member States, runs close to 90. Chapter 4.B discusses the far-reaching ramifications of having this large number of participants on the course of the meeting.

From the informal network which the European Council has created between the Heads of Government it arises that the discussions during the meetings can be very frank and, moreover, sometimes animated with no holds barred. Nevertheless the participants – not political rivals but rather amicable collegues – meet in a 'clubby' atmosphere and are in most cases on first-name terms with one another. On the other hand the political Heads of France, the UK and Germany often subliminally strive in the meetings for the informal political leadership and in doing so act simultaneously as partners and rivals. The degree of participation in the meetings is exceptionally high. Rarely does a Head of Government stay away.[28]

Box 13

The pecking order: from top dog golden pin holder to grass green badge

Brussels became the regular venue for European Council meetings in 2003. Meetings take place in the giant Justus Lipsius headquarters of the Council of Ministers in the Schuman district. The fifth floor, where the meetings take place, is divided in a section which is open to 'pinholders' and another one for 'red badges'. To be allowed access to the meeting room the Members of the European Council wear such a pinholder on their lapel or other garment. The Heads of Government and the President of the Commission wear a gold pinholder; the Ministers a silver one.

The Permanent Representatives and the Antici (for whom, see below) wear a red name badge. The other delegation members wear a blue name badge. The blue badge may be transferred to a high level official from the delegation. In addition each PM and FM has a gold floater in reserve which may be transferred to any delegation member. Each delegation has finally three non-named red floaters, valid only when together with a named blue or grey badge. Wearing the red badge a civil servant may advise their (Prime) Minister for one minute. After that he must leave the meeting room. The system also applies *mutatis mutandis* for the delegation of the Commission and the Council of Ministers. In 2005 the system was further fine-tuned with the introduction of the grey badges for 'non-official' or 'technical' delegation members. Finally the journalists covering the meeting (sometimes more than 2000) wear a yellow badge, whilst security staff and other service personnel wear a green one. Security officers wear mostly a green/yellow badge; drivers have a green one. All name badges include a photograph.

In the meeting, each delegation is allowed two seats: one for the Head of State or Government and one for the Minister for Foreign Affairs (or the Prime Minister). The delegations sit in the sequence used for the six-month rotation between the Member States of the Presidency. The number of other people with access to the meeting room is highly restricted. Each delegation has a suite in the vicinity of the meeting room from which national officials may be summoned as required.[29] (More details are given under 4. B.1.)

During the negotiations in Maastricht on the setting up of Economic and Monetary Union (EMU), the Finance Ministers secured the right 'to participate in European Council meetings'.[30] As a result, when EMU matters are on the agenda, which is mostly the case, EcoFin members are invited. Whenever the EcoFin Ministers participate in the meeting, the Ministers of Foreign Affairs have to give up their seats. In order to avoid this sensitive problem, the Presidency in the past sometimes made three seats available to each delegation. Still unsolved is the problem of the increasing number of Ministers for European Affairs who operate side by side with their Foreign Minister. They are not in the European Council meeting room and are therefore more or less marginalised during the meeting.

Bargaining power in the European Council

Heads of Government derive their bargaining power in the meetings from four sources. The first is of course the position of power their country has in the Union which is defined by the size of its territory, population, economic strength, commitment to European integration, military capabilities and its internal political stability. It is obvious that the Chancellor of Germany scores considerably higher than for instance the Prime Minister of Slovenia or Bulgaria. In addition there is the element of the issue-specific power of a Member State, which is defined by its resources, commitment, options and demands in a specific area. Spain (regional financial aid) and the UK (long-term budget) have with their justified demands in these areas on various occasions put their stamp on the course of important European Council

---

Box 14

A beehive

Meetings of the European Council sometimes happen to coincide with important football matches. Then the political Heads tend to make off for a while. In the June 2006 meeting during the World Cup, PM Tony Blair watched the TV coverage of the England versus Trinidad and Tobago encounter while his colleagues in the conference room debated the way forward for the European Constitution. Blair sent his Foreign Secretary, Margaret Beckett, as his substitute. Dutch PM Jan Peter Balkenende went looking for Blair by the TV screen in order to solicit British support for ditching the Constitutioninal Treaty, which had been rejected by the Netherlands in a referendum. This scene shows that a meeting of the European Council looks like a beehive where the busy negotiators swarm around.

meetings (as discussed in Chapter 3). France and the UK, to give another example, speak in the meetings with more authority on issues of foreign policy because they are the only ones with a permanent seat in the UN Security Council. Luxembourg has unusually strong bargaining power on issues pertaining to its vast system of banks and financial services. In most areas France and Germany dominated the European Council during the last century.

The course of the meetings also shows that bargaining power is dependent on the attributes of the individual Heads of Government. It takes a couple of years until a newcomer from a medium sized or small country can speak with authority in the meetings. As the longest serving member of the European Council, with wide experience in the course of the meetings and an ironcast standing in domestic politics, Luxembourg PM Jean Claude Juncker holds a powerful position, although the GDP of his country is only around 0.1 per cent of the Union's.

Finally the institutional setting represents the fourth factor. As a result of the required consensus in decision-making, each Head of Government has in most cases the option to block decision-making with a veto. But everybody realises, as one Prime Minister once said, that 'Luxembourg can issue a veto once in a decade and Britain once a week' (Tallberg, p. 16).

Does a privileged *inner circle* of the leaders of the largest Member States exist within the European Council? According to Belgian PM Wilfried Martens, only Chancellor Kohl and PM Thatcher were allowed to address President Mitterrand as François (Martens, p. 611) in the 1980s. How should one take it that at the reception of the Heads of State or Government in 2007 in Berlin the leaders of France, the UK, and Italy were cordially kissed by Chancellor Angela Merkel, but not those of the smaller countries? A marginal detail? Perhaps. Nevertheless it reflects the atmosphere between the political Heads in the Council.

National governmental leaders have throughout the Union's history been its most influential and powerful players, with the leaders of France and Germany to the fore. Looking back on one's coverage of more than thirty years of European Council meetings, (only) a few names linger in the memory as very important players. In the era of Chancellor Helmut Schmidt and President Valéry Giscard d'Estaing, who took advantage of their common use of the English language, the meetings 'provided a stage for the dazzling Schmidt-Giscard show that helped to maintain a modicum of integration during an otherwise inauspicious time' (Dinan, p. 75). Later, Helmut Kohl and François Mitterrand, followed by Jacques Chirac and Gerhardt Schröder, were for years the dominating persons of note.[31] Today Chancellor Angela Merkel and President Nicolas Sarkozy play that role. The roll of honour needs to be completed with Commission President Jacques Delors (1985-1995). The trio of Kohl, Mitterrand and Delors for years decided upon the agenda and for the greater part the course of the European Council. According to Belgium PM Wilfried Martens they also did so in order to prevent British PM Thatcher from putting spanners in the works. The Franco-German preponderance is marked by the fact that only seven, always French or German, members of the Council put their stamp on the results of 130 Summits during more than thirty years.

Box 15

The important aspect of 'seniority'

For the meetings to go well it is important that Heads of Government can boast many years of experience. Moreover, these Heads of Government are more familiar with their colleagues. Such 'senior people' therefore have a large influence, including those coming from the smaller Member States. The Heads of Government of the ten States which joined in 2004 still lack these characteristics. As a result they have played, with the exception of the Polish representative, a subordinate role in the meetings to date. Another reason is the rapid turnover of political leaders in these countries. This important aspect of 'seniority' elevates the list of those who have participated in the meetings for more than ten years to the *'roll of honour'* of the most influential members of the European Council.

Presidents François Mitterrand (1981-1995) and Jacques Chirac (1995-2007 and as PM 1986-1988), and Chancellor Kohl (1982-1998). Prime Ministers: Jacques Santer, Luxembourg (1984-1995 and as President of the European Commission from 1995-1999); Felipe Gonzales, Spain (1982-1996); Wilfried Martens, Belgium (1979-1992); Ruud Lubbers, the Netherlands (1982-1994); Margaret Thatcher (1979-1990) and Tony Blair (1997-2007), both UK: Anibal Cavaco Silva, Portugal (1985-1995): Leo Tindemans, Belgium (1974-1978 and as Minister for Foreign Affairs from 1981-1989); Wim Kok, the Netherlands (Maastricht 1991-1994 as Minister of Finance and PM from 1994-2002); Jean-Claude Juncker (Maastricht 1991-1995 as Minister of Finance and since 1995 as PM); Wolfgang Schüssel (1995-2006); Göran Persson, Sweden (1996-2007); Giulio Andreotti, Italy (PM in 1972-1973, several times FM during the 1980s and again PM between 1989 and 1992); Bertie Ahern, Ireland (since 1997). And, finally, Javier Solana Madariaga (1992-1995 Minister for Foreign Affairs of Spain and since 1999 High Representative for the CFSP/SG of the Council).

The former German Foreign Minister Hans-Dietrich Genscher, who attended the meetings from the beginning in 1974 until 1992, holds the record for attendance.

Since the creation of the European Council in 1974, no permanent or long-term political or personal coalition has been revealed other than the Franco-German one. The UK emerges as number three in the pecking order. But who is number four? That is open to question. 'Italy is not one of the four great Member States. Spain is trying to replace Italy, but it is not successful and Poland will have to admit that it is not part of these great Member States', an insider once stated (Tallberg, p. 15).

Prime Minister Juncker of Luxembourg has said: 'Sometimes some Heads of Government became edgy when without complaining they had to swallow once again a compromise set up by the French president and the German Chancellor. Twenty years ago such a French/German pre-agreement guaranteed a general agreement. Today, however, more Heads of Government demand to see their interest reflected in that compromise. There is also another side to the coin. Many Heads of Government, particularly of the smaller and medium-sized Member States, become really nervous when they see that the French/German couple fails to find the intended compromise. They then realise that probably no agreement will come about at all'.

I asked the Luxembourg PM whether in this large European Council a small country can stop the decision-making or, by seriously threatening to do so, influence the meeting decisively. Juncker answered somewhat evasively. 'Sometimes those larger Member States make the mistake of ignoring the vital interests at stake for a certain much smaller Member State. The Head of Government concerned feels he is being treated shabbily and becomes inflexible. He will eventually obstruct. For this reason, each President ought to be advised to treat all Member States, large and small, equally', said Juncker.

Let us now focus on the conduct of the meetings. They provide a striking contrast between the privacy of the meetings and the frenzied activity outside the rooms. There is an enormous contrast between the informal, flexible character of the meeting and the boundless ingenuity which the Presidency and the General Secretariat of the Council must show in order to provide translations in all the 23 official languages of the Union, security arrangements, secretarial assistance and information for the national delegations (with approximately one thousand members) sitting in adjacent rooms and for upwards of more than two thousand journalists covering the event.

It has been the practice since 1987 to begin the session in the afternoon with a speech by the President of the European Parliament. The President informs the European Council of the Parliament's position on the main issues at stake and, after a short discussion, leaves the room. The subsequent evening session is in many cases mostly reserved for questions related to the Community as such, whereas the session in the morning of the second day generally is devoted to foreign policy and common security issues plus the finalisation of the Conclusions.

The course of the really exciting European Council meetings differs from the foregoing scheme. On average there is such an extraordinary important meeting every two years. The most recent was the June 2007 meeting. It agreed on a mandate for a Reform Treaty (the Lisbon Treaty) to replace the defunct Constitutional Treaty (see Chapter 4.B.1.)

The President may, in very difficult negotiations, ask the advice of an 'ad hoc' group of like-minded Member States, 'the Presidency's friends', to help to come to an agreement. An example was the group the Dutch PM Jan Peter Balkenende gathered around himself at the meeting in Brussels in December 2004 in order to deal effectively with the candidacy of Turkey.

Finally, some specific aspects of the functioning of the European Council may be looked at.

Number of meetings

The number of meetings has been changed over the years. According to the TEU, the European Council meets 'at least twice a year'. In Seville (2002) it was decided in principle to meet four times a year, in practice twice in every six-month Presidency. Usually these meetings are held in March, June, October and December. Meanwhile experience since 2002 has taught that many October and March meetings are simply talking shops that fail to produce results. The meagre outcomes from these meetings caused damage to the reputation of the European Council. The UK Presidency of 2005 endeavoured to introduce changes. That took place through calling a so-called *informal meeting* at Hampton Court, southwest of London, on 27 October 2005. Informal meetings like the one at Hampton Court are not prepared by the Council of Ministers or the Coreper. The task in that case fell to the acting President, PM Tony Blair, and the 'sherpas' (see below) – the personal advisors for European affairs of the Heads of Government, plus the President of the Commission. At Hampton Court an attempt was made to set up an 'Energy Policy for Europe' and a 'Globalisation Adjustment Fund' in order to give financial assistance to workers who fall victim to globalisation (as the UK did earlier in the case of the Rover car plant). Those two initiatives are being further developed at present. Only time will tell whether the Hampton Court Summit will bear fruit.

Each Presidency is free to organise such an informal meeting wherever it likes. The informal meeting is an attempt to break away from the solemn massive plenary sessions. The Heads of Government and the Commission President need such consultation in a relaxing environment, without having to take immediately binding decisions. In this setting, the rules of the treaties concerning decision-making in the Union, their implementation and judicial review do not apply. It is remarkable that the formula of the informal meeting of only the Heads of Government (in most cases without ministers and without a large delegation) has over recent years sidelined the traditional Autumn Summit meeting. After the British started with the Hampton Court Summit in October 2005, the Finnish followed in October 2006 (in Lahti), the Germans in March 2007 (Berlin) and the Portuguese in October 2007 (Lisbon). These informal meetings are at times underestimated with regard to their importance. Economic and social problems and new agenda items are often the subject. Such meetings earn their importance by opening to discussion difficult or politically sensitive central issues, outside the slow functioning institutional framework of Commission, Council and Parliament.

Separate from the formal meetings and the meetings described as 'informal' or 'extraordinary' (Brussels, September 2001, after the terrorist attacks in the US), are the 'thematic' meetings, as for instance Tampere (Justice and Home Affairs) in 1999.

The preparation of these special meetings, which are generally concluded without written conclusions[32], is also primarily in the hands of the Presidency. The General Secretariat of the Council prepares a draft of the President's Statement (a kind of veiled Conclusions) for the final press conference. The acting President uses it at his pleasure, while also the President of the Commission draws his conclusions when facing the media representatives. In most cases these Statements are afterwards made available to the public.

Sometimes a Presidency uses such a meeting to tackle in a more informal atmosphere certain urgent priorities on which discussions are not making progress. At times this proves to be helpful. Such a meeting can also serve unexpectedly to isolate troublemakers and thus help to break their resistance. PM Thatcher for instance saw the informal meeting in Rome in October 1990 (rightly) as an attempt 'to pre-empt the outcome of the two IGCs on EMU and Political Union' (which she vehemently opposed). Sometimes the rhythm is the other way around. In 1987 in Copenhagen Thatcher managed to adjourn the discussion on what she saw as the money-devouring CAP. An extra informal meeting (in February 1988) was required to break the deadlock. That resulted in an agreement on setting legally binding controls on agricultural expenditure in order to reduce surpluses, which Thatcher had earlier advocated in vain.

Since 2001 a Tripartite Social Summit takes place in the hours before the Spring European Council meeting. This is a meeting between the Heads of Government of the current and two subsequent Presidencies and the representatives of the organisations of employers (for instance Businesseurope, formerly UNICE) and the unions (ETUC) in the EU.

The meeting place

Until 2003 the European Council had no permanent seat. From the first meeting in 1957 in Paris until 2003 most of the meetings took place in some 50 different capitals and cities located in the country of the acting President. Over time, in particular after the enlargement in 1995 to fifteen Member States, the European Council turned into a kind of 'travelling circus' which became ever more difficult to organise. Therefore the IGC decided in 2000 in Nice that 'when the Union comprised 18 Member States, all European Council meetings will be held in Brussels' (Declaration Nr. 22 annexed to the Treaty of Nice). The last regular meeting in one of the Member States was Thessaloniki (2003). It should be noted that the decision to meet in Brussels relates only to the *formal* European Council meetings; every President is free to organise an informal meeting in their own country.

Secretariat, minutes, 'Antici' and 'sherpas'

The secretariat for the meetings is provided by the SG/HR of the Council and his Deputy. The sessions are not recorded. There exist no minutes apart from the Conclusions. In many cases it is therefore not clear what exactly was agreed. Besides the Presidency, some Heads of Government and Ministers for Foreign Affairs also take notes for themselves. The Secretary-General of the Council is sometimes asked to disclose his notes in order to settle a disagreement between Member States.

The European Council knows no public debates, as distinct from the Council of Ministers where discussions and adoption of acts in the co-decision procedure take place during public procedures. The meetings of the European Council are strictly closed. Full interpretation is the rule during the meetings.

In meetings *'en petit comité'*, and the working dinner, it is possible for Heads of Government to be assisted by a whispering translator.

An interesting phenomenon in this context is the so-called *'Antici group'* (so named after its Italian originator). These *'agents de liaison'* are gathered in the room next to the meeting room of the European Council. Every delegation has one member, mostly a staff member of the Permanent Representation. The 27 Antici are responsible for guiding the flow of information coming from the meeting room of the European Council. Every quarter of an hour an official of the Council Secretariat arrives to tell the Antici in verbatim what has been discussed in the main conference room – such as who has taken the floor, what has been said and decided. Each individual Antici makes careful notes. Each sends his text by fax to his own national delegation room. Thus, after a certain delay, the delegations get to know what happens inside. They always anxiously await those faxes. Should the delegation sense trouble and wish to avoid their Head of Government getting embroiled in undesirable decision-making, then the delegation tries to intervene informally with its PM. For this purpose the Personal Advisors of the Prime Minister and of the FM, plus the Permanent Representative and the Political Director, have access to the conference room. However, this often happens too late, due to the progress of the meeting. In order to obtain advice more quickly each Head of Government has a red button in order to summon an advisor into the room for a few minutes. Prime Ministers or Ministers, moreover, sometimes walk out of the conference room in order to consult their national delegation. To the above should be added that thanks to the recent changes in the course of the European Council, with more negotiations by way of the 'confessional', the role of the Antici has somewhat diminished.

Operating invisibly, but important at crucial moments, are the *'sherpas'*, the so called *'proches collaborateurs'* of the Heads of Government. They constitute an informal, loose network, which officially does not exist but in which all Member States invest. Each Member State has two, being the private secretary or High Councillor for European Affairs of the Prime Minister and of the Minister for Foreign Affairs. While the members of the European Council meet or dine, these consultants stay together in an adjoining room. They have badges which allow them access to the Council meeting in order to give their PM or FM concise oral advice. Sometimes ahead of a European Council meeting a sherpa tries on behalf of his PM to find out in one or more capitals what the exact negotiating room is concerning a trying problem. Occasionally the sherpas play an important role in the preparation. That is particularly the case when a specific problem arises for the European Council. In autumn 1997 the European Council organised a special 'Jobs Summit', in order to tackle high levels of unemployment in some Member States. The European Council can deal with such a specific problem only on the basis of thorough preparation. In order to reach an agreement, each Member State had to appoint in advance a high official with responsibility in the area of unemployment. This sherpa had to coordinate their action internally with the national ministers concerned and subsequently with their Head of Government. In this way the Luxembourg Presidency succeeded in triumphantly completing this Jobs Summit. It would perhaps have failed through the usual channels of the General Affairs Council and Coreper since the required expertise is lacking there. In 2007, the sherpas (then called the 'focal points') played a central role in the preparation of the successful June meeting with a precise mandate for the IGC after the collapse of the Constitutional Treaty as an item on the agenda.

In 2000, at the launch of the Lisbon Strategy, these sherpas attempted to walk further away from the Community Method by the introduction of a 'Mr/Ms Lisbon' for this project. The Commission, with the backing of Coreper/the Council, prevented that. In some cases the sherpas played a role in the preparation of the meetings with the Lisbon agenda as its main subject because of the special responsibilities of the Heads of Government on this issue. Sometimes the Heads of Government request these officials to prepare a detailed report for them on an important matter.

Worth mentioning is that the Seville Rules of Procedure regarding the conduct of the European Council's meetings came about through consultation of the sherpas. In this case the national political leaders clearly insisted on putting their stamp on the future course of the meetings. Such a critical role of the sherpas, bypassing Coreper and the General Affairs Council, is exceptional though. Curiously the position of the national sherpas has been weakened by the setting-up of the Seville rules, the result being a more thorough preparation of the meetings in Brussels.

'Fireside chats'

'Fireside chats' in the past constituted another characteristic element of the phenomenon of 'summitry'. Important elements such as the personal contact of the Heads of Government, their informality and confidentiality, and a level of socialising were reinforced. The original purpose of the European Council was to provide an opportunity for Heads of Government to hold in their inner circle informal discussions on issues of common interest. At the same time the Heads of Government reinforced their personal ties. The 'fireside chat' followed the official dinner on the evening of the first day of the meeting. There the major EU and other cross-boundary issues and political taboos, not ripe or accepted for official discussion, were dealt with as were also the home affairs which bothered the top politicians. No doubt there was an extra stimulating effect for some participants to be found in the late hour, the cuisine and ambience, and the friendships among some of them. For nearly two decades these talks were a central and very important element in the meetings. In the late 1980s, however, the fireside chats slowly died out. The reason? A 'fireside chat' doesn't lend itself to a party of more than about twelve persons. It is obviously difficult to arrange such informal debate in a group of nearly 30 Heads of Government. The dinner-meeting, since 2002, of the members of the European Council plus the HR for the CFSP on the evening of the first day and the recently introduced yearly informal meeting may be viewed as attempts to come close to the 'fireside chat' of the original Summit meetings.

The European Council as a 'media spectacle'

To a European Council meeting the principle applies that what the press does not cover, has not happened! The Summit is a 'media spectacle'. When the Heads of Government meet, a road-show of journalists follows their proceedings, with wide coverage in the national press, TV and radio (De Vreese, p. 101). Therefore the pressure, especially on the President, to produce some measure of success is high. For this reason too, a series of national, Presidency and Commission press-briefings and press-conferences are held, and spokesmen and officials are permanently available by the dozen, with the confidentiality of the meeting little more than a fiction. Heads of Government play a public-relations game by giving out information, in particular to their national press, sometimes even after midnight. They do this in order as far as possible to choreograph the imprint the effects of the meeting have on their national public opinion. Each Head of Government tunes his report of the meeting to what his national audience likes to hear. Certain spokespersons for Heads of Government go to great lengths to confirm the impression that a meeting has been a success. It thus happens that after the meetings, due to the activities of those sources, Heads of Government in their newspapers sometimes read about 'discussed items' never examined in the meeting. This is evidence of the risks inherent in the massive publicity surrounding these meetings, which – especially for the President of the meeting – have to be seen at all cost as a successful event. Comparing daily newspapers from the Member States the day after the meeting one sometimes gets the impression that there was not just one meeting, but several, all ending with totally different results.

Despite this wave of unprecedented 'public diplomacy' (Van Grinsven, p. 153) the media present a reasonably true report. A meeting nowadays attracts sometimes some 4000 'participants'. Less than a quarter belong to the delegations. Most times there are more than 2000 media representatives from often more than 50 countries. Sometimes about 100 TV-stations are on the spot. The massive media attention forces the participants and, in particular, the President of the meeting to show their national audience results. After the closure of the meeting, a big press conference is jointly organised by the President-in-Office, the President of the Commission and the High Representative for the CFSP/SG of the Council. Such a press conference mostly takes place as early as on the eve of the first meeting day. Nevertheless the participants can leave unreported their (sometimes important) bilateral (or multilateral) deliberations about matters in the margin of the agenda. Of course, the journalists cannot cover all 28 simultaneously-held press conferences (27 Member States and that of the Presidency) at the conclusion of the meeting. They surmount that handicap after the conferences by comparing and swapping their notes. Moreover the reports of the media are bound to differ as a result of diverging national interests and hobby horses.

Pressure groups in the corridors

Finally the phenomenon of the pressure groups. Their influence in the Union is sometimes significant. They come in order to defend their point of view. If that fails via the European Council meeting, they try to seek attention from the countless media on the spot. Along the sidelines of the meetings one finds, depending on the agenda, representatives of differing groups and NGOs originating from all sectors of society.

C.3.   New developments in the activities of the European Council

Over the years an important shift has been noticeable in the role and activities of the European Council. Initially the European Council's most important activity was its function of taking care of 'overall consistency in the activities of the Communities and in the work on political cooperation'. This was the first important task laid down in the Council 'birth-certificate' (Annex 4 to this publication, point 2). But from the earliest days the Heads of Government also had to work as supreme arbitrator, or 'court of appeal', for the crucial political and sometimes even technical issues 'kicked upstairs' to the European Council. Take for instance the reforms of the Common Agricultural Policy by the European Council in the late 1970s and the 1980s. 'We did speak exhaustively about cheese and milk, but unfortunately spent not a single word on unemployment and inflation', complained Chancellor Helmut Schmidt immediately after the first European Council meeting in 1975, in Dublin. More than once during those years the Heads of Government entered into detailed technical discussions on very complicated matters such as the introduction of a system of national milk quotas and the elimination of the Monetary Compensatory Amounts. It fell to the European Council to elaborate this in detail because the Council of Agricultural Ministers lacked the courage to make far-reaching reforms because of their mutually opposed interests and their close ties with agribusiness (details in Werts, 1992, p. 220-224). Another example is the meeting of record length, a 'technical marathon', in 1978 in Brussels where final consensus was reached on the creation of the European Monetary System.

At the end of the 1980s the European Council returned to its original task, now, however, acting more as agenda setter. Since then the Heads of Government have, with the Commission President in many cases, taken charge of the important or disputed dossiers right from the start. Via guidance from the European Council, they now carry out a kind of progress control regarding the process of the different settlements in the Commission-Council-Parliament institutional triangle. In other words, the Heads of Government nowadays check meeting by meeting whether the specialised Councils are sticking to their brief. With such an approach, these Councils have more difficulties in bringing their insoluble problems before the European Council. This approach allows the European Council to avoid assuming its traditional role of arbiter or *instance d'appel*. 'Issues which otherwise might require an arbiter can thus be avoided through timely intervention', says Jean-Paul Jacqué, Director of the Legal Service of the Council of Ministers. This shift in the role of the European Council from arbiter to agenda-setter was mirrored in 2002 in Seville in the text of the newly agreed Rules for organising the Proceedings of the European Council (see Annex 5 to this publication).

Box 16

An example of the functioning of the European Council

An example of the new working method is the settlement in 2005-2006 of the hugely controversial issue of opening up the Union's services markets. The so-called Service Directivehas been designed to enable business to sell their services across borders as easily as they sell goods. 'The directive would have stayed on the shelf unless it became changed', said Commissioner Charlie McCreevy. Formerly the Heads of Government would only get involved with this dossier once they were called to arbitrate. But nowadays the European Council does not wait to let that happen. After its request of March 2005 of the Institutions that 'all efforts to be undertaken (...) in order to secure a broad consensus', Parliament responded with a draft Directive with far-reaching amendments. The European Council in its meeting in March 2006 welcomed this achievement. It asked the Commission to base its subsequent proposal of the Directive 'largely on the outcome of the European Parliament's first reading'. In the course of 2007 the Council of Ministers and the Parliament finalised deliberations on that basis. Directive 2006/123/EC will (without the contentious 'country of origin principle') come into effect on 28 December 2009.

The Dutch Minister for Foreign Affairs and former Permanent Representative, Dr Bernard Bot, has an explanation for the above shift in the European Council's activities: 'Thanks to the setting-up of more decision-making on the basis of QMV in the First Pillar (EMU, CAP, Transport etc.) where moreover the policy has largely been realised, the activities have since the turn of the century been moved to the Third Pillar (Justice and Home Affairs). As a result, the European Council comes more into the picture because (a) in the Third Pillar the Commission plays a restricted role just as the European Parliament does and (b) in the Third Pillar unanimity is required for decision-making in most cases, causing the Specialised Council to fail frequently.'

The undefined boundaries of the European Council

What determines whether or not a particular dossier will find its way to the European Council? Where are, in other words, the boundaries of its activities? A 'borderline' cannot be drawn regarding issues which do or do not reach the European Council. The review in Chapter 3 shows that the European Council has a series of 'set subjects'. They create a 'reserved area' by way of a monopoly position for the European Council/HSG Council. In other words these bodies as highest political authorities have taken upon themselves the decision-making regarding important parts of the Union's activities. Often these are subjects containing an important political aspect (such as enlargement) which determines the future development of the Union. Although the European Council has to respect the competences of the Institutions, as a 'multi-issue forum' it can discuss and, if necessary, decide pragmatically upon all matters inside or even outside the realm of the treaties. It is noteworthy that since 1975, as analysed in more detail in Chapter 3, the European Council, the HSG Council[33], and the Conference of the Heads of State or Government (IGC) have concerned themselves with some 500 widely varying issues. Experts at the Council of Ministers whom we questioned about this, could discover no 'dividing line' concerning subjects with which the European Council becomes involved or not. According to our research (see Chapter 3) the Heads of Government do indeed work in order 'to ensure progress and overall consistency in the activities of the Communities' (Annex 4 to this publication, point 2), by solving concrete problems (being their mission of 1974). In fact that often takes place on an *ad hoc* basis. In other words, the European Council, besides setting the agenda, tackles the problems which present themselves. Its activities cover, in summary, on the one hand the major strategic interests of the Union (such as the CFSP, the admittance of new Member States, the creation of EMU and Institutional development) and on the other hand the bottlenecks in the Council of Ministers, in the Commission and even sometimes in Parliament. Chapter 3 confirms that the Heads of Government discuss all matters which are of collective concern, whether they belong to the political or economic area, plus even sometimes matters within the confines of the political authority of the Member States, in other words the purely domestic domain of the Member States.

According to the father of the European Council, Jean Monnet, this process of broadening the limits would only stop where the frontiers of political power begin: at the border of the national political authority of the Member States.[34] But, as the example of Austria mentioned earlier in this chapter has shown, this thesis is today untenable. Another example was the refusal by Germany and France, the two most important members of the eurozone, to fulfil their obligations under the excessive deficit procedure of EMU at the beginning of this century. This refusal by the governments in Berlin and Paris threatened the functioning of EMU. Although an issue of a highly political nature with important economic consequences, this problem was never tabled for discussion in the European Council. The reason is that neither Chancellor Gerhard Schröder nor President Jacques Chirac would ever contemplate such a discussion.

This long series of tasks and functions assigned to the European Council is much more far-reaching than the Council of Ministers' 'power to take decisions' (Article 202 TEC), which is limited by the provision, 'in accordance with the provisions of this Treaty'.

(For a listing of the many future tasks of the European Council as laid down in the Lisbon Treaty, see Annex 6.)

Endnotes

1   TEC, Treaty establishing the European Economic Community (Treaty of Rome) and EAEC, the Treaty establishing the European Atomic Energy Community, both of which came into existence simultaneously on 1 January 1958; the Treaty establishing the European Coal and Steel Community

of 1951 which expired as planned on 23 July 2002; and SEA, Single European Act, which came into force on 1 July 1987. It made a number of amendments to the earlier Community treaties.

2   One of the rare studies is the lucid article by Professor Alan Dashwood, 'Decision-making at the Summit', *Cambridge yearbook of European legal studies*, 2000, 79-105 which provided some starting points for our research. For an extensive analysis of the legal nature and form of the European Council as it functioned before the coming into force of the TEU in 1983, see my earlier mentioned publication The *European Council*, Chapter III.

3   TEU Articles 4 (ex Article B) and 13.1 (ex J.8).

4   Answer to a question by MEP Hutton, OJ Annex, Debates of the EP, 2-356/191, 14.10.87; see also question by MEP Lord O'Hagan, OJ C.310/4, 10.12.79.

5   Jacqué and Simon, in Hoscheit and Wessels, (eds.), 123.

6   Monar in Curtin, Kellermann, Blockmans, 213 with some more examples of decision-making in legislative affairs by the European Council.

7   European Parliament, Corbett, Richard and Méndez de Vigo, Íñigo, *Report on the Treaty establishing a Constitution for Europe*, A6-0070/2004, 9.12.2004, par. 6.2. note 19.

8   The Consensus Principle was approved by the UN General Assembly in 1973. Decision-making by consensus, instead of voting by unanimity, is the rule in intergovernmental bodies. In the European Council consensus means an agreement between the Heads of Government without having to resort to voting.

9   As was the case with the process of decision-making for the creation of the European Monetary System (EMS) in 1978 and the launching of the so called Lisbon Process in 2000. More details under Chapter 3.F.2.

10   See for instance the 'agreement' on the creation of the EMS concluded at the Brussels 1978 meeting that afterwards temporarily stranded on unforeseen technical and political problems; details in Werts, 1992, o.c., par. 78.

11   For our systematic classification of the activities we combined (a) the functions as outlined in the Communiqué of Paris 1974, see Annex 4 to this publication; (b) the Tindemans Report on 'European Union', *Bull Suppl.* 1/76, see section V. (c) the paper regarding the 'Organization of European Council meetings' agreed at the London, 1977 meeting, *Bull* 6-1977, 2.3.1; (d) the 'Solemn Declaration on European Union', of the 1983 European Council in Stuttgart, *Bull* 6-1983, 1.6.1 (e) The Single European Act of 1987 (f) The Treaty on European Union (TEU) of 1993 (g) the Conclusions of Sevilla June 2002, *Bull* 6-2002, I.27. and (h) the Lisbon Treaty (not yet in force).

12   By way of derogation from the requirement of unanimity applicable for the CFSP, the Council of Ministers may act on the basis of QMV regarding some decisions. These are taken on the basis of a common strategy for the purpose of the implementation of a joint action (for instance the dispatch by the Union of a team of observers) or a common position or, according to Article 18(5) TEU, on the appointment of a special representative. Other examples are the negotiation and conclusion of international agreements implementing a joint action or a common position (Article 24(3) and the authorisation of enhanced cooperation in CFSP matters (Article 27a et seq. TEU). Article 40a(2) TEU and 11(2) TEC refer, in that order, to the authorisation of enhanced cooperation on Police and Judicial cooperation in criminal matters. In practice such decision-taking on the basis of QMV (Qualified Majority Voting) hardly ever takes place.

13   The Nice Treaty slightly reinforced the position of the European Council. The required unanimity for the appointment of the President of the Commission had become outdated. The Council meeting in the composition of the Heads of State or Government (Article 214(2) TEC) is regulating authority here and hence can make its selection by qualified majority.

14   For this parapraph see Busek, Erhard and Schauer, Martin (Hg.), '*Eine europäische Erregung. Die 'Sanktionen' der Vierzehn gegen Österreich im Jahr 2000'*, Wien, Böhlau Verlag, 580 pp. The tough sanctions were announced on the basis of a 'Statement from the Portuguese Presidency of the European Union on behalf of XIV Member States', of 31 January 2000. The governments of Ireland and Italy had unsuccessfully advocated a less confrontational approach. In a statement, 'Responsibility for Austria – A future in the Heart of Europe', published in several international newspapers, the Austrian Government protested strongly. 'The Federal Government works for an Austria in which xenophobia, anti-Semitism and racism have no place' and Austria 'acknowledges its special responsibility as regards the respectful treatment of ethnic and religious minorities' were its key phrases. Later Austria threatened to break out of its diplomatic isolation by holding a national referendum. That way the European Council was forced to a volte-face. The measures against Austria were quietly withdrawn

on 12 September 2000. The European Parliament had urged to do so. The question shows how the Heads of Government will even go as far as mobilising the HSG Council to condemn one Member State's policy.

15   At the 2001 Stockholm meeting, the Heads of Government and the Commission President during a ceremony with FIFA and UEFA signed an agreement on a new transfer and contract system negotiated between the Commission and the Football Associations.

16   For this detailed analysis, see Dashwood, 2000, p. 100-105 and further Jacqué in Dony and Bribosia (eds.), p. 143-144.

17   For an overview see R. Corbett, F. Jacobs and M. Shackleton, *The European Parliament*, 7th edn, London, John Harper Publishing, 2007, 52-53.

18   AE, 8 October 1999, 5. On 27 October 2005 at the informal Hampton Court meeting, the President of Parliament, Josep Borrell, was invited by acting President, PM Tony Blair; Borrell stayed during the whole meeting. His successor Hans-Gert Pöttering participated in full in the Lisbon informal European Council/IGC Conference on 18 and 19 October 2007. According to his spokeswoman this happened because Parliament had participated in the IGC.

19   Based on author's notes and countless media reports of the meeting published on 15 June 2006. According to these reports, the German Government persuaded the (German) leader of the Social Democrats, Martin Schulz, to withdraw his support for a change of the Parliament's seat.

20   Some frustration on the side of the Parliament played a part. Several months earlier the Heads of Government in their role as IGC had taken little notice of the urgent pleas from the Parliament to give it more say in the composition of the European Commission via the Constitutional Treaty (Article I-27).

21   Three Wise Men,   Report on European Institutions Presented by the Committee of Three – Biesheuvel, Dell, Marjolin – to the European Council, October 1979; not officially published, distributed by the Commission, 118 pp. For a summary see *Bull* 11-1979, 1.5.1. and 1.5.2. The main conclusions of the Three Wise Men have been confirmed, in 2001 by Poos, *Report on Reform of the Council*, European Parliament, Doc. Final A5-0308/2001.

22   After the 1978 Copenhagen meeting, for instance, President-in-Office Anker Jörgensen made a statement based on guidelines laid down by the Heads of Government on the position of the Nine regarding the Middle East. The Ambassador of Denmark in Cairo, had to inform the Egyptian Minister for Foreign Affairs submitting the text of the statement, but also pointing out that it was not a formal Declaration of the Nine. The statement has never been officially published.

23   See for instance Laeken (2001). This meeting had to spend considerable time to find agreement for its 'Declaration for the Future of Europe' (see Chapter 4). At the end of the meeting, after midnight, the Heads of Government had to start a discussion on the distribution of 22 agencies of the Union with a seat in the different Member Sates, such as instance the European Food Authority. It was no surprise that the meeting failed. This was due to the mistake by the President, Belgium PM Guy Verhofstadt, of putting on the agenda a very complicated issue not ripe for decision-making.

24   In Laeken in 2001, Austrian Chancellor Schüssel called for a Regulation for an extension of the ecopoints system. Austria used this system in order to restrict the transit flow of lorries through the environmentally sensitive Alps, a politically delicate matter in Tirol. When a promise to deal with the matter was not forthcoming, the Chancellor threatened to prevent the enlargement of the Union with the Eastern European Candidate Member States. Schüssel got his way. Schüssel repeated this trick in 2002, in Copenhagen. There he succeeded in subjecting the enlargement with ten new Member States to a continued restriction of the transit lorry traffic through the Alps. In 2002 in Barcelona more than one hour of precious time was lost when unexpectedly a discussion flared up regarding the reopening of the Sankt Gotthart tunnel, following a traffic accident.

25   The deaths provoked an initiative by France for a Framework Decision on reinforcing the penal framework to prevent the facilitation of unauthorised entry, transit and residence and the linked Directive defining the facilitation of unauthorised entry, transit and residence. Both were adopted in the Council of Ministers on 28 November 2002. The disaster, moreover, speeded up the Council Framework Decision on combating trafficking in human beings, adopted on 19 July 2002.

26   In Finland, for instance, the constitutional assignment of tasks between the President and the FA Minister in the European Council is unclear. In 1997 the Ministers for Social Affairs and those of Justice and Home Affairs made vain attempts also to gain admittance to the special Theme Summit about their activities. In 2002 European Council President PM Aznar prevented the Ministers for Social Affairs from being invited to the Barcelona meeting with its clearly social and employment

agenda. The Commissioner for Social Policy, Anna Diamantopoulou, and Belgium PM Verhofstadt had requested their participation. Opposition came especially from the Finance Ministers (themselves invited). In 2001 the Secretary-General of the Council – High Representative for the CFSP and former NATO Secretary General Javier Solana, clashed with his successor at NATO, Lord Robertson of Port Ellen, who wished to join the meeting. The dispute had its origins in NATO's surprise decision to invoke (for the first time in history) its famous Article 5 collective security agreement after the terrorist attacks on 11 September in the USA. The Belgium presidency refused to invite Robertson since he was not a member of the European Council.

27   The 'Rules of Procedure' of the Council of Ministers apply also to the HSG Council. According to these rules, the Commission has a standing invitation to attend Council meetings, although the Council may decide to meet without a Commissioner. The latter has never happened in the European Council. See Council's Rules of Procedure (CRP), JO, L106/22 of 15.4.2004, article 5.

28   In 2003 in the October meeting, when Chancellor Schröder and his FM Fischer had to return earlier to Berlin for a crunch vote in the Bundestag, the German political leader asked President Chirac to stand in for him. Leszek Miller, the Polish PM, arrived in December in Brussels in a wheel chair due to injuries he had suffered in a recent helicopter crash.

29   The setting during the years when France had a President whose political colour differed from that of his government (the so called 'cohabitation') was problematic. Due to their diverging political approaches towards Europe and moreover their personal rivalry, tensions and frictions ensued resulting in the Presidency's acting in a way which was at times unclear. Between 1986 and 1988, for instance, both the Socialist President François Mitterrand and the Prime Minister of the Right, Jacques Chirac, arrived along with their Minister of Foreign Affairs. As a consequence the latter was not allowed in the meeting room. The President and his PM in some cases adopted a completely different position on the same subject. The roll call at the Nice 2000 IGC meeting had President Chirac act as President of the meeting, while PM Jospin represented France's negotiating position. At the end of 1987 an important reform of the CAP was pending, a serious matter for France and its extensive agricultural sector. But, when the European Council convened in Copenhagen, the time clearly was not yet ripe for decisions. During the meeting President Mitterrand left the tough negotiations to his then PM Jacques Chirac. However at the subsequent Press Conference the President showed scant appreciation with the following remarks: 'Mesdames, Messieurs, Monsieur the Prime Minister will now explain why his proposals have come to nothing'. Then he leaned back with a broad grin. (With thanks to my collegue Frans Boogaard (*Algemeen Dagblad*, Rotterdam) who related to me the latter incident.)

30   Declaration No. 4 annexed to the Final Act on the occasion of the signature of the TEU. These EcoFin ministers in the past also wore a silver pinholder. Afterwards their position weakened a bit. Nowadays they wear a red name badge. The deputy ministers for European Affairs wear a red floater badge. That allows them through the second security ring into the coffee rooms outside the meeting room.

31   During the meeting in Vienna in 1998 Kohl became, after sixteen years' membership, Honorary Citizen of Europe. Kohl was the second (and until today the last) to receive this award. In 1976 the European Council had Jean Monnet (1888-1979), founding father of the Union and of its European Council, appointed as the first Honorary Citizen of Europe.

32   Nevertheless the informal meeting in Ghent on 19 October 2001 yielded three 'Declarations'. But none of them was – against the normal practice regarding meetings of the Council – published in the Bulletin of the EU.

33   The HSG Council has, moreover, the advantage in accordance with the Council's Rules of Procedure of being able to act formally under a written procedure. The requirement of Article 4 TEU that all the 27 Heads of State or Government are physically present (difficult to fulfil today) can in this way be circumvented.

34   Monnet, p. 770. An example is the policy of reconciliation of the former Federal Republic of Germany (FRG) with its Eastern neighbour State. Although this 'German Question" for decades was one of the most important political issues, it was never discussed in the European Council before the democratisation of Eastern Europe in the autumn of 1989. Even after the fall of the Berlin Wall, this subject could be discussed in the European Council only following a German request: see letter of the Dutch Minister for Foreign Affairs to the Second Chamber, Netherlands Parliament 1989-1990, No. 21416, No. 1, p. 3.

3   The most important successes and failures of the European Council

Introduction

This chapter provides a survey of the results of the major meetings since 1985.[1] In addition I try to highlight the activities of the European Council as analysed in Chapter 2, taking as a guide the package of its 'Functions and Tasks' – with the aim of clarifying which tasks and functions in the range of strategic functions of the European Council come to the fore.

The European Council has over the years discussed an endless number of important and less important topics. From those the author has dealt with a comprehensive selection. The choice of these events was to some extent a subjective exercise. Selected and described are the agenda items with a political scope which go beyond the meeting of the European Council itself since they affect the development of the Union. Moreover those agenda items are looked at which characterise the political course of affairs in the Union.

Although not everyone saw it as such at the time, 1989 was the year in which the European Council initiated its two biggest 'history making' projects ever. They concerned the accession of the Eastern and Central European countries and the creation of the Economic and Monetary Union (EMU) with the common currency of the euro. These events are described and analysed in this chapter as are other key events between 1989 and the signing of the Lisbon Treaty in 2007. Since institutional renewal has been an important item ever since 1985, I take this year as a starting point. The Economic and Monetary Union follows and after that the enlargements. These are also items which show up in the Conclusions of every meeting.

EMU and the euro became part of everyday life on 1 January 2002. Enlargement with the accession of eight former communist states in Central and Eastern Europe, plus Cyprus and Malta, was achieved on 1 May 2004 and with Bulgaria and Romania on 1 January 2007. Simultaneously the European Council dealt with two other important projects: the CFSP and the economic renewal/unemployment issue. In these projects as with institutional reform, the Council was clearly less successful. In this chapter I investigate why this was so. At Maastricht in1991, Amsterdam in 1997, Nice in 2000 and Brussels in 2004 the Heads of Government[2] failed to satisfy the expectations which had been created in respect of institutional renewal. I look at the reasons for this. I then analyse and describe the financing of the Union's activities, another big issue which has kept the European Council occupied during the last two decades. Finally, under 'Special European Council meetings' I focus on the meetings which dealt with economic and social issues, Third Pillar, terrorism and the important appointments in the Union.

A.   INTERGOVERNMENTAL CONFERENCES – INSTITUTIONAL AND PROCEDURAL QUESTIONS

A.1. Intergovernmental Conferences spanning three decades

The EU (and hence the European Council) has an obsession with its own institutional structure. Since its meeting in Brussels in December 1978, thirty years ago, the Council has been almost incessantly preoccupied with institutional reforms. In 1978 the Commission was already warning that 'with twelve members, the Institutions and decision-making procedures will be under considerable strain and the Community will be exposed to a possible stalemate' (*Bull* Suppl. 1/78 Nr.49) – in other words what remained the big problem thirty years later. In that 1978 meeting the Committee of the Three Wise Men was invited 'to consider the adjustments to the machinery and procedures of the Institutions which are required for the proper operation of the (European) Communities' (*Bull* 12-1978, 2.3.1). Yet this preoccupation certainly did not always result in success. Time and again the Heads of Government took on an ambitious challenge. According to most institutional experts and certainly the political world, the results were disappointing. But is that (with the benefit of hindsight) a true assessment? And if so, was the fact that the European Parliament and the Commission raised expectations far too high not an important factor? Why also have Heads of Government time and again fallen into the same trap of raising their expectations and solemn promises too high?

The Single European Act (in force since 1 July 1987) was a success, but suffered from the undeserved highly negative opinion of the European Parliament (Resolution of 17 April 1986). The achievement of the Treaty of Maastricht (in force since November 1993) became the next success. The subsequent Treaty of Amsterdam (in force 1 May 1999), however, was disappointing. Nice (in force since 1 February 2003) turned out slightly better, although the course of the IGC (Intergovernmental Conference) did not merit any great award.

The IGC dedicated to the Constitutional Treaty of 2004 finally also succeeded (unless one takes the view that the Heads of Government deserve the blame for the disaster of the referenda in France and the Netherlands).

Here I briefly sketch the IGC of 1985-86, resulting in the Single Act; the IGC of 1990 which resulted in 1991 in the landmark Treaty of Maastricht; the IGC of 1996-1997, which resulted in the Treaty of Amsterdam (1997); the IGC of 2000, resulting in the Treaty of Nice (in force since 1 February 2003); and the IGC of 2003-2004, which yielded the Constitutional Treaty. Finally the IGC of 2007 is analysed with as its result the Lisbon Treaty of 2007. In conclusion I attempt to answer the question to what extent the European Council has succeeded in its role as IGC.

A.2.   Milan 1985: 'separating the sheep from the goats'

'This European Council will stand in the history of Europe as a kind of turn-ing point', stated the President of the Commission, Jacques Delors after the Milan 1985 meeting. The Heads of Government decided to convene an IGC in order to draft a treaty on a Common Foreign and Security Policy and to include the amendments to the EEC Treaty that were needed to enable a series of institutional changes and an extension of the activities of the Community to be made.

In Milan, the Italian Prime Minister Bettino Craxi made history by 'sepa-rating the sheep from the goats', against the advice of more fearful delega-tions. Much against the liking of his British colleague Margaret Thatcher, PM Craxi pushed through an IGC by way of a surprising vote on the basis of a *majority decision*. The Council disguised itself, in accordance with Article 236 EEC, as Council of Ministers and called upon an IGC by way of Article 148.1 EEC (Thatcher, 1993, p. 551; Kohl, 2005, p. 385). This happened by means of a unique vote, or a 'confrontation' majority versus the minority (the UK, Denmark and Greece) which was unprecedented. The decision at the meeting to start an IGC was followed by an exceptional burst of applause. In Milan the Heads of State or Government acted as a Council ex Article 148(1) EEC. Craxi confirmed in Milan that recourse was made to the formula of a vote to 'escape the guillotine of unanimity: this was the only legal possibility' (author's notes in Milan). There was a link between the IGC and the acceptance in Milan of the Commission's White Paper 'Completing the Internal Market'. The acceptance of this latter project into the EEC's legal framework became a major step forward.

At the subsequent Luxembourg 1985 meeting, the Heads of Government reached agreement in principle on a reform of the Institutions and their pro-cedures. Qualified Majority Voting by decision-making in the Council was extended to four sectors vital to further development of the Community: the completion of the Internal Market; Technological Research and Development; Economic and Social Cohesion, and an improvement of the working conditions in the Community. Adoption by a qualified majority now became possible for two-thirds of all the decisions needed to create the Internal Market. The reform of the Community system and of EPC resulted in the first revision of the Treaty of Rome. This occurred via one 'Single European Act' (SEA), a reference to the fact that it contained both revisions of the treaties and a legal foundation for the EPC (European Political Cooperation, the forerunner of the CFSP). The decisions taken at the European Councils of 1985 in Milan and again regarding the calling of another IGC in 1989 in Strasbourg, and a few months later in Dublin regard-ing the creation of EMU, amounted to a breakthrough. All these important decisions were taken against the will of PM Margaret Thatcher (see Thatcher p. 760-763 for the broader view). The events indicated that no longer could a single Member State block progress in the Community, not even one of the largest.

The agreement in 1985 regarding the SEA encompassed moreover:

−   Increased powers for the Parliament through a new 'cooperation pro-
     cedure'. It involved the collaboration of the Parliament for legislation

concerning a number of activities, such as the measures concerning the
completion of the Internal Market by 1993;
- Compulsory cooperation on foreign policy matters (for the first time
  on a treaty base) through EPC;
- The establishment of a Court of First Instance at the Court of Justice;
- Delegation of more powers on implementation and management to
  the Commisson.

It was further agreed to incorporate provisions on monetary capacity via
a reference in the EEC Treaty to the EMS and to a further development of
the ECU (European Currency Unit). It was completed with another new
strategic term in the Community's dictionary, 'Cohesion' – a reduction of
the economic and social disparities between the regions by means of, especially, the European Regional Development Fund.

At the time of its signing the Single European Act was generally seen as a
failure. The SEA was far removed from its four preparatory documents: the
European Council's 1983 'Solemn Declaration on European Union';
Parliament's 'Draft Treaty Establishing the European Union' of 1984; the
'Report by the ad hoc Committee on Institutional affairs' written at the request
of the European Council; and the proposals of the Commission for the IGC of
1985. In its Resolution of 17 December 1985 Parliament underscored 'the ambiguities and shortcomings' of the Act. It concluded that 'it is very far from constituting the genuine reform of the Community that its people need'. Here the
European Parliament's outlook on the situation showed little realism. Looking
back, the meetings of 1985 and 1986 were *milestones*. The SEA opened at last the
way to completion of the Internal Market, thirty years after the Treaty of Rome
in which this key objective had already been defined. Moreover, the
Parliament overlooked that thanks to the SEA its own position in the institutional framework had clearly been reinforced.

A.3.   'Discussing... like a cabinet at a European level'

The meetings of the European Council in Madrid (June 1989), Strasbourg
(December 1989), Dublin I (April 1990) and Dublin II (June 1990) were cru-
cial in the process which resulted in EMU and the Treaty on European
Union (TEU).

The first meeting ever in Spain agreed at Madrid to set the stage for
Economic and Monetary Union (*Bull* 6-1989, 1.1.1.-1.1.24). A major point of
disagreement in Madrid was whether the European Council should commit
itself to the convening of an IGC, as a large majority headed by Mitterrand
wanted but which Thatcher opposed. At their Strasbourg 1989 meeting, the
Heads of Government finally cleared the way for the calling of an IGC,
although PM Thatcher (again) disagreed.[3]

The Heads of Government considered in Paris in November 1989, one
week after the fall of the Berlin Wall, the prospect of German unification.
Belgian PM Wilfried Martens noted that 'for the first time we were sitting
around the table discussing a political issue like a cabinet at a European
level' ('Watershed for Europe', *New York Times*, 22 November 1989).
President Mitterrand concluded on the basis of unanimity that 'we declare
ourselves ready to cooperate on everything which makes possible the recov-

ery of Eastern European countries (...); we are ready to contribute all our means to this restoration, (...) at the price, a *sine qua non* condition: the confirmed return to democracy' (AE, 20/21 November 1989, p. 3).

But two weeks later, at their meeting in December in Strasbourg regarding the prospect of German unification, Chancellor Kohl ran into considerable hesitation and even suspicion and hostility from all Heads of State and Government, except from the Spaniard Felipe González and the Irishman Charles Haughey (Kohl, 1996, p. 165; Cole, 1994, p. 153). They happened to represent the only two Member States which thanks to their geography had never been threatened by Germany. The opponents feared the creation of an economic (and hence political) superpower in the heart of Europe. Later Kohl would recall that during his many years as a member he never experienced a 'Summit meeting with such an icy atmosphere' (Kohl, 2005, p. 194). Due to this hesitation the meeting endorsed with a certain degree of reluctance the prospect of German unification. Since the expression 'reunification' was not liked by some Member States, this word was avoided in the Conclusions. In its Declaration on Central and Eastern Europe (*Bull* 12-1989, 1.1.20) the Council announced that it would 'seek the strengthening of the state of peace in Europe in which the German people will regain its unity through self-determination'. As an extra requirement it was laid down that unification 'has to be placed in the perspective of European integration'. This was a reference to the expectation that the FRG would compromise on its currency's dominant role in a future EMU. The Heads of Government promised in Strasbourg to contribute to the process of political and economic reform in the countries of Central and Eastern Europe by offering 'increased cooperation in all areas', with a pledge to aid those nations that were adopting a democratic government.

The foregoing should not give the impression that the European Union played a key role in the process of German unification. As a result of the reluctance in the Member States' capitals to recognise the urgency of such unification, the key roles in this historically important process fell to the Presidents of the USSR and USA, Mikhail Gorbachev and George Bush. Especially important was the acceptance by Gorbachev that a united Germany could be in NATO. In the European Council the Member States, led by France and the UK, drew the logical conclusion and welcomed the process once it became clear that German unification would go ahead anyway.[4] These crucial decisions had important side-issues, such as the question of the borders of a reunited Germany, in particular the border with Poland, and a possible reawakening of nationalistic aspirations and ethnic rivalries in Europe. As with the creation of EMU and the replacement of the national currencies by the euro (Chapter 3.B), these decisions of historic importance had been prepared in detail by the German and French leaders Kohl and Mitterrand. In 1991 in the run-up to Maastricht, six top-secret Franco-German bilateral meetings took place (Dyson, 1998, p. 47-55). With some exaggeration it could be said that these important decisions really concerned *Franco-German decisions* by '*la formidable machinerie franco-allemande*' (Lacouture, 1998, p. 395) that the other Heads of Government agreed with later. In the run-up to the meeting in the Spring of 1990, Mitterrand and Kohl sent a joint message to the other members of the European Council. They recommended that the European Community should achieve economic, monetary and, in a sense also, political unity by January 1993. One week later in Dublin the European Council agreed, and in so doing laid down the framework for the EC's programme for the rest of the century.

The feeling in many Western European capitals that with unification Germany might lose interest in European integration, or that a united Germany as a superpower would dominate the Community, was alleviated by Chancellor Kohl. He stated that, because 'German unity is only possible under a European roof', it 'must occur in very close cooperation and communication with the Community'. In other words German unification would 'mean a push and not a decline for the Community' (AE, Documents 27 March 1990, p. 2; Kohl, 2005, p. 1036), Kohl adding that unification would 'contribute to faster economic growth in the Community' (a quite remarkable argument).

All these decisions were taken during a period bristling with political tensions between France and Germany (for instance regarding the Gulf War and the wars in Yugoslavia). It has been suggested that in those days 'European integration became synonymous with the personality of Helmut Kohl himself – even more than those of Mitterrand or Delors' (Cole, 1998, p. 126).

Kohl wanted to realise three large projects in parallel and simultaneously: the unification of Germany, the achievement of EMU and the accomplishment of a Political Union (relating to foreign and security policy, interior and justice with more powers for the European Parliament). He succeeded regarding the former two, but failed to get the Political Union off the ground.

Mitterrand as well as various other Heads of Government, such as PM Thatcher, initially was sceptical regarding the German pursuit of quick unification (Thatcher p. 769 and p. 796-797; Kohl, 2005, p. 1042). Mitterrand feared that Kohl gave priority to Germany's unification. He even feared that the Germans might be prepared to cease membership of the European Community as a concession towards the Soviet Union in order to obtain unification (Genscher, p. 678). The French President considered EMU paramount. In those days Thatcher was (again) obstructive. She feared that EMU plus unification would drag Europe towards a Political Union which she abhorred (Thatcher p. 760-762).

A.4.   Maastricht 1991: a landmark in the history of Europe

The meeting in 1991 in Maastricht, under the Presidency of Dutch Prime Minister Ruud Lubbers, will remain a *landmark* in the history of Europe. The meeting had as an important background the recent German unification. The Heads of Government made an attempt in Maastricht to fit the reunited Germany into Europe's future power balance. Agreement on a draft Treaty on European Union (TEU) with EMU was the main result of the meeting. Maastricht can be seen as a dividing line between the original 'Common Market' and a broader European Union covering also non-economic policy areas such as defence, justice and home affairs migration. The treaty brought moreover the enhancement of the EP's powers by a new co-decision procedure (allowing the EP in the absence of an agreement with the Council of Ministers to veto a legislative proposal); an increased capacity of the Council of Ministers to take decisions by QMV; and the empowering of the Court of Justice to impose fines on Member States which do not comply with its verdicts. Provisions were laid down for a Common Foreign and Security Policy. Finally,

as a response to the possibility of creating an over-powerful EU, the introduction of the important principle of subsidiarity (*Bull* 12-1991, 1.1.1-1.1.4).

Prior to the meeting Chancellor Helmut Kohl had threatened in vain to
make a decision on Political Union a condition *sine qua non* in return for
Germany agreeing to Economic and Monetary Union. Kohl wanted an 'irreversible' process which would lead towards Political Union. He had to accept
in the end an *'interim solution'* since the UK especially could not agree with a
'pre-determined' path to further integration. From now on for Kohl the
achievement of EMU was the central basis for development of a Political
Union later.

British Prime Minister John Major succeeded at Maastricht in the drop-
ping of what was in his eyes the abhorred term 'federalism' in the treaty.
The (vague) pursuit of an 'ever closer Union' dating from 1957 remained the
final goal. French President Mitterrand calculated at Maastricht that a single
currency with a European Central Bank would allow his country a greater
influence over monetary policy which was always monopolised by the
German Bundesbank.

The UK, Ireland and Denmark received an 'opt out' clause.[5] Opting out (or:
differentiated integration) has since Maastricht been an important new
element in the development of the Union. PM Major saw this to be acceptance
of his *'Europe à la Carte'* and welcomed it in Maastricht with a blissful 'game-
set-and-match!' (author's notes in Maastricht). Since the UK could not accept
the articles in the social field, the Council decided to move forward via a protocol annexed to the treaty. This was a legal first. Since Maastricht differentiated integration makes it possible for Member States to choose not to join the
Union's main activities, or at least not to be obliged to do so.

Here we see an example of how important personal relationships are for
negotiations in the European Council. The proposal to separate the chapter
on Social Policy from the treaty in view of the resistance of PM Major came
from Chancellor Kohl. He would never have done that for Major's prede-
cessor Margaret Thatcher who in Dublin in 1979 had shown herself
intractable in the European Council with her unrelenting and repetitive 'I
want my money back, and I want it now' (Thatcher, 1993, p. 82).

There are further reasons to see Maastricht as an historic moment. From the
very first moment of striving for European integration there has been a tug of
war between supranationalism and inter-governmentalism. The Treaty on
European Union, the 'Maastricht Treaty', has consolidated this tug of war
over the shape of integration. The large First Pillar with EMU, the Single
Market and the series of common policies remains based on the original
Treaty of Rome which is founded on supranationalism. The Commission,
Parliament and the Court of Justice play a full-fledged role in these areas. The
two other pillars of Maastricht, the CFSP (Pillar II) and JHA (Pillar III), have a
more intergovernmental structure. In the CFSP and JHA the balance of
powers between the Council of Ministers, the Parliament and the Commission
is strongly in favour of the former. The Commission does not have here the
exclusive right to submit initiatives and Parliament is only consulted.

At Maastricht night-time negotiations took place, following the tried and
tested method of trying to deliver under the enormous pressure of time and
public attention. The Maastricht success came about thanks to the fact that

the political leaders had jointly invested a number of years in this operation. Apart from a number of important details most aspects of the agreement had been considered and agreed before the meeting.

Maastricht was followed by great *disappointment*. Nearly two years passed after the 1991 Maastricht meeting before the Treaty on European Union came into force on 1 November 1993. The critics of Maastricht were of the opinion that the EC had already over-stretched its authority. At the 1992 Lisbon Meeting the European Council had to express its 'determination to press ahead with European construction' in order to lend impetus to the ratification process for the TEU.

Half a year later in Edinburgh the Heads of Government again expressed frustration over the delays in ratifying the TEU. Denmark (after a negative referendum in June 1992) and France finally scraped through with narrowly won referenda on the TEU. To achieve that result, the Heads of Government in Edinburgh first had to win over Denmark with some institutional concessions. As a result of these setbacks which had not been foreseen at Maastricht, the Heads of Government had at their 1992 Birmingham meeting to discuss ways of reducing the gap between the EC bureaucracy and the citizenry. For that reason the Conclusions were free of jargon for the first time in years.

The 'Birmingham Declaration – A Community close to its citizens' foresaw measures aimed at improving access to the Council's work (until then closed and secret). In other words Birmingham saw the emergence of some transparency as a political concept. Subsequently it was decided that after a vote in the Council of Ministers the report of the vote would be published (*Bull* 10-1992, I.8; *Bull* 12-1992, I.24.; Council Rules of Procedure of 22 March 2004, article 8). Later, the Treaty of Amsterdam stated that decisions had to be taken 'as closely as possible to the citizen' (Article 1 TEU). In June 2006 the European Council agreed that in principle all legislative deliberations under the co-decision procedure (decision-making together with the EP) would become open to the public. Meanwhile in Germany the Federal Constitutional Court (Bundesverfassungsgericht) had to deliver a verdict in 1993 in order to silence the critics. The Court concluded remarkably that the two Houses of Parliament in Germany must retain powers 'of substantial weight' in relation to European integration. The judges warned that an 'over-preponderance of tasks and responsibilities' at EU-level would 'weaken democracy at state level'. After this verdict, the European Council acknowledged in October 1993 that 'there are many to whom Europe seemed distant, anonymous and interfering'. The verdict is of major importance, since the German High Court hereby to some extent questions the primacy of European law over national law.

A.5. Turin 1996 – Amsterdam 1997: unfulfilled intentions (I)

At the 1996 Turin Council, the Heads of Government amid great fanfare launched the formal go-ahead for a new IGC. Before that, a Reflection Group of representatives from each of the Member States prepared a modest agenda and reported it to the 1995 Madrid European Council. The Heads of Government ordered a review of the Maastricht Treaty in order to prepare for enlargement. The negotiators had the task of completing their work 'in about one year'. The reason for this revision was the fact that in Maastricht various important issues had remained unsolved. The Heads of Government pointed *inter alia* to:

–   the composition of the Commission;
–   the questions of the extent of majority voting, the weighting of votes and the threshold for qualified majority decisions;
–   a widening of the scope of co-decision, 'in truly legislative matters';
–   the creation of a 'more perceptible face and voice' for the CFSP via a High Representative;
–   the question of the contribution of national parliaments to the Union's tasks;
–   the introduction of 'flexibility' in order to enable a certain number of Member States to develop a strengthened cooperation;
–   the most effective means of simplifying legislative procedures.

We mention this series of tasks, largely leftovers from the insoluble questions in Maastricht 1991, because some of them would not be settled until the final negotiations for the Lisbon Treaty in 2007. The promises made by the Heads of Government in Turin took nearly a decade to materialise. Some important subjects, such as an important extension of majority voting in the Council are still under discussion now, more than fifteen years later.

Box 17

Member States divided into three groups

In terms of size the EU Member States can be divided into three groups. Six Member States have a population of over 40 million. Together they represent three-quarters of the population of the EU. The population of ten Member States ranges from eight to 22 million. Their share of the EU population amounts to one-fifth. Eleven Member States have less than five million each and together they represent seven per cent of the population. In this study we use the term *'larger Member States'* for the first category and *'smaller Member States'* for the rest.

The 1997 Noordwijk informal meeting (*Bull* 5-1997, I.1-I.2.) saw the arrival of Tony Blair as British Prime Minister in succession to John Major. Blair was very much centre stage in the discussions. The meeting had to be changed from Maastricht to Noordwijk at the request of President Chirac. The French President preferred not to come to Maastricht, because the treaty named after it had given Maastricht a bad name among the French. In Noordwijk a consensus emerged to postpone the planned limit on the size of the Commission to a maximum of twenty members. After the accession of Central and East European countries the five larger Member States would have to cede one of their two Commissioners. In Noordwijk it also became clear that smaller

Member States had little taste for a re-weighting of the votes in the Council of Ministers. Such a redistribution of the votes would have to favour the larger Member States. The smaller Member States were moreover absolutely not in favour of a much slimmer Commission with twelve to fifteen members instead of twenty, because then they would have to rotate. From then on, the smaller Member States began to distrust the 'Big Powers' more and more, particularly on those points in institutional matters.

Under pressure from the UK, the other Member States accepted in Noordwijk that Justice and Home Affairs would remain primarily a matter for intergovernmental cooperation. In return Blair seemed ready to accept that the European Court of Justice, the Commission and the European Parliament would start to play a very limited role in these areas.

The negotiations in the framework of the IGC resulted in June 1997 in the Treaty of Amsterdam. The two main aims of the negotiations were to bring the Union up to date by way of a modest revision of the Treaty of Maastricht and to prepare it for enlargement. The Amsterdam meeting (Langrish) appears to have achieved only the first of these aims. The two major aims of treaty reform, re-weighting of the votes and the future number of Commissioners, were postponed via a protocol. The meeting agreed in principle that the Commission should only consist of twenty members. *Flexibility*, also sometimes called 'enhanced cooperation' or *'coopération renforcée'*, was the most innovative institutional change at Amsterdam. A majority of the Member States (in Amsterdam eight Member States) may proceed with closer cooperation amongst themselves in certain areas. Flexibility was however not (yet) authorised in the Second Pillar (the CFSP).[6] Flexibility aims to avoid moving forward at the speed of the slowest partner (mostly the UK) in the European Union. After Amsterdam flexibility was heralded as an important innovation. But this new initiative has as yet not been used and there are no proposals to do so either.

For the first time the French interpretation of the so-called *Luxembourg Compromise* of 1966 (no qualified majority voting in the Council of Ministers 'whenever very important interests of one or more of them are at stake') was at Amsterdam recognised in certain parts of the treaty. Amsterdam strengthened the position of the European Parliament by an extension of the cases open for co-decision. Regarding environmental protection the important guiding principle was laid down that 'environmental protection requirements must be integrated into the definition and implementation of Community policies (...) in particular with a view to promoting sustainable development'. Article 100a, moreover, was amended in order to strengthen the possibility for a Member State to introduce national provisions based on new scientific evidence. Much publicised was the participation of the UK in the provisions formerly set out in the Agreement on Social Policy. The Community was given a new task in Article 3 EC of promoting coordination between the *employment policies* of the Member States with a view to enhancing their effectiveness by developing a coordinated strategy for employment. It was agreed that the European Council shall each year consider the employment situation and decide upon guidelines on employment policy. Some Member States took a critical stance on this. Therefore a formula was chosen excluding the transfer of financial resources.

Noteworthy at Amsterdam were the provisions on the Schengen Agreement, visas, asylum, immigration, refugees and other policies relating to free movement of people which were brought within the Community legal order. These decisions, comprising over one hundred new or amended treaty provisions, six protocols and twenty declarations, meant a clear strengthening of the JHA policies, since the ways in which and the means by which they should be developed further were set out in some detail. It is notable that the Court of Justice became competent for the Schengen acquis (the rights and obligations) in accordance with the rules relevant to Titles IV and VI. It was decided that within a period of five years after the entry into force of the treaty, measures should be adopted that would result in the progressive establishment of 'an area of freedom, security and justice' (Article 61) in which there would be free movement of persons within a common external border.

Regarding the CFSP, the most prominent development was the creation, initially under pressure from France, of the office of High Representative for the Common Foreign and Security Policy (CFSP). This was to be the Secretary-General of the Council of Ministers wearing another hat and would head a new Policy Planning Unit for the development of the CFSP. Furthermore, since Amsterdam, the Heads of State and Government acting as a Council of Ministers may determine that a Member State has committed a serious and persistent breach of the principles of liberty, democracy, respect for human rights and fundamental freedoms or the rule of law.

The results of the IGC of 1997 have generally been seen as disappointing. 'The changes most needed to prepare for enlargement were not achieved: Commission and Council reform was deferred to a later date' (Langrish p. 18). The Heads of Government at Amsterdam did not fulfil their promises made a year earlier in Florence. At the 1991 Maastricht meeting it was decided to hold the 1996 IGC because various important institutional matters had remained unresolved to the dissatisfaction of all parties. 'In 1996 we'll carry on', they said. But in 1991 the Heads of Government could not foresee *four important developments* of the 1990s, namely that:

–   the Treaty of Maastricht would not come into force until November 1993. Therefore 1996 was still too early for an evaluation;
–   the ratification of Maastricht would become a highly contentious operation in many Member States. In various Member States public opinion reacted with hesitation and even disapproval. That made further reforms an illusion;
–   from 1997 most members of the European Council would give priority to the overwhelming task of achieving EMU in 1999;
–   the 1990s saw no real urgency for institutional reform. Enlargement at that time was still too far away.

The numerous critics of Amsterdam, and especially the European Parliament, at the time overlooked the above developments. In Germany a very critical attitude towards European integration manifested itself in the Länder (regional States). 'More power for EU is not on the 1996 agenda', stated German FM Klaus Kinkel as early as two years before the meeting in Amsterdam (*The Times*, 7 July 1995). As a result of the above issues, the

Heads of Government could not fulfil their intentions at Amsterdam. What the critics, including the European Parliament, also ignored was that immediately following the start of the IGC at an informal meeting in October 1996 in Dublin, the Heads of Government had already diluted their former ambitions from Florence (*FT*, 6 October 1996, *FAZ* and *Le Figaro* 7 October 1995). That happened under French pressure with the support of Germany. It was also seen as a concession to the United Kingdom. As with Germany, France had other priorities in 1997. In France there was the defeat of Alain Juppé's right-wing government by the Socialists, which resulted in a weakened President Jacques Chirac. In Paris the Socialist leader and new Prime Minister Lionel Jospin questioned the EMU Stability Pact. Jospin threatened in Amsterdam to block approval of the Pact with its strict budgetary discipline. The meeting compromised by leaving the Pact intact while offering France language on economic growth and employment via two resolutions plus an extraordinary European Council on employment later that year (*Bull* 6-1997, I.6). In short, it was not illogical that, already in 1996 at the October Dublin meeting, Chancellor Kohl had speculated that the envisaged institutional reform package would not be accepted in 1997 but would take some years. Kohl calculated in Amsterdam (rightly) that the *achievement of EMU* rather than institutional reform was now the direction for the development of the EU. The German Chancellor was the one who at Amsterdam during the end phase at 2.00 a.m. proposed the postponement of reform towards a Political Union which he himself had urged earlier. Chirac and Blair immediately supported him. Then the meeting fizzled out after eighteen hours of negotiations.

At Amsterdam the single biggest success was something important that had nothing to do with institutional reform: the search for an agreement between France and Germany regarding the relationship between EMU and job creation. In other words, Amsterdam avoided a reopening of the discussion about the still contentious TEU.

A.6.   Berlin 1999 – Nice 2000: unfulfilled intentions (II)

At the start of the 1999 Berlin meeting, the Heads of Government moved swiftly to fill the power vacuum at the top of the Commission by nominating Romano Prodi. The former Italian PM would succeed Jacques Santer, who had resigned with the whole Commission a few days earlier following a devastating and demoralising independent report on nepotism, fraud and mismanagement. 'The Commission has an established culture that is secretive and authoritarian', stated Pauline Green, the British leader of the Socialist Group in the European Parliament. The nomination of Prodi came, especially for the leaders of the smaller Member States, unexpectedly soon. Massimo D'Alema, the Italian Prime Minister, hinted in Berlin that the leaders of the 'Big Three', Schröder, Blair and Chirac had prepared the decision to call Prodi to Brussels. The Parliament and the Commission at that moment had become embroiled in a hopeless clash. Perhaps the European Council wanted to show with a rapid reaction that it was more capable of handling the management of the Union.

In Cologne in 1999, two years after the failed IGC meeting in Amsterdam, the Heads of Government decided to call a new IGC early in 2000. It should

resolve 'the institutional issues left open in Amsterdam that need to be settled before enlargement'. Once again it would concern the three well-estab-
lished topics: size and composition of the Commission; a re-weighting of
votes of the Member States in the Council with the introduction of a dual
majority; and the possible extension of majority-voting in the Council. At
the 2000 Feira meeting the agenda of the IGC was broadened to other issues.

The subsequent meeting in Biarritz led to a new development in the shape
of an open fierce quarrel about institutional reforms between the larger and
the smaller Member States. Differences over the way the Institutions of the
Union ought to function would fester from then on. At the Barcelona meeting (2002) seven smaller Member States announced they would hold a separate Summit meeting in order to defend their interests in the context of
reform of the Institutions. The announcement was made by PM Juncker, on
behalf of the Benelux, Austria, Finland, Ireland and Portugal. The disagreements between the larger and the smaller Member States would continue
until the mid-June 2004 meeting with the agreement in the IGC on the
Constitutional Treaty. It was at Biarritz that the president of the meeting,
Jacques Chirac, opened the discussion with what was seen as a *'frontal attack'*.
Chirac stated that in a Union with 27 or more Member States the smaller
Member States would have to accept a European Commission in which they
on the basis of rotation would not be permanently represented. Furthermore
the weighting of the votes in the Council of the Union would have to change
in favour of the five 'big powers'. French Prime Minister Lionel Jospin
reminded the Heads of Government of the smaller States that they had
gained a much greater voice in world affairs thanks to the EU. 'Where would
you be without the Union?' he was reported as asking. The Prime Ministers
of Portugal, Finland, Sweden, Belgium and Luxembourg especially rejected
these ideas. 'There is a clear dividing line between the five big states and the
10 others', Danish Prime Minister Poul Nyrup Rasmussen said afterwards to
the media. The leaders of the smaller countries generally vented their frustration at Biarritz about the arrogant way France and particularly the
President himself conducted the IGC negotiations. 'EU reform deadlocked
after small states revolt' (*The Independent*, UK) was indeed a good headline
after this meeting. Seven weeks before the Nice Summit, where the IGC
would be concluded, the outcome did not look good.

In December 2000, during an exceptionally long session, the IGC reached
an agreement on the Treaty of Nice (results in *Bull* 12-2000, I.1 – 1.2.2.). The
meeting, presided over by President Jacques Chirac, first had to go through
the usual agenda of the European Council. For that reason the meeting
lasted four full days and a full night, in diplomatic parlance a 'five-shirt
Summit'. The 'leftovers' from Maastricht and Amsterdam were to a large
extent settled. This encompassed the future size and composition of the
Commission, the weighting of votes among the Member States in the
Council of Ministers, and a further extension of a replacement of unanimity
by qualified majority in decision-making procedures. Therefore there was
success in the basic goal of Nice, the removal of the institutional obstacles to
enlargement. The agreed treaty restricted itself to setting out the principles
and methods for changing the institutional system as the Union grew. The
number of seats in the European Parliament for the new Member States; the

number of votes allocated to them within the Council, and particularly the qualified majority threshold applicable in the future, were legally determined in the accession treaties. Since 1 November 2004, the Commission has comprised one national per Member State. The five larger Member States thus lost in 2004 their second Commission member. Other parts of the agreement in Nice were a new procedure for nominating the Commission, with increased powers for its President and an extension of the qualified majority vote in some areas where unanimity was previously required.

An important problem, which kept the Heads of Government occupied at Nice during the night, was the *re-weighting of the votes*. The distribution of votes in the Council of Ministers reflects the power balance between the Member States. Therefore it is a very sensitive matter. Since unification, Germany's population has increased to over one-third more than the three other big Member States, namely France, the UK and Italy. Until then the four big Member States each had uniformly ten votes. At Nice Chancellor Schröder wanted to introduce a 'decoupling' of the votes of Germany and the other big Member States. With the exception of France the other Member States wanted to honour this justified demand. France, in the persons of President Chirac and PM Jospin, was flatly against this, however. France could not accept the idea that Germany, with extra voting rights in the Union, could become more than *primus inter pares*. According to PM Jean-Claude Juncker, President Chirac was heard using unprecedented language. 'This century we have beaten Germany twice already. Moreover we have nuclear arms', Chirac threatened (interview by Frans Boogaard in Dutch daily newspaper *Algemeen Dagblad* of 18 December 2000).

The outcome was a complicated triple threshold for qualified majority voting in the Council of Ministers. The first requirement for decision-making is a threshold of votes of around 74 percent. Secondly, a majority of the Member States must agree; and finally, if requested, verification is allowed that this majority represents at least 62 percent of the total population of the Union. Under this last provision Germany could, with the help of two other big Member States, block all decisions taken on the basis of QMV. However, the population size of a combination of the three other large Member States (the UK, France and Italy) would in such a case not stop decision-making (Jacqué, 2005, p. 155). Since Nice the Commission has been forced to seek approval of its proposals in Berlin, London, Paris or Rome before launching them. 'Without highlighting it, *Germany's weight* has grown', Chancellor Schröder stated rightly (author's notes in Nice).

The Netherlands, with roughly 50 percent more inhabitants than neighbour Belgium, followed up by demanding more voting weight. It received an extra vote. During the course of the night the atmosphere soured. Displeasure grew among the Heads of Government of some smaller States, particularly Belgium and Portugal, in the face of unacceptable proposals by the Presidency. Finally the re-weighting was agreed. Belgium in particular was very dissatisfied with the decoupling of the Netherlands. (For more about Nice, see Clarisse and Quatremer, 141-160; AE, 11 December 2000, p. 4-5.).

Due to its weak leadership the French Presidency was unable to reconcile the strongly-held opposing positions. The meeting ended in a bad atmosphere. To soothe wounded Belgian feelings, the French President proposed that in future all European Council meetings should take place in Brussels instead of in the other Member States. The chaotic level to which a European Council sometimes descends was shown by the fact that not all Heads of Government were informed of the proposal when they left the meeting (AE, 27 January 2001, p. 3). For instance Swedish PM Göran Persson said he read the decision in his newspaper on the day after the meeting. Tough words were overheard as tired Heads of Government departed. Unprecedented outbursts of bad temper were reported to the press as having characterised parts of the meeting. After the meeting a storm of protest blew up in the media against the haggling in Nice and the arrogance of the French Presidency (which had, for instance, disregarded the Commission during the IGC negotiations, since its support was not required). Tensions had risen so much between France and Germany and also between the Netherlands and Belgium that special meetings had to be organised to soothe the wounds. To make matters worse, in the aftermath of the meeting sheer confusion came to light about what actually had been agreed. It concerned the voting rights of the Member States, a keystone of the agreement.

Box 18

Council of Ministers voting weightings since 2003

Germany, United Kingdom, France, Italy . . . . .29 votes
Spain, Poland . . . . .27 votes
Romania . . . . .14 votes
Netherlands . . . . .13 votes
Greece, Czech Republic, Belgium, Hungary, Portugal . . . . .12 votes
Sweden, Bulgaria, Austria . . . . .10 votes
Slovakia, Denmark, Finland, Ireland, Lithuania . . . . .7 votes
Latvia, Slovenia, Estonia, Cyprus, Luxembourg . . . . .4 votes
Malta . . . . .3 votes

Council acts shall require for adoption at least 255 votes cast by a majority of Member States. In case a decision is adopted by such a majority, a Member State may request verification that the Member States constituting the majority represent at least 62% of the total population of the Union. If that condition is shown not to have been met, the decision in question shall not be adopted.

After Nice it was concluded that the meetings of the Heads of Government would no longer be the appropriate forum to carry out the functions of an IGC. One of the main aims of the IGC, the improvement of the decision-making ability of the EU, had once again not been achieved. Hans-Gert Pöttering, the German President of the European People's Party-European Democrats (EPP-ED), the largest political group in the EP, considered the results for qualified majority voting and co-decision to be insufficient. His colleague, Enrique Barón, of the second largest group, the Socialists, also denounced the slippage of the IGC method. In the EP debate about the results in Strasbourg on 12 December the other political groups also vented their dissatisfaction and Parliament finally did not endorse the Nice Treaty.[7] Parliament was nearly unanimous in its view that the method of reforming the treaties by way of an IGC had reached its limits. Even Chirac in his role of President of the conference recognised that a better way had to be found.

A.7.   Laeken 2001 – Brussels 2004: a Constitutional Treaty

One year later in Laeken, a suburb of Brussels, during a meeting in the royal palace, the Council adopted the 'Laeken Declaration for the Future of the European Union' (*Bull* 12-2001, I.3.3 and I.27. More background information at Ludlow, 2002, 48-54). It begins with a claim that Europe is at a crossroads: The Union faces challenges within and beyond its borders. Within, the Union is perceived by some as 'a threat to their identity'. Beyond its borders the Union is confronted with a fast-changing, globalised world. 'What is Europe's role in this changed world?'

The document states that citizens in the EU now want 'more results, better responses to practical issues and not a European superstate or European institutions inveigling their way into every nook and cranny of life'. The declaration then raised more than fifty questions, as to what is Europe's role in this changed world? In summary, the declaration states that 'the first question is how we can increase the democratic legitimacy and transparency of the present Institutions'. The second question refers to the necessity of giving the national parliaments a role alongside the Council and the European Parliament. The third question concerns how to improve the efficiency of decision-making and the workings of the institutions in a Union of some thirty Member States. The fourth question relates to a possible reorganisation of the treaties: whether a simplification and reorganisation 'might not lead in the long run to the adoption of a constitutional text in the Union'. If so, 'what might the basic features of such a constitution be?'

By raising all these questions the declaration opened the way to yet another institutional reform. At the time the idea of the Heads of Government to convene a Convention on the Future of Europe was widely seen as a good one. Despite resistance from left-wing parties and from the (countless) other politicians who regarded the 75 year old former French President as 'a man of the past', the aristocratic intellectual Valéry Giscard d'Estaing was appointed as President of the Convention. This happened under the forceful persuasion of President Chirac, backed up by Chancellor Schröder. Giscard met with opposition but Chirac prevailed, thanks in part to the ambivalence about his own candidacy of Wim Kok, the highly regarded Dutch PM and 'doyen' of the Council. The former Prime Ministers of Italy, Giuliano Amato, and Belgium, Jean-Luc Dehaene, were added as Deputy-Presidents in order to silence the critics (details at Clarissen and Quatremer, p. 347-351).

It was 'the task of the Convention to consider the key issues arising from the Union's future development and to try to identify the various possible responses'. The final document would 'provide a starting point for discussions in the Intergovernmental Conference, which will take the ultimate decisions'. The French President self-consciously compared the Convention with the famous Philadelphia Convention that drafted the US Constitution. The Convention consisted of more than one hundred members. It was composed of 15 representatives of the Heads of Government, 30 members of national parliaments, 16 members of the EP and two Commission representatives. The 13 candidate countries moreover became 'fully involved' and were represented in the same way as the Member States. The candidates could take part in the proceedings 'without, however, being able to prevent any consensus which may emerge' (*Bull* 12-2001 Presidency Conclusions)'.

Finally it is worth mentioning that the meeting at Laeken ended prematurely following a fierce quarrel between various Heads of Government, which PM Guy Verhofstadt quickly silenced. At stake was the sharing out of a dozen new EU agencies, such as the European Food Safety Authority, the EU Maritime Security Agency, Eurojust or the EU prosecutors' office, the European Aviation Safety Agency, etc. Italian PM Silvio Berlusconi lost his temper in a squabble over the location of the European Food Safety Authority. This shows how the Heads of Government fiercely stand up for their national interest, even when it concerns secondary matters. But it was a sour end to the meeting.

At the 2003 Summer meeting in Thessaloniki, Convention President Giscard d'Estaing presented a draft Constitutional Treaty (OJ C 169, 18 July 2003; more details in Chapters 4 and 5). The meeting rated the text as 'a good basis for starting in the Intergovernmental Conference'. It fixed the calendar for finalising the reform of the treaties. The Council took upon itself in its role as IGC the task of agreeing on a Constitutional Treaty 'before the June 2004 elections for the European Parliament'.

Chancellor Schröder said that Germany was 'completely satisfied' with the draft. PM Blair, however, soon could be seen to question various aspects of the draft; certain important issues were not for discussion in his view. Heads of Government of smaller Member States demanded clarification of the role of the future long-term President of the European Council which, according to them, had the disadvantage of weakening the Commission. Poland plus nineteen small and medium-sized Member States demanded a substantial renegotiation of the draft in Rome on 4 October 2003 at the start of the IGC. Poland argued for retaining the system of weighted votes in the Council of Ministers as agreed in Nice in 2000. The nineteen and Poland insisted on a permanent Commissioner.

The December meeting in Brussels 2003 on the Constitutional Treaty ended according to its President PM Berlusconi 'in total disagreement' (see also Chapter 4.B.1). This collapse was attributable to a lack of political will by EU leaders and an Italian Presidency without the diplomatic skills to get a deal. The split over how votes (power) should be shared between the Member States ran so deep that Berlusconi needed nothing short of a miracle to reach an agreement. The greatest obstacle was the refusal of the Polish and Spanish political leaders to accept the introduction of a simple 50/60 double majority voting system in the Council of Ministers under which laws would be adopted and the refusal of the French and German leaders to seriously negotiate on this.

Under the envisaged system each Member State has one vote in decision-making in the Council of Ministers. Decisions taken by a qualified majority require a majority of Member States which, moreover, must represent 60 percent of the population of the EU. Berlusconi recognised that Poland and Spain were absolutely unprepared to make a deal. The French President for his part refused to cooperate with a watering down of the Constitutional Treaty by giving in to the Spanish and Polish demands to maintain the voting weight accorded these countries in 2000 at Nice. Rather than see the Convention text eroded further, Chirac wisely chose to wait for passions to cool. Moreover, a new timetable would have the possible advantage of dealing with a new Spanish leadership after national elections, perhaps enabling France and Germany to stick to the promised new 'double majority' system of decision-making. Berlusconi took his decision after a meeting with Chirac, Schröder and Blair. They agreed to call it a day. There was no criticism of the Italian PM for this decision from within the meeting but for the outside political world and the media it came unexpectedly. It was the first time in nearly thirty years of the European Council's existence that an IGC meeting finished before even bringing everyone round the table in plenary session. The course of the meeting confirmed that when the stakes are high, the Heads of Government of the larger Member call the shots.

The quick conclusion of the meeting by Berlusconi had the important advantage of avoiding a fight or a quarrel. Moreover, a repeat of Nice, an extremely limited reform of the treaties, was avoided. Exactly as in 2002 with enlargement and the decisions on the CAP (See 3.C.3), Franco-German cooperation determined the course of the meeting.[8]

On 18 June 2004 in Brussels the Heads of Government finally agreed on the Constitutional Treaty (*Bull* 6-2004, I). Curiously the wording of the agreement regarding the biggest point of contention, namely the distribution of voting power between the Member States in decision-making in the Council of Ministers, was almost similar to one of the proposals of PM Berlusconi in Brussels half a year earlier. In the June 2004 meeting Spain and Poland were both represented by a new Head of Government. They accepted that decisions should be taken when backed by a double majority of 55 percent of Member States representing 65 percent of the population of the Union. A 'yes' vote would require at least fifteen Member States and a minimum of four Member States would be required to block a decision, meaning that the three biggest Member States (the Big Three) were unable to do so alone. Spain and Poland accepted that this double majority system slightly weakened their power to block decision-making in the Council.[9]

The agreed 300-page Constitutional Treaty would replace the other treaties adopted over the course of 50 years. In addition to a streamlining of its basic rules and giving the European Union a legal personality, it would give the Union some new powers including fighting crime and terrorism. The treaty introduced a President of the European Council (see Chapter 4), a European Union Minister for Foreign Affairs, qualified majority decision making in some new areas (for instance regional development, asylum and immigration) and co-decision by the EP in areas like the CAP and regional development. National vetoes were retained over all the more sensitive political activities (such as defence, foreign policy, taxation, the EU budget, social security). Important parts of the draft Constitutional Treaty of the Convention had been watered down at the insistence of the British. Of the 80 sets of amendments, the

UK advocated 39. Therefore PM Blair had every reason to be satisfied upon his return to London.

A.8.   Berlin – Brussels and Lisbon 2007: a Reform Treaty

An important question, which arose immediately after this successful meeting, was whether all government leaders would succeed in getting the treaty ratified by their national parliaments, especially in those countries which were to hold referendums. In the event the treaty was rejected in referendums in quick succession in France (29 May 2005) and the Netherlands (1 June). It was clear that this major setback had also made ratification less likely in several other states, including the UK and Poland, where there was considerable opposition to the treaty. Following this the European Council decided in June 2005 on a *period of reflection* 'to enable a broad debate to take place in each of our countries' (document COM (2005) 0494). In 2006 it was decided to extend this period in order to take 'the necessary steps' to examine how to salvage elements of the Constitutional Treaty 'during the second semester of 2008' (*Bull* 6-2006, I, Brussels European Council). In the end only 17 out of the 27 Member States ratified the Constitutional Treaty. They were Austria, Belgium, Bulgaria, Cyprus, Estonia, Finland, Greece, Hungary, Italy, Latvia, Lithuania, Luxembourg, Malta, Romania, Slovakia, Slovenia and Spain. At the start of 2007, when it took on the six-month Presidency, Germany was still involved in the process of ratification. As President of the European Council, Chancellor Angela Merkel, in a meeting in Berlin on 25 March 2007 on the occasion of the 50th anniversary of the Rome Treaties, proposed a very tight timetable for securing a deal with a 'short and concentrated' IGC to agree a new treaty by the end of 2007. The German President would produce a 'roadmap' for settling the institutional problems at the subsequent June European Council.

The meeting in Brussels began on Thursday 21 June with Merkel ringing a bell. The busily chatting Heads of Government and the President of the Commission sat down like obedient school kids. During a marathon meeting lasting 36 hours the German Chancellor successfully used all options available to rope in all 27 Member States. The meeting was a kind of déjà vu for those who had lived through comparable long nights in Maastricht (1991), Amsterdam (1997), Berlin (1999) and Nice (2000). At dawn on 23 June at 5 a.m. a proud Chancellor presented the media with what was soon dubbed '*A Midsummer Night's Treaty*'. Merkel stated that 'negotiations had taken a lot of time but we have obtained what we wanted: a very detailed and precise mandate'. Although Merkel modestly refrained from drawing attention to it, this detailed mandate went much further than the vague roadmap, which some months earlier appeared to be the maximum obtainable. The Heads of Government had agreed to adopt a new 'Reform Treaty' for the European Union to replace the defunct Constitutional Treaty. This result was in line with ideas earlier proposed by French President Nicolas Sarkozy and approved by Chancellor Merkel and Prime Ministers Zapatero of Spain and Tony Blair (see article by Giscard d'Estaing in *Le Monde*, 15 June 2006, p. 23). According to legal experts the Constitutional Treaty had been of a 'genuinely constitutional nature' (Lenaerts and Van Nuffel, p. 74). Its provocative label 'Constitutional Treaty', 'the last rhetorical flourish of the idea of Europe as a

Federation' (Stephen Wall, PM Blair's advisor), was now abandoned. The new Reform Treaty would, nonetheless, according to the German Presidency 'preserve the substance of the Constitutional Treaty'. The IGC had to reach agreement on the Reform Treaty if possible in October or at the latest in December 2007. A fundamental difference with all previous IGCs was that the Heads of Government had meticulously laid down in their mandate the details of the changes in the existing TEU and TEC Treaties.

An important hindrance to an agreement was Polish resistance to the 'double majority' system of the Constitutional Treaty. Based on that formula a decision in the Council of Ministers would be taken when agreement was reached by 55 per cent of the Member States, representing a minimum of 65 per cent of the EU's population. Under the Treaty of Nice, Poland with a 40 million population has 27 votes and Germany with more than double the population only 29. The Poles wanted to fix voting rights according to the square root of the Member States' populations. In the new formula Germany would lose voting weight compared with Nice. The Polish President and the Prime Minister, the twin brothers Lech and Jaroslaw Kaczynski, said their plan 'is worth dying for'. In the end, however, they had to give up their fight.

In order to force Poland into a retreat Merkel announced during the meeting that the 26 other Member States would if necessary convene an IGC without Warsaw's assent. With the support of the Presidency, the three other most influential members of the meeting (newcomer President Sarkozy, outgoing PM Blair and old hand Juncker) began immediate negotiations with Lech Kaczynski in Brussels and, by telephone, with his brother Jaroslaw in Warsaw. Those three had also acted as brokers for the Presidency during the preparations of this crucial meeting (although this is unusual). The compromise proposed by Juncker, which was finally retained in the mandate for the IGC, accommodates the Poles. The introduction of the double majority system of the Constitutional Treaty, which reduces Poland's voting weight for decision-making and increases Germany's, will be slowed down. As a result Poland will benefit from the favourable provisions of the Treaty of Nice until 31 October 2014. The subsequent transition period will last until 31 March 2017. During that period each Member State may draw on the 'Ioannina Compromise'. This formula allows a small group of Member States that is narrowly outvoted by a qualified majority to demand re-examination of the text with a reasonable deadline. The formula was drawn up on the insistence of the UK and Spain during a Council meeting in Ioannina, Greece, in 1994.

Other Heads of Government and especially those of the countries that earlier had rejected the Constitutional Treaty or seemed likely to do so (France, the Netherlands, the UK, the Czech Republic) also gained important concessions.

The new Reform Treaty (the Lisbon Treaty) will, if ratified, amend the existing treaties, namely the TEU and the TEC. The latter will be renamed 'Treaty on the Functioning of the European Union' (TFEU). The term (European) 'Community' would in the treaties be replaced by 'Union'. There will be no 'Minister for Foreign Affairs', as intended in the Constitutional Treaty. The current High Representative of the Union for the CFSP will remain but will have the same authority as the intended minister. Nor will there be a referral to 'European laws', but maintenance of the terminology 'Regulation, Directive and Decision'. Except for the euro all nomenclature or symbols laid down in Article I-8 of the Constitutional Treaty will be scrapped in as far as they give the impression of the EU as a (super-) State: the blue European flag, the European anthem, the motto 'United in diversity', the celebration on May 9 throughout the Union of Europe Day and, moreover, the Article on the primacy of European law over national laws. Important was the decision taken, at the express request of PM Tony Blair, to make the Charter of Fundamental Rights in the Constitutional Treaty subject to opt out and opt in by Member States wishing to do so. London also won the right not to join police and judicial cooperation. The numerous novel key features in the rest of the Constitutional Treaty will be preserved including the nomination of a long-term full-time President of the European Council with increased powers.

During the final stages Belgian PM Guy Verhofstadt prolonged the meeting into the night (as he did also in the final stage in Nice in 2000 and in Laeken in 2001). He failed, however (again). Verhofstadt could not muster enough support from the leaders of the more integrationist Member States (here Italy, Luxembourg, Hungary, Slovenia, Greece and Spain) to block the concessions made to their more minimalist brothers.

As President of the European Council, Angela Merkel had stretched the options for compromise to the limits. Merkel was applauded from all quarters. 'We were not far from rupture. But France did not give up. Leaving a Member State from the East out, less than twenty years after the fall of the Berlin Wall and envisaging going forward with 26 instead of 27 countries would have provoked a crisis', President Sarkozy told the media after the meeting. 'Mrs Merkel and Mr Sarkozy represent a new generation of leaders of the big European powers. The scratchiness, frigidity and occasional pomposity of their predecessors, Gerhard Schröder, Jacques Chirac and Tony Blair, who between them have dominated European debate for around a decade, are a thing of the past', wrote *The Economist* (30 June 2007).

Far-sighted had been Merkel's decision as early as December 2006 to ask all Heads of Government to appoint two 'sherpas ' for confidential consultations in order to break the deadlock (AE, 16 December 2006, p. 6). The June 2007 meeting had been minutely prepared for half a year. Chancellor Merkel also paid attention to the former communist new Member States and the other smaller Member States. A small example demonstrates the importance of such methodical preparation. Merkel received each of the key players one by one with all due ceremony at the Barokschloss Meseberg, north of Berlin. Among them was the President of the Czech Republic, Václav Havel. He was one of the most vociferous critics of the Constitutional Treaty. But after the consultation in Meseberg, Havel no longer wanted to be a spoilsport. He sent his PM Mirek Topolánek to the Summit. Another clever move by Merkel was to start the Summit with an outstanding dinner party.[10] Each Head of Government there was offered the opportunity to highlight their own national hobbyhorses once more. Such an approach fits in with the media-focused nature of the European Council. Each of the political leaders gave a press conference for their national media. This way their priorities became front-page news at home, telling everyone that the national political leader was standing on the barricades in Brussels.

During their informal annex IGC conference meeting, held in mid-October 2007 in summery Lisbon, EU leaders breathed a collective sigh of

---

Box 19

'Unprecedented' references to Nazi massacres

Poland's PM Jaroslaw Kaczynski made during the June 2007 meeting what were called 'unprecedented references' to Nazi Germany's 'unimaginable' massacres. 'We are only demanding one thing: that we get back what was taken from us. If Poland had not had to live through the years of 1939-1945, it would today be looking at the demographics of a large EU country of 66 million people. It is due to the slaughter of 6.5 million Polish, nearly a quarter of our population, that we now have to compromise on our voting rights in the European Union' said the Polish PM. Although he employed a tactic regularly used by Israel for 60 years without any protest, the Polish references received general disapproval in the political world and in the media. Might a lack of historical knowledge of Poland's plight during World War II be at the base of the disapproval? Frank-Walter Steinmeier, the German FA Minister, said the move had been an unjustified example of 'historical prejudices'. The influential Berlin *Bild* tabloid spoke of the 'poisonous Polish dwarfs'. However the accusations of PM Kaczynski were not 'unprecedented', as the media thought. At the meeting in 1984 in Dublin there was a clash between Chancellor Helmut Kohl and Greek PM Andreas Papandreou. The latter blocked any agreement until Greece received 1500 million ECU in aid. The Member States offered a meagre 90 million. Kohl blamed Papandreou for the failure of the meeting. But the Greek PM disputed the Chancellor's right to speak as he did about Greece, given the massacre of thousands of Greeks during World War II.

---

relief (and drank champagne!) when during the small hours they agreed on the 'Treaty of Lisbon'. This Reform Treaty replaces the defunct Constitutional Treaty. It has to be ratified by all the Member States in the course of 2008 before it can enter into force in 2009. The treaty replaces the Treaty of Nice, in force since 1 February 2003. Should ratification fail once again, the Treaty of Nice will remain in force.

The new treaty is generally seen as the best possible institutional deal that could have been reached in the present circumstances. All in all around 90 percent of the Constitutional Treaty has been saved. The provisions regarding the upgrading and the future tasks of the European Council (see Annex 6 to this book) are reproduced in the new treaty. Certainly worth mentioning is the fact that it is thanks to the Convention (representatives of the national parliaments, the EP, the Commission, the national Governments) that the new treaty contains so many reforms. The Heads of Government would never have achieved so much through their traditional Intergovernmental Conference. Remarkable (and very wise) is the fact that the treaty does *not* include any '*rendez-vous clause*' for a future reviewing of its provisions, unlike the previous treaties. The Lisbon Treaty concludes an era of thirty years of uninterrupted treaty reform which began in 1978 (Wise Men Report), followed by the Single Act, the Treaties of Maastricht, Amsterdam and Nice, and the Constitutional Treaty signed in 2004.

B.   ECONOMIC AND MONETARY UNION (EMU)

B.1.   The beginning of the disappearance of the Deutschmark

The European Council decided in Maastricht in 1991 on the establishment by 1 January 1999 of a single currency which would be administered by a single, completely independent European Central Bank (ECB). The idea of linking the Single Market (internal market) to a single European currency was largely an invention by France. In those days there was talk of a 'historic compromise'. The creation of EMU meant Germany abandoning the D-Mark although an opinion poll showed that 75 per cent of Germans found that unimaginable.[11] Economic and Monetary Union had since the Summit meeting at The Hague in 1969 been an important project of the Heads of State and Government, especially of France and Germany. In 1989 in Madrid, after a bilateral agreement between Kohl and Mitterrand, the European Council had agreed to set the stage for Economic and Monetary Union.[12]

'Many people would claim that we live in a DM zone, which is not a good thing', according to President Mitterrand (Müller-Brandeck-Bocquet, p. 354). France and the other Member States accepted a reunited Germany as henceforth the economically and politically most powerful EU Member State, in exchange for the disappearance of the Deutschmark as the most important currency in Europe. German approval of EMU was apparently the price to be paid for the acceptance by the other governments, in particular France, of German unity. Following this line of thought the creation of a European Central Bank (ECB) was a very important achievement.

France and Germany reached a political compromise prior to Maastricht, that the ECB would function on the basis of strict price stability and operate generally along the lines of the Bundesbank. This was demanded by the Germans. In return, despite the hesitation of the Bundesbank, France had obtained at Maastricht a promise that the monetary union would start finally in 1999. Some doubt had arisen regarding this issue in Paris. There was uncertainty at the time as to whether unification in Germany might get priority over European integration.

The EcoFin was given competence to decide disciplinary sanctions against EMU-participating governments which ran excessive deficits. Under strong pressure from the UK and Denmark the Heads of Government created, as earlier mentioned, the possibility at Maastricht that Member States could opt out of certain important projects. Thus the British PM John Major acquired the right to decide whether to join the future common currency and to opt out of all new social policy provisions.

In accordance with Articles 121 and 122 TEC the Council in the composition of Heads of State or Government (HSG Council) took during the 1990s the series of decisions necessary for the transition to the third (final) stage of EMU. At its special meeting in Brussels in October 1993 to celebrate the coming into force of the TEU, the Council chose Frankfurt as the location for the European Monetary Institute, forerunner of the European Central Bank. This happened after months of wrangling and resistance from the UK, which feared that this choice would pose a threat to the City of London as an international financial centre. The decision was part of a wide-ranging agreement on the location of the EU Institutions and Agencies. According to Chancellor Kohl the choice of Frankfurt was necessary to reassure Germans about the loss of their D-Mark, the symbol of post-war stability. Kohl said that he saw in the choice for Frankfurt a recognition of the European engagement of the Germans. Kohl was at these negotiations 'motivated by German interests but defined these interests in terms of a vision of Europe' (Dyson, 1998, p. 37).

During the first phase of EMU (1990 – 31 December 1993) the Union had to contend with a serious economic, political, financial and monetary crisis. Low economic growth and the high costs of German unification were important causes. From September 1992 to August 1993 a currency crisis raged. The pound sterling and the Italian lira had to withdraw from the European Exchange-Rate Mechanism (ERM). A total unraveling of the ERM was in the air. These developments threatened the broader alignment of the European currencies and the successful creation of the EMU. Despite the serious problems caused by this to the Union, for months the Heads of Government took no notice of these developments in the European Council. At several meetings during 1992 and 1993 the general economic situation of those days (a deep recession) came up for exhaustive discussion in the European Council. However the problems around ERM did not. These monetary problems only featured as an item on the agenda during the meeting of October 1992 in Birmingham and again in 1995 in Formentor (Mallorca). These deliberations yielded little result. The Heads of Government passed on these major crises (which put in question whether the Union would meet its target of launching EMU on the sacrosanct date of 1 January 1999) to the EcoFin Council and to the other monetary authorities. One could argue that a European Council surrounded by intense publicity is not the forum to discuss market-sensitive currency issues. But such an argument ignores the fact that in 1978 two such meetings negotiated the creation of the European Monetary System EMS (Werts, 1992, p. 242-248).

It is therefore not true that the European Council always comes to the rescue as soon as the Union hits a major crisis, as one would expect in accordance with its brief under Article 4 TEU. The protracted crisis over the ERM, with all its attendant risks, was never discussed. Experience has shown that the Heads of Government in general avoid discussions regarding complicated monetary policy matters. Although these problems in most cases are connected with policy, the national political leaders prefer to leave these monetary issues to the EcoFin. This experience shows us that there are certainly limits to the choice of subjects for discussion in the European Council (see also Chapter 2.C.3).

B.2.   The long march towards a European currency

Although the Heads of Government have not been involved in crisis management regarding the ERM/EMU, they nevertheless discussed at every meeting during the 1990s and afterwards the progress towards creating EMU. At the 1995 Madrid meeting, it was decided to name the single (common) currency, to be used from 1 January 1999, quite simply as the 'euro'.[13] A suggestion by President Chirac to let the public choose the name of the currency by means of a European referendum was completely rejected by Chancellor Kohl. He foresaw, he said, that the Germans would reject EMU. In order 'to prepare Europe for the 21st century', a chronological sequence of events was agreed at Madrid for the changeover to the single currency. British PM John Major stressed at the meeting the danger of the single currency creating a permanent division in the EU between the two groups of Member States: those with the euro and those without it. Major spoke of Member States forming elitist groupings, the risk of trade wars within the EU and of the huge budgetary transfers that would likely be needed to cope with the strains of a fixed currency regime, both for those inside and outside EMU. But Chancellor Helmut Kohl chided John Major for being a pessimist (author's notes in Madrid). In December 1996 at Dublin, after lengthy and successful negotiations in the EcoFin on the eve of the European Council meeting, a compromise was reached on the Stability Pact for Europe urged by Germany (on French insistence officially the 'Stability and Growth Pact'). France obtained agreement that sanctions on Member States for excessive deficits remained a political matter by giving the Council of Ministers the right to decide (*Bull* 12-1996, I.3). Waigel here, as German Minister of Finance, insisted in vain that the Pact should mean 'automatic' sanctions on euro countries with a deficit larger than three percent of GDP, with exceptions only for a severe recession. In Dublin, the first glimpses were given of the euro banknotes, ranging from five to 500 notes, that citizens would receive by 2002.

The second 1997 Luxembourg meeting was characterised by hours of sometimes heated exchanges on the role of the *Eurogroup*. This is the monthly political monitor of macro-economic policy in the euro zone by the Finance Ministers of the States (and the ECB) participating in the single currency. It was at that time known as the Euro-X Council because the exact number of Member States joining the single currency was unknown. This Eurogroup pre-agrees all critical Council decisions with relevance for those Member States who have adopted the euro. It functions, moreover, as a forum where ministers decide on the overall orientation of economic governance in the euro area and establish common interpretations of EMU's core policy. Heads of Government in Luxembourg reconfirmed the EcoFin Council as 'the only body empowered to formulate and adopt the broad economic policy guidelines'. This was a symbolic concession to PM Tony Blair and his Finance Minister (Chancellor of the Exchequer) Gordon Brown, since the Eurogroup will continue to discuss whatever it wants. The UK would have liked to get access to its meetings as a euro outsider. A resolution was adopted on economic policy coordination, which had to complete the preparations for the third stage of Economic and Monetary Union (*Bull* 12-1997, Annex 1 to the Conclusions).

On 2 May 1998 in Brussels the HSG Council decided without debate to allow eleven Member States access to the single currency on 1 January 1999 (Press Release Council EU 8170/98). The eleven Member States recommended by the Commission were Austria, Belgium, Finland, France, Germany, Ireland, Italy, Luxembourg, the Netherlands, Portugal and Spain. The United Kingdom and Denmark had notified their intention not to move to the single currency. The Council noted moreover that Greece and Sweden at this stage did not fulfil the conditions. Greece was accepted at the 2000 Feira meeting. The decision was a crowning moment for EMU. It marked the accomplishment of Economic and Monetary Union according to the timetable set at Maastricht in 1991. It may cause amazement that such a far reaching, crucial and indeed historic decision passed through the meeting of the Heads of Government only once and moreover without debate, as if it were only a formality. What does seem odd is that an issue with such sweeping consequences in accordance with article 109(j4) TEC could be taken on the basis of QMV instead of unanimity which is normally the rule for all decisions with significant consequences for all the Member States. Indeed, 'such things ought to be done by unanimity in a constitutional order of States' (Dashwood, 2000, p. 97).

In our view this can be explained in three ways. The EcoFin had already reached agreement on this issue. In addition the record of the Council in dealing with EMU shows us, as earlier said, that the Heads of Government have a tendency to delegate monetary discussions (even if they contain obvious political aspects) to the Finance Ministers and other monetary authorities, such as the national central bankers. It is important also to note that during the years of the construction of EMU (1991-1999), the Finance Ministers were present at the meetings of the European Council whenever the subject of EMU was dealt with. Finally the Heads of Government, operating under the spotlight of publicity, tend to avoid painful discussions about whether or not to admit Member States. The same attitude prevailed during the decision-making over enlargement (Chapter 3.C).

The previous paragraph begs the question as to why the Heads of Government would decide upon the details of EMU if they would rather avoid such technical monetary issues. The answer is perhaps that the introduction of EMU required a huge leap from being a Common Market to becoming a European Economic Union with the transfer of basic national decision-making powers in the economic policy area to supranational institutions. National political leaders had to *legitimise* this far reaching operation, particularly during the construction stage of the EMU. This course of events does mean that the introduction of EMU via the European Council and the HSG Council has created an important precedent. It is no longer imaginable that fundamental decisions which stamp the process of European integration could be taken without involving the European Council.

It was interesting to see how during the 1999 Cologne meeting the Heads of Government fell over each other regarding a publicity policy for the euro. During the previous weeks the single currency had been severely devalued. The President of the meeting, Chancellor Schröder, advised his colleagues to leave any comment exclusively to the ECB president who would be responsible for the exchange rate. In the meeting the Heads of Government accepted his advice. But outside the conference room they returned to giving their own opinions to the media. In a leaked draft of the Conclusions the European Council had stated that (despite the persistent fall of the euro) it was 'not at all concerned' about the low exchange rate. At the last moment however this phrase was deleted. As a result of all those machinations the value of the euro against the dollar plummeted to a new depth. The lesson of Cologne: Heads of Government must remain tight-lipped about the exchange rate of 'their' euro. The Heads of Government learned their lesson at Cologne. They never have returned to the subject.

The meeting in Brussels in June 2006 was enlivened by a new controversy. Here a dangerous new area of tension between the Heads of Government came to light. *'New Europe'* (the new Member States which entered in 2004) collided with *'Old Europe'*. The HSG Council rejected Lithuania's bid to join the euro zone. The refusal was based on nothing more than Lithuania's inflation rate, which was 0.07% above the official criterion of the inflation target set in Maastricht in 1991. Lithuania's other macroeconomic indicators were comfortably in line with the criteria and, moreover, far better than those of some countries in the euro zone. During a troubled discussion the new Member States reminded 'Old Europe' of the fact that an excess of the same criterion by one percent for several years in succession by France and Germany hardly had any political impact.

The new Member States concluded that they were measured by a different standard. The same Maastricht criteria were interpreted quite flexibly in the past to allow 'old' Member States such as Italy and Belgium to join the euro zone. The dispute revealed a widespread feeling among the new Member States that they were being treated unfairly (based on author's notes at the meeting).[14]

B.3.   A difficult new item on the agenda: taxation

The Helsinki 1999 meeting added an item to the permanent agenda of the European Council: taxation. It was agreed that 'all citizens resident in a Member State of the European Union should pay the tax on all their savings income'.[15] The measures were intended to prevent tax evasion by people who put their deposits in non-reported or secret accounts abroad. This happened massively in Luxembourg and Austria, where banking secrecy regulation is in force. Because of the divergent interpretations of this principle, the Heads of Government had to give themselves more time to reach a position on an EU-wide savings tax. At Helsinki Prime Minister Blair blocked any decision for various reasons including dissatisfaction with the French refusal to lift the blockade on the import of beef from the UK (see also box 25). The meeting in Feira (Portugal) in the Summer of 2000 saw a new attempt to reach agreement. The European Council was landed with the problem after the EcoFin, during a three-day marathon meeting on the eve of the Summit, deadlocked on the tax package. 'There are still some 50 technical issues the Council has not debated', said Luxembourg's Prime Minister Jean-Claude Juncker, one of the opponents (AE, 21 June 2000, p. 8). A final agreement on the tax package of measures, to combat harmful tax practices with regard to the taxation of savings and company taxation, was not reached then in the Council of Ministers until 2003. As a result of problems with non-EU states, such as Switzerland, the tax package entered into force not earlier than 1 July 2005 (OJ L 157, 26.6.2003).

By way of conclusion: have the Heads of Government done a good job?

Have the Heads of Government done a good job of shaping the Economic and Monetary Union, in line with the important tasks which they imposed upon themselves on the basis of the TEU in Maastricht?

The long march (1991–2002) towards a European currency was handicapped by obstruction from three Member States, including the UK. In spite of this handicap, the range of serious decisions which the Council had to take has been entirely completed according to the timetable chosen in 1991. Moreover the creation of EMU meant a weakening of the sovereignty of the Member States. Great sensitivity surrounded the disappearance of national currencies. Finally, nearly all participating Member States were forced to cut their budgets, with often painful economic effects on their populations, in order to comply with the Maastricht criteria. For many years the Heads of State and Government dedicated themselves to the successful operation of EMU. This happened under the guidance of Chancellor Kohl, Presidents Mitterrand and later Chirac and Commission Presidents Jacques Delors and Jacques Santer. The 'common' Council of Ministers, here the EcoFin, could never have completed this long and difficult course exactly according to schedule. Given these facts the Heads of State of Government acting together in the Council, have certainly satisfied expectations.

C. ENLARGEMENT

C.1.   Edinburgh – Essen: arrival of the Eastern Europeans

The end of the Cold War raised the prospect of an unprecedented enlargement with applicant Member States from very different backgrounds. Three groups of countries were in the picture: a number of newly independent Central and Eastern European States who saw the Union as the path to democracy and prosperity; neutral States no longer constrained by the Cold War (Austria, Finland, Malta, Sweden) and other European States who now followed the herd instinct of the political world and jumped on the bandwagon (like Malta, Cyprus, Norway and Turkey). The Union was at that time ambiguous about the prospect of a doubling of its membership, with France especially fearing in the long run a diminution of its powerful position. The UK and Denmark were strong supporters of enlargement because it would ultimately weaken the Union and slow down the idea of a Political Union. Germany in particular, centrally situated in Europe, had much to gain (security, new markets) with enlargement. Despite their initial apprehensions, the Commission, Parliament and the Member States soon realised that enlargement on a large scale was inevitable. With the Cold War over, the Union could not restrict itself to Western Europe.

European Council meetings provided the important milestones on the path to enlargement, notably in the meetings held in Brussels in the Spring of 1985, in Dublin in 1990, Copenhagen in 1993, Essen in 1994, Madrid in 1995, Luxembourg in 1997, Berlin and Helsinki in 1999, Nice in 2000, Copenhagen in 2002 and Brussels in 2004. The European Council decided in accordance with Article 49 TEU every detail on the process of enlargement with thirteen new Member States.

Before each enlargement the European Council has laid down the conditions. In 1992 in Edinburgh the decision was taken to open negotiations from 1 January 1993 with Austria, Sweden and Finland. They became members on 1 January 1995, whereas the Norwegian people rejected membership in a referendum on 28 November 1994. In 1993 in Copenhagen the foundation was laid for a new wave of accessions, this time with the associated countries of Central and Eastern Europe. The *'Copenhagen criteria'* (*Bull* 6-1993, I.1-I.13) became famous since they established principles that have been applied for all subsequent enlargement negotiations. The terms require that the candidate country has: (1) achieved stability of institutions guaranteeing democracy, the rule of law, human rights and respect for and protection of minorities plus the administrative capacity to cope with the obligations of membership; (2) a functioning market economy; and (3) the capacity to cope with competitive pressure and market forces within the Union.[16]

The meeting in Essen in 1994 saw the first arrival of the Heads of Government of the acceding countries (Austria, Finland and Sweden) and, for part of the proceedings, of the six associated States (Bulgaria, Czech and Slovak Republics, Hungary, Poland and Romania).[17] The Essen meeting introduced a regular 'structured dialogue' between both sides with an annual meeting of the Heads of Government of current and future Member States. The Essen Summit was 'a historic moment'. Here, for the first time, twenty-one Heads of Government gathered together without, as President Mitterrand said, 'any difference between East, Centre and West'. 'Anyone who, five years earlier had said that a meeting of this kind was to be organised would have been considered mad', stated Chancellor Kohl, President of the meeting, at his press conference. The meeting approved a 'pre-accession strategy' proposed by the European Commission for the six. They received moreover the pledge that they would 'become members of the European Union'. 'Accession will take place as soon as the associated country is able to assume the obligations of membership by satisfying the economic and political conditions required'. Noteworthy was former President Giscard d'Estaing's remark that this meeting was a success for Germany because Berlin preferred a large Europe of which Germany would be the centre to a small Europe of which it would be on the outskirts (*'une Grande Europe dont elle serait le centre à une Petite Europe dont elle serait le bout'*, quoted by Weinachter, 2001, p. 451).

In Madrid in 1995 (*Bull* 12-1995, I.25) the European Council launched a first timetable for the achievement of enlargement. Chancellor Kohl pronounced a clear preference for accession of the neighbouring countries – Poland, Hungary and the Czech Republic – ahead of the other candidate countries. Kohl rebuffed an effort by Sweden and Denmark to ensure that the Baltic States would start negotiations at the same time as the other Eastern European countries.

C.2.   Luxembourg 1997 – Nice 2000: towards a 'Big Bang'

The second meeting in 1997 at Luxembourg entered history as the 'Enlargement Summit' (*Bull* 12-1997, I-1-I.6). The Heads of Government took the monumental decision to start the 'enlargement process (…) finally putting an end to the divisions of the past', with all ten Central and Eastern European applicants plus Cyprus. Various Heads of Government, surely all mature politicians, could hardly control their tears after the historic decision had been taken. PM Jean-Claude Juncker as President of the meeting then asked his Central European colleagues what they were doing exactly ten years earlier. 'Out of those eight, six replied that they were then in prison', Juncker said later.

From now on the Commission had to report yearly on all the applicants' progress. Negotiations on membership were announced with Estonia, the Czech Republic, Hungary, Poland, Slovenia and Cyprus. The Union began official enlargement negotiations with the aforementioned countries in the Spring of 1998. A *European Conference* proposed by France for all European States including Turkey would be held in March. Greece (due to territorial disputes) backed by Germany (fearing an extra influx of migrant workers) led a drive to exclude Muslim Turkey. Ankara therefore rejected the invitation for the Conference because Turkey was not added to the list of pre-accession States.

In December 1999 in Helsinki the important decision was taken to open negotiations with Bulgaria, Latvia, Lithuania, Slovakia, Romania and Malta (*Bull* 12-1999, I.3.10- 12). In Helsinki Turkey attained the status of being a full candidate for Union Membership.

Box 20

The 'waiting airplane tactic' of Heads of Government

The President of the meeting in Helsinki in 1999, PM Paavo Lipponen, and the High Representative for the CFSP, Javier Solana, had to fly to Ankara from the Summit meeting to convince Turkish PM Bülent Ecevit to board the plane in order to come to sign the agreement. Putting pressure in this way on the European Council from Ankara became known as 'the waiting Turkish airplane tactic'. Such 'make-or-break' tactics have been used on other occasions in crucial European Council meetings. In 1983 in Stuttgart there was a hard battle between the French President, Mitterrand, and the British PM, 'Iron Lady' Thatcher, on the anniversary of the Battle of Waterloo (18 June). The negotiations on Britain's budget dragged on to within 10 minutes of President Mitterrand's departure. In 2006 FM Abdullah Gül waited in the Turkish capital until the Heads of Government in Brussels conceded his demands. Gül then flew to the Brussels Summit to accept its decisions.

After a decision by the 2002 Copenhagen meeting 'to encourage Turkey to pursue energetically its reform process', in December 2004 it was decided to open accession talks under certain conditions in October 2005. Turkey's premier Bülent Ecevit said in Helsinki that the decision was a 'landmark event not only for Europe, but for the world'.

Upon the insistence of the UK and Italy in particular, the Nice 2000 meeting announced its intention to allow participation of the first new Member States in the European Parliament in 2004 (*Bull* 12-2000, I.II.6), which was greeted with joy by the applicants. It meant enlargement at the latest in early 2004 by way of a 'Big Bang', in other words with ten new Member States at once (all the applicants besides Bulgaria, Romania and Turkey). It is worth mentioning that at Nice it still sounded like futuristic music to which many in the EU listened with scepticism. But Anna Lindh, Swedish FM and President of the Council of the EU for the first half of 2001, announced in Nice the 'firm intention' of pushing the negotiations forward faster than planned by the Commission in its Road Map of 2000 (a comprehensive time table for the negotiations). At the Spring 2001 'enlargement' meeting in Göteborg the important intention was announced 'to complete the negotiations by the end of 2002 for those candidate countries that are ready' (*Bull* 6-2001, I.4.9) with the objective of those countries becoming Member States early in 2004. Which countries would be chosen was still an open question in 2001. The candidate Member States nevertheless reacted enthusiastically. Hungary, the Czech Republic, Slovenia and Cyprus were the favourites at that moment. Germany only wanted to cooperate if neighbouring Poland would also become a Member State in 2004. The 2002 Barcelona meeting saw the first full participation in a European Council meeting of the Heads of Government of the thirteen candidate States.

C.3. Circumventing all official EU procedures

It was under the Danish Presidency of PM Anders Fogh Rasmussen that half a year later in October 2002 in Brussels (*Bull* 10-2002, I.2-I.9) the Council agreed upon the conditions applicable to the ten future Member States regarding the CAP. An important issue was how to integrate Poland, which had by far the largest farming sector of the candidate Member States, into the Common Agricultural Policy without exceeding agreed spending limits. A certain limitation on expenditure on the CAP had, therefore, become an important requirement for enlargement. In particular the Netherlands insisted that simultaneously with the '*phasing in*' of direct financial aid to the agricultural sector in the new Member States, a '*phasing out*' would start in order to gradually end this kind of support throughout the whole of the EU. A pre-accord in the Brussels Conrad Hotel concluded by Chancellor Schröder and President Chirac, several hours before the start of the Council, delivered the foundation for a general agreement. For the umpteenth time the Franco-German 'engine' had protected the European Council from failure. The Council introduced a ceiling on CAP expenditure from 2006, with an annual inflation coefficient of one percent. Because inflation often exceeds one percent, the latter provision implied a sliding scale element. Another element was agreement on an envelope with €23 billion in structural aid (regional development) for the new Member States. That was €2.5

billion less than the Commission had urged. 'The Summit has placed us in the situation of concluding negotiations with candidate countries in Copenhagen, with a view to signing the Accession Treaties in March 2003', Chirac was pleased to say (AE, 27 October 2002, p. 2). During the meeting President Chirac and PM Blair had a stand up row. The French President was incensed by the PM's attempts to water down the Franco-German agreement on agricultural policy. Chirac therefore cancelled an imminent Anglo-French Summit.

At the subsequent meeting in Copenhagen the Council sealed an historic deal with the ten candidates.[18] This closed the circle of enlargement: from the European Council's Copenhagen Criteria of 1993 to its closing of the negotiations, again in Copenhagen, in 2002. The agreement came at the end of a meeting where PM Leszek Miller of Poland, the largest and most demanding of the new countries, accepted a calculated final financial package. It eased financial problems in Warsaw without substantially raising the cost to the Fifteen. The President of the meeting, 'enlargement superhero' Rasmussen (FT, 16 December 2002), had the advantage that his eurosceptic public at home was in favour of enlargement. In Denmark he was able to cash in on the success of 'his' Summit. Rasmussen in an emotional final speech seized the opportunity to underline the special nature of the moment. Referring to the 1945 division of Europe into Soviet and Western spheres of influence, Rasmussen described the decisions as the 'end of separation in Europe'. Most governmental leaders were euphoric. Italian PM Berlusconi declared to the press that he was in favour of a Europe that incorporated Moldova, the Ukraine, Belarus, the Russian Federation and Israel. Only Luxembourg PM Jean-Claude Juncker stated with more foresight that 'the new Europe will be difficult to manage' (author's notes in Copenhagen).

Tinkering with the rules by the Heads of Government

The Danish Presidency, in the run-up to the meeting of December 2002, played a remarkable role through their ambassador to the EU, Poul Christoffersen, together with the Commissioner for enlargement, Günter Verheugen. The Brussels October 2002 Summit had reduced the enlargement budget by €2.5 billion. On that basis Poland refused to accede because it would result in a reduced amount of financial aid. Christoffersen and Verheugen then used all kinds of tricks to clandestinely add back in again the earlier €2.5 billion which had been cut.[19] They ignored the protests of the Permanent Representatives of the EU Member States, and even those of the Council of Ministers. Presidency and Commissioner aimed at a *fait accompli* in the subsequent meeting of the European Council. The Heads of Government had to succeed at their 'Champagne Enlargement Summit' for a New Europe in December 2002 in Copenhagen. They could do no less than take on board this unpaid bill and that is exactly what did happen.

How can all this tinkering be tolerated despite solemn, published agreements? The lesson to be drawn is that a European Council is not only about the agreements. More important is what parts get executed. The Heads of Government form Europe's highest political negotiation body. Because of their function they automatically enjoy their Governments' mandate. At any

moment they can operate at will, even circumventing all official EU procedures. In this way do they often succeed. The political leaders of the EU
Member States were determined to achieve enlargement in 2004 after more
than ten years of intense negotiations. Therefore they had to remove all
obstacles. Such a 'Big Bang' by 2004 had been seen to be impossible through
the classic diplomatic negotiating channels: Coreper (the ambassadors), the
Council of Ministers, the Commission. The enlargement operation may be
compared with the complicated creation of the euro/EMU. There the
European Council also cut through the obstacles over a period of roughly
twelve years.

D.   FINANCIAL RESOURCES AND BUDGETARY
CONTRIBUTION

D.1.   Brussels 1988 and Edinburgh 1992: two successful
Delors packages

The Union's budget has always been a source of conflict in the European
Council. An important task, which has regularly absorbed the European
Council since 1975, is the consensual adoption of the multi-annual financial
framework. In 1984 at Fontainebleau the European Council created, after a
nine-year long budgetary struggle, the 'British rebate'. The UK would
receive 66 per cent compensation of the difference between what it paid in
VAT and what it received from the Community budget. Such a problematic
course as took place in Fontainebleau, and which later repeated itself, has
indeed a basis in logic. On the one hand there are the interests of the 'net
contributors', in other words the richer Member States which have to pay
much more into the Union coffers than they receive under various programmes (for instance Germany, the Netherlands). On the other hand are
the poorer Member States, which receive much more than they pay thanks
to various regional policy instruments, the Structural Funds, and the
Common Agricultural Policy. This is the famous disputed *burden sharing*
among the individual Member States. The spending limits agreed by the
European Council often go side by side with important policy changes
within the Structural Funds and the Common Agricultural Policy, by far the
biggest budget items of the Union.
    The so-called *Financial Perspectives,* or seven-year budget of the Union, lay
down, subject to the ceilings on own financial resources assigned to the EU,
maximum amounts by major heading of expenditure within which the
annual budget must be established over the period in question. After the
European Council has agreed on the exact figures in the Financial
Perspectives on the basis of a proposal by the Commission, the European
Parliament must give its consent by the majority of its component members.
    The 1988 Brussels and the 1992 Edinburgh meetings, after tough nego-
tiations, partly due to severe public expenditure constraints in several
Member States, reached a comprehensive deal on the EC budget for the
period from 1988 to 1992 (Delors I package) and from 1993 to 1999 (Delors
II package or Financial Perspectives).[20] In Brussels this was achieved after a
heated discussion, particularly between Chancellor Helmut Kohl and Prime

Minister Thatcher, in an almost uninterrupted meeting of 38 hours' length. The Brussels agreement meant the end of a nine-year long budgetary struggle with the UK about its financial contribution in which Thatcher reportedly during these negotiations from time to time slammed her palm and ring on the conference table. She also threatened to suspend unilaterally the UK's payments to the Community. In Edinburgh a so-called *Cohesion Fund* first saw the light as a financial instrument intended to reduce the gap in the economic performance of the Member States and especially to help the poorer Member States: Ireland, Greece, Portugal and Spain. They saw roughly a doubling of the amount of money they received for their development. This achievement was largely attributable to the insistence of Spanish Prime Minister Felipe González. The UK achieved in Edinburgh a renewal of its approximately £2 billion budget rebate, negotiated in 1984 in Fontainebleau. After the meeting different Heads of Government praised John Major's Presidency as 'elegant and effective'.

D.2.   Agenda 2000: a perfectly operating European Council

At their December 1998 meeting in Vienna the Heads of Government set the timetable for negotiations over Agenda 2000. This 1300 page study (doc. COM(97) 2000; Galloway, 1999), presented in 1997 by the Commission President Jacques Santer, encompassed:

–   a new financial framework to cover the years from 2000 to 2006;
–   a reform of the arable crops, beef, veal and milk production sectors in the CAP plus modifications to CAP financing and of the Structural Funds and Cohesion Funds;
–   a complicated process for enlargement (details at Galloway, 1999, p. 9-35).

Germany, the Netherlands, the UK, Sweden, Austria, France and Denmark (being in this order the relatively largest contributors in the financing of the Union) called in vain for a freezing of the Union's spending. The proposal met with resistance in particular from Spain, Portugal, Greece and Ireland, the largest beneficiaries of EU funds. It had already been decided at Cardiff in Spring 1998 to agree on Agenda 2000 by way of a *series of meetings*. A total of ten such meetings were held in 1998-1999 in the space of less than twenty months, a record number for the European Council. The aim was a political agreement on Agenda 2000 in March 1999 with final adoption of the whole package 'before the next European Parliamentary elections in June'. In hindsight this clear planning contributed to the satisfactory result.

The informal meeting in February 1999 at Petersberg near Bonn at first appeared to have no substance. Worse still: the only result was a new clash about the long-debated issue of budgetary reform. But behind the scenes the reality was different. The incoming President of the Council, Chancellor Gerhard Schröder, had called for the meeting in an attempt to settle aspects of the reform of the CAP and of the Structural Funds. A few days earlier 30,000 farmers from across the EU had staged a demonstration in Brussels against the price cuts on agricultural products proposed in Agenda 2000.

Germany proposed that the Member States should pay for their own farmers via co-funding the CAP aid. President Chirac, however, flatly ruled out such system. This refusal was a setback for Schröder but he took revenge on Chirac a year later. At Nice in the IGC in 2000, Schröder claimed (and obtained) for Germany more voting weight than France in decision-making in the Council. This disengagement cut through the important traditional principle of the equality of France and Germany in European integration.

The detailed decision-making about the gigantic Agenda 2000 package meanwhile took place at the Council of Ministers for Agriculture and the EcoFin. The Ministers responsible for the CAP, who had the toughest nut to crack, were urged at Petersberg to take decisions. At the same time the Heads of Government tried (although initially in vain) to reach agreement on their varying priorities. An important element was the presentation by the Presidency of a skeletal pre-draft of what eventually would become the Berlin European Council Agreement. On the basis of this first framework a process of successive drafts would gradually firm up a final text. This method mirrored that used in the Edinburgh meeting which in 1992 had agreed the Delors II package. In hindsight the Petersberg meeting was a useful one. It showed how the European Council controls and directs a difficult decision-making process. Agenda 2000 ultimately came into being precisely on schedule thanks to this approach.

At their successful March 1999 meeting in Berlin the Heads of Government reached an overall compromise on Agenda 2000: a reform of the CAP and of the Structural Funds; the Union's budget until 2007 and a financial aid package for the newly acceding countries, including the period after enlargement (details in *Bull* 3-1999). 'Our agreement sketches the outlines of the EU for the next seven years, on the financial and political levels', concluded a proud Commission President Jacques Santer. The agreement, 'one of the most complex packages ever processed through the institutional system' (Galloway, p. 34), had to be a balanced result that should neither have 'big losers nor big winners'. In that framework everything revolved around achieving a balanced share-out between individual Member States of the financial benefits and burdens resulting from EU membership. On the second day of their meeting, the Heads of Government spent their time largely on bilaterals and so called 'confessionals' (bilateral meetings between the Presidency and the principal protagonists). The plenary meeting was not resumed until late in the evening on the second day. This session ran into stalemate due to Spanish PM José-Maria Aznar. He demanded an extra billion ECU for the Cohesion Fund. The meeting dragged on until dawn on Friday 25 March. By six o'clock in the morning Aznar had got his way. Agenda 2000 was agreed.

The 1999 Special Berlin Summit was a threefold success: agreement about Agenda 2000; the smooth appointment of Romano Prodi as Commission President; and important decisions regarding the CFSP (see next chapter).

The hallmark of this Summit was the detailed preparation and the commitment of all participants to clinching a deal. The meeting can therefore be added to the list of truly successful European Councils. That was thanks in particular to Germany's relatively new Chancellor, Gerhard Schröder, who faced in Berlin an important test of leadership. Some days before the Summit

he lost his Finance Minister, Oskar Lafontaine, who quit. At the same time the
EU faced a crisis due to the sudden and unprecedented stepping down of the
European Commission (see Chapter 3.A.6). In addition on the first night of the
meeting NATO started its air strikes against Yugoslav forces in Kosovo. The
Chancellor had to appear on German national TV to explain why German sol-
diers in Kosovo were engaged in their first battle since World War II. It was
'urgent to conclude Agenda 2000 to save the European Union, in the eyes of
the public at least, from a deep crisis', Schröder had written to his colleagues
in his invitation to the meeting. The Chancellor passed the test *cum laude*. But
the price was high. Chancellor Schröder had earlier said that Europe's problems could not and should not be solved with a German chequebook. But in
Berlin he finally had to dampen his hopes for a substantial reduction in contributions to the EU budget.

Box 21

'Gift scheme' in order to hand out 'sweets' to all

Negotiations in the European Council preferably end in a win-win
situation. Important negotiations more or less require that everyone
returns home to his national capital as a 'winner'. It is worth examining the following list, which was drawn up at the last moment in
Berlin in 1999. This 'gift scheme' for the Member States has deliberately been designed to enable nearly each Head of Government to
hand out 'sweets' at home. This list must be seen as an addition to
the important and far reaching financial decisions in the framework
of Agenda 2000. The extras were of course designed to win approval
from hesitant government leaders. The list reflects the problems
faced at Berlin. In particular the Netherlands, Germany, Austria and
Sweden had to receive a reduction of their financing share.

- 500 million euro for Portugal, the Lisbon region;
- 500 million for the peace process in Northern Ireland;
- 695 million for Ireland's cities and regions;
- 500 million for more jobs in the Netherlands;
- 500 million for regional development in Sweden;
- 100 million for 'specific problems' in East-Berlin;
- 96 million for Italy;
- 79 million for some regions in Belgium;
- 300 million for the Highlands and Islands of Scotland;
- 450 million for Greece and Portugal; 200 million for Spain and
  40 million for Ireland, 'in order to maintain to 2006 the overall
  average level of per capita aid';
- 350 million for Austria and 550 million for the Netherlands
  (both unspecified);
- Special attention for the areas of the Italian Abruzzi (unspecified).

An interesting additional aspect of the decision-making in Berlin was the fact that the tensions in Europe caused by the Kosovo conflict contributed to the European Council smoothly taking some very important decisions that year. That was perhaps also due to the fact that in those days no less than thirteen of the fifteen governments of Member states were social demo-cratic-oriented and therefore politically in the same boat.

Agreement after 'amazingly complicated negotiations'

Seven years later in December 2005 in Brussels, this pattern was repeated, now with Luxembourg PM Jean-Claude Juncker and later British PM Tony Blair as acting Presidents. The difference from Agenda 2000 was that nego-tiations for the Financial Perspectives 2007-2013 did not go together with serious revisions of the policy of the Union. Nevertheless the Member States (and hence the European Council) split into two blocs during the tense negotiations of 2004-2005. One bloc was led by Tony Blair and the other by his sparring partner President Jacques Chirac. The former again wanted revisions with a view to a leaner and more competitive Union that could cope with the challenges of globalisation by refocusing spending on R&D in science and technology, whereas the latter preferred to safeguard the CAP in order to protect his large national rural society which saw itself threat-ened by globalisation.

In February 2004 the Commission launched its proposals. For the period 2007-2013 it wanted to earmark €1025 billion, or 1.14 percent of GDP of the EU. Next the Parliament came up with €975 billion. Both the Commission and the Parliament disregarded the poor state of public finances in most Member States and completely ignored the warnings of the six largest net contributors – Germany, the UK, France, the Netherlands, Sweden and Austria. They accounted for three-quarters of the net payments and wanted to retain spending at the much lower level of 1% of GDP.

After a failed run-up to the 2005 June meeting (Chapter 4. B.1) the Heads of Government managed to reach agreement in the small hours of 17 December. This happened after 'amazingly complicated negotiations' (PM Blair at his press conference in Brussels) during months of acrimonious disagreements. The overall budget for the period 2007-2013 was agreed at €862.3 billion (1.045% of EU GDP). That is hugely less (even exceeding one full annual budget) than the €1025 billion proposed by the Commission which had the support of Parliament. The outcome highlighted the relatively small influ-ence of the Commission and the European Parliament regarding the size of the budget of the Union. The final amount lay midway between the lower proposal of Blair and the higher one on which the European Council had got bogged down half a year earlier, under the guidance of PM Juncker. The six thrifty Member States thus put their stamp on the final agreement.

The agreement was a result of the excellent role of 'honest broker' played by the new German Chancellor Angela Merkel in cooperation with President Jacques Chirac. Her compromise proposal especially helped the new Member States and came close to meeting the ultimatum by Poland, which had said it would not accept any figure less than 1.05 percent. An important part was also played by Council President Tony Blair who, after initially refusing to give ground on this issue, eventually agreed to cut the

British rebate by €10.5 billion over the seven year period. Another element was the relaxation of conditions under which the new Member States could draw from EU funds. One arrangement gave these States the option to deploy so-called 'non-reimbursable VAT' to provide extra funds. To meet the requirements of the four largest contributors (the Netherlands, Germany, Sweden and Austria) the deal altered the VAT rate for these countries and also provided a lump sum for them.

Finally an important Review Clause was initiated by Commission President José Manuel Barroso. This encompassed a commitment to a 2008 review looking at all aspects of the budget. On the basis of this clause Tony Blair could claim that his condition for reaching agreement – a review of the costly Common Agricultural Policy – was part of the agreement. President Chirac, in contrast, could maintain that the policy of not changing the CAP, which was essential for his country, would remain unaltered until 2013, since France could use its veto in the European Council. Like Chancellor Schröder did in 1999, PM Blair now persuaded the other Heads of Government by offering each of them a sweetener. With these extra funds, largely intended for their national regional policy or R&D, the PMs could return home gloriously. Thus the Council laboriously arrived at the required consensus.

The foregoing report of the final days of these very complicated negotiations in the European Council is a good example of its method of working. Unusually (but understandably) the tension of months-long negotiations finally broke at the end of a nearly 34-hour meeting with spontaneous applause.

E. COMMON FOREIGN AND SECURITY POLICY (CFSP) – EXTERNAL RELATIONS

E.1.   The CFSP: a highly declaratory foreign policy

For almost forty years of European construction the very expression *common foreign policy* found no place in the treaties. After the failure of the proposed European Defence Community in 1954, *economic integration* became the preferred option. From October 1970 the Member States endeavoured to consult one another on major international policy issues. This 'European Political Cooperation' (EPC) occurred, as earlier mentioned, on the basis of a decision by the Heads of State or Government taken in December 1969 in The Hague. In 1986, the Single European Act (SEA) formalised this system of intergovernmental consultation. The Treaty of Maastricht (TEU, in force 1993), unlike the Treaty of Rome (1958), made collective security a goal for the European Union. In accordance with Title V TEU the Common Foreign and Security Policy (CFSP) belongs to the prerogative of the European Council. Articles 11 to 28 are now devoted specifically to the CFSP and include also a common security policy. However, these policies are at present in their infancy. For the future the formula applies that the Member States consult one another within the European Council 'on any matter of foreign and security policy of general interest in order to determine a common approach' (Article 17a TEU as amended by the Lisbon Treaty). The structure chosen resembles the intergovernmental approach that French President Charles de Gaulle had put forward in vain in the Fouchet Plan of 1961.

At European Summit meetings (1957-1974) and later on in the European Council (from 1974), the external problems facing Europe constituted a substantial part of the agenda. The European Council, in the role of policy-maker conferred on it by the Amsterdam Treaty (1999) working on the basis of unanimity, lays down the principles and general guidelines of the CFSP. The decisions in the framework of the CFSP, which the Council has adopted in this area, concern in particular:

- international security and disarmament;
- transatlantic relations;
- relations with Russia, Latin America, Asia, and the Mediterranean area;
- major international political conflicts such as in former Yugoslavia and the Middle East.

The European Council has laid down a common position regarding the Union's foreign policy through a number of specific landmark declarations. Such a 'Declaration by the European Union' (or, the European Council) reflects its position vis-à-vis a third country or an international issue. France especially, moreover, saw these statements and declarations as an expression of Western Europe's independence vis-à-vis the United States. The whole approach has a highly *declaratory character*. These landmark declarations have of course no legislative basis. The EU cannot impose its foreign policy statements on real international situations. Some examples are the Middle East problem (Venice 1980), détente with the Soviet Union (London, 1981), South Africa (The Hague 1986), the USSR and Eastern Europe (Madrid and Strasbourg 1989), the unification of Germany (Strasbourg 1989 and Dublin April 1990), the use of force in Yugoslavia (Berlin 1999) and the fight against international terrorism (Brussels 2001).[21]

In addition to these widely published declarations the European Council also deals confidentially with countless matters relating to the Union's foreign policy. These talks do not necessarily always lead to agreement. Sometimes the matter is complicated by the fact that one or more Member States are militarily involved in an international conflict. But even if there is agreement, it may be kept quiet.

At the Rhodes 1988 meeting, the Heads of Government agreed a statement on the 'international role of the European Community'. They welcomed the emerging readiness of Eastern European States to develop relations with it, in order 'to overcome the division of our continent and to promote Western values'. As outlined earlier in this chapter, the Heads of Government were to be granted their wish sooner than expected with the spectacular turn of political events in Eastern Europe in the Autumn of 1989.

Thus far CFSP has not fared well despite earlier intentions and declarations. Member States often divide when faced with an important international conflict. The larger Member States, moreover, (understandably) prefer to discuss important foreign policy matters in a small circle. Finally there is the refusal of the USA to consult the EU-27 in advance via the

Presidency regarding any big international conflict (for instance after September 11). These factors have resulted in influential ad hoc groupings coming into being outside the official framework of the CFSP. Examples of this are the Contact Group on Bosnia (with Germany, France and the UK and Russia) in the 1990s, and the Quintet, a restricted leadership group comprising the four largest Member States and the USA. This development on the face of it weakens the CFSP. On the other hand such ad hoc groupings may deliver positive results – for instance when a group of Member States sharing interests in a certain country or subject prepare a policy and introduce it into the Council. It is possible to speculate that a long-term President of the European Council whose task regarding the CFSP is to 'ensure the external representation of the Union' could play a key role in such a development, together with the High Representative for the CFSP.

During all five foreign political crises of the last two decades (the Gulf War, the breakup of Yugoslavia in the early 1990s, Afghanistan, the Iraq war and the Kosovo question) Europe was seriously divided. Throughout each of these situations the political leaders of the UK, France and Germany preferred to take their own positions. This puts in perspective the meaning of the CFSP. In other words the CFSP did not impose new constraints on the Member States in making their own foreign and defence policy.

E.2.   1999 – 2003: towards a European Security Strategy

At the 1999 Cologne meeting the Heads of Government approved a landmark document that formally marks the creation of a European Defence Community by way of a European Security and Defence Policy (ESDP) as part of the CFSP (*Bull* 6-1999, I, Annex 3). The political breakthrough had already occurred a year earlier, in December 1998, when a Franco-British Summit in St. Malo called for strengthening of the CFSP through the creation of a European Security and Defence Policy. A key clause in the document agreed in Cologne read as follows: 'The Union must have the capability for autonomous action, backed up by credible military forces, the means to decide to use them and a readiness to do so, in order to respond to international crises without prejudice to actions by NATO'. With the latter phrase the Heads of Government emphasised their striving for a certain independence from the US, which as is well-known dominates NATO.

The Council in Cologne in 1999 gave the Union a decision-making and military planning capacity and the ability to take decisions on the full range of conflict prevention and crisis management tasks defined in the Treaty on European Union, the 'Petersberg tasks'[22], which were taken over from the Western European Union. It was on this basis that continued efforts led to the establishment of permanent political and military structures and to the development of civilian and military capabilities, including the formulation by the EU of a set of crisis management concepts and procedures. The arrangements allow the Union to have recourse to NATO's assets and capabilities.

Later in 1999 in Helsinki (*Bull* 12-1999 Conclusions) a military '*Headline Goal*' was agreed. Under the flag of the Union the Member States must be able to deploy within 60 days military forces of up to 50,000 to 60,000 persons sustainable for at least one year. Meanwhile the Union developed the concept of multinational '*battlegroups*'. Battlegroups will be employable across the full series of tasks listed in Article 17.2 of the TEU and those identified in the European Security Stategy. Examples are humanitarian and rescue tasks, peacekeeping, crisis management and peacemaking. With these battlegroups of battalion-size of approximately 1500 troops, the Union will be able to undertake autonomous rapid response operations. Since 2007 the EU has been able to undertake two concurrent single battlegroup-sized rapid response operations. The Union has agreed as a global actor to take direct responsibility for collective Petersberg peace-keeping tasks in a series of places. The Union's troops have successfully been deployed in operations in, for example, Macedonia, Congo, Bosnia, the Middle East, Indonesia (Aceh) and the Horn of Africa. For EU-led operations, the EU will on a case by case basis determine whether it will conduct them using NATO assets and capabilities or without recourse to NATO.

In Feira in 2000 and Göteborg in 2001 mechanisms were launched that were designed to facilitate civilian crisis management. The European Council decided to create a Committee for Civilian Aspects of Crisis Management with its own headline goals, such as the deployment of 5000 police and judicial officials. Their tasks encompass four areas: police, strengthening the rule of law, strengthening civilian administration and civil protection. By 2006 the European Union was engaged in eleven such operations. In 2008 an EU Rule of Law Mission was sent to Kosovo with 1900 police officers, judges, prosecutors and customs officials plus approximately 1100 local staff. The objective was to support the Kosovo authorities with a view to fostering self-sustainable judicial and administrative systems in Kosovo.

In order to fulfil the real objective of ensuring that the Union speaks with one voice on issues of foreign and defence policy, in Amsterdam in 1997 the post was created of a High Representative for the CFSP. According to the Vienna European Council (1998) this HR/CFSP should be 'a personality with a strong political profile'. The HR/CFSP is also the Secretary-General of the Council of Ministers. The 1999 Cologne meeting appointed NATO Secretary-General General Javier Solana Madariaga to the new post. His appointment could be welcomed by the USA whose former Secretary of State Henry Kissinger once famously quipped that in a crisis he would not know whom to contact because 'Europe' has no telephone number to get in touch with. High Representative Solana, known since 18 October 1999 as '*Mr. PESC*' after the French acronym for the CFSP, is burdened with a complicated working method. The HR/CFSP acts at the request of the rotating Presidency of the Council by helping to make and implement political decisions. He must try and find common ground with the European Commissioner for External Relations – currently Benita Ferrero-Waldner – who has a similar brief. Meanwhile HR Solana has clearly given the CFSP more significance and presence. While all too often Member States are tempted to play the national card, Solana does what he can to act as catalyst of a European foreign policy. In so doing Solana has already put into practice what is intended to become policy with the coming into force of the Lisbon Treaty, with its reinforcement of the position of the HR/SG and the creation of the European External Action Service.

Within the CFSP, with reference to Article 25 TEU, a Political and Security Committee (PSC, or more commonly with the French acronym COPS), consisting of national representatives based in their respective Permanent

Representations in Brussels, was also set up for defence policy (Council Decision 2001/78/CFSP). PSC/COPS meets at Ambassadorial level and has as its function to monitor crises and to advise the European Council. Furthermore a European Union Military Committee (EUMC), with the chiefs of defence staffs of the EU Member States and a small EU Military Staff (EUMS) were created, all located in Brussels, plus an Institute for Security Studies based in Paris.

The political message sent out from the Cologne meeting was that the European Council in the future, in close cooperation with NATO and the United States, would try to tackle Europe's security problems. The sugges-tion by France, Germany, Belgium and Luxembourg that a separate EU headquarters be created was replaced by the decision to create a liaison between the EU Military Staff and NATO's SHAPE (Supreme Headquarters Allied Powers Europe) in Mons.

And so it can be seen that defence in the EU depends greatly on inter-governmental cooperation. Decision-making in the European Council requires consensus. Neither the Commission nor the Parliament have such an important role in this area.

The Cologne meeting finally agreed on a common strategy for Russia with a system of permanent consultation. It was the first time that the Treaty of Amsterdam was used to put such a strategy in place. Such 'common strategies' for the CFSP were moreover agreed in Helsinki in 1999 for the Ukraine and in Feira in 2000 for the Mediterranean Region. The Cologne meeting coincided with the surprising announcement by the President of Yugoslavia, Slobodan Milosevic, that his government had accepted terms for a proposed G8 peace settlement in Kosovo. As mentioned before, 72 days earlier in March, just before the Berlin meeting began, NATO's military action had begun with intensive bombardments.

In the meantime the terrorist attacks of 11 September 2001 took place in the US. Soon it became clear that these threats and the dangers posed by Saddam Hussein's Iraq as well as other so-called 'rogue States' were perceived in sig-nificantly different ways by Europeans (although divided between them-selves) on the one hand and Americans on the other. The EU and the US are often at loggerheads on important foreign policy questions such as North Korea, the Middle East, the Kyoto protocol, the International Criminal Court, environmental issues, trade issues and the role of the many international Institutions of the UN. 9/11 meant that as a result several Member States expressed greater interest in the CFSP and the ESDP 'in order to promote European unity rather than Western unity' (Shearman and Sussex, p. 62).

In Barcelona in 2002, the Heads of Government, despite internal divisions, managed to avoid a debate about the prospect of an American war against Iraq. When Belgian PM Verhofstadt attempted to raise the issue, his col-league Aznar, President of the meeting, told him politely to shut up. A year later in February 2003 in an extraordinary meeting in Brussels[23], and again in March during their regular Spring meeting in Brussels, which coincided with the outbreak of the war in Iraq, this was repeated. Under the banner of their Common (?) Foreign and Security Policy two almost equally large groups of Heads of Government opposed each other squarely. The oppo-nents of military intervention closed ranks with Germany and France, and the proponents sided with the UK, Spain and Italy. In February 2003

President Chirac launched in the European Council an unprecedented sting-ing attack on Eastern European applicant Member States, saying they had missed a great opportunity to shut up when they issued pro-American state-ments on Iraq. Chirac's rant against the Union's candidate members con-tained words such as 'infantile' and 'dangerous'. The French President saw in their alignment with the USA 'a certain lightness'. Chirac, moreover, dis-approvingly underscored the fundamental difference in importance between the existing Member States and the applicants. At the subsequent meeting in March the greatest opponents, President Chirac and PM Blair, sat face to face (by chance) and kept silent for a long time. Eventually the sub-ject of Iraq was opened for discussion by means of a common call 'to address the major humanitarian needs that will arise from the conflict; the EU is committed to be actively involved in this field' (*Bull* 3-2003 I.45.67). A proposal to note in the Conclusions that Europe was divided concerning Iraq was rejected. The CFSP is one of the most important tasks of the European Council. But scenes such as these above show that this CFSP is a phantom as soon as important matters arise.

In 2003 in Thessaloniki it was decided to establish the European Defence Agency (EDA)[24], to support the Member States in their effort to force Europe's splintered defence industries into more coherence and to improve European defence capabilities in the field of crisis management.

The 2003 December meeting in Brussels endorsed a rather vague *European Union Security Strategy* (ESS). The draft came from SG/HR Javier Solana. There is a key phrase worth noting: 'As a Union of 27 States with over 450 mil-lion people producing a quarter of the world's Gross National Product, the European Union is inevitably a global player'. The Union identified three main threats to global security: terrorism, weapons of mass destruction and the consequences of failed States (in which the central government is perma-nently weakened by warlords and militias). 'The European Union has the potential to make a major contribution, both in dealing with the threats and in helping realize the opportunities. An active and capable European Union would make an impact on a global scale. In doing so, it would contribute to an effective multilateral system leading to a fairer, safer and more united world' are the final words of the ESS. It will be interesting to see to what extent the European Council in the coming years will give meaning to this Security Strategy.

F. SPECIAL EUROPEAN COUNCIL MEETINGS: ECONOMIC AND SOCIAL ISSUES – THIRD PILLAR – TERRORISM – APPOINTMENTS

Economic and Social Issues

F.1.   An Employment Pact as a face saving 'solution'

At the 1993 Brussels meeting Commission President Delors presented at the invitation of the European Council an important initiative, a White Paper, 'Growth, Competitiveness, Employment. The Challenges and Ways Forward into the 21st Century' (*Bull*. Suppl. 6/93).

Box 22

High foreign visitors never yield results

In the course of the 1990s the custom developed of decorating a meeting with the presence of an important political leader from elsewhere. Such visits never yield real results. Sometimes one has the impression that Presidencies seek to employ them as a diversion to deflect attention from their own lesser level of ambition. The visitors attract lots of media attention. They take up a lot of time and on many occasions distract attention from the really important subjects of the Summit. An example is the meeting in Lahti (Finland) in 2006 which turned ugly due to the divisive statements by the invited President of the Russian Federation, Vladimir Putin. Before Putin had arrived in Lahti, the Finnish President Tarja Halonen was criticised for having hijacked Putin out of the EU arrangements by sharing a car ride with him. That was followed during the meeting by declarations in which the Polish and Latvian Presidents, the PMs of Sweden and Denmark and the President of the EP decried the state of democracy in Russia. The besieged Russian President responded that his country was no more corrupt than Spain and that 'mafia' is an Italian word, not a Russian one. In short, this was another useless invitation, which did not improve the EU-Russian relationship.

Visitors were:

- **Corfu 1994:** Boris Yeltsin, Vice-President Russian Federation
- **Cardiff 1998:** Nelson Mandela, President of South Africa
- **Pörtschach 1998:** Yasser Arafat, President of the Palestine Authority
- **Brussels, 1999:** Kofi Annan, Secretary-General of the UN
- **Lisbon, 2000:** Ernest Zedillo Ponce de León, President of Mexico; Thabo Mbeki, President of South Africa
- **Biarritz, 2000:** Vojislav Kostunica, President of Yugoslavia
- **Göteborg 2001:** George W. Bush, President of the USA
- **Stockholm 2001:** Vladimir Putin, President of the Russian Federation; Boris Trajkovski, President of the Former Yugoslav Republic of Macedonia
- **Barcelona 2002:** Vojislav Kostunica, President of Yugoslavia; Milo Djukanovic President of Montenegro
- **Athens 2003:** Kofi Annan, Secretary-General of the UN
- **Brussels, November 2004:** Ijad Allawi, Prime Minister of Iraq
- **Brussels, December 2004:** Recep Tayyip Erdogan, Prime Minister of Turkey
- **Lahti 2006:** Vladimir Putin, President of the Russian Federation.

The Union expected in 1994 a level of unemployment of 20 million people, the equivalent of the combined population of Denmark, Belgium and Ireland. On the one hand Delors envisaged large-scale investments in the European infrastructure, partly financed by the budget of the EU. On the other hand he wanted a series of measures to combat unemployment. The paper required an estimated funding over the next ten years of ECU 150 billion in order to create 15 million jobs by the end of the century. Delors wanted the European Union to issue 'Union Bonds' as an extra source of finance for large-scale European infrastructure projects. This proposal met immediately with resistance from the UK, Germany and the Netherlands. However there was also a lack of interest from private investors. The European Council decided to implement an alternative 'action plan based on specific measures'. Each year, beginning in December 1994, the Council would 'take stock of the results' and 'at the same time take any measure it deems necessary'. Of all these plans, projects and promises hardly anything has materialised.

It happened in Brussels that Delors tried to by-pass the thrifty 'economical accountants' of the EcoFin Ministerial Council who had to provide the required finances for his plan. To get rapid approval for his proposal, the Commission President wanted it dealt with directly by the European Council. But his attempt fell foul of the President of the EcoFin, Dutch Minister Wim Kok. He could refer to Declaration No. 4 annexed to the TEU which states that the President invites the EcoFin Ministers 'when the European Council is discussing matters relating to Economic and Monetary Union'. This course of action confirms that the European Council as a general rule will not put on its agenda proposals from the Commission which have not been discussed in the Council of Ministers.

A year later, the 1994 Essen meeting (*Bull* 12-1994, I.1-I.55) decided upon the list of priority large-scale Trans-European Networks or TENs (motorways, rail infrastructure, airports, port infrastructure, electricity, gas) essential to Union development. In so doing the European Council initiated an ambitious plan to integrate the mode-oriented national transport networks into a single so called Trans-European Network. For this purpose the guidelines identified projects of the order of ECU 400 billion.

The meeting introduced moreover the 'Essen procedure', an annual report to the European Council in December by the EcoFin and Social Affairs Council and the Commission. This procedure was later confirmed in Article 109 Q of the Treaty of Amsterdam. As a consequence each meeting of the European Council since 1994 has paid attention to employment issues. This does not mean, however, that the European Council has played an important role in tackling unemployment in Europe, since the annual report is strongly repetitive in nature.

Although at the 1995 Madrid meeting the Heads of Government affirmed that the 'the fight against unemployment' was their 'priority task', they had in Essen shelved Delors' White Paper. Delors later remarked that the Netherlands, Sweden, Denmark and to a certain extent also the UK and Spain have followed his recommendations on a national scale (Delors, 2004, p. 471-472). In the 1990s trimming deficits to meet the Maastricht Treaty targets became more important than spending billions in order to create jobs. Chancellor Kohl, PM Kok, PM Major and the new Spanish PM José Maria

Aznar stated in 1996 in the European Council that it was not up to public administrations to create jobs.

At their first 1997 Luxembourg meeting (*Bull* 11-1997, I.1-I.79) the Heads of Government tried once again, during a lengthy debate at a special *'Jobs Summit'*, to find an answer to the unrelenting high unemployment rate in the Union (seasonally-adjusted, 10.6%). This happened mainly upon the insistence of France. The meeting launched a coordinated strategy for national employment policies. It consisted in defining guidelines for employment at EU level whose achievement would be regularly monitored according to a common procedure or result assessment. These guidelines, once adopted by the Council of Ministers, were to be inserted in national plans for employment drawn up by the Member States. The emphasis in the European employment policy therefore was put on coordination of the policies which each Member State conducts for itself. Each year the Council of Ministers reports to the European Council on the way these guidelines have been transposed into national policies. The approach mirrors the one laid down in the Maastricht Treaty, which sought to use peer pressure to stimulate Member States to meet the so-called Maastricht criteria regarding their governmental budget. Secondly, the (non-binding) promise was made to offer every unemployed young person in the Union a 'new start' in the form of a job, training or work practice, before reaching six months of unemployment. Unemployed adults were in the same framework offered 'a fresh start' also by one of these means.

Reasons behind the minimal results of the job strategy

By 1997 the Heads of Government had for more than five years pledged at every single meeting to reduce unemployment. Against that background and given the ambitions stated in the 1993 Commission White Paper, the results in Luxembourg were minimal. By way of conclusion, the question arises why the European Council should year after year use its meeting for solemn intentions and pledges and finally accept such a face- saving agreement?

Most Member States did not want a policy aimed at employment targets, certainly not in an EU framework. As in the 1970s and 1980s, the European Council refused to start debating specific measures to fight unemployment. They considered this to be a national issue. Secondly, many governments in 1997 considered the realisation of the so called 'Maastricht criteria' for accession to the EMU more important than a Keynesian employment-stimulating policy. Helplessness was a further element. Perhaps that is why the 'Jobs Summit' in Luxembourg did not reach agreement until the European economy was already recovering. In 1998 it improved further. One year after Luxembourg, at the 1998 Vienna meeting, the Heads of Government happily noted that 'for the first time since 1992, the unemployment rate has fallen below 10%'. This opened the way for a face-saving exit. Subsequently, at their 1999 Cologne meeting, the Heads of Government endorsed a non-binding *'European Employment Pact'* (*Bull* 6-1999, I.5.7), bringing together all the Union's employment policy measures. The pact was based on earlier meetings of the European Council and therefore the first pillar was called the Luxembourg Process, the second the Cardiff Process (a reference to the structural reforms in for instance labour, product, services and capital markets in order to bind the various policy sectors together agreed in Cardiff in 1998) and the third the Cologne Process (an improvement in the interaction between wages and monetary, fiscal and budget policy). For 2000 a special Spring Summit was announced on economic reform, employment and social cohesion. This 'Employment Pact' came about at a time when it was already becoming clear that due to an upswing in the world economy the problem of unemployment would soon be largely solved in many Member States.

F.2.   The Lisbon Strategy: aiming too high

Knowledge, innovation and jobs in a cohesive society were the benchmarks measured at the 2000 'dot.com' Summit in Lisbon. The Council launched a decade-long strategy for economic reform and social and environmental renewal (*Bull* 3-2000, I.1-I.19). The main aim was stated thus: '*to become the most competitive and dynamic knowledge-based economy in the world*'. The European Council would devote its Spring meeting to economic and social questions. The basic documentation for these meetings includes a 'synthesis report' by the European Commission and the 'Key Issues Paper' on the broad economic guidelines. Since Lisbon, the Commission reports annually on the achievements made. On the basis of specific indicators the areas of employment, innovation, economic reform and social cohesion are looked at. The European Council here takes fully on board its coordinating role regarding the whole of the social and economic policies of the Union and of its Member States. The formula is based on Article 99 TEC.

An important aim was to halve the unemployment rate in the Union. Lisbon seemed to open up a better world. One spoke of the 'Consensus Summit'. The meeting progressed especially smoothly because all concrete targets regarding employment had disappeared from the strategy, at the request of some Heads of Government. Moreover the Lisbon Strategy contains no sanctions.

In Lisbon in 2000 Europe moved unnoticed (and without mention of a treaty amendment) in an intergovernmental direction. The President of the meeting, Portuguese PM António Guterres, did not expect that the Union's Institutions would be able to achieve the Lisbon Strategy. Therefore the Council itself took on the role of coordination and monitoring. During the final press conference the acting Council President talked about the new *Open Method of Coordination* (OMC) to be applied to topics where no treaty-based rules exist (for instance the financing of the national pension systems), coupled with a stronger guiding and coordinating role for the European Council.[25] He noted 'a true revolution in our working methods, (...) hinging between national policies around European objectives'. In short 'an effective method of coordination'. Lisbon introduced operational recommendations for the Member States on the basis of 'benchmarks', 'best practices' and 'peer review'. Commission President Romano Prodi also sat there, beaming. He happily talked about 'a turning point'. Lisbon introduced moreover, according to political sources there, a system of 'naming and shaming' by ranking the Members States' achievements. But the latter element has never been brought into practice because the larger Member States especially would never accept such chastisement coming from 'Brussels'. After the meeting it was said that the Heads of Government from now on wanted to be seen as being in charge of the whole spectrum of EU economic and social policies. Since Lisbon in 2000, the principal Commission reports regarding the Single Market take the 'Lisbon Strategy' as their starting point. This is a perfect example of how the European Council deprived the Commission of its right of initiative.

It was soon to become apparent that the European Council – just as earlier the Commission with its White Paper on the fight against unemployment – had aimed too high. At their first stocktaking meeting in Stockholm in 2001, during a meeting characterised by an avalanche of preparatory documents, the leaders failed miserably to deliver on their promises. This painful failure was masked by a further embellishment of the Lisbon agenda. The problems of the EU's ageing population and resultant pensions burden, the role of biotechnology in economic growth, sustainable development and a plan to create a common market for financial services and risk capital, were added to the Lisbon agenda (*Bull* 3-2001, I.1-I.26). During this meeting new action plans, committees, taskforces, procedures and scoreboards were launched. The political leaders here, again, were very self-satisfied, as their comments show.[26] 'If we do it well, we shall be able to take over the leading role of the United States', Guy Verhofstadt was quoted as saying. The Belgian PM reflected in his statement the general mood in the meeting. In his report to the European Parliament, Commission President Romano Prodi warned of the risk of a multiplying of 'unfulfilled promises'.

A year later, the 2002 Barcelona meeting tried to relaunch the struggling Lisbon process. There were attempts to produce some additional agreements about a package of liberalisation reforms in the energy sector. Little had materialised of the solemnly declared 'effective monitoring of progress' of 2000. Spain's PM José-Maria Aznar spoke in his role as President of the meeting of an 'extraordinarily important package'. Most other Heads of Government and Commission President Prodi also issued in Barcelona euphoric statements (author's notes in Barcelona and AE, 17 March 2002, p. 1-5). The German weekly *Die Zeit* characterised the meeting aptly as the '*Gipfel der Heuchler*' (the Summit of Hypocrisy).

The March 2005 meeting, under the guidance of Luxembourg PM Jean-Claude Juncker, gave short shrift to this project. Against the urgent advice of the overwhelming majority of the European Parliament (Press Release EP of 21 March 2005), the Lisbon Strategy – which according to the President of the European Council had been ignored and 'lamentably implemented' – was largely abandoned, and the target of 2010 dispensed with. Under the new flag of 'A Partnership for Growth and Employment', Lisbon was replaced by 'national action programmes' to boost employment and growth. It was now made clear, more than it had been earlier, that the reforms – of labour markets, social welfare systems, business regulation and pensions – largely lie outside the competence of the Union and within that of the Member States. The Lisbon agenda has to be carried out largely at the national level. With its change of policy in 2005, 'the European Council helped to transform Lisbon from a race which had to be completed by a particular time, into a reform process which will be continuous and in the course of which the contradictions can be managed' (Ludlow, 2005, p. 37). It will be an important test of the credibility of the Heads of Government, whether they will be able to successfully conduct and complete what is after all an extremely important project.

The same applies to the ambitious climate plan as a measure against global warming which was agreed at the Spring meeting of 2007. The Council reached agreement on a *binding commitment* (a new term in the European Council's vocabulary!) to produce 20% of the Union's energy from renewable sources, such as wind or solar power, by 2020. In addition the Council set a binding minimum target of 10% to be achieved by all Member States for the share of biofuels in overall transport petrol and diesel consumption by 2020. Moreover the Council announced unilaterally that Europe would be transformed into a highly energy-efficient and low greenhouse gas-emitting economy. Within this framework the European Council promised 'to achieve at least a 20% reduction of greenhouse gas emissions by 2020'. Commission President José Manuel Barroso called this new 'Energy Policy for Europe' (EPE) 'a historical result'. 'The most ambitious package ever agreed by any organisation on energy security and climate change', said Barroso. However, insiders saw these far-reaching commitments as being a near-replay of the March meeting of 2000 when the European Council launched its much-touted Lisbon agenda to become the world's leading economy by 2010, a promise that could not be achieved as it later turned out.

Justice and Home Affairs Issues

F.3.   The Tampere milestones: a difficult project to evaluate

The meeting in Tampere in the autumn of 1999, a Special meeting of the Heads of Government to discuss their internal affairs, was 'an idea' developed by Commission President Jacques Santer. The meeting, under the outstanding Presidency of Finnish Prime Minister Paavo Lipponen, paved the way for the creation of an Area of Freedom, Security and Justice as laid down in the Treaty of Amsterdam (today Article 61 TEC). The meeting stated that the Heads of Government would 'place and maintain this objective at the very top of the political agenda'. In this context, the European Council agreed on a number of common policies, policy guidelines and priorities. For example, with regard to asylum it was decided to pursue the objective of a common European system entailing special protective measures for people fleeing from persecution. The 'shopping list' with agreed ambitious projects, the 'Ten Milestones of Tampere', contains among other things a Common European Asylum System, equitable treatment for third-country nationals, measures against the trafficking of human beings, the mutual recognition of judicial decisions, measures regarding the fight against crime and money laundering and a call for the creation of a 'Europol' unit composed of national prosecutors.

Although there was no agreement in Tampere on the vexed and urgent question of how to share the burden of mass influxes of refugees, the Heads of Government called it a resounding success. The Council, the Commission and Parliament were invited to keep under constant examination the progress made and respect the deadlines set out. 'The European Council will keep an eye on that', said Finnish PM Paavo Lipponen as President of the meeting at the final press conference (author's notes in Tampere).

Is Tampere, with hindsight, an example of a largely failed project? A large part of its objectives has indeed not been realised to date. In the Autumn of 2007, eight years after the Tampere meeting, the Commission circulated four alarming communications about the very poor implementation of the Tampere Programme by nearly all the Member States. For instance the Framework Decision of 2002 on Joint Investigations Teams, as called for in Tampere, was applied in 2006 by only one out of the 27 Member States! (AE, 29 June 2006). On the other hand Justice, Freedom and Security have been on top of the Union's agenda for the last five years. This has resulted in an enormous increase of activity in an area always zealously guarded by the Member States as their national fiefdom. In the meantime, the Member States have reached a very important agreement in principle on far reaching mutual recognition of their judicial decisions. In a variety of areas of civil and criminal law the 27 Member States are increasingly and successfully looking for alignment. In practice, what has been realised since Tampere has been largely based on what was scheduled there in 1999 with the European Council as the agenda-setter.

As an insider has noted 'it was naive to think that, for instance, after Tampere a completely integrated refugee policy would be realised, when the realisation of the Internal Market took 50 years.' Ratification of the Lisbon Treaty will undoubtedly lead to an acceleration in decision-taking. The reason is that, among other things, in regard to most JHA matters decision-making on the strict requirement of unanimity will make way for qualified majority voting.

The reasons for the initially somewhat disappointing results are interesting because they show how the European Council should not operate.

Soon after the meeting the Tampere policy turned out to be politically entirely unobtainable. Tampere wanted a step-by-step approach, which at an earlier time had successfully led to the achievement of EMU and the Internal Market. This time it failed.

The first reason relates to the fact that in Tampere the Council agreed to priorities which were not matched by actual political reality in the Member States. This was soon shown by the non-cooperation of the Justice and Home Affairs Council (JHA). At their first meeting subsequent to Tampere on 29 October 1999 most JHA Ministers did not even turn up. They took revenge for the fact that they, the politicians most involved, had not been welcome in Tampere. Secondly, the Heads of Government finished their meeting in Tampere very early, leaving many contentious issues unresolved. That was unwise. Justice and Home Affairs belong to the hard core of the sovereignty of the Member States. It may have been unintended but Commission President Prodi in Tampere referred to a third reason. Prodi said that only a small part of the envisaged measures would be taken at the level of the European Union. According to him most matters regarding Justice and Home Affairs would be left to the Member States and the other levels of government.

In the opening years of this century JHA affairs – combating drugs, organised crime and illegal immigration – became for European citizens issues of the greatest political concern. The European political elite has understood that very well. The conclusions of the European Council (particularly those of the December meetings) show that the Heads of Government fully comply with their solemn promise of 1999 to keep the 'Milestones of Tampere at the very top of the political agenda'. In 2002 the European Council tried in Seville to revive 'the spirit of Tampere', but in vain. In 2004 the JHA Council, in a move remarkable for a Specialised Council, took upon itself the role of the European Council by the creation of Tampere II or 'The Hague Programme' which again spelled out the priorities. In November 2004 under the Presidency of the Netherlands, the European Council endorsed this Hague programme (*Gen Rep*, 2004, XIII). The strategy included special Dutch interests in particular regarding asylum, integration policy, and soft drugs policy (a most sensitive issue in Dutch politics). It now is a matter of wait and see as to whether the Hague programme will be executed in the years to come. Meanwhile it is certain that this programme will see a follow-up in the coming years.

F. 4.   Terrorism: an action plan with mixed results

On 21 September 2001, 'totally supportive of the American people', the European Council approved in Brussels an action plan against terrorism (*Bull* 9-2001, I.1-I-21). The meeting was held in order to stop the 'cacophony' in the Union and analyse the international situation following the September 11 terrorist attacks in the United States. The plan consisted of 30 or so measures such as enhancing police and judicial cooperation, developing international legal instruments, putting an end to the funding of terrorism, strengthening air security and a better coordination of the Union's global action. It was decided to introduce:

–   fast-track extradition on an EU-wide scale for those suspected of supporting or planning terrorist acts. The meeting decided on the introduction of a European Arrest Warrant (EAW) for serious crimes that would supplant the current system of extradition between the Member States;
–   a common EU definition of terrorist acts, a particular challenge since before 11 September only six Member States had defined terrorism as a specific crime;
–   the freezing of assets which might be used for terrorists' activities;
–   increased cooperation between the operational services responsible for combating terrorism.

The importance of this meeting lies in the fact that under pressure from the Heads of Government, the Ministers of Justice and Home Affairs of a number of Member States immediately had to give up their resistance to EU fast-track extradition. The European Council took away from various JHA Ministers the possibility of their blocking the aforementioned measures on the grounds of civil liberties and constitutional concerns. The EAW is seen as one of the most important pieces of legislation ever agreed upon in the European Council, since it encroaches deeply upon the sovereignty of the Member States. It implies a very high level of trust in the legal systems of the other Member States.

Further significant developments followed. One month later at a meeting in Ghent, 79 policy initiatives were agreed as part of a big action plan against terrorism. The Heads of Government went so far as to fix deadlines by which the JHA Council had to comply with their wishes.[27] The meeting also prompted the European Parliament to develop specified actions.

The 2001 meeting in Ghent was overshadowed by a totally unusual *'Petit Sommet des Grands'* staged there some hours earlier. In other words, Ghent saw two Summits: one limited to France, Germany and the UK and held on the initiative of President Jacques Chirac and the broader one held on the initiative of the Belgian Presidency. This was unprecedented. During the meeting of Chirac, PM Tony Blair and Chancellor Gerhard Schröder, the situation in Afghanistan and the elimination of the Al Qaida terrorist organisation were discussed. The larger Member States in so doing took a tighter grip on proceedings. The leaders of Italy and the smaller Member States raised the spectre of a threatening *'Directorate'* for the really important issues. Commission President Romano Prodi made a critical statement and was visibly unhappy with the event. The Ghent Summit(s) showed that the EU Member States were strongly divided over a fitting reaction to September 11, as soon as the military aspects were raised.

Nearly three years after September 11, in the wake of new terrorist attacks in Madrid, the Brussels 2004 Spring meeting made a renewed effort to speed up the poor progress within the EU regarding the agreements on anti-terrorist measures. The European Council appointed the Dutch former President of the Group of Liberal Democrats in the EP, Gijs de Vries, as Counter-Terrorism Coordinator. He would have to try to improve the often inadequate exchange of sensitive information. Furthermore De Vries had the task of chasing up the seven Member States that had missed the agreed date for introduction of the European Arrest Warrant.[28]

Appointments

F.5.   Clashes over important appointments

According to Article 112 TEC (accord of the Heads of State or Government) and 214 TEC (HSG Council) the Heads of State or Government decide on the most important appointments in the Union: the President of the Commission[29]; the President, the Vice-Presidents and the other members of the Executive Board of the European Central Bank (ECB); the High Representative on the CFSP (Article 207.2 TEC). Under the terms of Article 289 TEC the Heads of Government also determine the seat of the Institutions.

These appointments do not always run smoothly. For obvious reasons the Heads of Government have a tendency to regard appointments via the European Council as an instrument to reinforce their own national position, although the treaties require the appointed leading officials to operate independently.

After the coming into force of the Treaty of Maastricht in November 1993, there followed in the summer of 1994 at Corfu (Greece) the most important event of that year in institutional affairs. It was the British veto of the appointment of Belgian PM Jean-Luc Dehaene as the successor to Jacques Delors. British PM John Major rejected Dehaene on the ground that he was an avowed federalist, with *'a centralising attitude'*. Dehaene, strongly pushed by France and Germany, had received the support of many other Heads of

Government. In the run up to the meeting, Chancellor Helmut Kohl had waged a diplomatic campaign against the candidature of Dutch PM Ruud Lubbers who in 1989 had made some critical remarks regarding the urgency of German reunification. Lubbers had strong credentials as an avowed European integrationist with impressive accomplishments during his twelve years as PM. In addition the Netherlands was in those days one of the few Member States close to fulfilling the requirements for EMU. Kohl's action, which resulted in Lubbers withdrawing his candidature, offended the Dutch government and Dutch public opinion. Furthermore the request to Belgian PM Dehaene to become Commission President totally ruined the relations between the two Benelux Member States. The Chancellor's rejection of PM Lubbers received the backing of President Mitterrand who in 1989, as earlier outlined, fully shared Lubbers' critical opinion regarding German unification. Later the Greek Presidency asked Delors in vain if he would consider prolonging his term by one year. In mid-July, at an extraordinary meeting in Brussels, it was agreed as a last option to make as an appointment from the Benelux group, Luxembourg's PM Jacques Santer (*Bull* 7/8-1994, I).

Four years later at the 3 May 1998 meeting in Brussels there occurred another momentous event. Due to messy preparations by Council President Blair and the unattainable demands of France regarding the Presidency of the ECB, the meeting nearly ended in a total fiasco. A major point of contention was the appointment of the first President of the Executive Board of the ECB. Only after a record twelve hour working lunch with a lot of unfruitful debate was agreement reached. Pursuant to the TEU the President is appointed for a non-renewable term of eight years, in order to protect the independence of the ECB. On this Saturday afternoon PM Tony Blair had to broker a deal between the French, the Germans and the Dutch concerning the candidates. It involved the Dutchman Wim Duisenberg, president of the European Monetary Institute, the forerunner of the ECB, and Jean-Claude Trichet, Governor of the National Bank of France. The way in which this drawn-out Saturday afternoon passed by shows once more the extent to which purely *national interests*, the urge to *score points* and the *personal prestige* of the individual Heads of Government sometimes win out in these Summit meetings.

Duisenberg was not planning to serve his full eight-year mandate, given his age (62). President Chirac was only prepared to accept the Dutchman if there was absolute certainty that Duisenberg would give way to Trichet, if he were to step down prematurely. At that moment this demand was politically and legally difficult to realise. To break this deadlock Chirac, Kohl and the Dutch PM Wim Kok had agreed with Blair that the latter would do some play acting for the other Heads of Government (Quatremer and Klau, p. 18-30). Blair would propose to appoint Duisenberg for a fixed eight-year term with Trichet as his successor, again for another eight-year term. Once that was agreed, Blair would return to the meeting later with the announcement that Duisenberg was unwilling to complete his term in office. Next the Heads of Government should decide that Trichet would succeed Duisenberg after a number of years. This play-acting was intended to disguise that the prescribed eight-year term would be ignored. However Blair had failed to consult Duisenberg first. During the course of the meeting it became clear that Duisenberg wanted to retain full freedom to decide at which point during his eight-year mandate he would step down. Chirac, threatening a veto, held the meeting at bay for hours. He insisted that Duisenberg should appear before the meeting in order to break the deadlock. Duisenberg finally came and declared that he 'alone and entirely of my own free will' had decided 'not to serve the full but a shortened term' (Press Release Council 8170/98). At that moment everyone realised that Duisenberg more or less had been forced to make this unusual statement.

The French finally were given a written political commitment that Trichet would be Duisenberg's successor. When Chirac, after the meeting at the press conference in Brussels, emphasised the voluntary aspect of Duisenberg's statement, there was spontaneous incredulous laughter. The President justified his behaviour by saying: 'One has to protect one's own interests. We are in a system of a Europe of Nations. Each of them has to defend its interests'. This presidential statement went too far for Dominique Strauss-Kahn, the French Minister of Finance. He pushed a scribbled note to Chirac. Next the President corrected himself by saying: 'A Frenchman isn't there in the French interest but to run the common currency'. Mockingly the editor wrote his analysis in the *Financial Times* under the headline 'Wim-Claude Trichenberg'.

Observers claimed that the deal had violated the Maastricht Treaty (TEU). Chancellor Helmut Kohl had favoured a full term for Duisenberg. Some remarked that Kohl had been too soft with the French and thus 'played tricks' with the conditions of EMU. Chirac, visibly irritated, tried to protect Kohl from the fall-out, by saying: 'This was not a Franco-German quarrel but a Franco-Dutch problem' (author's notes). The whole course of events led an experienced observer to conclude that 'the new ECB was to have its functional independence, but like everything else in the EU, it would ultimately be responsible to Europe's nation states and would reflect a balance among them' (Calleo, 2001, p. 286).

The background to the quarrel was that France had earlier lost the site of the ECB to Germany. Moreover it had failed to persuade its partners of the need for a permanent secretariat for the Eurogroup. The Heads of Government in Brussels 'demonstrated their amateurism, and Jacques Chirac his biases' according to Francis Woerling, a high-ranking expert in monetary affairs at the European Commission. After Chirac's antics the ECB was faced with a credibility problem. 'What happened in Brussels has neither contributed to the expectation nor the necessity that the euro will be a real supranational and apolitical currency', said German Bundesbank President Hans Tietmeyer in an acid comment (DPA/AFP/Reuters, 6 May 1998).

Precisely as in Corfu in 1994 the European Council in June 2004 in Brussels again failed to reach agreement without a major clash over the appointment of a Commission President, this time in succession to the retiring Romano Prodi. According to the Council President, Irish PM Bertie Ahern, there were no less than eight or nine candidates. President Jacques Chirac and Chancellor Gerhard Schröder proposed the Belgian liberal PM Guy Verhofstadt. But several hours before the Council meeting, the EPP-ED group, which was the biggest in the newly elected EP (and in the European Council), proposed Chris Patten, the Conservative British EU Commissioner who was fully backed by Tony Blair. Chirac and Schröder made it clear to the European Council that they could not support Patten. Blair, backed by six other Heads of Government, shot down the candidacy of the Belgian PM. It was remarkable how the Franco-German candidate became the subject of an ugly public spat. The background to the dispute was the tensions in 2003 between the UK on the one hand and the French and Germans on the other, over the US-led war in Iraq, and also over the future of the Nice Treaty and the necessity of CAP reform. Such tensions sometimes led to remarkable bullying tactics via the European Council. Thus Chirac at his June 2004 D-day anniversary celebrations deliberately placed PM Blair next to Verhofstadt at the lunch table. That was an embarrassment to both men given the political tensions between them. For the first time in its 40-year history the European Council was confronted with an action by a major political grouping (the EPP-ED) which it could not ignore. It was something new that a European political party claimed the Presidency of the Commission. After a two-week search, Council President Ahern proposed Portuguese Prime Minister José Manuel Barroso during a brief Council meeting in Brussels on June 29. The 48-year old Thatcherite reformer of EPP-ED background was appointed unanimously.

Barroso was appointed notwithstanding the fact that in 2003 as PM of Portugal he had figured in the most serious crisis ever in the CFSP: the split to the bone regarding the necessity of the American invasion of Iraq (Chapter 3.E.2). Shortly before the start of the American military action Barroso hosted a Summit with US President George W. Bush, UK PM Tony Blair and the Spanish PM José Maria Aznar. They supported the Iraq war despite the opposition of a large number of other Member States. When deciding on their position Barroso, Blair and Aznar ignored the obligatory consultation within the Council of Ministers 'on any matter of foreign and security policy of general interest' as required by Article 16 TEU. In those days Barroso was described in the media as a 'butler' to the larger powers.

On three occasions the UK has vetoed a Franco-German candidate for the Presidency of the Commission. In 1984 French FM Claude Cheysson became the victim of Margaret Thatcher's veto; in 1994 PM John Major rejected the candidature of Belgian PM Jean-Luc Dehaene; and in 1999, Dehaene's successor as PM, Guy Verhofstadt, suffered the same fate as the result of a veto from PM Tony Blair.

G. Conclusions

By way of a conclusion to this chapter the first question to answer is to what extent the European Council has succeeded in its objective, ex Article 4 ex D TEU, to *provide the Union with the necessary impetus for its development* and to *define the general political guidelines thereof*. A second question concerns the effectiveness of the meetings of the Heads of Government in the role of an Intergovernmental Conference. A third question concerns the role and significance of the European Council as executor of the Articles and Provisions laid down in the TEU. In summary we focus in particular on the CFSP, EMU and the Third Pillar, as well the yearly discussion of the 'broad guidelines' of the economic policies of the Member States.

The European Council is today the highest political body of the EU. For more than two decades the Council has been the initiator and the highest decision-making body of the Union. The beginnings can be traced to after the meeting in 1984 at Fontainebleau, where a definitive agreement was reached on the British 'rebate'. This British problem had fully involved the European Council since the first meeting in 1975 and had almost incapacitated the EC. Examples of the enormous scope of its activities are:

- the review of the treaties in 1985, 1991, 1997, 2001, 2004 and 2007;
- the complicated enlargement operations in 1981, 1986, 1995, 2004/ 2007, bringing in a total of 18 new Member States;
- the successful settlement of the financing of the Union in 1984 and in 1988, 1991, 1998 and 2005, since 1988 by way of the Financial Perspectives;
- the launch, elaboration and realisation of EMU;
- the initiation of a considerable amount of secondary legislation.

There are numerous examples of decisions of the European Council with a highly technical and at the same time political character on a national level for which the Ministers for Foreign Affairs (the GAERC) were unable to find a solution. Examples of this include the introduction of the very complicated milk quota in London (1981), or the technically difficult introduction of a system of information exchange about the taxation of non-residents, in Feira (2000).

Our earlier study, completed in 1991, showed that the Heads of State or Government, right from the beginning in 1975, took decisions as 'supreme arbitrator' or '*instance d'appel*' regarding matters which had left the Council of Ministers in stalemate. In the course of the 1980s and especially since 1991, the European Council became even more omnipotent. It took the core problems of the Union upon itself. These were solved, generally appropriately, in complicated negotiations often going on for several days and nights. This development shows that from the beginning in 1975, the European Council did not restrict itself to its core function 'to define the general political guidelines'. At the same time the Heads of Government besides functioning as *instance d'appel*, charged themselves with the political decision-making on other important political projects. Chapter 4 will, however, trace a shift in this area.

Our analysis shows that the European Council in acting in this way offers coherence to the varying tasks and activities of the Union. The European Council has become an organisation which in fact promotes European integration. This takes place at an intergovernmental level but – as we will show in Chapter 4 – with a strong dependence on the famous Community Method of decision-making of the Union (for this method see box 2).

Government leaders enjoy travelling to these meetings. It confers an aura upon them. Absenteeism is rare. See, for this, the memoirs of those political leaders who have participated in the Council as President. Or consider, for instance, the Netherlands and Belgium. Traditionally these countries have been very critical towards the European Council. They prefer the Institutions – Commission, European Parliament, Council of Ministers – to fully play the part assigned to them in the treaties. During every IGC they have advocated a reduction in the number of meetings of the European Council. But once the Netherlands or Belgium themselves preside over the Union, these governments organise extra European Council meetings as greedily as the French, as their record reveals.

Next the question regarding the functioning of the meetings of the *political*

Heads in their role as an IGC with the main task of updating the treaties. Since the 1950s every decade has seen an important step in the direction of European integration (for an overview see Werts, 1992, p. 177-178). Since 1985 the Heads of Government, in the guise of an Intergovernmental Conference (IGC), have six times reviewed the institutional structure of the Union. In Luxembourg in 1985, Maastricht in 1991, Amsterdam in 1997, Nice in 2000, Brussels in 2004 and again in 2007 – on each occasion a process of long-term negotiations was completed. However, only twice were expectations satisfied, namely by the successful conclusion of the Single European Act in 1985 and in 1991 with the Treaty of Maastricht (TEU). How can this be explained?

Previously in this chapter we examined why the IGC of 1996-1997 did not yield the expected results. The European Council had already indicated in Noordwijk (1997) that the agreement reached at Amsterdam would not result in bringing about the institutional renewal on which the European Parliament and the Commission counted. The time was not right. There was no imperative need in 1997 to adapt the institutional functioning of the Union for an enlargement which still lay several years in the future.

In Nice (2000) there was indeed the urgency of institutional renewal. At the subsequent IGC in Brussels (2004) even more urgency was required. These two IGCs show how politically difficult institutional renewal can be. Is it not significant that the carefully prepared IGCs in Amsterdam (1997), Nice (2000) and Brussels (2004) and again Brussels (2007) were concluded after marathon meetings on the basis of a lowest common denominator with last-minute compromises on the most sensitive questions at 2 a.m., 4 a.m., 6.00 a.m. and 4.50 a.m.? After Nice the general feeling was that the European Council is no longer the appropriate forum in its role of IGC. Therefore the European Council in June 2004 agreed a Constitutional Treaty by a Convention, composed of parliamentarians, governmental representatives, ministers and members of the Commission.

Only at Maastricht did that rare moment occur when a seriously changed international political situation (the collapse of the communist regimes of Eastern Europe) created the climate for far-reaching expansion of the activities of the Union at the same time as institutional renewal. Germany, France, Italy, and the Benelux, who were in charge in 1991, were ready for the serious decisions that Maastricht produced: the Treaty on European Union and the path to Economic and Monetary Union. Moreover Maastricht was the only IGC meeting with the stimulating influence of the Franco-German tandem of Mitterrand and Kohl. On the next occasion, in Amsterdam in 1997, Kohl's position had been weakened too much, due to the internal opposition of the SPD and of several Länder (which must approve every treaty revision). Public opinion in Germany at that time was largely sceptical over the loss of the D-Mark which (in their eyes) could possibly lead to the arrival of a European Super State (Hefeker p. 39-71). In Amsterdam the Chancellor was even obliged to veto any meaningful extension of QMV, although his own CDU/CSU had argued in favour. Three and a half years later in Nice there was no longer talk of a Franco-German coalition, which has always been a requirement for a successful treaty revision (Wiegel). Finally in December 2003 in Brussels at the negotiations for a Constitutional Treaty, President Chirac defended the idea of a *two-speed Europe* with 'pioneer groups', whereas Chancellor Schröder talked of a 'practically inevitable failure' of that crucial IGC meeting (AE, 14 December 2003, p. 3-5).

Another important reason why the European Council failed was that expectations were too high. Time and time again the European Commission, the European Parliament and some Member States were too ambitious and created unrealistic expectations. The European Parliament especially is always very assertive as regards the need for far-reaching reforms.[30] In Parliamentary resolutions since 1985 the approach of the European Council has consistently been criticised as too narrow. Parliament, however, fooled itself. As earlier remarked, in 1985 Parliament underscored 'the ambiguities and shortcomings' of the Single European Act (SEA). 'Strasbourg' proved to be remote from political reality. Parliament did not see that the SEA opened the way to completion of the key objective of the Single Market and, moreover, clearly strengthened its own position in the institutional framework. Time and time again Parliament misjudged in its resolutions after the IGCs the political willingness of the Member States to approve serious change.

Some Member States made the same mistake. Let us compare for instance the expectations of Belgian PM Guy Verhofstadt as articulated at the meeting in Laeken (2001) with the results laid down in the Constitutional Treaty agreed in Brussels two and a half years later. Verhofstadt, who was at that point the President of the European Council, wanted a big increase in majority voting; a directly elected Commission President to be 'the President of Europe'; the transfer of the High Representative for the CFSP from the Council to the Commission; the introduction of a direct EU tax paid by the citizens into the EU coffers; and a redefining of the sharing of competences entailing a larger role for the EU concerning defence and foreign policy (author's notes in Laeken). But this call by the Belgian PM subsequently proved to be over-ambitious and a misjudgement of the political situation. Not one of the above proposals materialised in the Constitutional Treaty, let alone the subsequent Reform Treaty.

Moreover after every treaty revision portrayed as a failure by the EP and other faultfinders (Amsterdam, Nice, Constitutional Treaty) it turned out that the Union was still able to operate acceptably without any of the demanded far-reaching institutional renovations. That fact puts into perspective the 'failure' of the European Council in its role as Intergovernmental Conference. In other words: the Heads of Government have not failed in their permanent struggle since 1985 for institutional reform, given what was politically achievable and really necessary. The failure to ratify the 2004 treaty reform was to an important degree due to its being designated a Constitutional Treaty. Its naming was not a suggestion of the European Council, but of former French President Giscard d'Estaing as President of the Convention that drafted the treaty.

That brings us to the third question: the role and the meaning of the European Council as *executor* of the Articles and Provisions laid down in the TEU. The Union has had a frontier-free single market since 1 January 1993. Since that date the focus of its activities has shifted to three core tasks of the Maastricht Treaty: EMU, the CFSP and the Third Pillar, the last of these comprising such matters as asylum policy, judicial cooperation in criminal and civil matters, immigration, terrorism and control of the Union's external frontiers.

The central role in the execution of these three core tasks does not lie with the European Commission (as was the case with the single market) but with the European Council. With regard to EMU, the CFSP and the Third Pillar of the Union, the European Council is the main mover as laid down by the treaties. Moreover since Maastricht these core functions have been extended to more and more national 'hot potatoes', subjects such as the budgetary situation in the Member States, energy security, climate change, fiscal matters, industry policy, the Lisbon objectives, Trans-European (traffic and energy) Networks, peace-keeping outside the Union and, regarding the Third Pillar, questions like immigration, asylum, terrorism, organised crime and the admission of foreigners. In all these highly sensitive matters the Union penetrates deeply into areas of national autonomy and domestic policy. In the areas mentioned above, the Union is only authorised to act when the Member States agree unanimously. Therefore, since Maastricht the Union very often deals with questions which the Member States prefer to discuss together. In this context, in every Member State the Head of Government features as the national coordinator. In conclusion: the need for effective leadership by the European Council increases.

The fourth central theme (after EMU, the CFSP and the Third Pillar) for the Union nowadays is its financing. As shown earlier in this chapter, the European Council has drawn this series of very important subjects successfully into its competence. All the policies of the Union mentioned, except for the CFSP, are very adequately covered by the European Council and generally handled with some success.

Next to foreign policy. The European Council in the 1970s and 1980s sought to define a role for Western Europe on the global political scene (details in Werts, 1992, p. 204-220). This occurred by means of Statements regarding the most pressing international problems which, however, remained in most cases without further action. According to Article 13 TEU, since 1993 the European Council has to define the principles and general guidelines for the Common Foreign and Security Policy, including matters with defence implications. In striving for this ambitious goal the CFSP is not very successful, as shown in the previous analysis. Notwithstanding their obligations regarding the CFSP, most Member States claim the right to conduct their own foreign policy. In practice, it is not European but – in many cases for understandable reasons – national interests that supply the driving force. The various Member States have different perceptions of their national interests. Foreign and security policy goes right to the heart of what it means to be a Nation. These issues rapidly run into clashes around the sovereignty, identity and independence of the Member States. In a Union of 27 Member States, with as many Ministers for Foreign Affairs and with the requirement of unanimity, this results in problematic decision-making. For the European Council this means that little credit can be gained from the CFSP.

Another handicap for the CFSP is the lack of leadership within the 27 Member States. France and the UK, both permanent members of the UN Security Council, and Germany, politically and economically the most important EU Member State, can offer that leadership jointly. But these three dwell upon their own divergent opinions and interests. For France the

CFSP serves as an instrument to turn Europe into a rival of the US. The British adhere to their special relationship with Washington. Indeed, 'so long as France, Germany and Britain are confused about their own roles in Europe, so long will Europe be mixed up too' (Chris Patten, former European Commissioner for External Relations, p. 24). However, should Germany, France and the UK create a 'Directorate', in order to prepare decision-making, this would immediately raise the hackles of the other Member States. Finally, there is the factor that smaller Member States such as, for instance, the Netherlands, Portugal, Ireland and the Central and Eastern European countries, show a classical preference for a good relationship between Europe and America. These Member States are not in need of a CFSP when this thwarts their preferences.

Endnotes

1   For our extensive survey of the results and description of the earlier meetings, see Werts, 1992, Chapter IV.

2   In this publication, in line with the approach taken by the 1974 Paris Summit meeting where the European Council was created, whenever we henceforth mention, with reference to 'the European Council', 'Heads of Government', this stands for the whole membership of the European Council: the Heads of State or Government of the Member States of the Union plus the President of the Commission; 'Commission' stands for the Commission of the European Union; 'Council' stands for the Council of Ministers of the European Union; 'Parliament' stands for the European Parliament. The name 'Heads of Government' also includes the Presidents if they are a member of the delegation of a Member State in the European Council (such as the President of France, of Poland, Cyprus and Romania).

3   *Bull* 12-1989, 1.1.1. ; Thatcher, 1993, p. 760-762. At the Dublin 1990 Summer meeting, the European Council agreed to start the IGC on EMU on 13 December 1990 in Rome. It was intended that this conference and that on Political Union should conclude rapidly with, as its objective, a ratification of the results by the Member States in the course of 1992, see *Bull* 6-1990, I.10-I.11.

4   Küsters, p. 514. The blueprint for the swift integration of the GDR in the EU was adopted at the special meeting of the European Council on 28 April 1991 in Dublin, *Gen. Rep.* 1990, 18. The Report on Economic and Monetary Union in the European Community (Delors Plan) was at the 1989 Madrid European Council adopted as the basis for launch of EMU, *Gen Rep* 1989, 8.

5   Opting out is an exemption granted to a State that does not wish to join the other Member States in a particular area of Union cooperation as a way of avoiding a general stalemate. The United Kingdom, for instance, asked to be allowed not to take part in the third stage of Economic and Monetary Union (EMU). Similar clauses were agreed in Maastricht with the UK and Ireland for the abolition of all measures of internal border controls and the free movement of persons, and with Denmark as regards EMU, defence and European citizenship.

6   The Treaty of Nice introduced in 2001 flexibility in the CFSP.

7   Corbett, Jacobs and Shackleton, p. 352; author's notes at debate European Parliament 12 December 2000; AE, 13 December 2000, p. 5-7; telexpress European Commission, 11 December 2000, Edition No. 2.; *The Times*, 12 December 2000, Blair to EU: 'We can't go on like this'.

8   In Brussels a provocative statement of the six founding Member States was in the air, inspired by President Chirac. They threatened to form a 'Two Speed Europe'. The six 'Founding Fathers' would then move ahead as a core group to integrate further and faster among themselves.

9   On joining the European Union, Spain was accorded medium/large country status. It received eight votes in Council under the weighted voting system as against Germany's ten, and two Commissioners, the same as Germany, France, Italy and the United Kingdom. In the Commission, therefore, Spain was treated on a par with the biggest members. Spain and later Poland, both of similar size, needed months to accept that this would change in the Constitutional Treaty (and subsequently in the Reform Treaty).

10   Rollmop of char with Frankfurt green sauce and wild herb salad - Artischoke filled beef olive and Werderaner chilled soup of sour cherries with vanilla rice pudding. A selection of German and Spanish wines.

11   FT, 7 December 1991, p. 3; see also Delors, 2004, p. 364. For a selection of the official texts referred to in this Chapter see European Commission, *Economic and Monetary Union. Compilation of Community legislation*, Luxembourg, Off. Off. Publ., 1991, 258 pp. For a detailed analysis of the extensive past history of the EMU within the European Council see my publication 'The European Council', par. 78.

12   Earlier, in Hanover in 1988, after a Franco-German pre-agreement, the European Council laid the first foundations of EMU by the creation of the Delors Committee. It was composed of central bank Governors and other monetary experts who had the task 'to study and propose concrete steps that would lead towards economic and monetary union', see *Gen Rep*, 1989, 137. The Delors Committee set the framework for the later EMU negotiations.

13   *Bull* 12-1995, I.1 - I.7. According to my notes in Madrid and also to Quatremer and Klau, p. 270-271, the idea came from Theo Waigel, the German Finance Minister. Most governments had preferred to retain the classic 'European Currency Unit' or ecu, but Germany refused, since 'Ecu' in the German language sounds like 'kuh', or cow. The European Council moreover agreed that Member States who joined the EMU would begin issuing their negotiable debt, in other words all bonds traded in the market, in euros as of 1 January 1999, whereas the bills and coins would be introduced by 1 January 2002 at the latest.

14   The HSG Council decided at the same meeting to allow Slovenia to be the first 'new' Member State to join the euro zone from 1 January 2007. See Press Release 10452 - 06 Council of the EU; AE, 17 June 2006, p. 9.

15   Given the general inclination of governments to tax residents, as opposed to non-residents, there was a concern that every EU country would simply become its neighbours' tax haven. The biggest problem was that EU measures could seriously harm the City of London's financial centre and Luxembourg and Austria because of their profitable tradition of banking secrecy.

16   A new requirement for enlargement was added in 2006 with the decision of the European Council 'that the pace of enlargement must take the Union's absorption capacity into account', see *Bull* 6-2006, I Brussels European Council. This addition was generally seen as an attempt to slow down the process of enlargement with candidates like Turkey, Croatia and the Western Balkans.

17   See *Bull* 12-1994, I.13. Five other candidates, Estonia, Latvia, Lithuania, Malta and Cyprus, were allowed to participate for a part of the subsequent meeting in June 1995 in Cannes (France). This meeting provided the first vision of a European Council with 26 Heads of Government; see also *Bull* 12-94, I.2. In Essen the European Council by means of consultation with Spanish PM Aznar avoided a threatening and sharply political conflict concerning Spanish fishery rights. Aznar had threatened to block the accession of Austria, Finland and Sweden by 1 January 1995.

18   For details regarding the agreed €40.8 billion budgetary aid package for future Member States see *Bull* 12-2002, I.16, Annex I and AE, 15 December 2002, p. 2. Regarding Bulgaria and Romania it was decided to try to accept them as Member States in 2007. For Turkey the launch of negotiations for membership would take place 'without delay', if at the end of 2004 it 'fulfils the Copenhagen political criteria'. This postponement disappointed Ankara since it wanted a specific date. Energetic lobbying by US President Bush in favour of having NATO ally Turkey inside the EU had no effect.

19   Ludlow, Peter, *The Making of the New Europe. The European Councils in Brussels and Copenhagen* 2002, Brussels, EuroComment, 2003, p. 298-305.

20   *Bull* Suppl. 1/87; *Bull* 2-1987, 1.1.12-1.1.16; *Bull* 3-1987, 2.3.1 and *Bull* 12-1992, I.1 and Part C.

21   Detailed examination of the rather fragmented development of the CFSP and ESDP as well as the diverging results of these policies lies beyond the scope of this book.

22   In 1948 the Western European Union (WEU) was created as a response to the Soviet Union's moves to exercise power over the countries of Central Europe. In 1992 the ministerial Council of the WEU widened in the 'Petersberg Declaration' its sphere of activity to include peace-making, peace keeping, humanitarian and rescue tasks. The Maastricht Treaty (TEU) declared in Article J.4 the WEU to be 'an integral part of the development of the Union'. The EU was moreover here invited to 'elaborate and implement decisions and actions of the Union which have defence implications'. In 1993, with the entering into force of the TEU, this series of tasks became an integral part of the Union's activities.

23   After this meeting the leaders issued a joint statement concerning Iraq, *Bull* 1-2, 2003, I.1.

However, at their separate press conferences following the meeting, the Heads of Government differed in their explanations of this common declaration. Based on author's notes and AE, 19 February 2003, p. 3-8; see also Schröder, p. 228-229 and p. 238-239.

24   *Bull* 6-2003, Conclusions of the Presidency, VIII.I .25.65. EDA includes an embryonic military planning staff attached to the Council of Ministers as well as to NATO military headquarters. The latter was necessary, since 'the transatlantic relationship is irreplaceable'. Its task is to advise the European Council on strategic developments. Based in Brussels, EDA became operational in 2005, with a limited staff of approximately eighty people and HR/SG Solana as its Head.

25   *Bull* 3-2000, Conclusions of the Presidency, I.2 - I.19. In Göteborg in June 2001, the Council launched the Union's sustainable development strategy as an addition to the so-called 'Lisbon process', *Bull* 6-2001, I.2.1.

26   AE, 23 March 2001, 1-3. The failure of the Lisbon process was largely due to a lack of guidance from the European Council: see Michalski, 2004, p. 26-27 and p. 40-42.

27   7 December 2001 was laid down as the deadline for the European Arrest Warrant, for the common definition of terrorism and for the freezing of suspected financial assets and 'the end of the year' for drawing up a list of terrorist organisations; more details in AE, 19 and 20 October 2001. The Council Framework Decision on combating terrorism followed on 13 June 2002 (2002/475/JHA).

28   The EAW entered into force on 31 December 2003, but only eight Member States – Belgium, Denmark, Finland, Ireland, Portugal, Spain, Sweden and the UK – met the deadline. In August 2005 it was announced that all the Member States had now replaced their extradition procedure by the EAW; European Commission, Memo/05/278, 2 August 2005. Counter-terrorism coordinator De Vries was in September 2007 succeeded by Gilles de Kerchove, a director at the Council Secretariat.

29   The Nice Treaty slightly reinforced the position of the European Council. The required unanimity for the appointment of the President of the Commission had become outdated. The Council meeting in the composition of the Heads of State or Government (Article 214(2) TEC) is regulating authority here and hence can make its selection by qualified majority.

30   Apparently out of touch with political reality Parliament required in 1997 that 'integration will have to be measured against the requests and expectations expressed by the European Parliament', Resolution on the Amsterdam Treaty, AE, Documents, 3 December 1997; see also for instance European Parliament, *Resolution on the preparation of the reform of the treaties and the next intergovernmental Conference* (C5-0341/1999 - 1999/0825 (CNS)).

4   The role of the European Council in a Union of 27+ States

Introduction

This chapter deals with the position of the European Council in a European Union consisting of 27 or more Member States. An important issue is the future role and functioning of the European Council in this enlarged Union. I will therefore consider the structure laid down in the Lisbon Treaty, still to be ratified, which introduces a long-term full-time President. The upgrading of the European Council to an official Institution of the Union as introduced by Valéry Giscard d'Estaing, President of the Convention on the Future of Europe, is relevant here. I propose to follow this line despite the rejection of the Constitutional Treaty by referenda in France and the Netherlands, since this upgrading and the coming of a long-term President has been reproduced word for word in the replacement Lisbon Treaty.

The establishment of the European Council as an Institution serves more-over as an example of how the French are pushing their governmental model, featuring the Heads of State or Government in the leading role. Giscard d'Estaing imposed upon the Union a structure which fits seamlessly into the way Paris thinks about Europe. The French took the lead in this regard in 1974 with the creation of the European Council. In the Constitutional Treaty and the subsequent Lisbon Treaty this is repeated through the installation of a long-term full-time President with their own administrative apparatus in Brussels. Seventeen smaller Member States together with the European Commission and the European Parliament were squarely against this 'Dictate of the six big Member States'. This chapter shows why they lost that battle, first in the Convention and later the IGC of 2003-2004. The subsequent analysis shows that in the future the national Ministers for Foreign Affairs and in a certain sense the European Commission will only be partially involved with the activities of the European Council. This fits in with the French proposals of Michel Debré in 1953 and Charles de Gaulle in 1961 (see Chapter 1). In their day these proposals did not stand a chance with the other Member States. Under the current structure the European Council as a Conference of the Heads of State or Government as initially proposed by Debré decides on the entire policy. Thus the French vision of fifty years ago has now been completely realised.

The Lisbon Treaty will turn the European Council into the most important power centre in the Union. Does the upgrading of it mean a frontal attack on the Community Method as is often supposed? Or does a reinforced European Council lead to reinforcing the Community Method rather than undermining it? A Community Method which functions better under the umbrella of the intergovernmental European Council? That is the central issue of this chapter.

A. HOW THE EUROPEAN COUNCIL HAS UPGRADED ITSELF

A.1.   Justifying a 'President of the Union'

An important moment in the discussion about the role of the European Council in the new treaty was the publication of the joint Franco-German proposal on 17 January 2003 in the Convention on the Future of Europe (Convention doc. 489/3; AE, Europe Doc., 17 January 2003). The two biggest Member States introduced a long-standing full-time President of the European Council instead of the current part-time President which rotates on a six-monthly basis. The idea originated with the 'Three Wise Men' in 1979 and President Giscard d'Estaing in 1984. In his book *'Deux Français sur trois'*, Giscard suggested creating such a semi-permanent President (Giscard d' Estaing, p. 98-100). President Jacques Chirac presented this idea on 17 March 1995 in *Le Monde*. The creation of a permanent President was also promoted by the Prime Ministers of the United Kingdom and Spain, Tony Blair and José-Maria Aznar. In 2002 the former President of the Commission, Jacques Delors, argued that 'we are at a serious turning-point for Europe'. In his view, the EU must find a realistic way of working with 27-plus members. Otherwise 'the three big countries – perhaps tomorrow, four or five – will remove their cards from the table and choose to play alone' (*The Economist*, 14 February 2002, p. 34).

Since the Franco-German proposal got the backing of the larger Member States, it was immediately an important point of departure in the Convention. This development was in line with the views of Giscard d'Estaing. Originally the Commission saw itself as being the future 'government' of the Union. However, according to Giscard, that had proved to be a big mistake. History took a different turn with the founding of the European Council in 1974. In 2001 the former French President argued before the Institutional Affairs Committee of the European Parliament that within the Union the European Council and not the Commission ought to become the executive power (Marhold, p. 463-481).

In April 2003 Giscard launched remarkable Draft Institutional Proposals (published in Norman, p. 343). He wanted to upgrade the European Council substantially and referred to Jean Monnet, one of the 'founding fathers' of the EU. Monnet had told him of his own mistake when he initially relied on the European Commission to develop gradually into a European government (interview in *Le Monde*, 16 October 2001). Giscard proposed to the Convention that the European Council should be formally elevated to the most important Institution and the highest decision-making authority of the Union. The European Council was to get a President to be chosen by qualified majority voting (QMV) by the Heads of Government for a period of two and a half years, renewable once. This possible five-year period would be in line with the duration of the mandates of the European Parliament, the

Commission and the Union's High Representative for the CFSP. The President would 'prepare, chair and drive' the activities of the European Council; ensure its continuity and moreover represent the EU in the wider world. It has been said that Giscard himself once hoped to become the first 'President of Europe' (Weinachter in Bitsch p. 442).

In his famous Report on European Union, Belgian Prime Minister Leo Tindemans advised as far back as 1976 of the need to ensure that the European Council functioned as an efficient Institution. Taking this approach, Giscard dealt with some weak elements in the functioning of the Council. The first is that the Heads of Government sometimes lose themselves in an overloaded agenda. The second weak point lies in the preparation. All successful Council meetings show the evidence of detailed preparation. A full-time central leading figure would be capable of thoroughly preparing the meetings in pre-consultation with the national capitals.

Arguments pro a permanent President

The following further arguments can be made by those who favour the introduction of a full-time President of the European Council.[1]

–   The starting point of the Treaty establishing a Constitution for Europe/Lisbon Treaty is enabling the Union to operate effectively in the context of an expanded membership of 27+ states. For this the Union requires a power centre in which all Member States are represented at the highest level. Their common representative, the full-time President of the European Council, will become the figurehead of Europe. As the leading figure, the President will be afforded the necessary space and authority. An additional point is that the big countries, especially France, the UK, and Spain, like to play the game via the European Council. That will certainly be the case in a Union with 27 or more Member States;

–   a second argument of the larger Member States lies in the development of the Union. At the start the EEC/Common Market concerned itself mainly with economic cooperation. As already mentioned, the Union's agenda today comprises more and more national 'hot potatoes', subjects like the budgetary situation in the Member States, fiscal policy, energy policy, employment, industry policy, the Lisbon objectives, Trans-European (traffic and energy) Networks, terrorism, and peacekeeping outside the Union. In these matters the Union penetrates deeply into national autonomy and domestic policy. The Union in other words deals very often with questions which the Member States prefer to discuss together. In this setting, today more than earlier 'based on the involvement of the member states in every phase of decision-making' (Rood, 2003, p. 122) in every Member State the Head of Government features as the national coordinator;

–   an important consequence of enlargement is an increased complexity of coalitions. With 27 or more Heads of Government[2] around the table, the European Council has changed its nature. An assembly of this type undergoes the influence of what the French call 'l'effet nombre': the simple fact that the more Member States the Union has, the more difficult decision-making will become. Such a large meeting can no longer solve a difficult problem only by negotiation in a meeting with limited time available. This applies even more since the European Council has to take its decisions by consensus. In addition, the natural informal leadership of the former trio of Kohl, Mitterrand and Delors which was accepted by the other members of the Council, no longer exists. There is now need of a leadership figure sitting at the apex of the Institutions. Such a person must have a long-standing mandate. Their office would enhance the consistency in the setting of tasks by the European Council and in the representation of the EU abroad;

– the current six-month rotating Presidency, in which each Member State gets its turn, is not quite functioning. Moreover, on a six-month rotation of 27 Member States, the intervening period will be 13 years. Each Government taking on the Presidency will henceforth have to see it through (both administratively and politically) without experience and without the institutional memory of the previous period;

– an important part of the tasks of the President is moulding decision-making and searching for a compromise in an urgent matter by means of a game of give and take, prior to the meetings, in order to gradually arrive at the required consensus. The President has to keep an eye on the initiatives of the Commission and the national delegations, draft Presidency papers and proposals and keep in touch and secure consensus with countless Heads of Government. This involves touring the 27 capitals before each meeting. For a six-month rotating President cum Head of State or Government this would be impossible.

Finally, one can point to the lack of supervision of the execution of decisions. The Heads of Government regularly launch important plans without organising their execution at the same time. The Specialised Councils fail time and again to execute urgent requests of the European Council. An example is the European Community Patent, from which the business sector expects many advantages. As early as its Lisbon meeting in 2000 the European Council urged the Council of Ministers to ensure the availability of such a system 'by the end of 2001'. However, some obstructing Member States ignored the request by raising technical and political objections. As a result there is still no single EU-wide patent. Naturally, such a course of events diminishes the standing of the European Council. The advocates of a full-time President expect (or at least hope) that such a debacle as that over the Community Patent could not occur with a permanent full-time President in place. The full-time President would have the task of ensuring the preparation and continuity of the activities of the European Council and that its Conclusions were being executed. Heads of Government of obstructing governments would be confronted with the agreements made in the European Council. At the same time the President would see to it that politically unfeasible projects (such as the Community Patent) no longer turned up in the Conclusions. He would suffer political damage should the execution of various decisions escape from his grasp time and again. In other words, such a permanent President would mount the barricades. That is exactly what is now missing from the functioning of the European Council.

What the proponents could not yet achieve

Before moving on to the arguments of the opponents of an upgrade of the European Council in the following section, 4.A.2, we look first at the hopes which Giscard d'Estaing as Convention President could not realise. These elements are important, since they point to the direction in which the Council will unavoidably develop in the future. This theory supposes that France, supported by other larger Member States, will get its way anyhow, sooner or later.

Giscard proposed in 2003 to reinforce the European Council with a political and administrative body via a Board. This permanent *'Bureau'* would be constituted as follows. Firstly the President would have a full-time role. During the negotiations in the Convention it was generally expected that the President would usually be from one of the larger Member States. Secondly, a vice-president would be appointed, coming from one of the smaller Member States. The vice-president would lead the General Affairs Council, which supervises all intra-EU affairs. Then would come the High Representative for the CFSP of the Union. Further members of the permanent Bureau would, according to these proposals, be the President of the Economic and Financial Affairs Council (EcoFin), the President of the Council on Justice and Home Affairs (JHA), plus two members chosen from the European Council.

Another novel proposal was to *trim the authority* of the European Commission by making it responsible not only to the European Parliament but also to the European Council. Both Institutions could pass a motion of censure. Giscard made no mention of the Commission in its role as the Union's coordinator or executive. His proposals were unclear as to whether the Bureau of the European Council would meet regularly with the Presidents of the Commission and the European Parliament in order to ensure consistency.

Thus the Commission and its President as well as the Union's High Representative for the CFSP would only be partially involved with the activities of the European Council. Giscard's approach – to upgrade the European Council to the executive of the Union with the European Commission as its lower administrative branch (see interview in *Der Spiegel*, January 1979) – fits in with the proposals of French Prime Minister Michel Debré in 1953, President De Gaulle in 1961, President Pompidou in 1973 (see Chapter 1) and the (also French) President of the Commission Jacques Delors in 1994. In this approach the Conference of the Heads of State or Government decides on the entire policy.

The United Kingdom and Spain were ready to elevate the European Council even more. They proposed a full-time President who, besides preparing and presiding over its meetings, had 'to ensure the follow-up of decisions adopted, for which purpose he or she could also chair the General Affairs Council of Ministers, to give added profile to the external representation of the EU' (Convention doc. 591/03). Moreover the President was to be charged with directing the Presidency of the Specialised Councils.

In the subsequent IGC of 2003-2004 the Union's Institutions succeeded in strengthening their own position in the Constitutional Treaty and this was carried over to the subsequent Lisbon Treaty. Therefore the influence of the

Member States on the Union was reduced. The strengthening of the European Council is to be seen as a compensation for this development. It seems certain that the large Member States, after the introduction of the full-time President in the Lisbon Treaty, will continue to pursue the upgrading of the European Council.

A.2.   The defeat of the smaller Member States and the Commission

Opposition emerged to the intergovernmental approach adopted by the larger Member States and Convention President Giscard d'Estaing. In December 2002 a strangely elaborate 'Draft Treaty' was published, entitled *Penelope*. The red bound booklet was offered by the European Commission services in all the Union's languages. Yet, according to a spokesman, it was no more than a feasibility study, produced by high Commission officials 'at the request of President Prodi'. Internally the Commission was too divided to be able to take a common stance on Penelope. Penelope, in summary, tried to elevate the Commission to the status of a European Government. It relegated the European Council to a 'Council meeting at the level of Heads of State or Government' (Article 42). Its right to designate the President of the Commission was taken away by Penelope. That became the Parliament's prerogative. Penelope met immediately with insurmountable objections from the Member States.

In the first months of the Convention most of its members could be considered natural allies of the European Commission. In their eyes that was the Institution watching over the preservation and enhancement of the Community Method of decision-making in the Union. But by launching the wrong proposals the Commission wasted its credit. The Commission's internal discord over the reforms required and the subsequent clumsy introduction of Penelope resulted in a marginal role for the Commission in the Convention (Lamassoure, p. 50). In its official position document (COM (2002) 728) regarding the Convention, the Commission totally rejected the idea of a long-term President for the European Council. The Presidency must rotate every six months between all Member States. Furthermore, in order to give the Commission more executive scope, an obligation of its democratic accountability not only to the European Parliament but also to the European Council was proposed.

In those days the European Parliament (Resolution of 24 September 2003) also rejected the plans to upgrade the Council. Parliament took the view that 'the election of the President of the European Council cannot in itself solve all the current problems affecting the functioning of that institution and could entail unforeseeable consequences for the institutional balance of the Union'. Parliament considered moreover that 'the role of the President must be strictly limited to that of a chairperson in order to avoid possible conflicts with the President of the Commission or the Union's Minister for Foreign Affairs and not to endanger (....) the Commission's role in external representation, legislative initiative, exclusive implementation or administration'. Another authoritative source, Christiaan Timmermans, Judge at the Court of Justice of the EU, although having a positive attitude regarding the functioning of the European Council, warned in 2004 that it was essential that its semi-permanent President should not be able to develop his own administration which would then necessarily be competing with the Commission (Timmermans p. 346-347).

Next, the smaller Member States showed their opposition. They had as central complaints, besides their own marginalisation, the risk of a permanent leadership rivalry between the two Presidents (of the European Council and the Commission) and an upset of the institutional or power balance between the Union's Institutions to the advantage of the largest Member States. 'The Commission's role as a self-steering and independent political force will be devaluated to become that of a dependent administrative secretariat (…). The long-term President will undermine the influence of the smaller Member States', according to the Dutch Ministers J.G. de Hoop Scheffer and A. Nicolaï, 7 March 2003 (my translation). The smaller Member States insisted that the Commission must remain the guarantor of the common interest, the initiator and independent honest broker with important executive and representative tasks. The smaller Member States saw incoherence between the roles of the Presidents of the European Council and the Commission, whose areas of responsibility both fall within the scope of the executive branch and which overlap. A full-time President with powers of initiative and coordination has tasks currently attributed to the President of the Commission. The coordination between the two Presidents with executive tasks may lead to lots of arm-wrestling, confusion of powers, competition, friction and conflict. Dutch European Affairs Minister Nicolaï, referred to the new President as an omnipotent 'Sun King' (*De Telegraaf*, 18 January 2003) not accountable to any parliament.

During the Convention debate 79 out of 91 speakers rejected a full-time President, noted Dutch Christian-Democrat MEP Hanja Maij-Weggen (Press Release 21 March 2003). Some wondered whether such a President also was to provide political day-to-day leadership. Quite a few members of the Convention questioned the democratic legitimacy and accountability of such a President (Convention doc. 508/03). The Austrian MEP Johannes Voggenhubber said that Europe was not waiting for another 'Napoleon'.

For the first time in history the Heads of Government of the smaller Member States clubbed together in Spring 2003. Jointly they acted, on the initiative of Luxembourg, against Giscard's plans. The Benelux countries plus Austria, Finland, Ireland and Portugal, immediately dubbed the 'Seven Dwarfs', saw the feared vision of a 'Directorate' of the larger Member States running the Union. In April the highest political leaders of seven smaller Member States held their own two Summit meetings, first in Luxembourg and later in Athens. On the morning of the Athens European Council, 16 April 2003, at a 'Benelux breakfast' a coalition of seventeen smaller Member States agreed to refuse to accept a long-term Council President. Austrian Chancellor Wolfgang Schüssel made a strong appeal for maintaining the rotating Presidency. According to Dutch Prime Minister Jan Peter Balkenende the meetings served 'to give a clear signal to Giscard d'Estaing and to the larger Member States' (author's notes at these meetings). At the meeting of 15 May, shortly before the conclusion of the Convention, sixteen smaller Member States called for the retention of the rotating six-monthly President, for almost half a century the symbol of equality between the Member States.[3] Moreover they asked to maintain the rule that every

Member State permanently has a seat in the European Commission. They argued that this maintains equality amongst them.

A second major difficulty for the smaller Member States was the division of labour between the High Representative for Foreign Affairs of the Union and the full-time President of the European Council. It is expected that a President would be the logical interlocutor with the President of the United States, Russia, China and Japan. What then would be the role of the Union's 'Foreign Minister'?[4]

How the parliamentarians saved the European Convention

Eventually the national and European parliamentarians who formed the majority in the Convention were the ones who saved it.[5] The Italian liberal former PM Lamberto Dini, Dutch Christian-Democrat senator René van der Linden, and German Social-Democrat parliamentarian Jürgen Meyer took the first step. They recognised that the smaller Member States would reluctantly have to accept the idea of a long-term President. Otherwise the larger Member States would have scuppered the entire Convention. Beginning in June 2003, the three persuaded their co-parliamentarians in the Convention to accept along with other new proposals the introduction of a 'President of the European Council'. Their motivation was: (a) preventing the failure of the Convention and (b) preventing the larger Member States further undermining the Community Method of decision-making. At the same time the Benelux countries ceased their opposition.[6] The 'Seven Dwarfs' pulled back. It is interesting to see how the trio Dini-Meyer-Van der Linden acquired the support of a coalition of integration-minded national parliamentarians and MEPs. They enabled Giscard d'Estaing to conclude the Convention successfully. The Convention agreed to a substantial upgrading of the European Council. Giscard's proposals, as sketched above, were subsequently adopted by the Convention and later included in the Lisbon Treaty, despite the resistance of the smaller Member States. At the time leading German MEP Elmar Brok spoke rightly of 'a dictate of the six big Member States'.

The upgrading of the European Council as laid down in the Constitutional Treaty, later duplicated word for word in the Lisbon Treaty, is a clear victory for the larger Member States (AE, 11 July 2003; Bunse, Magnette, Nicolaïdis, p. 294). Giscard d'Estaing and the largest Member States wanted to achieve two elements: a stronger European Council (as a future European Executive) and a smaller Commission. They got their all-powerful European Council as an official Institution of the Union with a permanent President located in Brussels. In addition the number of Commissioners was reduced – the IGC arrived at a number equalling two-thirds of the number of Member States. Finally the general task of the European Council has been tightened up. While the TEU stated rather vaguely that it had to 'define the general political guidelines', the Lisbon Treaty speaks of 'the general political directions and priorities thereof' which offers more clarity. This reinforcement of the task of the European Council is in accordance with the wishes of the larger Member States.

The larger Member States achieved moreover a limitation of the

Commission's political and legislative initiating role. The President of the Commission will no longer be the personification of the Union. The President of the European Council is the future real *'patron de l'Europe'*. The system is comparable with that of the Fifth Republic. The new President defines the strategy and presents the big projects of the Union to the public. The Commission President in that vision would become the *'Premier of Europe'*. When friction or a conflict occurred the President of the European Council would naturally triumph, according to Robert Badinter, former President of the Conseil Constitutionnel in France (*Le Monde*, 12 February 2003). Such a President moreover suits perfectly our *'société médiatique'*. 'In the long term I hope that the President will be elected directly by the people', says Giscard d'Estaing (interviews in *Le Point*, 28 April 2005, p. 50 and *Les Echos*, 25 May 2005, my translation).

Why do smaller Member States do a better job as President?

Talking about 'big versus small' raises the question of whether the smaller Member States really play a minor role in the European Council, as is always assumed. Furthermore, were the representatives of France (especially Giscard), the United Kingdom, Spain and Germany in the Convention right to claim that smaller Member States would be less capable of conducting the Council Presidency? (see Norman, p. 138, for a summary of opinions of the larger Member States).

Our previous investigation covered the years 1969-1991. On the basis of various examples we arrived at the conclusion that during nearly a quarter of a century with 60 meetings the leaders of the smaller Member States never played the leading role. My conclusion in 1991 was 'that although government leaders of Italy and the smaller Member States sometimes revealed their willingness to accept one, a lasting crucial role was never set aside for them' (Werts, 1992, p. 303).

It is now remarkable that this has changed since around 1990 (see Chapter 3). The Heads of Government of smaller Member States such as Belgium (1993), Ireland (Stability Pact for EMU and draft revision of the Maastricht Treaty in 1996), the Netherlands (Treaty of Amsterdam in 1997), Finland (excellent Presidency in 1999), Denmark (similarly with the enlargement in 2002), Belgium and Ireland (Constitutional Treaty), have meanwhile played a leading role at crucial moments. Prime Ministers of smaller Member States who, according to our analysis in Chapter 3, have played such a role between 1990 and 2007 are: Bertie Ahern (Ireland), António Guterres (Portugal), Wim Kok, Ruud Lubbers and Jan Peter Balkenende (the Netherlands), Paavo Lipponen (Finland), Anders Fogh Rasmussen (Denmark), Guy Verhofstadt (Belgium) and not least Jean-Claude Juncker (Luxembourg) with his influential role in general. Balkenende, for instance, as a newcomer in the meeting in October 2002 rejected the important Franco-German so-called 'Conrad Agreement' regarding expenditure under the CAP to 2013. Although the Dutch PM was isolated, he managed to force the meeting into a substantial extra reduction of expenditure. The claim that the European Council must have a full-time President because the Prime Ministers of the smaller Member States can no longer cope with this position in the current six-monthly rotating system is therefore wrong.[7]

> **Box 23**
>
> ## President Chirac: 'the arch villain of the piece'
>
> In the European Council President Jacques Chirac often did not look beyond French interests. Moreover the President was sometimes rather rude to his colleagues. Reportedly he treated Commission President Jacques Santer with considerable disregard and even disrespect (Peterson p. 62). Chirac sneered in 1987 that PM Margaret Thatcher was a 'housewife'. In February 1988 in Brussels Chirac made an unprintable remark about the British PM (Thatcher 1993, p 730) which may be found in Clarisse and Quatremer (p. 170). Chirac operated poorly as President in 1995 (Cannes) and in 2000 (Biarritz and Nice). He was generally criticised because of his arrogance and haughtiness. According to a participant in the meeting in Biarritz, Chirac as President of the Council started by presenting his own Conclusions. Next a round table was held with diverging opinions especially from the smaller Member States, following which the unflinching French President repeated his own Conclusions as a summary of the debate. In Nice in 2000 Chirac 'exploited his position in the chair to promote the interest of France and the other big countries' (leader in FT, 11 December 2000). After the meeting Europe's press almost unanimously blamed the 'fiasco' on Chirac. The President was, according to Simon Taylor in his analysis in *European Voice* of 14 December 2000, *'universally seen as the arch villain of the piece'*. French authors revealed a deliberate ignoring by France of the wishes of the other Member States. The word 'amateurish' was even used for the French set-up in comparison with the utmost rigor of the machinery deployed by Finland in 1999. In Nice, France 'engendered the antipathy not only of the small member states but also of Germany, her traditional partner in the EU'.[8] At the meeting in February 2003 Chirac launched a stinging attack on the East European candidate Member States, saying they had missed a great opportunity to shut up when they issued pro-US declarations on Iraq. Finally Chirac produced the sound bite of the day in 2006 in Lahti (Finland). Heads of Government had confronted the invited Russian President Vladimir Putin with the worsening human rights situation in Russia. But Chirac let his colleagues down. 'There is business on one hand, and then there are the human rights. These issues should be treated separately', Chirac said to his astonished audience.

The really important decisions taken since 1990 in the European Council were often shaped under the Presidency of a smaller Member State. Take for instance Ireland. Dublin since its debut in 1975 has exclusively chalked up successful Presidencies. It started back in 1979 with the agreement about the Dublin mechanism for compensation for the financial contribution of the UK. In 1984 important decisions were taken in Dublin regarding the completion of the Single Market; in 1990 regarding EMU and enlargement; in

1996 the Stability and Growth Pact; and in 2004 the Constitutional Treaty (see also Quaglia and Moxon-Browne, p. 349-368).

The words *'arrogance – incompetence – spin'* were used to describe the 1998 Presidency of another big Member State, the UK. The UK's subsequent Presidency, in 2005, was generally viewed as poor. PM Blair spent so little time as President on the European stage that 'yesterday a cheeky MEP launched a missing person's search for him'. The UK Ambassador to the EU had to express his 'wholehearted regret' after poor logistics and bad organisation of two Council of Ministers' meetings.[9] The failure of Italy in 2003 (failed December IGC meeting, see Chapter 3.A.7) provides another example of the various larger Member States which since 1990 have offered poor leadership.

An important exception was the successful Presidency of Germany in 2007 under the leadership of Chancellor Angela Merkel. Together with her Minister for Foreign Affairs Frank-Walter Steinmeier she has put Europe *'back on track'* with a detailed agreement on institutional renewal. It resulted in the Lisbon Treaty which retained all essential parts of the rejected Constitutional Treaty. At the Spring meeting of 2007, Merkel won approval for an ambitious *climate plan* as a measure against global warming.

Why, then, do smaller Member States nowadays make a better job of managing the Presidency, showing more leadership? Perhaps the answer lies in the fact that since the departure of President Mitterrand (1995), who had the construction of Europe as the *leitmotiv* of his presidency (Haywood, p. 269-282; Müller-Brandeck-Bocquet, p. 349-357) and of Chancellor Kohl (1998) 'another lifetime advocate of European integration' (Dinan, p. 236), none of the larger Member States has had a political leader who has given comparable priority to European integration. A second reason may be that the fear of failure makes the smaller Member States more caring, more careful and more dedicated. The latter point was confirmed by Costa, Coudivat and Daloz who stated that larger Member States such as France often have other priorities than the EU Presidency. The Heads of Government of the smaller Member States frequently have an advantage in the meetings, because they are better prepared. According to Luxembourg PM Jean-Claude Juncker these leaders have somewhat more time and somewhat fewer assistants. Hence their personal, more thorough, study of the agenda. Thanks to their better preparation they can improvise more creatively when looking for a compromise.

Finally, it is worth mentioning that since the emergence of the European Council, for three decades none of the smaller Member States has ever complained about having an inferior role in the European Council.

None of these foregoing arguments should be misinterpreted. The prominent role of the Prime Ministers of smaller Member States as President of the meetings does not diminish the fact that the larger Member States, and Germany and France in particular, have no small influence on the results of the meetings. This was confirmed for instance in the important meetings in Fontainebleau in 1984 (after secret meetings between Bonn and Paris) and again in 1989 and 1990 with the unification of Germany and the achievement of EMU. Fontainebleau was a triangular deal among the 'Big Three': the UK, searching for a significant and lasting reduction of its financial contribution; the FRG pressing for compensation for its farmers which would not be, strictly speaking, in accordance with the official rules, and President

Mitterrand fighting for a successful Presidency. The paramount influence of the larger Member States was confirmed in December 2003 (the collapse of the Intergovernmental Conference negotiations), December 2004 (the opening of accession talks with Turkey), December 2005 (the agreement on the Financial Perspectives 2007-2013) and in June 2007 (the agreement on a precise mandate for the Reform Treaty). As described under Chapters 2 and 3, at the moment when crucial European Councils are threatened with ending in stalemate, the Presidency forms an inner circle with the 'Big Three', the German Chancellor, the French President and the Prime Minister of the UK, seeking to find the final basis for a solution.

A.3.   The lost alternative – a better solution

At the Convention, some had suggested a better, more Community- based solution: the creation of a *single post* combining the Presidency of the European Council and of the Commission. Such an integrated President for the Union – for the European Council as well as for the Commission – would not disrupt either the meaning or the equilibrium of the Institutions. The same logic which lies behind the future combination of the functions of the High Representative for the CFSP and the Commissioner in charge of Exterior Relations, also supports the notion of such a single President. In the long term such a 'President of Europe' (as a permanent President would be restyled) would at the same time provide the political initiatives for the external representation of the Union, for guiding the European executives (European Council and European Commission) and for dialogue between the Institutions.

An interesting aspect is that this approach is neither completely communitarian, nor supranational, nor intergovernmental. It reflects, moreover, the trend not to confer new powers upon the Commission and, moreover, the increasingly cross-pillar and multi-faceted nature of most of the Union's policies.

The idea of having a single President at the head of both the European Council and the Commission follows the blurring of the lines of recent years between the functions and roles of the Commission and the Council of Ministers (including its influential General Secretariat). Originally the Commission had the prescriptive and normative role in the institutional framework, whereas the Secretariat of the Council had as its priority task to help to broker the broadest possible agreements. But the Council, with its countless specialised committees and its mostly very active Presidency, developed itself much further. It became in the course of the decades a powerful competitor in the institutional framework instead of an interlocutor. This process was strengthened by the parallel development of the Committee of Permanent Representatives (Coreper). Javier Solana, the Council Secretary-General, also holds the position of High Representative for the CFSP, so that the General Secretariat is headed by a political figure. He has his own institutional tasks under the TEU. The SG's active political role, backed by his influential deputy Pierre de Boissieu, is spilling over into other fields, in particular in areas where working parties are chaired by the Council Secretariat. The result of these changes is a blurring of the differences between the Commission and the Council Secretariat.

A possible difficulty for such a permanent President would be that he would have to serve three masters: the Heads of Government; the Commission over which he presided; and the Parliament. That could make his position vulnerable as soon as a conflict arose between the European Council (the Governments) and the Commission or the Parliament. However, against that, the fusion of the roles of the Presidents of the European Council and the Commission could provide the central place for overall coordination and for the much needed synergy between the Commission and the European Council. With one President, the Commission as a powerful Institution and the European Council would together form the heart of the European Government. It is certainly worth mentioning that the text of the Lisbon Treaty leaves open the possibility for the European Council to appoint the President of the Commission as its chair.

The idea of a single President was launched in the Convention in vain by Pierre Lequiller (p. 51-58), representing the French National Assembly and Lamberto Dini, the representative of the Italian Senate. Giscard d'Estaing supported the fusion of the functions and tasks of the current President of the Commission, those of the Council and those of the High Representative for the CFSP in such a President (interview in *La Croix*, 19 September 2002). During the negotiations in the Convention it was clear that the advocates came from all quarters. They included the former President of the Commission Jacques Delors; German FM Joschka Fischer; the French Commissioner for Institutional Affairs and later FM, Michel Barnier; and MEPs Pervenche Berès, Jean-Louis Bourlanges and Andrew Duff. Others were Belgian PM Guy Verhofstadt; former Belgian PM and, moreover, President of the EPP/ED, Wilfried Martens; Belgian FM Louis Michel; and Italian Deputy Prime Minister Gianfranco Fini. Also in favour were the former Presidents of the Commission Jacques Santer (1995-1999) and Romano Prodi (1999-2004). There is much to be said, seen from the perspective of either the larger or the smaller Member States, in favour of a future fusion of the functions of President of the European Council and President of the European Commission. In the future, one may expect, there will be a return to this radical thought in the debate on the future structure of the Institutions.

A.4. Provisions of the Constitutional Treaty/ Lisbon Treaty

The Lisbon Treaty currently awaiting ratification maintains the earlier described competences and functions of the European Council and also its way of decision-making and composition as laid down in the TEU, with some new specifications. Article 62 TFEU as amended by the Lisbon Treaty for instance gives it the explicit task to 'define the strategic guidelines for legislative and operational planning within the area of freedom, security and justice'. In terms of defining the general political orientations the Lisbon Treaty offers some concrete details, without excluding other initiatives. The European Council has to *define the broad guidelines* of the economic policies of the Member States and of the Union (Article 99 TFEU as amended by the Lisbon Treaty); to *adopt conclusions* regarding the employment situation in the Union (Article 128 TFEU as amended by the Lisbon Treaty) and to define the general guidelines and '*adopt the necessary decisions*' for the CFSP (Article 13 TEU as amended by the Lisbon Treaty).

Secondly, often in the early years it was customary that 'when discussing matters within the scope of the Treaties, (...) the European Council may, in accordance with the said Treaties, act in the capacity of Council within the meaning of Article 2 of the Merger Treaty'.[10] This option to act like a Council of Ministers (Council in the composition of the Heads of State or Government or HSG Council) and *take legally binding decisions* is not to be found in either the Constitutional Treaty or the Lisbon Treaty. In 1993 the TEU had confirmed the possibility of the Council acting as a decision-making body 'to meet in the composition of the Heads of State or of Government'. With the coming into force of the Lisbon Treaty this power will disappear. As a result of the absence of the HSG Council in the Lisbon Treaty the European Council may only act in the normal way.

Nevertheless, it is my belief that the structure of the Lisbon Treaty will assist the European Council to sidestep its handicap of not being legally the decision-making body since it will be able to present its agreement on an issue as a *political accord*. Shortly after the political accord, follows the legally-binding decision-making through the interplay of Commission, Parliament and Council as laid down in the treaties. It remains remarkable that this way of operating has been common practice since the emergence of the European Council in 1974, although it is not foreseen in the treaties.

With the exception of the common strategies as set out in Article 13.2 TEU (i.e. acts with immediate legal consequences), the other decisions, guidelines, declarations, etc. of the European Council under the Lisbon Treaty remain of a political character. These actions have I believe nevertheless a legal status in *statu nascendi* because they are in many cases aimed at the creation of Community law through the action of the Institutions.

Consensus remains the rule, except for cases which expressly diverge. This concerns in particular the election of its own President (Article 9b (5) TEU as amended by the Lisbon Treaty); the choice of the candidate for President of the Commission (Article 9d (7) TEU as amended by the Lisbon Treaty); the ascertainment of the existence of a serious and persistent breach of the values of the Union by a Member State (Article 7 TEU as amended by the Lisbon Treaty); regarding procedural questions and the adoption of its Rules of Procedure (Article 201a TFEU as amended by the Lisbon Treaty); and the appointment of the members of the Executive Board of the European Central Bank (Article 11 of the Statute of the European System of Central Banks and of the European Central Bank). It is a remarkable characteristic of the European Council that in all the cases mentioned above a vote has never been taken in the past. In summary, the European Council decides by consensus, whatever the treaties may pretend.

The Lisbon Treaty in some specifically indicated cases refers the final decision to the European Council. It holds the important function of '*emergency brake*' where a Member State concludes that its essential interests are affected as a result of a decision from the Council of Ministers. According to Article 42 (b) TFEU as amended by the Lisbon Treaty, a Member State that considers that a proposed law would affect 'important aspects' of its social security system may request that it be referred to the European Council. The European Council then has the option of requesting the Commission to submit another proposal or referring the draft back to the Council for final decision-making. A somewhat similar system is introduced in Articles 69e TFEU and 69f TFEU as

amended by the Lisbon Treaty where a Member State considers that 'fundamental aspects' of its criminal justice system would be affected by a proposed
European law. The European Parliament considers this as an example where
the European Council interferes 'in a virtually decisive manner in a legislative
procedure' (EP, 2008, par. 6.2).

Finally, the 'simplified revision procedure' laid down in Article 33 TEU as
amended by the Lisbon Treaty is important. This, known in French as the
passerelle' ('bridge'), allows the European Council to decide, with the consent of the European Parliament, to switch a legal basis from unanimity to
QMV, or from a special legislative procedure to the ordinary (co-decision)
procedure. Every national Parliament has the right to block such a decision.
Nevertheless this competence is far reaching since it allows the European
Council to change the decision-making in the Union by circumventing the
usual required, difficult to achieve, process of ratification by all the Member
States. This *'passerelle'* clause is also applicable in a number of other cases
referred to in the Lisbon Treaty, for instance the adoption of the multiannual
financial framework (Article 270 a TFEU as amended by the Lisbon Treaty).

How the smaller Member States were fobbed off in 1974 and 2003-04

The long-term President of the European Council (Article 9b (6) as amended
by the Lisbon Treaty, not yet in force) will have tasks set out as follows:

–   to chair the European Council and drive forward its work;
–   to ensure its proper preparation and continuity;
–   to endeavour to facilitate cohesion and consensus within the European
     Council;
–   to present a report to the Parliament after each meeting;
–   to ensure the external representation of the Union regarding its CFSP.

The smaller Member States hope with this delineation of the job to prevent the emergence of an all-powerful full-time President. I do not believe
that this will be the case. In order to put his dominant position in perspective, the smaller Member States developed their own minimalist view on the
role of the future President. They extracted the condition that the new
President should act more like a *chairman* than a President. The President
should only prepare the meetings of the European Council and monitor the
execution of the decisions. Since the future President of the European
Council 'shall not hold a national office' (Article 9b(6)(d) TEU as amended
by the Lisbon Treaty), this approach 'begs the question as to how this senior
figure is going to occupy himself or herself for the remaining three hundred
and fifty days or so of the year?' (Milton and Keller-Noëllet, p.76). Moreover
such a role as simply chairman applies only to the First Pillar of the Union.
The smaller Member States have here forgotten the fact that the tasks of the
full-time long-term President encompass the entire political management of
the Union. The President will be central to the running of the Council of
Ministers as a whole, the setting of the wider agenda of the Union and the
overseeing of its implementation on the political level.

The proposed full-time President has a totally different function than the
current semi-annually rotating President. At present, every six months on
the basis of rotation among the Member States a Head of State or

Government who is by definition already heavily charged, takes on this additional task. He or she does not have, as their full-time successor will have, their own permanent staff (as part of the General Secretariat of the Council) and European Council offices with large meetings centre in the prestigious Résidence Palace at Brussels. The job description of the full-time President to 'prepare, chair and drive', as drafted by Giscard d'Estaing, gives the holder a policy space and political influence which go much further than those of the current rotating President.

This job description has to be seen as an example of nebulous phrases in the treaties, which later become invested with a meaning which earlier they never possessed. The latter was confirmed by the French connoisseur of the European Council, Pierre Lequiller, President of the delegation for the EU in the French National Assembly, in *Le Figaro* of 6 February 2008. The limitations laid down in the job description in the Constitutional Treaty and the subsequent Lisbon Treaty are merely politically symbolic for the benefit of the protesting small Member States. Exactly the same thing happened at the creation of the Council in 1974. Then there was no indication whatsoever (see Chapter 1), that the European Council would turn into a decision-shaping and decision-making body. The opposing Benelux countries were guaranteed that nothing would change the whole decision-making process. Yet, as outlined in Chapter 1, the decision-making process changed profoundly. Right from the beginning, the European Council took decisions as 'supreme arbitrator' or *'instance d'appel'*, regarding matters which had left the Council of Ministers in stalemate. Since 1991 the European Council has become even more omnipotent. It took the central activities and problems of the Union upon itself. These were solved, generally appropriately, in complicated negotiations.

In other words, over the course of the years the Heads of State or Government have given their creation an ever wider and deeper influence. As outlined in Chapters 2 and 3, comparison of the promise made in Paris (1974) with the actual development of the European Council leads to the conclusion that any agreement on a restricted job description for the new President in the IGC is of little consequence. Surely this is a remarkable point of departure.

The parallel fashion in which the protests of the objecting smaller Member States were dealt with both in 1974 and 2003 is striking. In 1974 the creation of the European Council by France and the other larger Member States was combined with an agreement on the future direct election of the European Parliament, viewed as a federalist countermove. This move was seen as a response to the protests of the smaller Member States but it proved only for the sake of appearances. The French Conseil Constitutionnel ruled that such direct European elections were not a problem for France, 'because the European Parliament possesses no real powers'. In 2003 the protesting Member States, the Parliament and the Commission were fobbed off in the Convention (and thus in the subsequent treaties) with the promise of election of the President of the European Commission by the European Parliament. That election, however, is restricted to a candidate chosen by the European Council. In short, in 1974 and in 2003 the protesting smaller Member States settled for a *consolation prize*. This allowed the elevation of the European Council to the Union's most important institution at the initiative of the largest Member States and especially France.

In the Convention in 2003 President Giscard d'Estaing ensured that there would be no special working group for institutional matters.[11] He purposely kept this bone of contention outside the working procedures of the Convention. Not setting up a working group on the Institutions is more than remarkable since this subject in particular went to the core of the objectives of the Convention. Moreover, in the EU it is most unusual that an important innovation such as the introduction of a 'President of Europe' gets pushed through without any preparatory study and against the wishes of both the European Commission and the European Parliament as well as the large majority of the Member States.

To sum up: the smaller Member States have been awarded the booby-prize by their 'Big Brothers' both in 1974 and thirty years later in 2003-2004.

B. AN ALL POWERFUL EUROPEAN COUNCIL

B.1. The new method of working of the European Council

Over the years the European Council has undergone a great metamorphosis. The meetings between the nine Heads of Government during the 1970s were in the nature of 'confidential chats', without political 'taboos', held in great privacy (details at Werts, 1992, p. 80 and 96-97). From this beginning has grown (as provided in the Lisbon Treaty) an official institution of the European Union with 27 or more Heads of State or Government. In the following paragraphs I will try to outline the future working method of the European Council in a Union with 27 or more Member States.

The European Council for three decades, since its creation in 1974 until around 2004, met and decided in most cases in plenary session. During these many years the Heads of Government arrived at their decisions while they sat at the same big table. At times the President and some Heads of Government would precede the meeting *'en petit comité'* in order to solve the most difficult problems.

As earlier mentioned, the Seville European Council in June 2002 agreed on a number of important operational measures designed to improve the effectiveness of the European Council. Seville did not come too soon. Since the expansion to 27 Member States in many cases roughly 90 persons crowd around the meeting table: 27 Heads of Government, plus their Foreign Affairs Ministers and sometimes their Ministers for Finance, plus the President of the Commission and one or two of his Vice-Presidents, plus the Council Secretary-General cum High Representative for the Common Foreign and Security Policy and the Deputy Secretary-General of the Council. On a separate row sits the Secretary-General of the Commission, a very small number of senior Presidency, Commission and Council officials, and some technical staff. These numbers clearly exceed the maximum acceptable number of participants for joint deliberation and decision-making. As a result the Heads of Government no longer have the eye and voice contact required for negotiations. The crucial negotiations nowadays take place of necessity outside the main conference room and so outside the plenary meeting.

Seville (2002) was thus an important moment for the conduct of the meetings. Previously the President laid down the agenda items for discussion in his traditional letter to the Members of the Council, some days before the event. But one never knew whether Heads of Government would turn up with additional items. Often France and Germany together would put forward their own priorities shortly before the meeting. In addition, the President previously kept the draft Conclusions close to his chest. On the first day of the meeting he avoided discussing them. Not until the early morning of the second day would all delegations find the draft Conclusions of the Presidency slipped under the door of their hotel rooms. During the morning hours the meeting would then as a collective editorial board compose the final text. 'The final result was really a lottery with surprises. It was simply not professional', an insider claims.

Nowadays the adoption of the Conclusions is a much faster process. The General Affairs Council and in particular Coreper finalise the draft Conclusions in advance, except for some important remaining points. However this system also has shown up disadvantages. They boil down to the fact that in the national capitals all Ministers involved in the European Council and their top civil servants take part in the discussions. That results in a vaguer compromise text because everyone has to come on board. Previously, under the pressure of time and unhindered by experts, the Heads of Government in their closed final session sometimes came up with surprisingly creative or ambitious agreements in their Conclusions. The Specialised Councils had no option but to swallow and execute those agreements. Another disadvantage of the present working method is the threat of the return of the 'Christmas tree'. Twenty-seven national delegations each try to include their own priorities in the draft Conclusions. A shopping list of unattainable wishes threatens to be the result.

The European Council at present strongly experiences the so-called 'effet nombre', which is the negative effect of the tripling of the number of participants. From ten members initially (1975) the number has grown to 29 (27 national political leaders, plus the Commission President and the SG of the Council). A simple 'tour de table' with 29 participants today takes approximately three hours! Such a large gathering impedes decision-making in the plenary meeting concerning every issue requiring negotiations.

Little attention has been paid to the far-reaching influence of 'l'effet nombre' on the functioning of the European Council. Yet this is a serious problem which does not exist in the other Institutions. The European Parliament solves the problem in the Lisbon Treaty with a decrease of the maximum number of members (from 785 to 751). The number of seats in the Commission has, according to Article 213 TEC, been reduced to 20. Moreover, within the Commission there exists day-to-day coordination in order to bridge disagreements before they reach the plenary meeting. Putting a similar limit on the number of members of the European Council is politically unachievable and therefore impossible. As long as the European Council exists it must comprise as many members as the number of Member States. The conclusion is that the impact of the different enlargements on the character and the functioning of the European Council is serious.

In the Lisbon Treaty, neither the Ministers for Foreign Affairs nor the Ministers of Finance are mentioned in the articles regarding the European Council. This is in line with the historic aspiration of France to further strengthen the position of the Heads of State or Government (Chapter 1.A.1 and 1.B.2). According to Article 9b (3) TEU as amended by the Lisbon Treaty, the members of the European Council, when the agenda so requires, 'may decide each to be assisted by a minister and, in the case of the President of the Commission, a member of the Commission'. This opens the door to ending the traditional rivalry between the Ministers of Foreign Affairs and their EcoFin colleagues who traditionally both claim the right to participate. The Head of Government of every Member State will in the future decide which of his ministers will come along to the meeting. In practice, though, little will change. The Ministers for Foreign Affairs remain participants. But in so-called *'thematic meetings'* it becomes possible that the Heads of Government could be accompanied by, for instance, their Agriculture or Justice and Home Affairs Ministers.

The meeting really starts after the taking of the 'family photo'

Nowadays a meeting with an important complex compromise at stake runs as follows. The official opening around 17.00 hours is followed by the traditional speech of the President of the European Parliament and a brief session. After the taking of the 'family photo' the Members of the European Council and the Ministers for Foreign Affairs have separate working dinners. Dinner is now the only place where the Heads of State or Government are alone. According to the Commission Secretary-General Catherine Day this means the discussion there is more free and open. 'What often happens is that the Presidency introduces the subject, and then gives the floor to the President of the Commission. He sets out a scenario or an approach, and then the European Council has a discussion around that.' At meetings with a really important issue at stake the President and some Heads of Government break out of the dinner rather quickly. Groups or pairs of Heads of Government discuss their diverging priorities, often outside the meeting room, while the dinner conversations continue. Meanwhile the President begins his private consultations, bilateral and trilateral, later followed by the so-called *'confessionals'* (bilateral meetings between the Presidency and the principal protagonists) about the really important political issue on the agenda, which requires decision-making after tough negotiations. He begins with the Heads of Government whose agreement is vital. These will be the Member States which tabled objections during the preparation of the meeting. The plenary meeting frequently shows that when discussing a vital item on the agenda five to seven Member States, for example, have a pressing problem. In order to clear the last hurdles, the President summons the Head of Government of each obstructing Member State in turn. Each delegation has to specify its *minimum conditions* for an agreement. At the same time the President wants to know what concession each Government leader is prepared to make in return. Meeting face-to-face an obstructive PM is prepared to disclose his minimum position, but not in the plenary meeting. On the basis of this 'confessional' procedure, the President arrives at a final balanced proposal.

These consultations are followed by meetings in groups where the real decision-making takes place. The President of France, the Chancellor of Germany and the Prime Minister of the UK get fully involved there as does, depending on the subject, the President of the Commission. Often the leaders of the other larger Member States, Italy, Spain and Poland also get involved. All specific interests of the Member States are then taken into account by the President to the maximum extent possible, so that nobody can reject the final proposal for a compromise out of hand. That way the meeting gets very close to an agreement. In this manner the concept of a compromise develops gradually, destined for the plenary. Or it may become clear that the issue at stake as the most important item for the European Council cannot be solved this time. At this point the meeting has often lasted for two whole days and half a night or more. Under pressure of time (and lack of sleep) the Heads of Government often reach consensus during the small hours.

The meeting as described here runs along totally different lines than during the 1990s and before. In those days the negotiations largely took place during the plenary meeting. As a result of these developments the European Council nowadays convenes in plenary for much shorter periods than previously. Take as an example the important meeting of the European Council of December 2005 with the complex negotiations on the Union's Financial Perspectives for the period 2007-2013. This meeting was stretched over three days of haggling and waiting, number-juggling and arm-twisting. In reality the Heads of Government only met for about two hours in plenary.[12]

A further comment needs to be made on the course of meetings where a complex compromise is at stake. Before the meeting can be resumed in the early evening of the second day after a suspension, a night will pass and often part of the following day before definitive Conclusions are drawn up. For Heads of Government not directly involved with that process of negotiating in a small circle, being left out of the search for a compromise leads to irritation. Huge irritation at times. They sit waiting aimlessly for hours at a stretch. What then happens is that those members of the Council start consulting each other. Via various channels they try to discover what is happening in the closed room of the President. Sometimes they don't like what they are hearing. Then these outsiders try to influence the deliberations in the President's room their way, through bilaterals and trilaterals. This new formula governing the course of the meeting means that nowadays nobody has an overview of the entire negotiating process as soon as really important political problems present themselves. Not even the President of the European Council, even though he has of course the most complete picture.

The use of 'confessionals' as the ultimate means to an agreement raises new problems. During the (failed) meeting in June 2005 about the Financial Perspectives, for instance, various Heads of Government in the large group of smaller Member States complained that they were forced to give their opinion on a final compromise which had only been discussed with the largest Member States plus the Netherlands and Sweden (as major troublemakers). Partly for that reason Finland rejected the final compromise. 'Here we run into a new problem for the European Council arising from the fact that today no less than 27 Heads of Government sit around the table. A compromise born in a small grouping, will in future give rise to a new problem. How do I sell this compromise to the other Heads of Government?', noted Dutch Minister of Foreign Affairs Bernard Bot. At the same time European Council President Jean-Claude Juncker complained after the Brussels meeting that he had spent 65 hours talking in consultations with the Heads of Government.

The difference with the past (see photos on pp xviii and xix) is remarkable. In my previous study of 1992 I concluded as follows: 'In the small setting of the European Council, Heads of Government negotiate in a committed, and even undiplomatic, open way'. Initially the twelve Heads of Government and the President of the Commission sat around a table with nothing else in front of them but their file. Nowadays the meeting room is larger than a tennis court with the huge oval meeting table in the centre. The room is so large that each leader has a helpful flat-screen monitor in front of them, so they can see who is speaking on the far side. These monitors reveal however that eye contact and body language, both essential elements of tough negotiations, are absent. The oval table for the 28 Members of the Council is encircled by rows of tables and chairs for the Ministers for Foreign Affairs. This is an important break with the past. These Ministers for Foreign Affairs are often better informed about European details. However they are in some cases no longer seated next to their national political leader, but further back. Therefore they can no longer prompt their master. It has happened also that a Head of Government was unable to properly take part in the discussion because his own Minister of Foreign Affairs had failed to brief him properly (because of political rivalry). Belgian PM Wilfried Martens complains about that in his memoirs. The opposite also happens. Former British Foreign Secretary Geoffrey Howe complained about having had 'to spend more time on managing, informing or finessing Number 10 than on getting the whole rest of the world into line' (Howe, p. 7). Should an (exceptional) vote take place, the results appear on a screen in the same fashion as during the Eurovision Song Contest. This set-up of the meeting is in no way comparable with an informal gathering such as the European Council clearly was in the early days. 'In the former small informal setting the members of the European Council spoke their mind, but those days are gone' notes an insider at the Council. In other words in this new setting the course of the meetings has lost its former spontaneity. This is an important difference.

In addition the procedural requirements have changed beyond recognition. The official 'arrivée protocollaire', which nowadays would require at least one hour and a half due to the number of participants, has been abolished. Also abolished in 2004 was the three-decades-old 'tour de table', the opening round offering everyone a say which set the political tone of the meeting. 'Yet every Head of State or of Government would like to be given the floor at least once during such a meeting', reckons Hans Brunmayr, Head of Protocol and DG at the Council Secretariat.

A typical example of the course of the proceedings was the November 2004 European Council. Prior to the meeting nearly all of the comprehensive five-year plan 'The Hague Programme for Strengthening Freedom, Security and Justice in the European Union' had been prepared in detail by Coreper, agreed by the Council JHA and confirmed by the General Affairs Council, on the initiative of the Dutch Presidency.

Confessionals, bi- and trilateral meetings also characterised the meeting, held under the Presidency of Dutch PM Jan Peter Balkenende in December 2004, regarding the decision to start accession negotiations with Turkey. Three core items remained open for discussion and decision-making. They were the date to start entry talks, the potential outcome of such negotiations (with the option of not ending with full fledged accession) and finally the required recognition of the Republic of Cyprus. When matters came to a head, Turkey's PM Recep Tayyip Erdogan entered into the 'get the engines of my plane warmed up, I'm leaving' tactic. Then the Big Three, PM Blair, Chancellor Schröder, President Chirac and moreover, the two Member States with special interests in this case, Cyprus (President Tassos Papadopoulos) and Greece (PM Konstantinos Karamanlis), had to become involved. During meetings with Erdogan and his Minister for Foreign Affairs Abduallah Gül they salvaged the situation. The final negotiations were aimed at persuading Erdogan to accept an indirect recognition of Cyprus via the signature of an EU-Turkey Association Agreement. Here we see, moreover, how a non-European Council Member takes a full part in the negotiations. This fact made the outcome more obscure. It caused irritation among some Heads of Government who themselves had to wait for hours for the results.

Another example of this new-style conduct is how PM Silvio Berlusconi as President of the Brussels IGC in December 2003, with the Constitutional Treaty at stake after a night of haggling, closed the meeting before time, but with good reason. Berlusconi sensed perfectly that it was still too early for a compromise. Then look how in June 2004, after careful preparation Ireland's PM Bertie Ahern, as President surveyed the scene of his greatest political triumph, by leading two meetings to brilliant agreements, comprising both the Constitutional Treaty and the appointment of José Manuel Barroso as successor to Commission President Romano Prodi. The negotiations and decisions regarding these issues materialised outside the meeting room by way of a series of one-to-one confessional meetings between the Irish PM and his fellow Heads of Government. At the end of it, PM Ahern made up his mind and concluded there was enough support for his Portuguese collegue Barroso as new President of the Commission.

Observe further how Luxembourg's Prime Minister Jean-Claude Juncker came unstuck as President in June 2005. On the eve of the referendum in his country about the Constitutional Treaty Juncker attempted to force through a compromise on the Financial Perspectives 2007-2013 even though the deadline for decision-taking regarding this matter was not due until 2006. No wonder he failed. At the final press conference Juncker made an unusual attack on the troublemakers, his colleagues from the Netherlands and the UK. In the meeting Juncker had manipulated the sequence in which Heads of Government gave their opinions about his draft compromise. The French President and the German Chancellor had the immediate opportunity to give their fully disapproving reactions to the positions taken by Dutch PM Balkenende and UK PM Blair. After Balkenende had pronounced this to be 'totally unacceptable' he was followed in the same vein by Blair. Relations were soured and this also diminished the chance of an agreement under the subsequent Presidency of the UK.

Tony Blair, Juncker's successor as President, had to organise an extraordinary meeting on 27 October 2005 at Hampton Court (near London) in order to move away from the poisonous atmosphere that prevailed when talks broke down in June. Blair succeeded. He and French President Chirac, who were at daggers drawn at the foregoing meeting in June, worked closely at Hampton Court on the meeting's theme of how the Union should respond to globalisation (author's notes at Hampton Court). At the subsequent December 2005 meeting with the decision about the Financial

Perspectives 2007-2013, the crucial moments were two trilateral meetings (one just before the start and another just before the end) between Blair, Chancellor Angela Merkel and President Chirac.

In summary one can say that nowadays, in cases where an important and politically difficult problem is at stake, it is common that five or six Heads of Government largely decide on the course of the meeting. Those involved include the President plus the Head(s) of Government of the Member State(s) with special problems (the 'troublemakers'), the German Chancellor, the French President and often also the British Prime Minister. The composition of this group in other words varies as per meeting and per subject.

The role of the President of the Commission at this crucial moment of decision-making depends on the subject and on the room for manoeuvre the Commission is given by the Presidency. In the so-called 'confessional' formula as outlined earlier, the President of the Commission may sometimes play only an insignificant role. In other cases where issues are being negotiated that are of a very technical character and where there are sharp differences of opinion between the Heads of Government, the Commission is indispensable. During the final negotiations on the Financial Perspectives in the meeting in December 2005, for instance, it became clear to the Heads of Government that they would never succeed without the involvement of the Commissioner for Financial Programming and Budget, Dalia Grybauskaité, and her DG for Budgetary Affairs, Luis Romero Requena. Without the cooperation of these experts it was impossible in this very complicated matter to walk the last mile to the final deal. In contrast, during the more political discussion in the European Council about the renewal of the British rebate the Commission played a less important role.

Why the results of a meeting are always 'gloriously uncertain'

Now I will focus, finally, on some special elements of the European Council.

An interesting development is that nowadays more than before various Specialised Councils prefer to settle their own matters. They use the European Council as a kind of internal lever, or bogeyman. This way these Specialised Councils prevent the European Council encroaching on their decision-making.

Take for instance the EcoFin. For several years now that Council has sought to solve the most difficult problems itself. Often that happens under the pressure of deadlines, shortly before the meeting of the European Council. For that purpose the EcoFin usually holds a parallel session to discuss matters of urgency. After this meeting these Finance Ministers often join the European Council meeting for a session to take part in the discussion or the decision-making. By this means the EcoFin in 2004-2005 kept the politically sensitive violations by five of the twelve euro-area countries and the subsequent review of the Growth and Stability Pact away from the European Council. Jean-Claude Juncker claimed that as President of the EcoFin he threatened four times to refer the issue to the European Council, which the Ministers did not like at all.

In 1995 the EcoFin Ministers at the European Council meeting in Cannes rejected a proposal to install a group of 'Wise Men' under the guidance of the former French President Giscard d'Estaing. The group was to seek solutions for the problems, the timetable and other questions surrounding the preparation of the introduction of a European currency. The EcoFin preferred to keep that job in its own hands (*Bull* 6-1995, 1.11 and author's notes in Cannes).

A comparable development occurred in the Council of Ministers for Agriculture. Since the first meeting in 1975, the CAP has been a theme on the agenda of many European Council meetings. Ever since the arrival of two highly capable and influential Commissioners for Agriculture, Ray MacSharry (1989-1993) and Franz Fischler (1995-2004), the Agricultural Ministers have not accepted being bulled. The Agriculture Council takes careful note that the European Council does not take off with their dossier. The same applies to the Council for Justice and Home Affairs (JHA). Its 'Hague Programme for Freedom, Security and Justice' (Tampere II) was – unlike the earlier-mentioned Tampere Programme produced by the European Council of 1999 – the result of a series of informal and formal JHA Council meetings, held between June and November 2004 at the request of the European Council. The Programme was immediately confirmed in the European Council of November 2004. This is an interesting development: a Specialised Council taking the job off the hands of the 'higher' European Council!

Box 24

An example of 'Summit-fatigue'

Sometimes European Council meetings are held in a climate which the Germans call *'Gipfelmüdigkeit'*, or 'Summit-fatigue'. This was for instance the case in the Summer of 1990, which witnessed within the space of only two weeks a European Council in Dublin, a NATO Summit meeting in London and a Western Economic Summit in Houston, Texas. Four Member States' leaders had to attend all three of these meetings, which seriously overlapped not only in their participation but also in the subjects discussed (based on author's notes at coverage of these three Summits).

Sometimes the acting President employs the technique of 'blaming and shaming'. In 2004 an impasse was reached regarding the harmonisation of penalties for polluting ocean-going vessels. Agreement required unanimity in the Council of Ministers. The three Member States with the biggest fleets and the most polluting ships, Cyprus, Malta and Greece, obstructed. The Presidency could only solve this problem (via a compromise) by threatening the Heads of Government of the troublemakers with putting the matter on the agenda of the European Council. Malta, Cyprus and Greece were not amused. Their Government leaders would then be pilloried in the European Council, with all the negative publicity to boot. The three Heads of Government were keen to avoid that. So they keeled over and accepted a compromise of the Presidency before the European Council meeting.

In 1992 I concluded my study with a statement of Commission President Jacques Delors. He pointed out that the results of the meeting are always '*gloriously uncertain*' due to their highly political character. Nowadays a large part of what will happen in the meeting is fixed in advance. The items on the agenda offer less surprises than before the arrival of the Seville Rules of Procedure in 2002. But due to the above-mentioned disjointed course of the meeting and the doubling of the number of participants, the actual results nowadays are still as unpredictable as before without the Seville rules.

For years now the Heads of Government have taken the most important political initiatives. At every meeting they ask the Commission and the Specialised Councils to follow up case by case with suitable decisions, often with a deadline. Thus the Council has evolved from an *'instance d'appel'*, cutting through problems unsolved at a lower level, into an all powerful European Council. Today at every quarter the Heads of Government in their meetings keep tabs on progress and monitor the decision-making in the Institutions of the Union.

B.2.   The position of the future 'President of the European Union'

From a constitutional point of view the full-time, long-term President of the European Council will boast an unprecedented status. The President will be at the apex of the EU's political process. He will, moreover, be the external spokesman on the international political scene on behalf of the Union. In that capacity he has 'to ensure the external representation of the Union on issues concerning its common foreign and security policy' (Article 9b(6)(d) TEU as amended by the Lisbon Treaty). He will act on behalf of the 27 Member States. It is from their endorsement that the position of President will derive its democratic legitimacy. That is impressive. Compare that with the President of the Commission. When the latter speaks on behalf of the Union, he does so, from the constitutional perspective, on behalf of the citizens, insofar as they are European citizens. That is surely a nebulous concept (Van Middelaar, p. 138).

To the outside world the President will conjure up the image of being the EU's supreme authority, who oversees the work of the other Institutions. This image will encapsulate both the intent of the bigger and the fears of the smaller Member States. His 'image building' will happen both within the EU towards the political world and the citizenry and outside towards the rest of the political establishment. In summary: there are no prizes for guessing who of the two 'Presidents of the EU' will receive the warmest welcome at the White House. This would indeed be a new departure.

The 1979 reference by the Three Wise Men to the *dual role* of organisational control and political impetus of the President (at p. 35) is to date fully relevant. According to the academic literature the Presidency has to be carried out impartially, efficiently and effectively. It requires good knowledge of EU affairs (process expertise, content expertise) and political credibility. Another requirement for success as President is a good relationship with the Commission, Parliament and the Council Secretariat as well as with the Member States. Researchers (Schout and Vanhoonacker, p. 1052-1054; Quaglia and Moxon-Browne, p. 349-368) identify not only the requirement of political leadership but also of task-oriented leadership (taking the necessary steps to get the job done), group-oriented leadership (sounding out helpful positions, creating a good atmosphere and giving direction for a compromise) and finally transformational leadership (looking for long-term alternative compromises). These requirements will certainly be important for the long-term President since his or her term in office will be ten times longer than that of the six-monthly rotating President

The new President will manage the political agenda of the Union. Such a Presidency entails great political and organisational responsibilities. The President has the dual role of organisational control and political impetus. The package of tasks encompasses, besides the management and chairing of the diverse business of the regular European Council meetings and the representation of the Union abroad, a great many activities such as agenda-setting and agenda-manipulation (including raising the awareness of neglected problems), coordination, mediation in a Union with 27 Heads of State or Government all with their own national interests, brokering (sometimes in cooperation with the President of the Commission), taking political initiatives and providing the contact point for the Heads of State or Government and the President of the Commission. Prior to all meetings the President has to check the position of each Member State regarding every point on the agenda and visit the 27 capitals personally. According to two former General Secretaries of the Council of Ministers, Niels Ersbøll and Jürgen Trumpf (in Arnaud, p. 16), a President through debate, mediation and persuasion has to work with each of the Heads of Government in order to improve the chances of an agreement. The development of this highly personal process depends to a large extent on the style, the personality and the general attitude of the President. Such leadership 'concerns thinking through the consequences of proposals, finding new solutions and addressing short-term value problems in making the solutions feasible'. It requires 'thorough preparation, familiarisation with various national positions and frictions' and, moreover, 'understanding future trends and the capacity to convince other delegations to give up short-term stakes for wider EU interests' (quotes taken from Van Hoonacker, Schout, p. 5).

The unavoidable field of tension between the 'two Presidents of Europe'

Will the series of tasks of a long-term full-time President of the European Council interfere with the rather fragile institutional balance or power balance between the Council, the Commission and Parliament? And will there be incoherence between the Presidents of the European Council and of the Commission, whose areas of responsibilities will overlap? These are interesting questions which at the moment are difficult to answer. Nonetheless there are some observations which can be made.

In the future the European Council, the General Affairs Council created by the Treaty of Lisbon (separated from the Foreign Affairs Council) and the European Commission will all have a role in the preparation of decisions, decision-making and implementation of decisions, in short the management of the Union. In their joint analysis of 'the destruction of what could be called the *unity of the Presidency'*, three leading Brussels based think-tanks – CEPS, Egmont and EPC (p.46) – noted that in the future the Presidency would be split up into no fewer than five levels of somewhat unconnected responsibility, namely:

1.   The President of the European Council;

2.   the group of three Member States in the new eighteen-month Presidency-
        Team (see explanation under Annex 2);
3.   the Member State in the team holding the six-month Presidency;
4.   the High Representative for the CFSP, President of the Foreign Affairs
        Council;
5.   the President of the Eurogroup.

The Commission expects that this will 'create confusion as to how
responsibility is shared' (doc. COM(2003) 548, 14). This is particularly relevant because the President of the European Council, in addition to the task
of chairing the meetings, has amongst his tasks the organising of the
European Council's work. The General Affairs and External Relations
Council (GAERC), under the presidency of the High Representative for
Foreign Affairs (Article 9e (3) TEU as amended by the Lisbon Treaty), has
also to prepare and ensure the follow-up of the European Council meetings.
This happens 'in liaison with the President of the European Council and the
Commission' (Article 9c (6) TEU as amended by the Lisbon Treaty). It may
be unavoidable that this fragmentation of Presidencies will have a negative
effect on the *preparation* of the meetings and the *effectiveness* of the European
Council as an Institution of the Union.
    A comparison of the wording of Article 9b TEU and Article 9d (1) and (7) as
both amended by the Lisbon Treaty, shows that the new treaty reserves the
more prominent leadership function for the European Council. According to
Giscard d'Estaing, the President of the European Council will be a sort of
primus inter pares recognised and accepted by his peers, possessing indis-
putable political acumen and intellectual dexterity. Giscard put it thus: 'He
wouldn't have any direct authority over the others but he would certainly have
influence. The Commission President's profile is different. The role calls for
someone capable of making proposals, of giving impetus to a system and of
running the machinery, someone similar to what you might look for, actually,
in a prime minister' (interview with *Le Figaro*, 22 January 2003). The position of
the President of the European Council versus his colleague in the Commission
is in other words strongly influenced by his widely diverging brief.
    The President of the Commission in addition faces problems because expe-
rience shows that the management of this complicated Institution almost
requires witchcraft, given the involvement of 'representatives' from 27
Member States on all levels. Moreover the President of the Commission has to
find agreement with both the Heads of Government of all the Member States
and with the European Parliament. Both bodies like to blame the Commission
and its President for failures in the Union. The European Parliament sometimes saddles the President of the Commission with politically unobtainable
and therefore unrealistic tasks. At the same time the Heads of Government
claim the honour for successful projects. Since the departure of Jacques Delors
in 1995, his successors Jacques Santer, Romano Prodi and José-Manuel Barroso
(all three former members of the European Council) have had a rough time as
President of the Commission. The question is however whether *any* President
of the Commission, given the climate in which he must operate and the extensive package of difficult tasks which he must execute, could have performed
any better.
    In comparison with the President of the Commission the President of the

European Council will get an easier job. He does not have to justify himself anywhere other than in the European Council. Not even in Parliament. The only obligation towards the European Parliament is laid down in Article 4 TEU: the European Council shall submit to Parliament a report after each of its meetings. When examining the relative position of the two Presidents a distinction must, however, be made between on the one hand the First Pillar (Internal Market, EMU, CAP, etc.) and on the other hand the Second (CFSP) and the Third (JHA) Pillars. The First Pillar has been founded on the Community Method with the strong involvement of the Commission, Parliament and the Council of Ministers. In the Second and Third Pillars the Commission President is in a weak position because there the Community Method is largely lacking. In those two pillars the Member States take the initiative and it is they who give instructions to the Commission. In the Second and Third Pillar the President of the European Council will therefore certainly become most influential.[13]

Another notable aspect is the choice which the European Council itself will make in the future in selecting its own President and the President of the Commission. Will it choose a politically strong President for itself and a somewhat less robust Commission President? Or the reverse: a Council President who may be swayed by the European Council and a strong Commission President who will not be outwitted? The latter option does not seem probable. The larger Member States will aim for the appointment of a politically cast iron President of the European Council. That is appropriate for their strategy to direct the Union by means of the European Council.

Finally consider that Article 9b (5) TEU as amended by the Lisbon Treaty states that 'the European Council shall elect its President by a qualified majority'. In the rare cases where the European Council has to decide by a (qualified) majority, a smaller Member State has the same voting power as a larger. Does this mean that the large majority of smaller Member States gets a relatively heavy weight in the appointment of the President? Nominally, in such cases the larger Member States can easily be outvoted by the smaller ones. In practice the appointment of the permanent President will be steered beforehand by the larger Member States. Without the approval of the 'big boys' there will be no President. Even if the majority of the smaller Member States should put forward their own candidate, he himself would realise that he would be unable to function without the support of the 'big boys', let alone get reappointed. The permanent full-time President will have to be acceptable to the larger Member States.

It must moreover be noted that decision-making in the European Council is rarely or never a matter of large versus small but much more dependent on changing coalitions of larger and smaller Member States. Logic dictates that the President will ensure the maintenance of good contacts with – if at all possible – all Heads of Government in the Union. From this departure point he will consequently build a position of power as befits his function. If it is true that 'public relations, negotiations with governmental leaders, and the conceptualisation of new policy initiatives' are the main tasks of a Commission President (Endo, quoted by Dinan, p. 242), than these tasks should also fit perfectly into the job description of the new President of the European Council. Under pressure of the smaller Member States and the Commission, this President must in accordance with Article 9b (6b) TEU as amended by the Lisbon Treaty prepare the meetings 'in cooperation with the President of the Commission'. In spite of this, the permanent European Council President can greatly obstruct his Commission colleague – for example by taking political initiatives which are (or, will be) approved by the Heads of Government of especially the larger Member States. The series of tasks of the permanent President sketched out earlier in this chapter confirms that the President of the Commission will end up among the 'threatened species'.[14] At the same time, however, a discussion has meanwhile begun about the 'balance of power' between the two Presidents. The opinion that the two will (have to) find common ground was coming more to the fore at the time of writing.

An unknown element in the appraisal of the future power base of the permanent President of the European Council is whether he will be provided with a strong administrative apparatus. Will a sufficient budget be made available? The President can at any rate rely on the extensive resources of the General Secretariat of the Council. Its experts have a good understanding of the various aspects of the countless sensitive dossiers. The President will have full access to them.

All these elements together have certainly raised some important open questions of future constitutional practice. Much of the success of the new 'President of the European Union' will, moreover, depend on the ability of the first incumbent 'to exploit the considerable influence which the job could wield, and so gradually carve out a distinctive role which complements rather than competes with that of the President of the Commission', as two insiders in the negotiations for the Constitutional Treaty, Milton and Keller-Noëllet (p. 126), noted.

Nothing in the Lisbon Treaty prevents the President from establishing the necessary structures in order to bring his position in line with the requirements of his task: to deliver leadership at the highest level. An alternative line of development, however, could see the President's function modelled upon that of the Secretary-General of NATO: a very high ranking official who is strongly influenced by the largest Member States and who has a ready ear for all the Heads of Government. In that scenario however the intended reinforcement of the power of the European Council would fail to materialise. The current rotation system makes use every six months of the total dedication of yet another enthusiastic Head of Government as a fly-wheel. A Secretary-General-type of officer as President would lack political power. Such a type of officer is incapable of enforcing decisions in the way, for example, a German Chancellor or French President can do when acting as President of the Council. Behind the neutral text of the Lisbon Treaty there are indeed *two opposing concepts* of the long-term full-time President. Time alone will tell which concept will prevail, as it will also show how the relationship will develop between the newly-created President and both the Union's High Representative for Foreign Affairs and the rotating Presidency of the series of Specialised Councils.

B.3   The ingredients of a successful meeting – winners and losers in the European Council

The ingredients of a successful European Council meeting may be deduced from the preceding analysis. First of all, a President who can act as, and be seen moreover by the other Heads of Government to be, an independent mediator. Secondly thorough preparation is required, especially by the President. *'Un sommet réussi est par définition un sommet bien préparé'* (A successful Summit is by definition a well-prepared summit) according to former French Minister for European Affairs, Pierre Moscovici (in Marhold, p. 137). Third: the nucleus of a growing consensus, which should emerge during the course of the preparation of the meeting by way of productive pre-Summit contacts beforehand between the key players. Fourth: the absolute necessity to reach an agreement in accordance with the point of view (the interests) of the large majority of the Member States, in other words the pressure of a deadline.[15] Fifth: the absence of national domestic barriers or national elections, which limit the room for manoeuvre for participant Heads of Government. The sixth requirement is that the Presidency should have been able to reduce the number of points of difference to a mere handful during the important preparatory phase. Finally it helps under certain circumstances when the President can produce during the final hours from his inside pocket a carefully prepared 'shopping list' to win over the remaining trouble makers.

Box 25

The 'mad cow' Summits

Sometimes the entire apparatus of the European Union is dominated by a single event. The European Council also gets caught up in it. During the entire Spring of 1996 it seemed that all the Institutions in Brussels were exclusively concerned with BSE (mad cow disease). The 1996 Turin Spring meeting was totally overshadowed by the crisis resulting from the EU's worldwide ban on British beef because of the risk of BSE. UK Prime Minister Major, referring to the devastating effects on British agriculture, attacked this ban in Turin and asked for solidarity and financial aid. In May 1996 Major threatened to stop all consultation and meetings by the UK with the EU for as long as the export ban was not lifted. At the subsequent Florence meeting, the European Council endorsed a 'Mad Cow Pact' presented by the Commission for the eradication of BSE and the phasing-out of the embargo on British exports. The BSE crisis shows how an internal political problem in one of the Member States can completely spoil the atmosphere in the European Council and stagnate all decision-making on the other important items on the EU agenda.

The course of the meeting which took place in December 2005 concerning the Financial Perspectives 2007-2013, clearly demonstrates what takes place during an important European Council. As mentioned before, in such a large assembly it is no longer possible to negotiate in plenary. The encounters between acting President Blair, Chancellor Merkel and President Chirac were crucial to the outcome. At a given moment the Luxembourg PM Jean-Claude Juncker and Austrian Federal Chancellor Wolfgang Schüssel joined in. The former, as previous President of the Council, played a key role in the production of the agreement. The latter was the incoming President who had to lead the consultations over the Financial Perspectives with the European Parliament. This group made it clear to PM Blair that disaster loomed unless he agreed to accept a further significant reduction in the UK's rebate. Blair climbed down a peg or two. He offered a reduction of €2 billion, freeing the way for a general agreement.

As soon as matters come to a head, in other words, when Heads of Government defend their own national interests over a specific item on the agenda, a President is required who will act as independent mediator and trustworthy honest broker. That demands far-reaching skills and qualities. Such a President must dare to put the success of the European Council above his own narrow national interests. Take for example President François Mitterrand who in 1984 in Fontainebleau accepted reforms of the CAP which his rural population saw as a stab in the back. See further PM Tony Blair who, as I have just pointed out, at the final negotiations on the Union's budget for the years 2005-2013 had to give up part of the sacrosanct British rebate.

Traditionally the rule applies that a meeting with an overloaded agenda will not succeed. What leaders need to do in such a meeting is just take note of certain reports and concentrate on a few key themes. The management of the course of the meeting is exceptionally demanding now that the Council, even at its most restricted extent, numbers approximately thirty members. For this reason some Presidencies have experimented with the introduction of so-called lead speakers. Selected Heads of Government make presentations to the meeting, sometimes on behalf of a group of 'like minded' Member States, or because they have specialised interest or knowledge in a carefully delimited subject.

Take for instance the November 2004 meeting. The President sought to initiate discussions about economic reforms. These followed a strictly directed and detailed format. Three members of the European Council had been asked beforehand to speak. This 'subcommittee' within the Council started with a presentation by former Dutch PM Wim Kok, the Chairman of a High-Level Group advising the European Council regarding the Lisbon Strategy. In the same meeting Slovak PM Mikulas Dzurinda explained the new Member States' views on Lisbon. German Chancellor Gerhard Schröder then gave a presentation of the views of the 'old' Member States regarding the implementation of the Lisbon Strategy, and Finnish PM Matti Vanhanen outlined the (successful) experience of the Nordic States with economic reform. This approach by way of the leaders who had relevant expertise was fruitful. The Heads of Government of the new Member States told the other political leaders that their policy of a 'low tax economy' matched by a very low corporate tax would be a necessity for them. Such a result proves that, if well-prepared, a meeting of 27 Heads of Government can indeed result in a degree of consensus concerning a politically charged subject.

In Biarritz in 2000 President Chirac introduced for every participant a five minute speaking time limit. The introduction of such a general limitation (such as the one applying in the European Parliament) is impossible within a forum such as the Heads of State or Government. According to an expert in the conduct of the European Council it is not acceptable, for example, to limit the speaking time of the President of France in favour of the PM of, say, Portugal. The latter for instance spent a quarter of an hour making a speech which had little relevance to the meeting during the March 2007 European Council.

Franco-German cooperation as the cardinal point of the European Council

As outlined in Chapters 2 and 3, cooperation between France and Germany has constituted the driving force behind the European Council. This cooperation has continued during the whole long period of European Summit meetings and the European Council, with the exception only of the Brandt/Pompidou term (former Chancellor Helmut Schmidt, 1990, p. 163) in the early 1970s. It is based on closely knit personal bonds between the President of France and the Chancellor of Germany. However, can the Franco-German duo remain the pivot of decision-making? In 2004, with the appointment of a successor to Romano Prodi as President of the Commission, President Chirac and Chancellor Schröder suffered an awkward defeat. Their candidate, Belgian PM Guy Verhofstadt (member of the Alliance of Liberals and Democrats for Europe, ALDE) was faced with a very large group of Heads of Government in the European Council who came from the Christian Democratic and Conservative tradition (the EPP-EDD). They opposed his appointment (see 3.F.5). From approximately 2000 onwards British PM Blair (despite being the leader of the the social democratic Labour Party) began to exert a remarkable counterforce by solidly working in coalition with his centre-right Italian and Spanish colleagues Berlusconi and Aznar who shared his opinion on the necessity of more economic reforms. According to British newspapers, diplomats were calling it 'Blairlusconi' (*The Independent*, 16 March 2002 and *The Times*, 18 March 2002). As I have outlined, this trio had already attempted to put a spanner in the works of the Franco-German cooperation.

For a successful Franco-German duo a new requirement comes into the picture today. For decades the assent of France and Germany was required for an agreement in the First Pillar (EMU, internal market, Financial Perspectives, CAP, etc.) The other Heads of Government were therefore obliged to lobby via the Franco-German axis if they wanted a result. Meanwhile the focus of activities has increasingly moved to the Second Pillar (CFSP) and the Third Pillar with Justice and Home Affairs in particular. In the CFSP, besides the Franco-German axis, close cooperation is also required from the United Kingdom. In the Third Pillar a pre-agreement between France and Germany no longer guarantees an agreement with 27 Heads of Government around the table.

On the other hand there are current signs that Franco-German cooperation remains very important for the functioning of the European Council. An important requirement is a mutual liking between the German Chancellor and the President of France. Chancellor Merkel and President Sarkozy, although they have very different characters and political styles, seem to live up to this. For the rest it is remarkable that Commission President Barroso dares not take an important initiative without the prior (mostly tacit) consent of Paris and Berlin. In conclusion, the Franco-German pairing remains a very important driving factor within the European Council.

Apart from that it is a fact that each important agenda item creates ad hoc coalitions within the European Council. Bilateral and trilateral relationships within larger groups have always played a role. Logically the formation of coalitions depends hugely on the Member States' own interests and opinions. Take, for example, the December 2004 European Council. It promised Croatia accession negotiations under the strict condition of full cooperation with the International Criminal Tribunal for the former Yugoslavia. The moment Croatia failed to cooperate, the Council GAC postponed the start of entry negotiations. Immediately the formation of a coalition was seen within the European Council comprising Austria, Slovakia and Hungary as champions of the accession of Croatia. Accession negotiations with Croatia were ultimately opened on the same day as for Turkey, 3 October 2005.

A peculiar pattern to the results of the meetings

A peculiar pattern to the results of European Council meetings has been apparent to the author right from the start in 1975. After a successful meeting, the following meeting either tends to take on a more task-setting role, or else it is a failure, after which a third or fourth meeting in the chain once more is successful. And so it seems that the European Council operates without any 'grand design' and does not necessarily follow the precedent of the previous European Summit meetings (1957-1974) but instead adopts a rather *problem-by-problem* approach. For the really important issues one or more European Councils are always scheduled. Take for example the meeting held in Biarritz in the run-up to the agreement on a new treaty at Nice, less than two months later. Or take Noordwijk in 1997, two months before the Treaty of Amsterdam. That meeting led to the 'crystallisation' of opinions on a number of important issues, according to the President of the Commission, Jacques Santer. Noordwijk further produced a list of issues that might be stumbling blocks, according to the President of the European Council, Wim Kok (author's notes in Noordwijk). Or take the meeting at the Petersberg (Bonn) in 1998 held as the run-up to the Cologne meeting which resulted in Agenda 2000; the collapsed Brussels December 2003 meeting on the Constitutional Treaty followed by the successful Summer 2004 meeting; the failed June 2005 meeting on the Financial Perspectives 2007-2013 as a run-up to the subsequent successful Brussels December meeting.

Such an extra meeting offers the Presidency the opportunity to (a) work out what exactly should be done, (b) discover which Heads of Government are prepared to commit themselves to compromises, (c) create a general feeling following previous failures that after such long and agonising negotiations a deal becomes a necessity.

All the important agreements (for instance the creation of the EMS and later of EMU, enlargement, the agreement on a rebate for the UK in 1984, the Delors Package of 1988, the agreements on a calling of the IGCs of 1985 and 1990, the successful meeting in Maastricht in 1991, Agenda 2000) emerged from such a series of meetings. The extremely important negotiations every seven years about the future financing of the Union, the so-called Financial

Perspectives, concluded in Edinburgh in 1992, Berlin in 1999 and in Brussels in December 2005 following such a series of meetings.

Let us take as an example of a good functioning of the European Council the meeting in June 1998 in Cardiff, which was apparently not such a very important meeting. There a deadline of March 1999 was set for wrapping up the complex Financial Perspectives (Agenda 2000) package for 2000-2006. That decision put great pressure upon the several Specialised Councils and the Commission for the next nine months. And such was the pressure that finally an agreement was indeed reached in March 1999 in Berlin according to the schedule set down.

In addition to the cyclical character of the results of the meetings there is the fact that the President always calls 'his' meeting a success, even if this is untrue. Take for instance the IGC meeting in which the Treaty of Nice was set up. 'This meeting was long and difficult, but I said you'll see, this Summit will remain in the history of Europe as a great Summit by the scale and complexity of the problems involved', said President Chirac at 5.00 a.m. on Monday 11 December, at his final press conference in Nice. The meeting was generally regarded as a failure. The quotation is worth mentioning here because it confirms our experience that the President of every European Council always claims that 'his' meeting has succeeded whatever the evidence to the contrary.

The rhythm of success and failure of the meetings

This process-driven character of the European Council is of the utmost importance. The question of whether a meeting has succeeded, therefore, may not be judged entirely on a case-by-case basis, although this is always done. After each failure both politicians and media commonly over-react. Consider for instance the disastrous meeting in December 2003 with the Constitutional Treaty as the starting point. Along with Convention President Giscard d'Estaing, the Heads of Government pronounced at the conclusion of the meeting that the crisis would be long-lived. Leading European publications, as for example *Financial Times Deutschland* and the *Common Market Law Review* (2004/1), even predicted a deep political crisis.

Box 26

Letter to the Editor in The Times of 19 June 2007

Sir, the European Union suffers from one massive self-inflicted problem: the six-monthly summit. The host nation's leader always feels the need to have a 'successful' summit. That does not mean letting the EU tick over nicely, but taking some great new initiative – a treaty, a constitution, inevitably one that 'strengthens' the Union (i.e., takes more power away from its members). Get rid of the revolving presidency and the regular Summits, and you get rid of half the conflict that bedevils the institution.

ROBERT STONE, Worcester

But as with various previously 'failed' European Councils the Heads of Government went on to reach complete agreement in June 2004 following an 'intermediate Summit' in March 2004 which, according to the President, Irish PM Bertie Ahern, demonstrated 'a new willingness to compromise'. Exactly the same happened in 2005 with the failed attempt by the Luxembourg Presidency regarding the EU budget for 2007-2013. Juncker as President and other Heads of Government then saw 'a deep crisis'. Half a year later in December 2005 the European Council succeeded. Much earlier, in 1980, the Luxembourg Spring meeting, originally seen as a failure, may with the benefit of hindsight be cited as the key to the most important project of the European Council in the 1970s, namely the creation of the EMS, and that of the 1980s, the achievement of the Single Market by 1993.

The fact that the media totally fail to recognise the rhythm of success and failure of European Council meetings must be mentioned. Indeed, the Heads of Government also fail to recognise this rhythm and have mistakenly often judged a particular meeting as a 'historic failure' (or a 'resounding success') on its own. The history of the European Council is sometimes mystifying. An instance is the 1974 Paris meeting (described in Chapter 1.B.2.). Future scholars are likely to regard this Summit as the most significant one ever held. However, at the time, assessments were low key and were summarised by the headline 'Modest Summit in Paris: Something for Everybody'.[16]

Another example is the 1993 Copenhagen European Council. This meeting is today, as I have mentioned, generally regarded as very important. It set out the conditions for the accession of the countries of Central and Eastern Europe. In December 2002, again in Copenhagen, the European Council concluded the accession under the banner 'From Copenhagen to Copenhagen'. But when analysing news coverage of the 1993 meeting, one sees that 'Unemployment and the economic recession eclipsed all other items at Copenhagen', according to the Bulletin of the European Community. The meaning of this meeting escaped the European Parliament as well. The headline of the report in the 'EP European News' read significantly: 'Summit rights deck chairs on the Titanic'. The media all over Europe in 1993 told the same story regarding the meeting. But ten years later, the same media, the same Parliament and the same European Heads of Government elevated the 1993 Copenhagen meeting to the historic 'Enlargement Summit'.

Box 27

The most successful Summits and European Council meetings

A number of crucial decisions taken at Summits and European Council meetings mark the development of the Union. The meetings mentioned below can be considered the most successful. They deserve this designation because the decisions taken there are regarded as milestones, which determined the development of the European Union. While any selection is to some degree necessarily arbitrary and subjective, taken as a whole the list demonstrates that

continued on the next page

continued from the previous page

the European Council is the engine providing power for the process of European integration.

1. **The Hague, 1969.** Agreements on enlargement and reform of the CAP and financial resources; foundation of European Political Cooperation (EPC).
    Key players: Chancellor Willy Brandt and President Georges Pompidou.
2. **Paris, 1974.** Creation of the European Council; direct election of the EP and the setting-up of the European Regional Development Fund agreed.
    Key player: President Valéry Giscard d'Estaing, founder of the European Council.
3. **Bremen, 1978.** The creation of the European Monetary System.
    Key players: Chancellor Helmut Schmidt and President Giscard d'Estaing.
4. **Fontainebleau, 1984.** Budgetary agreement with the UK after a nine-year-long budgetary struggle which had almost incapacitated the EC; introduction of budgetary discipline, and an increase in the EC's own financial resources. Accession of Spain and Portugal.
    Key players: President François Mitterrand, PM Margaret Thatcher, and Chancellor Helmut Kohl as 'paymaster'.
5. **Milan, 1985.** Decision to rewrite the EEC Treaty by way of a majority vote.
    Key player: Italian PM Bettino Craxi as President of the meeting.
    The loser: British PM Margaret Thatcher, who had to accept the new treaty.
6. **Luxembourg, 1985.** The 'Single European Act' with majority-voting in the Council of Ministers and 'Project 1992': the completion of the Internal Market (with abolition of border posts). Foreign Policy, Monetary Policy and Environmental Policy become part of the Community's legal system.
7. **Brussels, 1988.** Delors I Package with financial resources until 1992; creation of an Agreement between the Institutions on the budgetary procedures; doubling of the Structural Aid; extension of the British rebate.
8. **Maastricht, 1991.** Historic meeting: Treaty on European Union (TEU) with Economic and Monetary Union (EMU) and a Common Foreign and Security Policy (CFSP).
    Key players: British PM John Major who succeeded in dropping the (for British people) dreaded term 'federalism' and received important opt-out clauses and, moreover, the President of the meeting Dutch PM Ruud Lubbers who bro-

continued on the next page

continued from the previous page

         kered 'the biggest milestone in the European Community's 34-
year history' (FT, 15 December 1991).

9.   **Edinburgh, 1992.** Financial Perspectives 1993-1999; creation
of the Cohesion Fund (Delors II Package); Denmark exempted
from key aims of Maastricht Treaty; start of entry negotiations
with Austria, Sweden and Finland.
Main winners: Spanish PM Felipe González (regional aid) and
Danish PM Poul Schlüter.

10.   **Berlin, 1999.** Agenda 2000 or Financial Perspectives 2000-2006;
a reform of the CAP and the Structural Funds, including aid for
the acceding countries. Creation of a European Defence
Community.
Key player: Chancellor Gerhard Schröder as President of the
meeting.

11.   **Nice, 2000.** Treaty of Nice, with the removal of the institu-
tional obstacles to enlargement. More votes for the larger
Member States in the Council, whereas they lose their second
Commission member.
The loser: President Jacques Chirac since the meeting was gen-
erally seen as 'a disaster for the Presidency'.

12.   **Brussels – Copenhagen, Autumn 2002.** Agreement on
enlargement with ten former communist Central and Eastern
European States, plus Malta and Cyprus.
Key players: Chancellor Gerhard Schröder, President Jacques
Chirac (brokers) and PM Anders Fogh Rasmussen as President.

13.   **Brussels, June 2004.** Constitutional Treaty that would
replace the older treaties.
Key player: Irish PM Bertie Ahern as President.

14.   **Brussels, June 2007.** Reform Treaty which replaced the
Constitutional Treaty.
Key players Chancellor Angela Merkel (President), newcomer
President Nicolas Sarkozy, old hand PM Jean-Claude Juncker
and Polish PM Jaroslaw Kaczynski. They brokered a deal
between the majority that had accepted the Constitutional
Treaty and a minority which could not accept it.

B.4.   The European Council as rescuer of the Community Method

Will Brussels get a French-style Elysée with the coming of a permanent
President of the European Council with his own offices, staff and spokesmen? Does reinforcement of the European Council indeed mean the end of
the Community Method as the Commission and the European Parliament
predict? Will the European Council be all-dominant? And if so, does that
matter? Will the European Commission and its largely unknown President
pale by contrast into insignificance?

During more than 50 years of European integration the question 'who wields the ultimate power?' has been the subject of battles. In the future, the full-time President will provide the Union with a recognisable supreme authority. Initially the highest point of reference was the High Authority of the European Coal and Steel Community and its successor, the European Commission. That was during the build up of the Single Market (from 1953 to roughly 1988). Thanks to increased political cooperation between the Member States' national leaders during the 1980s and 1990s, the European Council began to take over this role. Developments within the Union since 1975 have been inextricably linked to the position of the Heads of Government at the political centre of gravity.

Over the years the European Council has worked its way into the Union's decision-making process by *changing the institutional balance*: the position of the Commission, the Parliament and the Council of Ministers vis-à-vis each other. During the 1990s it took upon itself, apart from decision-making in most major areas, the preparation and even the monitoring of the execution of the major projects. In doing so the European Council offers coherence to the varying tasks and activities of the Union. The European Council is today the body which decides the agenda for the future shaping of the Union, as well as for the execution and supervision of the decisions taken. This takes place on an intergovernmental basis but – as we will show in the following paragraphs – is always tied into the Community Method of decision-making of the Union.

The European Council goes far beyond the tasks allocated to it by the treaties: 'to provide the Union with the necessary impetus and to define the general political guidelines'. In many areas it has absorbed competences and tasks of the Commission, the Council of Ministers and in some cases even the European Parliament. The European Council has undermined the right of initiative of the Commission. Another important aspect is the non-existent relationship with the Parliament. The European Council obstructs the Parliament in the full execution of its responsibilities. In 2006, for instance, it was generally observed that it was the German government led by Chancellor Angela Merkel which, behind the scenes, drafted the compromise for the survival of the politically very delicate Directive on Services in the European Parliament (Dana Spinant, Editor-in-chief, *European Voice*, 16-22 February 2006, p. 1 and many other press reports in that week). To sum up, the balance of power in the Union has been shifted towards the Member States by the European Council.

Extremely important now is the question whether this shift of power impacts negatively on the Community Method of decision-making. Is it true that 'if the new style president quits his national duties [as is the case in the Lisbon Treaty], this would mean the end of the Community Method and a triumph for the intergovernmental method'?[17]

By way of its regular meetings, the European Council allocates various tasks to the Council of Ministers. This method envisages that the national Ministers must arrive at an agreement (often with a deadline) regarding various Commission proposals. Should they fail, as is frequently the case, the European Council itself will take the necessary decisions. In its continual striving for the acceptance of its proposals, the Commission has therefore found a valuable partner in the European Council. This is an important aspect (and an important benefit) of the functioning of the European Council. From the previous chapters and observation of the current state of affairs in the Union, it can therefore be concluded that the European Council is a welcome, and indeed indispensable, *addition* to the Community Method. The results of the meetings as analysed in Chapter 3, show that the emergence of the European Council has improved the Community's decision-making process to a significant extent. (See also Chapter 1 for a detailed elaboration of the favourable difference in the decision-making process resulting from the arrival of the European Council.)

Since its creation the European Council has moreover brought to the EU a common political orientation framework. Under pressure from the European Council and thanks to the efforts of the Heads of Government the Community Method of decision-making now functions better.

The Lisbon Treaty stipulates that the European Council 'shall not exercise legislative functions' (Article 9b (1) TEU as amended by the Lisbon Treaty). That Article offers some clarity about the boundaries within which the European Council operates. This ban on exercising 'legislative functions' also contributes in my view to a confirmation of the Community Method.

Thorough preparation is, as has been said, the key to successful decision-making in the European Council. This means that the Institutions, especially the Council of Ministers with Coreper and the European Commission, play a very important role in the development of the activities of the European Council. Without detailed and thorough cooperation from the Council and the Commission, a European Council cannot succeed in breaking deadlock. See for instance the far-reaching Agenda 2000 agreed upon in 1999 in Berlin. No less than four preparatory European Councils were required. Meanwhile during all those months the various Councils (the General Affairs Council, EcoFin, Agriculture) negotiated intensely. Only on the basis of the Commission's large package of proposals, other intensive ground work carried out by the Commission and Coreper, and finally the progress made in the Specialised Councils, was the European Council able to go the 'last mile': arriving at a final agreement (and in so doing receiving the honours!). In other words, without a well-framed preparation along the lines of the Community Method, no successful decision-making can take place in the European Council.

Time and again approaches taken by the European Council have been based on initiatives originating from the European Commission and sometimes from the Parliament or the Council of Ministers. This fact confirms that the European Council is closely interwoven with the Union's institutional framework. In short it is untrue, as critics of the European Council persist in claiming, that this phenomenon undermines the legislative procedure based on the trio of the Commission, the Council and the European Parliament. On the contrary. Chapter 3 offers various examples showing that due to the emergence of the European Council a stronger Community Method has been developed. To sum up: the fact remains that the Community Method, as a phenomenon of an integrationist approach, and the European Council as an intergovernmental body whose functioning is mingled with the Commission and the Council of Ministers, supplement each other. One might conclude that the Heads of Government in 1975 with their creation of the European Council have saved the Community Method, which in those days had totally stagnated.

The European Council as a bridge to public opinion

Another element of importance is that the European Union is remote from the citizens. For the majority 'Europe', as it is understood by the Institutions and other insiders, might as well be on the Moon. The citizens do not understand the countless mechanisms and Institutions, neither the many procedural details nor the complexities of decision-making. That explains the rather poor interest of the media in the activities of the Commission and the European Parliament. The big exception is the European Council. During its more than thirty years in existence it has enjoyed permanent media attention. The Heads of Government with the President of the Commission function like a cabinet at a European level gathered around a large table where they deal with the big political issues in a more or less polemical fashion. This simple formula explains why the European Council is the organ of the Union which is best understood and followed via large media coverage by the general public. This characteristic is also of great importance for the integration process.

For more than thirty years the Heads of Government have in essential matters in the European Council never ignored their national interests in order to arrive at a common solution in their striving for European integration. These national political leaders operate here above party politics. In this way the Council has confirmed its role as a competent decision-taking body in matters which left the Council of Ministers and the Commission in stalemate. Nearly all the fundamental problems confronting the Union have passed via the European Council. As soon as a delicate matter arises, the Heads of Government deal with it. That suits the EU fine.

The Heads of Government regularly work with the President of the Commission to solve the biggest problem that faces the Union at any particular time. They then enter discussions in extended and exhausting (nighttime) sessions, sometimes a marathon. Thus does the disputed agenda point become an event in itself, partly due the vast media attention. The failure of such Summit meetings can have an enormous political impact. Therefore sometimes the Heads of Government accept any compromise at all – as for instance at Nice in 2000. This meeting produced the Treaty of Nice with which the EU now functions with few problems since the enlargement in 2004/2007 from 15 to 27 Member States. With the benefit of hindsight the storm of criticism over Nice, for example in the European Parliament, was exaggerated. The result of such a meeting tends to be whatever is most *politically feasible*. Thanks to the European Council, in other words, the EU usually gets what it wants, be that Monetary Union or enlargement or a reform of fundamental policies.

Endnotes

1   For a summary of the various underlying intentions of the Member States with the European Council, see Michalski and Heise, p. 8.

2   As already mentioned earlier, in this publication 'Heads of Government' stands for the whole membership of the European Council: the Heads of State or Government of the Member States of the Union plus the President of the Commission.

3   Six EU members, Austria, Denmark, Finland, Ireland, Portugal and Sweden, and all twelve

Candidate Member States with the exception of Poland and Romania; see Press Release EP 15 May 2003 and the reports by the Press Agencies AFP, DPA and Lusa of 16 May 2003.

4   For an analogous moot point, made by a very qualified observer, see Jean-Claude Piris, Director General of the Legal Service of the Council of the EU, o.c. 93 and 184.

5   Based on Norman, on the book of the vice-president of the Convention former PM of Belgium Jean-Luc Dehaene, that of French insider Alain Dauvergne and confirmed by my own reporting. British journalist Peter Norman wrote the definitive book on the Convention.

6   'In the Union nothing can be achieved without agreement of the bigger Member States. Therefore one should not get locked into the group of small countries. Moreover, as a Dutch politician I think one's preference should be the French-German or rather a French-German-British combination'. This post-Convention statement made by Van der Linden, mirrors the opinion of the Benelux countries. He explains why the smaller Member States could never win their fight against an upgrading of the European Council. When tensions ran high, their leader, the Benelux countries, favoured cooperation with the bigger neighbours. That was an important moment during the Convention.

7   For more details see Magnette and Nicolaïdis; Nugent 1996, p. 4; Lamassoure, p. 28; Peel.

8   Dinan, p. 289. The other quotes taken from Costa, Couvidat and Daloz, p. 121-134.

9   Quotes in this paragraph taken from Stephen Castle, *The Independent*, 1 July 2005, 20 September 2005, and FT, 13 October 2005, 12. See further 'We must get off the Euro-fence', leader in *The Observer*, 14 June 1998; *Die Zeit*, 15 December 2005 and the French newspaper *La Croix*, 19 December 2005. See also in Chapter 3.F.5 the disastrous May 1998 meeting.

10   Answer to a question by MEP Hutton, OJ Annex, Debates of the EP, 2-356/191, 14.10.87; see also question by MEP Lord O'Hagan, OJ C.310/4,10.12.79.

11   The Presidency only launched the discussion paper convention doc. CONV 477/03, followed by a plenary debate, see CONV 508/03, which yielded no clear conclusions. For a brief summary of how this question was rushed through the Convention, see Craig, p. 52-56.

12   The first day half an hour was dedicated to the President of Parliament followed by a meeting of about half an hour. The following day saw a plenary lunch lasting half an hour. The following morning saw the concluding night session of approximately half an hour during which everyone accepted acting President Tony Blair's compromise proposal.

13   It is worth noting that in the Lisbon Treaty the Third Pillar will also largely be functioning on the basis of the Community Method, in other words giving a stronger role to the Commission and its President.

14   For a contradictory opinion see Alan Dashwood and Angus Johnston, 'The Institutions of the enlarged EU under the regime of the Constitutional Treaty', CMLR, 2004, 1511, who see 'a certain degree of creative tension' as 'a healthy feature of the constitutional order'.

15   The meeting on 2-3 May 1998 (Chapter 3.F.5), had as a point of contention the appointment of the first President of the European Central Bank. It almost ended in a fiasco mainly because none of the three just-mentioned requirements had been satisfied.

16   *Time*, 23 December 1974, 8. Other typical headlines after the meeting on 12 December 1974: 'Le modeste succès de la réunion des Neuf est surtout dû à des concessions françaises' (The modest success of the meeting of the Nine is above all due to French concessions), *Le Monde*; 'Das Pariser Europa-Treffen lässt viele Fragen offen' (The European meeting in Paris leaves many problems unsolved), FAZ; 'Parijse top geen mislukking en geen overtuigend succes' (The Summit of Paris no failure but also no success), *Het Financieele Dagblad*. See for this paragraph also AE 9, 10, 11 and 12 December 1974 and Gazzo p. 34.

17   Editor-in-chief Ferdinando Riccardi of Agence Europe, before the negotiations in the Convention started, AE, 17 January 2003, p. 3. See also Rossi, 2

5. Conclusion and policy recommendations: the European Council beyond the 2009 horizon[1]

The European Council has been *'the source of all the major decisions taken over the past quarter of a century'*, Jacques Delors, longest-serving President of the European Commission (1985-1995).

Introduction

In this concluding chapter, a series of main conclusions is offered. A thread running through this work has been: 'Who leads the European Union after the unstoppable march of the European Council?' An important question is to what extent the European Council/Heads of Government (HSG) Council undermines the institutional balance: the relationship between the European Commission, the European Parliament and the Council of Ministers. What are the consequences for the Community Method in which these Institutions of the Union play the key roles?

Does the further upgrading of the European Council by means of the Constitutional Treaty and the subsequent Lisbon Treaty mean a frontal attack on the Community Method as is often supposed? Or does a reinforced European Council lead to reinforcing the Community Method rather than undermining it?

My conclusion is that the fear of the smaller Member States and of the supranationalists/federalists that the European Council would devalue the famous *'méthode communautaire'* was unfounded. The concept of involving the Heads of Government fully in the policy-making of the Community was already very much alive in France during the 1950s, but was forcefully opposed elsewhere. This French formula, as this study shows, has finally won the day. This concept will now be formalised in the Lisbon Treaty with the appointment of a permanent full-time President of the European Council.

This chapter will end with a number of policy recommendations. These apply mostly to decisions which the Heads of Government can take on their own initiative without changing the treaties, in order to improve the functioning of 'their' European Council.

The first question to answer is to what extent the Council has succeeded in its objective, laid down in Article 4 D of the Treaty on European Union, to 'provide the Union with the necessary impetus for its development' and to 'define the general political guidelines thereof'. Next there is the question regarding the functioning of the meeting as Intergovernmental Conference (IGC). Thirdly, what is the role and the significance of the European Council/HSG Council as executor of the Articles and Provisions laid down in the TEU? Do the larger Member States prevail in the European Council, as is presumed in the circle of the governments of the smaller Member States? How does the European Council operate in practice? Which are its greatest successes and biggest failures? What are the requirements for a successful meeting? How does the European Council fit into a future Union consisting of more than 27 states?

1. The European Council: a necessity

'The European Council is the Union's supreme political authority. It possesses a legitimate power of decision', once stated Javier Solana, High Representative and Secretary-General of the Council of the EU ('Preparing the Council for Enlargement', 11 March 2002). For a quarter of a century (especially since the 1984 Fontainebleau meeting) it has been the initiator and the highest decision-making body of the Union. By means of its general political guidelines, the European Council decides and controls the future development of the Union at the highest level every three months. More than thirty years of experience with the European Council show that the regular Summit meetings are the ideal forum to weave together into a single fabric the multiple needs of 27 Member States with mostly contradictory interests in and views on European integration.

By means of its arbitration the European Council regularly eliminates threatening obstructions. Examples of its enormous scope of activities are:

–   the review of the treaties in 1985, 1991, 1997, 2001, 2004 and 2007;
–   the complicated enlargement operations in 1981, 1986, 1995 and 2004 with a total of fifteen Member States;
–   the successful settlement of the financing of the Union in 1984, 1988, 1991, 1998 and 2005, since 1988 by way of the Financial Perspectives;
–   the launch, elaboration and realisation of the EMU;
–   the initiation of a significant body of secondary legislation.

Unaltered in its basic structure for fifty years the European Union has been based on four Institutions: the Council of Ministers, the European Commission, the European Parliament and the Court of Justice. From the beginning however this structure lacked an overall European political leadership. The European Council filled the void. The 'missing link' at the highest political level was a potent representation of the Member States in the complicated and multi-layered government of the Union. The European Union is neither a classical international organisation, nor a European State in *statu nascendi*. The foregoing analysis of 50 years of 'Summitry' in the EU confirms this. It shows that the countless Governmental bodies of the Member States and the Union's Institutions do not act autonomously but in common, day by day. The national governments play the key role in this process. Given the *'sui generis'* character of the Union as a mix of supranational and intergovernmental elements, the Heads of Government will also in future play an important role.

The process of the creation of the European Council in 1974 was guided by French President Valéry Giscard d'Estaing. Its creation was in many ways *a compromise* based on a package deal and a system of give and take. In order to overcome potential opposition, the Communiqué of the meeting in Paris announced the setting up of a European Council as a top intergovernmental organ managed by the governments of the Member States, and on the other hand the direct election of the European Parliament. The direct election of Parliament was in those days seen as a federalist (or supranational) countermove in order to compensate for the coming of the intergovernmental working European Council. The cooperation between President Valéry Giscard d'Estaing and Chancellor Helmut Schmidt here was of fundamental importance. Both men were sceptical about the capacity of the European Community Institutions to take responsibility in a crisis.

In 1974 the European Council had become a necessity due to a series of events and changes in the domestic, international, economic and Community environment.[2] Central to this development was the stagnation of the integration process in that era due to a crisis in decision-making. In the Council of Ministers the hammering out of every compromise, however unimportant, was the result of one or several night sessions. In 1974 crises had developed in the EEC and according to the European Commission 'the Community was not sufficiently equipped to cope with these (crises) properly' (*Gen Rep*, 1974, 1). Given this situation, the Commission lost all the dynamism that it ought to demonstrate as political initiator. Secondly, the larger Member States began to seek political consultation and decision-making at the highest level. Thirdly, the Community was disrupted in 1973 by successive monetary crises with the risk of dangerous currency devaluations, a rise of commodity prices (especially oil), restrictive trade measures, enormous inflation and negative political developments in the Middle East. The developments resulted in an economic slowdown and in growing domestic political problems within the Member States.

These issues resulted in a Community based on 'leaderless pluralism' (Drake, p. 259) which needed a solution by way of a more personalised role for the Heads of State or Government. It is only they who have the political power by way of a 'package deal' in an EU Summit Conference to reconcile their different domestic interests. Therefore a Council of Heads of Government meeting regularly became a necessity. It opened the way to 'make the best use of possibilities for cooperation between the nine Governments' (statement by the European Council, *Bull* 11-1976, 2501).

2. A 'Provisional European Government'

Chapters 2 and 3 set out the important achievement that was the introduction of the European Council: the foundation of a needed '*autorité européenne*' consisting of the highest representatives of the Member States. Jean Monnet called it in 1978 a 'Provisional European Government' (although dependent on the Member States of the Union). As the previous chapters show, the Member States never intended to establish any other type of European Government than one dependent on the Member States.

Since 1975 the European Council (including in its composition as Heads of State or Government Council, HSG Council) has acted as the highest policy and decision-making body and, indeed, as supreme arbitrator. Generally speaking, the European Council has developed itself as the *agenda-setter* of the Union, taking the major political initiatives. In practice, the European Council involves itself with every main issue and, if desired, with each detail of European integration. Besides its main tasks (to define the general political guidelines plus the principles of the Union's policies and the general guidelines of the Common Foreign and Security Policy) the Heads of Government[3] have for instance acted as the creator of Economic and Monetary Union. Since Maastricht (1993) they, moreover, have been involved in the important appointments in the Union. In this combination of roles the European Council may be seen to involve itself in what is known in French as a mixture of *'la politique'* (day by day power politics, where individual political careers are made) together with *'le politique'* (changing the nature of society through ideas on the basis of ideals) with the emphasis on the latter.

From an institutional point of view, Heads of State or Government are the most recognisable political leaders. Because the members of the European Council operate as a fraternal legislative cum executive body at the Union's highest level, a 'Provisional European Government' has indeed come to manifest itself. It has, besides its strategic and political guiding roles, a function as the Union's agenda-setter and highest political decision-maker. Its discussions are a combination of the Community Method – the classic structured decision-making debate based on the rules of the treaties – and bilateral talks between the Heads of Government. These talks are based on direct bargaining between the members of the Council as opposed to the much more formal negotiations with a more bureaucratic character which take place in the Council of Ministers.

Examining the authority which the European Council has, one only has to think of a hypothesis such as the following. Imagine the Union is faced with a sudden large threat which cannot be warded off by a single Member State and from which the US keeps itself aloof. Which Institution will be expected by everyone to jump into political action? The European Commission or the Council of Ministers? The High Representative Solana? Put another way, which body other than the European Council could have dealt so excellently with the politically risky fall of the Berlin Wall, followed by the unexpected process of German unification? Where else could the anger of PM Thatcher, the exasperation of PM Lubbers and the panic of President Mitterrand in the aftermath of 9 November 1989 have been soothed without causing serious damage? (Eijsbouts, p. 76-77).

The 'secret of success' of the European Council

What then is the 'secret of success' of the European Council? A very difficult question! Yet, something can be said. The European Council deals with problems which are deadlocked as the result of divisions between the Ministers for Foreign Affairs or for Finance or another Specialised Council. For this situation two scenarios exist. In the first one the Presidency threatens the Council of Ministers that the controversial question will be dealt with in the European Council. This scares the Ministers. By passing on a problem labelled 'insoluble', they would admit to being incompetent.

Moreover (not being allowed to participate in the European Council) these Ministers fear losing their grip on finding an appropriate solution to 'their' urgent problem. This threat scenario has frequently worked and forced the Ministers to find a compromise solution. The subsequent second scenario, which is also frequently applied, is to table the problem globally in the meeting of the European Council. This in some cases results in an immediate solution and in other cases the European Council offers some suggestions or reaches a 'political agreement' on main principles. On that basis the Specialised Council concerned can still look for an agreement, frequently after months of negotiations. This scenario has often worked well too.

Luxembourg PM Jean-Claude Juncker is the *'doyen'* of the European Council. Asked for his general opinion about its functioning, Juncker said that he misses depth in the debate in the European Council.

> 'The politically sensitive subjects the Heads of State speak about in this forum and on which they must sometimes decide, are often deliberately couched in woolly language. Subsequently often the Conclusions of the meeting do not reflect the genuine political priorities and therefore the required measures are not taken. The real problems are too frequently avoided. Moreover, the European Council gives innumerable tasks to the Commission. By means of reports and studies the latter must make proposals or look more closely into urgent questions. Per meeting one needs two cases to take all the Commission reports to the next meeting. But subsequently those reports hardly get talked about in the European Council. As a result, the follow-up stays out. Moreover, where the European Council has taken a decision, such decision in some cases is not carried out. This, however, does then not lead to a thorough discussion in the European Council'.

Another European Council insider nevertheless maintains that the countless reports for the preparation of each and every meeting mentioned by PM Juncker do get ample attention in Coreper, in the Council of Ministers and in Parliament.

A special function of the European Council is its close connection to *public opinion*. The Council operates in a way the citizen can recognise. The reason is that even apolitical citizens know the name of their Head of State or Government who plays a full part in the European Council meetings. The fact that the citizens are able to understand the Council is based on its simple structure: a round table conference of the highest political leaders. The media cover these meetings intensively. One of the major tasks facing all Heads of Government is the creation of an overall Union structure that the citizens can more or less understand. Only then will the problem of the lack of democratic legitimacy in the integration process be solved. 'States are perceived by their citizens as the natural ground on which to play democratic games' (Dashwood, 1998, p. 216). Their survival is likely to inhibit the development of a genuinely interesting game at the level of the Union's political leaders. Departing from that idea, a well functioning European Council will bring some legitimacy.

Most Heads of Government are (in some cases directly) elected politicians. Without exception they have a bond with the citizenry of their country. As the highest elected representatives of the Member States' peoples, they take their own collective initiatives, preparing and making decisions, coming together as an executive body. At the conclusion of every meeting each Head of Government gives an account in his parliament. Often there is also preparatory consultation in the national parliament before the meeting.

How the European Council has developed in stages

With the benefit of hindsight it can be seen that the European Council has developed in stages. Each decade brings a new phase. At the genesis of the European Council in 1974 the Heads of State or Government recognised in their communiqué 'the need for an overall approach to the internal problems involved in achieving European unity and the external problems facing Europe'. They therefore decided to meet 'three times a year and whenever necessary'. During the 1970s the European Council was, apart from the creation of the European Monetary System, important mainly as a forum for informal consultations. Nevertheless it was foreseen from the beginning that the European Council would also act as a decision-making body in the framework of the Council of Ministers. In order to facilitate the latter, the European Commission's participation in the meetings was not expressly laid down in so many words. In 1977 its function 'to produce decisions' (*Bull* 6-1977, 2.3.1) was confirmed. The problem-solving function of the European Council developed in the wake, primarily, of the Fontainebleau meeting in 1984.

1987 brought the second phase in the Council's development. Article 2 SEA set the European Council within the framework of the treaties. But only the composition 'the Heads of State or of Government of the Member States and the President of the Commission' and the number of meetings, 'at least twice a year', were laid down in the treaty.

In 1991 in Maastricht, with the Treaty on European Union (TEU), a 'pillar' structure was introduced. Then began the third phase of development of the European Council. Spanning the three pillars of the TEU is the European Council as the leading body. With the coming into force of the TEU in 1993, the European Council was no longer able to operate as a decision-making body in the framework of the Council of Ministers. Yet, various Articles of the TEU afforded the Council, as a decision-making body, the possibility 'to meet in the composition of the Heads of State or of Government' (HSG-Council).

The fourth phase began around the start of the new millennium. In the European Employment Pact of Cologne (1999) and, further, at the Lisbon Summit in 2000 the European Council quietly extended its authority. An important announcement was made in Lisbon: 'The entire process will be underpinned by the European Council taking on a pre-eminent guiding and co-ordinating role to ensure overall coherence and the effective monitoring of progress'. With this kind of jargon the European Council in Lisbon took the right to develop the policy lines away from the Commission which from now on acted as secretariat and coordinator of the Lisbon Strategy.

Until then one could claim that the European Council scarcely concerned itself with the implementation of its own decisions. In the Employment Pact and the Lisbon Strategy, the Heads of Government take responsibility not only for the preparation but also for the supervision of the implementation of their decisions. In so doing, while the Commission here is given an important role in orchestrating policy, the European Council nevertheless took the right to develop the policy lines away from the Commission. After the meeting in Lisbon it was said that the Heads of Government from now on wanted to be seen as being in charge of the whole spectrum of the Union's economic and social policies.

The next and possibly final phase will start if the Lisbon Treaty comes into force as expected in 2009. In this treaty the European Council is confirmed to be the highest authority of the Union vested with the task of taking crucial decisions. It foresees a long-standing full-time President who will 'prepare, chair and drive' the activities of the European Council (and so of the European Union), ensure its continuity and moreover represent the EU in the wider world. This means in practice that the permanent President will supervise an improved implementation of the decisions of the European Council. The twice-yearly rotating President hardly gets involved with that. The poor supervision of decisions taken is at present a weak element in the functioning of the European Council and does harm to its credibility. The Commission and the Council of Ministers, as has already become the case, will merely have to implement the decisions of the European Council in important areas such as EMU, the financing of the Union, JHA and the CFSP.

When it comes to the crunch the Heads of Government negotiate until the finish in the early hours. More than once (for instance in Maastricht 1991, Amsterdam 1997, Berlin 1999, Nice 2000, Brussels June 2004, December 2005, June 2007) we have seen the exhausted and visibly run-down Heads of Government limping from the 'arena' often between six and nine o'clock in the morning; entirely washed out by their efforts to reach an agreement. They have been eager to defend the results when faced with 'their' national media. Over a period of thirty years I know of no example of such an exhausting European Council meeting ending in failure. In Nice in 2000 they even took the very tough decision to allow Germany to have more power in decision-making in the Council than France or any other Member State. They do find a solution, always. The positive effect on European integration of this persistent and total dedication of the highest national political leaders, time and time again, can hardly be overestimated.

3. How the European Council changed the Institutional balance

'Contrary to expectations, shortly after its emergence the European Council worked its way into the Community's decision-making process without deeply undermining the institutional balance: the position of the Commission, the Parliament, and the Council', I concluded in my earlier work in 1992. That conclusion has with the passage of time become untenable.

The European Council has since then worked its way into the Union's decision-making process by undermining the institutional balance: the position of the Commission, the Parliament and the Council. It has modified the role of these Institutions and changed essential parts of their tasks. The famous 'méthode communautaire', of giving autonomous and direct competence to the Institutions of the Community, has been, for many important decisions, sup-

plemented by a system based on cooperation between Member States 'prepared to exercise their sovereignty in a progressively convergent manner'
through the European Council (statement European Council, *Bull* 11-1976,
2501). The original classic, triangular development of legislation, i.e. a proposal
by the Commission, an opinion by the Parliament and a final decision in the
Council of Ministers has, as analysed in Chapters 2 and 3, been changed.

The European Council has itself taken the initiative on a number of key
issues which, according to the text of the treaties, should be done by the
Commission. It is customary for the European Council at each meeting to
ask the Commission to present proposals or develop certain issues and projects. This undermines the independent position of the Commission as
described in the treaties. In this approach, the Commission loses to the
European Council its role of honest broker or 'institutionalised mediator'
between the Member States. The European Council moreover sometimes
prepares the process of decision-making, originally done by the
Commission and the Council of Ministers, and subsequently takes the crucial political decisions which, according to the treaties, should be done by
the Council and the Commission. Commission President Barroso has
emphasised 'a real danger of seeing Governments settling the problems
among themselves, without taking into account the opinion of the
Institutions' (interview by Bernard Bulcke, Belgium daily *De Standaard*, 6
October 2007, my translation). To summarise, due to the development of the
European Council, the European Commission may no longer be seen as the
embryo of a future Government of Europe.

Next let us look at the Parliament. No productive relationship has been
established between the European Council and Parliament. The European
Council's activities are not controlled by Parliament. It is the only one of the
three Institutions which, though deeply involved in the legislative procedure, does not attend the European Council meetings. By laying down the
limits of the budget (the so-called Financial Perspectives), which in practice
hardly gives Parliament opportunities to intervene (see Chapter 3.D), the
European Council has curtailed Parliament as the budget authority.

In the relationship between the European Council and the European
Parliament there has not been much progress other than (since 1981) the
speech of the President of the Parliament at the start of each Council meeting and the verbal report of the Council President to the plenary after every
meeting in Strasbourg (since 1987). The European Council vis-à-vis
Parliament moreover operates entirely on its own conditions. That leaves
the Parliament in a weak position.

Finally there is the Council of Ministers. By way of its regular meetings,
the European Council gives various tasks to the Council of Ministers. They
boil down to the fact that the national Ministers must arrive at an agreement
(often with a deadline) regarding various Commission proposals. The
Council duly obeys. In so doing, the European Council has eroded the position of the Council of Ministers as decision-maker of last resort. In 1974
when the European Council was created, the Heads of Government gave the
Ministers for Foreign Affairs (nowadays the General Affairs and External
Relations Council GAERC) the role 'to act as initiators and coordina-

tors'(…), 'in order to ensure consistency in Community activities and continuity of work'. It is curious that those Ministers went on to neglect that task.
The conclusion is that as a result of the arrival of the European Council, the
Council of Ministers has lost its key political role. The real political debates
no longer take place there.

Finally it is noteworthy that the ascent of the European Council, over the
years absorbing important tasks of the Commission, Parliament and
Council, could take place without a prior inter-institutional discussion. To
summarise, the important institutional balance in the Union has been
shifted towards the Member States by the European Council.

4. Why the larger Member States do not entirely dominate the European Council

The question remains to be answered whether the larger Member States
entirely dominate the regular meetings of the European Council. Is the
European Council for these Member States an instrument to try and fix
Union business their way?

In the European Council, unsurprisingly, there is a 'pecking order' that
influences the results of its meetings. In 1992 the present author reached the
conclusion that 'the European Council meetings held under the Presidency
of a smaller Member State have proved to have less chance of resulting in an
important agreement or a break-through than the meetings organised under
the leadership of the FRG or France'. At that time I concluded that 'Summit
and European Council meetings held in France never miscarried'.

It is remarkable to note that this has changed since around 1995. The
Heads of Government of smaller Member States such as Finland (excellent
Presidency in 1999), Denmark (similarly with the enlargement in 2002) and
also Belgium (2001) and Ireland (2004), both with a key role in the negotiations for the Constitutional Treaty, have meanwhile played a leading role.
The Netherlands (2004) and Portugal (2007) did the same as President. Since
1995 some larger Member States on the other hand have offered poor leadership. Jacques Chirac did not cover himself in glory in 1995 and 2000 on
behalf of the French Republic. For the UK, another big Member State, 'arrogance - incompetence - spin' (see Chapter 4.A.2.) were words used to
describe its Presidency in 1998. Italy in 2003 (following the failed December
IGC meeting) is another example. The claim that the European Council must
have a full-time President because the PMs of the smaller Member States can
no longer cope with these situations is therefore wrong.

None of this should be misinterpreted however. The prominent role
which some PMs of smaller Member States have displayed in the Presidency
does not diminish the fact that, according to the longest-standing current
member of the European Council, Luxembourg PM Jean-Claude Juncker,
larger Member States have more influence. 'We never acknowledge it but
one has to agree that geography, economics and demographics are playing
an important role'. In other words the European Council 'is by definition
dominated by the Heads of Government of the larger members' (Pijpers, p.
11), with Germany and France in the key role. This was confirmed in the
important meetings of Fontainebleau in 1984 (the end of a nine-year budgetary struggle with the UK), in October 2002 (at the extremely important

Council concerning the future financing of the Common Agricultural Policy), in December 2003 (the collapse of the Intergovernmental Conference negotiations), December 2004 (the opening of accession talks with Turkey), December 2005 (the agreement on the Financial Perspectives 2007-2013) and in the meetings of 2007 (agreement on the Lisbon Treaty). At the moment when such important Councils are threatened with ending in stalemate, the Presidency forms an 'inner circle' with the 'Big Three' – the German Chancellor, the President of France and the Prime Minister of the United Kingdom – in order to come up with a solution.

The creation of the aforementioned 'inner circle' in order to draft the final deal together with the President should in my view, despite the fears of the smaller Member States, not be seen as proof of the coming of a 'Political Directorate' of three or more of the largest States who would control decision-making. Such a three-way permanent 'Political Directorate' has failed to emerge partly because managing a triangular relationship is much more difficult than managing a bilateral one.[4] Even more important is that the interests of the larger Member States in most cases are not in line with each other. The prominent role of the Governmental leaders of the 'Big Brothers' does not mean that the smaller Member States are subordinate to them. The European Council sanctioned the principle of equality of the larger and smaller Member States, which is such an important principle for the development of the Union. That is confirmed by our research into the 130 meetings since 1957. Finally it is worth mentioning that since the emergence of the European Council, for three decades, none of the smaller Member States has ever complained about its role.

The question remains as to what is the cause of the stronger role of the smaller Member States as President, since the beginning of the 1990s. The answer is elusive. At least two factors have changed the picture. One important element was certainly the notably diminished interest in European Union affairs shown by the leaders of France (Jacques Chirac) and Germany (Chancellor Gerhard Schröder) in comparison with their predecessors Mitterrand and Kohl. Confident of his top-dog status, Schröder failed to conceal his boredom at many Summits, slipping outside to smoke cigars. Chirac could be bulldozer-like in pursuing his own national demands; at the same time he seemed on occasion to prefer conversation with beautiful young women in the margin of the meeting. The presence of British PM Tony Blair was not always very helpful either. Blair often left his officials ashen-faced by conceding small points in pursuit of what he considered the big picture, according to *The Economist* (23 June 2007, p. 36).

5. The European Council to the rescue of the Community Method

During more than 50 years of European integration the question 'who wields the ultimate power?' has been the subject of battles. A future European Council with a full-time long-term President with his own offices and staff in Brussels will provide the Union with a recognisable highest power centre. Does such a reinforcement of the Council indeed mean an alteration of the famous Community Method, the cornerstone of decision-making in the Union, to the advantage of the Intergovernmental Method as the Commission, the European Parliament and most smaller Member States expect? Will the European Council in other words become all-dominant? And if so, does that matter? Will the European Commission and its comparatively unknown President in comparison pale into insignificance? Is it true that a full-time permanent President means the end of the Community Method and a triumph for the Intergovernmental Method?

Opening the conflict between the larger and the smaller Member States in the Convention on the Future of Europe was the fundamental question of whether the Union relies on an intergovernmental or a Community structure. Taking the former approach, the interests of each of the Member States comes to the fore. In the supranational structure, the overall interest of the Union as such has a greater sway. In the latter approach the negotiating process takes place by way of the Community Method in the so-called institutional triangle consisting of the Commission, the Parliament and the Council, whilst in the first formula the European Council is the highest authority of the Union. Most smaller Member States favour the Community Method because they expect it to offer them the opportunity to exercise more influence (particularly via the European Commission).

The European Council is today the centre which decides the agenda for the future shaping of the course of action of the Union, plus (as described in more detail in Chapter 3 in particular) sometimes the decision-making, the execution and supervision of the implementation. This takes place intergovernmentally but – as we will show in the forthcoming paragraphs – with a strong connection with the Community Method of decision-making. In this way the Heads of Government certainly play a key role in the intensive process of 'Europeanisation' in which significant national actors 'create an irreversible process of pooling and merging policy instruments' with 'checks and balances between national and EU Institutions in preparing, making, implementing and controlling binding decisions' (Mittag and Wessels, p. 446).

It is my belief that the structure of the Lisbon Treaty will assist the European Council to sidestep its handicap of not being legally the decision-making body since it will be able to present its agreement on an issue as a *political accord*. For shortly after the meeting follows the legally binding decision-making through the interplay of Commission, Parliament and Council as laid down in the treaties. It remains remarkable that this way of operating has been *common practice* since the emergence of the European Council in 1974, although it is not foreseen in the treaties.

The Commission has never protested against the European Council assuming such powers. Its underlying motivation in treading warily with the European Council may be that in alliance its proposals enjoy the support of the highest political leaders of the Member States. In its continual striving for acceptance of its proposals, the Commission has found a valuable partner in the European Council. Thanks to its emergence, the Heads of Government have delved into the complicated technical details of policy-making and decision-making, which they might otherwise not have done. The fact that these Heads of Government direct the Council of Ministers each quarter to settle certain Commission proposals reinforces the position of the Commission.

As mentioned above, an American researcher (Johnston, p. 132-133) put it clearly: 'While the Commission became more politically competent, the

European Council became more technocratically competent'. Her experience is in accordance with mine in covering the meetings since 1974. In conclusion, the Heads of Government with their far-reaching 'meddling' have in the end reinforced the role of the Commission in the entirety of the Union's activities. Seen from the outside, it can even seem as if the two bodies today form a tandem. A tandem with, to mix a metaphor, the Commission clearly playing second fiddle. This is an important aspect, and an important benefit, of the functioning of the European Council. It can therefore be concluded that the European Council is a welcome and indeed *indispensable addition* to the Community Method. Under pressure from the European Council and thanks to the efforts of the Heads of Government, the Community Method of decision-making now functions better.

A second vital element, which underpins this conclusion, is the importance of *thorough preparation* as essential to successful decision-making in the European Council. This means that the Institutions, especially the Council of Ministers with Coreper and the European Commission, play a very important role in the development of the activities of the European Council. Without detailed and thorough cooperation from the Council and the Commission, no European Council can succeed in breaking through deadlock. Only on the basis of the Commission's proposals, other preparatory activities of the Commission and Coreper, and finally the progress made in the Specialised Councils is the European Council able to go the 'last mile': arriving at a final agreement (and in so doing so receiving the honours). In other words, without efficient preparation based upon the Community Method, no successful decision-making will take place in the European Council.

In short it is untrue, as critics of the European Council would claim, that this phenomenon undermines the legislative procedure based on the relationship between the Commission, Council and European Parliament. On the contrary. Chapters 2 and 3 offer various examples of where a stronger Community Method has been developed due to the emergence of the European Council. The Community Method, in other words the integrationist approach, and the European Council as an intergovernmental body supplement each other. The danger, as set out thirty years ago in the famous Report of the 'Three Wise Men', that the European Council would represent a weaker form of commitment of the Member States which would undermine the institutional development of the Union, has not materialised. It might be said, to the contrary, that the Heads of Government in 1974 by creating the European Council have saved the Community Method, which was at that time in danger of stagnation.

6. How the French concept of European integration won the day

The European Council had its origins some fifty years ago even though it was only officially launched in 1974. It was in 1953 that the French Gaullist Michel Debré, in the Constitutional Commission of the Assembly of the European Coal and Steel Community, unsuccessfully proposed the idea of a purely intergovernmental Political Union, with a Conference of the Heads of Government. Debré followed the approach of the future President of France, General Charles de Gaulle. Six years later, in 1959, Michel Debré as new French

Prime Minister declared it to be France's policy to have regular consultations between Heads of Government of the Member States. The French never abandoned this idea. The phenomenon of intergovernmental cooperation, eliminating the original supranational character of the European treaties, was later to reappear time and again. President de Gaulle was, as described earlier, undoubtedly the most important initiator of periodical Summit meetings. Surprisingly, the federalist Jean Monnet (as detailed in Chapter 1) emerged with President Valéry Giscard d'Estaing and Chancellor Helmut Schmidt as one of the so called 'fathers' of the European Council. It was always at the initiative of France that the leaders of the Member States of the European Economic Community (EEC) and Euratom met whenever the need arose between 1957 and 1974. They clocked up eight Summit meetings.

In 1974 President Giscard d'Estaing with the creation of the European Council imposed upon the Union a structure which relies heavily on French thinking about Europe since the early days of striving for European integration. In the Convention and the IGC of 2003-2004, at Giscard's insistence the European Council was further upgraded through the installation of a full-time President with his own administrative apparatus. Seventeen smaller Member States together with the European Commission and the European Parliament were squarely against this. Chapter 4 shows why they lost that battle.

The upgrading of the European Council in the defunct Constitutional Treaty, later reproduced word for word in the Lisbon Treaty, serves as an example of how the French always pushed their governmental model, featuring the Heads of Government in the leading role. The Lisbon Treaty will turn the European Council into an official Institution of the Union, with a permanent President. Here the European Council is, by way of a reform of the TEU, confirmed as being at the centre of power in the Union. One should not forget that this upgrading came into being at the insistence of the same Giscard d'Estaing who in 1974 as President of France had launched the European Council. In the new structure, the European Council as a Conference of the Heads of Government, as initially proposed by Debré in 1953, decides on the entire policy. As soon as the upgrading of the European Council as laid down in the Lisbon Treaty becomes effective, the French ideas of fifty years ago will have been completely achieved.

7. The ingredients of a successful meeting – why European Council meetings generally succeed

Chapter 3 gave an analysis of the most important successes and failures of the European Council. In short, it boils down to the fact that the Heads of Government did not operate very successfully when a reform of the Union's Institutions and their functioning was on the table. A clear example is the Constitutional Treaty, from 2005 until 2007 in abeyance after the negative referenda in France and the Netherlands. Six times (in 1985, 1991, 1997, 2000, 2004 and 2007) in the guise of an Intergovernmental conference (IGC) the Heads of State or Government reviewed the institutional structure. Only once were expectations satisfied, namely in 1991 by the successful conclusion of the Treaty of Maastricht (TEU). How this can be explained has been described under Chapter 3.

Since the TEU came into force in 1993, the European Council has been the executor of three new core tasks of the Union: EMU, the CFSP and the Third Pillar (in other words the activities regarding Justice and Home Affairs such as asylum, terrorism and judicial cooperation).

Let us consider first Economic and Monetary Union. Has the European Council made a good job of *shaping EMU*? During the 1990s and afterwards, the Council discussed the progress of this project at nearly every meeting. Under the terms of the TEU the European Council had to take numerous difficult, politically far-reaching and technically complex decisions in the run-up towards the creation of EMU. An extra complication was that four Member States did not accept EMU. The meeting in Dublin in 1996 achieved a compromise on the difficult subject of a Stability and Growth Pact. On 2 May 1998 the Heads of Government decided that eleven Member States would introduce the single currency system on 1 January 1999. The long march towards the accomplishment of Economic and Monetary Union passed off exactly according to the timetable set in Maastricht in 1991. It should be acknowledged that the EcoFin, together with the Commissioner for Economic and Monetary Affairs, played a key role in this process. Nevertheless this is a fine example of the successful operating of the Heads of Government. This success is particularly significant because EMU meant the end of national currencies and an attack on the sovereignty of the Member States.

Another success was the European Council's decision-making on the subject of *enlargement*. Before each enlargement the European Council laid down in concrete terms the criteria for accession. In 1992 in Edinburgh the decision was taken to open negotiations with Austria, Sweden and Finland. In 1993 in Copenhagen the foundation was laid for a new wave of accessions, now with the associated countries of Central and Eastern Europe. The Essen 1994 meeting saw the first arrival of the Heads of Government of the acceding countries (Austria, Finland and Sweden) and, for part of the proceedings, of the six associated States: Bulgaria, the Czech Republic, Hungary, Poland, Romania and Slovakia.

It was very important for the Union to restructure its own working methods and policies, ahead of the conclusion of negotiations with the twelve applicant States (besides the six just mentioned: Cyprus, Malta, Estonia, Latvia, Lithuania and Slovenia). In October 2002 in Brussels the European Council agreed upon the conditions that would be applied to the ten future Member States regarding the CAP. A limit on expenditure for the CAP in general had become an important obstacle to enlargement. A pre-accord in the Brussels Conrad Hotel concluded by Chancellor Schröder and President Chirac, just before the start of the European Council, established a foundation for a general agreement. For the umpteenth time Franco-German collaboration had protected the European Council from failure. At the subsequent meeting in Copenhagen in December 2002, the Council sealed an historic deal with the ten candidates. The successful enlargement process achieved by the European Council equalled the complicated creation of the euro/EMU. In both cases the European Council cut through obstacles that had built up over a period of roughly twelve years.

Another task, which the European Council has carried out admirably for three decades since 1975, is the consensual adoption of the multiannual *financial framework*. In the early 1980s a fierce budget struggle raged in the European Council, following the demands of the UK's then PM Margaret

Thatcher. This debate resulted in 1984 at Fontainebleau in a permanent rebate. Time and again since then the European Council has managed to produce an acceptable compromise by way of a complex package under the slogan 'no losers, only winners'. This operation 'Financial Perspectives' was kicked-off in 1988. It was repeated in Edinburgh in 1992. In 1999 in Berlin it came through a comprehensive package called Agenda 2000, which the European Council completed perfectly under the guidance of Chancellor Schröder. In 2005 the Council succeeded in Brussels yet again, this time with considerably more effort and political fuss, to produce a budget for the years 2007-2013.

A look back on somewhat less fruitfully executed activities

Not so successful has been the *Common Foreign and Security Policy*, the CFSP. This is because Member States have diverse perceptions as regards their foreign policy interests. In a Union of 27 Member States, with the requirement of unanimity, there is bound to be problematic decision-making. A second handicap is the lack of leadership within the 27 Member States. France and the UK, both permanent members of the UN Security Council, and Germany, politically and economically the most important EU member, can offer that leadership jointly. But these three rather tend to nurture their own divergent opinions and interests. Under these circumstances, the European Council can gain little credit from the CFSP.

Also less successful have been, moreover, the large projects decided upon in 1993 and, again, in 2000 for *employment, economic reform and social and environmental renewal*. In 1993 Commission President Jacques Delors, at the invitation of the European Council, presented a White Paper on the fight against unemployment and economic stagnation. Hardly anything has come of these detailed proposals. It is noteworthy that during the 1990s most governmental leaders considered the realisation of the Maastricht criteria for accession to EMU as being more important than the Keynesian policy of the European Commission.

In 2000 Europe once again was experiencing economic restraint. At that time the European Council decided in Lisbon after scant discussion that the EU would in 2010 'become the most competitive and dynamic knowledge-based economy in the world'. The programme aimed at halving the unemployment rate in the EU, involved far-reaching reforms of labour markets, social welfare systems, business regulation and pensions. Five years later in 2005 the European Council was forced to admit to having aimed too high. The Lisbon Strategy was replaced by some more limited goals. The big advantage of the Lisbon Strategy was that the European Council put globalisation squarely on the table as the most important problem and the biggest challenge facing the Union. The Heads of Government cannot be blamed exclusively for the lack of immediate and tremendous success. As soon as public opinion understands this challenge, politics can follow. It will be an important test of credibility as to whether the European Council will be able to complete successfully this extremely important project. The same applies for the very ambitious climate plan as a measure against global warming agreed at the Spring meeting of 2007.

The Third Pillar, or *Justice and Home Affairs* (JHA), is another example of policy activities which the European Council has taken on, once again with rather limited success. In Tampere in 1999 the European Council paved the way for the creation of an Area of Freedom, Security and Justice. The meeting agreed on a number of common policies, policy guidelines and priorities, for instance a Single European Asylum System. The agreed ambitions, the 'Ten Milestones of Tampere', were placed 'at the very top of the political agenda'. Is Tampere an example of a largely failed project? Certainly many of its objectives have not been realised to date. On the other hand Justice, Freedom and Security have been on top of the Union's agenda for the last six years. This has resulted in an increase of activities in an area always zealously guarded by the Member States as their national fiefdom. The various activities during the past years in this field (Chapter 3.F.3) have all resulted from the decisions in Tampere and their renewal by the European Council in Brussels in November 2004.

A series of requirements for a successful meeting

The ingredients of a successful European Council meeting may be described as follows. For every meeting to be successful there is the '*necessité d'un enjeu*' (the necessity to have something at stake). Concentration of discussion on a limited number of precisely defined points is a condition. A third requirement, as has been outlined earlier, is thorough preparation by the President of the Council. It has been shown over time to be important either that the nucleus of a growing consensus should emerge during the preparation of the meeting or that there should be an absolute necessity to reach an agreement from the point of view of the Member States. There should be no domestic barriers or national elections, which limit the room for manoeuvre for those Heads of Government who are most involved. In general, it is important for the Council to fix realistic aims, which receive support from the large majority of Member States. Time has shown that things tend to go wrong as soon as the European Council takes upon itself tasks which the Member States want to retain at the national level (as with the CFSP) or when it goes for objectives which are not realistic (such as with the decisions in 2000 regarding the Lisbon agenda).

The analysis especially in Chapters 2 and 3 has indicated that Franco-German cooperation may be seen as the kernel of the functioning of the European Council. At important moments, France and Germany have developed their own parallel bilateral Summits at which they prepare for decision-making. It is hard to find an area in which the common perception of the President of France and the Chancellor of Germany in the preparation and decision-making in the European Council was not decisive.

An interesting exercise would, moreover, be to see if the negotiating process in the European Council follows along the lines of the political parties in Europe. In my research and over the course of 35 years covering the meetings it was very rare to find any trace of ideological conflict (or of harmony either). The purely national interests of Member States and of their governmental leaders have been the main forces.

Our research brings to light the fact that the Heads of State or Government and the President of the Commission sometimes *tinker with the rules*. But that happens only in exceptionally difficult situations. When these arise the European Council will interpret the rules creatively and may circumvent earlier agreements in order to reach agreement (see Chapter 3.C). How can this be so? It is important to recognise that a European Council is about more than political technicalities and arrangements. More important is what gets done. The Heads of Government form Europe's highest political negotiating body. Consequently they have as the 'Provisional European Government' the power to find a way around official EU procedures should the need arise. In this way do they often succeed.

8. The new method of working of the European Council

Over the years the European Council has changed character in two important ways. Firstly the Council changed from a 'court of appeal' or 'supreme arbitrator', having to deal with the issues of the day or the issues which had left the Council of Ministers in stalemate, into the central agenda-setter of the Union. Next, the method of decision-making changed with regard to crucial questions. The decision-taking moved from the plenary meeting to the so-called 'confessional'. Let us illustrate these two important aspects.

During the 1970s and 1980s, the Heads of Government had to delve into detailed technical discussions on very complicated matters such as the introduction of a system of national milk quotas and the elimination of the Monetary Compensatory Amounts. Later, however, little by little, they began to take on the role of agenda-setter. More and more in the course of the 1990s they were to take charge of the most important or most disputed dossiers right from the start. The Heads of Government now take control regarding many of the processes within the three European Institutions: the Commission, the Council of Ministers and the Parliament. An example is the settlement in 2005-2006 of the hugely controversial issue of opening up the Union's service markets, as earlier described.

The Heads of Government nowadays check on a meeting by meeting basis whether the Specialised Councils stick to their brief. With such an approach these Councils have less opportunity to drop their insoluble problems at the door of the European Council. This shift from arbiter to agenda-setter was recognised in 2002 in Seville in the text of the new Rules of Procedure of the European Council.

The second fundamental change concerns the course of a meeting with a very important subject on the agenda. Nowadays the meeting room is larger than a tennis court with a huge meeting table in the centre. Political leaders no longer speak their mind at such a large gathering. During negotiations, eye contact and body language reveal a great deal. Those aspects no longer have any relevance given the size of the gathering and it would clearly be impossible to negotiate complicated matters in plenary session.

The contrast with the past is truly remarkable. Initially the twelve Heads of Government and the President of the Commission sat around a table with nothing else in front of them but a file. My previous study of 1992 noted as follows: 'In the small setting of the European Council, Heads of Government negotiate in a committed, and even undiplomatic, open way'. The most important reason for creating the European Council was to escape the rigidity of the institutional framework of the Union. Committed direct negotiations in a small setting between the national political leaders sitting as the

European Council has broken many a deadlock over the decades. During the 'fireside chat' or get-together, in the small circle of what was then twelve national political leaders and the Commission President, on the evening of the first day of the meeting, they could also deal with political 'taboos' or with issues not yet ripe or accepted for official discussion. Important decisions were taken there informally. As a consequence of the growing number of participants from the mid-1990s this important element of the meetings has been rendered unworkable.

What has become more important than before is the so-called *'confessional'* procedure. In order to clear the last hurdles, the President will summon in turn the Head of State or Government of each obstructing Member State. Each delegation has to specify its minimum conditions for an agreement. At the same time the President wants to know what concession each governmental leader is prepared to make in return. On the basis of this 'confessional' procedure the President arrives at a final balanced proposal for the plenary. At this point the meeting has often lasted for two days and perhaps half a night or more. Under pressure of time (and sleep) the national political leaders will then often reach consensus in plenary during the small hours. This formula has become the hallmark of those meetings with difficult items on the agenda, particularly since the 2004 enlargement. In those meetings five or six Heads of State or Government largely decide on the course of the event.

9. The inevitable coming of a permanent 'President of Europe' and its consequences

A crucial moment in the discussion as to the future role of the European Council was the decision in 2004 in the IGC to introduce a long-term full-time President located in Brussels. The tripling of the number of members of the Council over the course of the years was an important driving force behind this far-reaching decision, which was proposed by France, Germany, the UK and Spain. In addition, a Union with some 27 or more Member States has an increased complexity of competing interests and allegiances and hence of problems with its decision-making. The larger the group, the more difficult it is to arrive at an agreement (which at European Council level must be based on consensus).

A full-time leader at the centre would be in a position thoroughly to prepare the meetings in pre-consultation with the national capitals and the President of the Commission. Another factor behind the call for creating a long-term full-time President of the European Council lies in the development of the Union's agenda. Today there are increasing numbers of national *'hot potatoes'*, such as the budgetary situation in the Member States, fiscal policy, energy policy, employment, industry policy, the Lisbon objectives, Trans-European (traffic and energy) Networks, terrorism and peace-keeping outside the Union. Dealing with these matters, the Union penetrates deeply into national autonomy and into domestic policy. The Union in other words often becomes involved with questions which the Member States prefer to discuss together. In such a setting the Head of Government of each Member State features as the national coordinator.

The European Council is not in a position fully to keep track of its own programme and follow up activities. At the moment the European Council is in great need of supervision for the execution of its own decisions. A full-time permanent President would bring an urgently required continuity to the work of the European Council and hence to the EU. That would be another important advantage.

Chapter 4 lists the most frequent arguments put forward by the proponents of a permanent full-time President. However there is a further strong argument that is rarely mentioned. That is the lack of consistency in the Conclusions: firstly, the regular repetition of previous solemnly declared intentions and accords which the Institutions fail to implement, sometimes for years at a stretch; and secondly, the reversals of position on topics over which the European Council has changed its mind. Examples of the latter, as described earlier, are employment policy in the 1980s and 1990s, the CFSP, and the Lisbon agenda. Such examples illustrate that the European Council is a grouping with the consistency of quicksand. That is partly attributable to the fact that the Council meets only three or four times a year. A body of this type, without a full-time President with backing apparatus, has difficulty in being a reliable pilot for the Union. The most important task of the upcoming full-time President will be to tackle these issues of consistency and follow-through.

It should be noted that the need for a permanent President is disputed by the smaller Member States, by the Commission and by the European Parliament. A full-time President with powers of initiative and coordination would take over tasks currently vested in the President of the Commission. Such a President would moreover acquire new administrative powers for himself, having functions that are partially carried out by the Commission. As has been set out in Chapter 4, opponents fear that by upgrading the European Council, the Commission's role as a self-steering and independent political force would be devalued. A permanent President would provide Europe in the future with two centres of preparation and implementation of its decisions, in short, of the management of the Union: the European Council and the European Commission. The latter expects a permanent rivalry between its President and the permanent full-time President which will create confusion as to how responsibility is shared. These arguments are real ones. The radius of action of an extra full-time President with extensive powers of initiative and coordination will overlap with that of the President of the Commission. Coordination between the two Presidents (and also with the Minister for Foreign Affairs of the Union) may prove to be difficult.

Why the smaller Member States had to swallow 'two captains on one ship'

So why then propose two captains on one ship? The upgrading of the European Council by way of its permanent President has been sought by the six largest Member States. It has grown from observation of the increased complexity of allegiances and interests in a Union approaching 30 Member States, as are fully set out in Chapter 4.A.1. The smaller Member States fear that this development will undermine their influence. They anticipate that the new President will play ball with the largest Member States, since the President can hardly consult with approximately thirty Heads of State and Government. In 2003 at the end of the Convention it became clear, however, that the smaller

Member States would have to accept a permanent President. Otherwise the largest Member States would have scuppered the entire Convention. In those days one spoke rightly of *a dictate* of the six larger Member States.

Would the arrival of a full-time President change the nature of meetings of the European Council? As seen above, the Heads of Government of the largest Member States have played a key role since the beginning in 1974. Equally, analysis of the course of the meetings shows clearly that the smaller Member States also get their say. One must acknowledge the objections of the smaller Member States to the proposed upgrading of the European Council. But the functioning of the European Council since the enlargement of 2004 (see Chapter 4.B.1) and the absolute priority which it gets from the larger Member States, shows that the coming of a permanent full-time President is inevitable.

The full-time permanent President will become the *figurehead of Europe*. To the outside world he will take on the appearance of the European Union's superior authority, who oversees the work of the Institutions. This image conveys both the intent of the larger and the fears of the smaller Member States. Everything points to an important innovation.

It is the case that the new President will have a vague and at the same time wordy job description. The President has to chair the European Council and drive forward its work; to ensure its proper preparation and continuity; to endeavour to facilitate cohesion and consensus within the European Council; to inform Parliament and to ensure the external representation of the Union regarding its CFSP (Article 9b (5) TEU as amended by the Lisbon Treaty). The smaller Member States, together with the European Commission and the European Parliament who oppose the creation of a permanent President, hope with this job description to prevent the emergence of an all-powerful President.

Indeed, 'only practice will show whether these provisions are adequate', as the European Parliament stated (2008, par. 6.2.). I do not believe that the above-mentioned job description will limit the radius of action of the permanent President. It is merely a political gesture for the benefit of the protesting small Member States. The permanent President will have a totally different function from that of the bi-annual rotating President. At present, every six months an already heavily charged Head of Government from amongst the Member States takes on this additional task. A full-time successor to this rotating President will have their own secretariat and staff and a European Council office in Brussels situated among the Union's Institutions. The functions of the full-time President will bestow far greater political influence. The tasks of the new President will encompass in fact the entire political management of the Union. Regarding all kinds of important agenda items the President will chase up both the Commission and the acting President of the Council of Ministers in its different compositions.

The smaller Member States have been left with an *illusory concession* in the shape of a restricted job description that turns out to have no reality. Exactly the same thing happened with the creation of the European Council in 1974. Then there was no indication whatsoever that the European Council would turn into a decision-shaping and decision-making body. The Benelux countries, which were strongly opposed to the creation of a European Council, were guaranteed that nothing would change in the whole decision-making process.

Yet, as outlined in Chapter 1, the decision-making process changed profoundly. Right from the beginning, the European Council took decisions as 'supreme arbitrator' or '*instance d'appel*' regarding matters which had left the Council of Ministers in stalemate. Since 1991, the European Council has become even more omnipotent. It has taken upon itself the core activities and problems of the Union.

It is striking to note the parallel fashion in which the protests of the objecting smaller Member States were dealt with in 1974 and 2003. In 1974 the creation of the European Council at the initiative of the larger Member States coincided with an agreement on the direct election of the European Parliament. The latter concession was in 1974 meant to assuage the protesting smaller Member States. In 2003 the protesting Member States, the Parliament and the Commission were fobbed off in the Convention with the election of the President of the European Commission by the European Parliament (as laid down in the Lisbon Treaty). That election, however, is restricted to a candidate chosen by the European Council!

As outlined in Chapters 2 and 3, an examination of the promises which were made in Paris in 1974 and in Brussels in 2003 (in the IGC) in conjunction with the further development of the European Council leads one to conclude that any agreement on a restricted job description for the new President is of little consequence. The smaller Member States have been awarded the booby prize by their 'Big Brothers' first in 1974 and again thirty years later in 2003-2004. Surely this is remarkable.

10. Ten policy recommendations

The European Union is at present confronted with at least three challenges which threaten to jeopardise its functioning. Firstly, it has to search for a solution to dealing with a much larger number of Member States. This will change the nature of the Union. Secondly, nowadays the national interests of the Member States dominate the Union more than in the past. This makes decision-making cumbersome. Thirdly, there is the lack of support from an important part of public opinion, as shown by the rejection of the Constitutional Treaty.

The European Council is the most appropriate organ to deal with these powerful challenges. Its regular meetings (surrounded by intense publicity) offer the ideal forum for testing the adaptability of the whole of the Union to politically or economically changing situations and for taking fitting decisions. The organisation of most European Council business is fully within the competence of the Heads of Government themselves. In the coming years they might carry through the following practical policy recommendations without time-consuming reform of the treaties.

1.   A weak point of the European Council is its obsession with the Union's institutional structure. Since its meeting in Brussels in December 1978, the Heads of Government have almost incessantly been involved with institutional reform. In 2007 we witnessed the seventh Intergovernmental Conference since 1985! This fixation on institutional reforms urgently requires a break. The European Council ought to decide on a moratorium regarding internal reforms until 2015 at the

THE EUROPEAN COUNCIL BEYOND 2009

earliest. This applies all the more since the Lisbon Treaty offers the option to introduce new, far reaching institutional modifications by a unanimous decision of the Heads of State and Government, bypassing the official (laborious) way of the IGC.

2. An important problem now threatening the proper functioning of the European Council is the fact that Italy, Poland and Spain are outside the inner circle (the 'Big Three'), which in reality takes the decisions. As described in Chapter 3, these Member States vent their frustrations by regularly obstructing or delaying the decision-making process. The author sees no solution to this problem, since an 'inner circle' almost by definition consists of three countries, or four at the most. Here lies a task for the upcoming full-time permanent President of the European Council.

3. The smaller Member States would be seriously mistaken to underestimate the importance of the coming permanent President. The secretariat of this President will have an important role to play in the preparation of the decision-making and the implementation of the decisions. In particular the smaller Member States would be advised to ensure that suitable officials are placed in that secretariat right now and reinforce their regional cooperation (Benelux, Visegrad, Nordics, Baltics).

4. The Heads of Government should have more informal profound debate and in-depth exchanges of view. Keep the standard March, June and December meetings, but cancel the October meeting. Organise instead an informal meeting in the Autumn. Implement in this meeting, whenever possible, the motto of former German Chancellor Helmut Schmidt: *'Keine Papiere'* (no documents). Then the Heads of Government may sound out their mutual political positions concerning crucial problems.

5. Specialised Councils and individual Ministers (such as Justice and Home Affairs, Internal Market, Agriculture, Transport, etc.) would do well to take into account the fact that the European Council after its 'upgrading' in the Lisbon Treaty will also get involved in their activities, more so than today. These Specialised Councils and also the Ministries should in their own interest try to play a role in the preparation of the meetings of the European Council.

6. The Heads of State or Government should examine their working method. Every six months each President tries to launch 'something pleasant' or 'something new'. That threatens to result in an abundance of politically unfeasible projects. The permanent President should see to it that the European Council, in line with the Institutions, begins to function on the basis of a five-year programme.

7. The new President should moreover keep a keen eye on the exact execution of the decisions made. The European Council gives the Commission countless tasks. By means of its communications, analyses, reports and studies the Commission does a lot of preparatory work. But subsequently these reports are hardly talked about in the next meeting of the European Council. As a result, follow-up is missing.

8. The Lisbon Treaty confirms the proliferation of opt outs of Member States (exemptions from treaty provisions like the EMU, immigration and asylum policy, CFSP, etc). The reason for that is a fundamental

disagreement between the Member States on the political objectives of
the Union. The advantage of 'opting out' and 'opting in' by way of a
multi-speed integration is that all Member States will feel more at
home in the Union. The disadvantage is that the Member States are
legally allowed to observe the treaties differently. It is up to the full-
time President of the European Council to direct this process and preserve the overall institutional structure.

9.   With the coming into force of the Lisbon Treaty the Union's character
       will clearly take a parliamentary turn. Decision-making will in future
       mostly take place on the basis of parliamentary co-decision. This
       requires some adjustment of the traditionally laborious relationship
       between Parliament and European Council. Herein lies another point
       of action for both the permanent President and the European Council.

10.   Little noticed is the strongly process-driven character of the European
       Council. The Union on average every two years witnesses an import-
       ant and successful meeting. Due to the laborious decision-making such
       Summits are always preceded by one or two so-called failed meetings.
       At their conclusion the Heads of Government, the EU's Institutions,
       politicians and also the media all over Europe jointly react bitterly.
       Nearly every year they predict a crisis. That crisis however never
       materialises. Let us therefore stop shouting about yet another crisis in
       Europe each time there is a 'failed' meeting!

Endnotes

1   2009 is my frame of reference because, according to the Conclusions of the European Council
meeting of 21 and 22 June 2007, the new Lisbon Treaty that replaces the Constitutional Treaty rejected
by France and the Netherlands has to be ratified 'before the European Parliament election in June
2009'. The Intergovernmental Conference of 2007 has in between taken the necessary steps. It created
an institutional structure for a Union comprising 27 or some more Member States, instead of the
former 15.

2   For more background regarding the creation of the European Council see besides Chapter 1, my
previous study of 1992, *The European Council*, p. 56- 74.

3   As already mentioned in earlier chapters, in line with the approach taken by the 1974 Paris
Summit meeting where the European Council was created, whenever, with reference to 'the
European Council', 'Heads of Government' is mentioned, this stands for the whole membership of
the European Council: the Heads of State or Government of the Member States of the Union plus the
President of the Commission. The name 'Heads of Government' also includes the President of the
French Republic, plus, since 1995, the President of Finland and, since 2004, the President of Cyprus.
In some cases Bulgaria, the Czech Republic, Lithuania, Poland and Romania are also represented by
their President instead of the Prime Minister.

4   At the conclusion of this research there were reports (from Paris and other capitals) that France
and Germany contemplate having former British PM Tony Blair appointed as first permanent
President of the European Council. However, for the smaller Member States this would mean that a
directorate of the Big Three led the Union.

Annex 1

LIST OF SUMMIT MEETINGS (*) AND EUROPEAN COUNCIL MEETINGS

Presidency - Topics discussed and significance of meeting

1. PARIS*   18-20 February 1957   Guy MOLLET
Agreement on 'left overs' from negotiations for EEC and Euratom Treaty.

2. PARIS*   10-11 February 1961   Charles DE GAULLE
Political Union with regular meetings of Heads of Government envisaged.

3. BONN*   18 July 1961   Konrad ADENAUER
Discussion on Political Union, later pushed aside by the Fouchet Plan.

4. ROME*   29-30 May 1967   Aldo MORO
Commemorative Summit for the tenth anniversary of EEC/Euratom.

5. THE HAGUE*   1-2 December 1969   P.J.S. DE JONG
France lifts its veto on British accession and obtains CAP finances.

6. PARIS*   19-20 October 1972   Georges POMPIDOU
'European Union' and 'Economic and Monetary Union' envisaged.

7. COPENHAGEN*   14-15 December 1973   Anker JOERGENSEN
Failure to react with Energy Policy on worldwide oil crisis.

8. PARIS**   16 September 1974   Valéry GISCARD d'Estaing
'Summit picnic' - Decision about more regular Summit meetings.

9. PARIS*   9-10 December 1974   Valéry GISCARD d'Estaing
Creation European Council - EP to be directly elected - Regional Fund created.

10. DUBLIN   10-11 March 1975   Liam COSGRAVE
Renegotiation of UK membership terms agreed.

11. BRUSSELS   16-17 July   1975   Aldo MORO
Talks between oil producer and consumer countries envisaged.

12. ROME   1-2   December 1975   Aldo MORO
European elections and the European passport agreed.

13. LUXEMBOURG   1-2 April 1976   Gaston THORN
Tindemans Report discussed; no breakthrough.

14. BRUSSELS   12-13 July 1976   J. DEN UYL
Allocation of seats in EP to each Member State - Jenkins appointed.

15. THE HAGUE   29-30 November 1976   J. DEN UYL
Attack on Japanese trade policy.

16. ROME   25-26 March 1977   James CALLAGHAN
Smaller States win agreement on participation of the EC in the G7.

17. LONDON   29-30 June 1977   James CALLAGHAN
Statement on 'the need for a homeland for the Palestinian people'.

18. BRUSSELS   5-6 December 1977   Leo TINDEMANS
Introduction of the European Currency Unit as of 1978 – Rebate for UK.

19. COPENHAGEN   7-8 April 1978   Anker JOERGENSEN
Starting point agreed for introduction of European Monetary System (EMS).

20. BREMEN   6-7 July 1978   Helmut SCHMIDT
Decision to create the European Monetary System (EMS).

21. BRUSSELS   4-5 December 1978   Helmut SCHMIDT
'Three Wise Men' commissioned to report on the Institutions.

22. PARIS   12-13 March 1979   Valéry GISCARD d'ESTAING
Immediate start of EMS after delay due to unexpected political problems.

23. STRASBOURG   21-22 June 1979   Valéry GISCARD d'ESTAING
Arrival of PM Thatcher - Agreement on CAP prices - Debate on energy.

24. DUBLIN   29-30 November 1979   Jack LYNCH
Thatcher's famous demand: 'I want my money back' (Rebate UK).

25. LUXEMBOURG   27-28 April 1980   Francesco COSSIGA
British budget problem - EMU and Internal Market on the horizon.

26. VENICE   12-13 June 1980   Francesco COSSIGA
Declaration on the Middle East – US President Carter criticised.

27. LUXEMBOURG   1-2 December 1980   Pierre WERNER
International politics and worsening economic situation.

28. MAASTRICHT   23-24 March 1981   A.A.M. VAN AGT
Gloomy conclusions on economic situation - disagreement over CFP.

29. LUXEMBOURG   29-30 June 1981   A.A.M. VAN AGT
Arrival of President Mitterrand - Variety of issues but no breakthrough.

30. LONDON   26-27 November 1981   Margaret THATCHER
Long discussion on milk quotas - Accession of Portugal and Spain.

31. BRUSSELS   29-30 March 1982   Wilfried MARTENS
25th anniversary EEC/Euratom - Urgent problems avoided.

32. BRUSSELS   28-29 June 1982   Wilfried MARTENS
Debate on European-American relations; variety of other issues.

33. COPENHAGEN   3-4 December 1982   Poul SCHLÜTER.
Arrival of Chancellor Kohl - Variety of issues, no breakthrough.

34. BRUSSELS   21-22 March 1983   Helmut KOHL
New exchange rates EMS (pre-agreed by Governors/Ministers).

35. STUTTGART   17-19 June 1983   Helmut KOHL
Solemn Declaration (Action Plan) on European Union adopted.

36. ATHENS   4-6 December 1983   Andreas PAPANDREOU
First European Council meeting to end in 'total failure'.

37. BRUSSELS   19-20 March 1984   François MITTERRAND
New VAT resources, budgetary discipline, Mediterranean discussed.

38. FONTAINEBLEAU   25-26 June 1984   François MITTERRAND
Settlement of the British budget problem and on EU own resources.

39. DUBLIN   3-4 December 1984   Garret FITZGERALD
Organisation of the wine market - Row on aid, Greece versus Germany.

40. BRUSSELS   29-30 March 1985   Bettino CRAXI
Agreement on Integrated Mediterranean Programmes.

41. MILAN   28-29 June 1985   Bettino CRAXI
Convening IGC by qualified majority voting – Cockfield White Paper.

42. LUXEMBOURG   2-3 December 1985   Jacques SANTER
Single European Act (SEA) and completion of the Single Market agreed.

43. THE HAGUE   26-27 June 1986   R.F.M. LUBBERS
Variety of issues; no agreement on sanctions against apartheid.

44. LONDON   5-6 December 1986   Margaret THATCHER
Variety of issues, no breakthrough.

45. BRUSSELS   29-30 June 1987   Wilfried MARTENS
Working programme agreed for better financing of EC.

46. COPENHAGEN   4-5 December 1987   Poul SCHLÜTER
Groundwork for reform of CAP - Doubling of Structural Funds - UK rebate.

47. BRUSSELS   11-13 February 1988   Helmut KOHL
Delors I (budgetary) Package with doubling of Structural Aid agreed.

48. HANOVER   27-28 June 1988   Helmut KOHL
Committee invited to draw up report on creation of EMU (Delors Report).

49. RHODES   2-3 December 1988   Andreas PAPANDREOU
Variety of issues, no breakthrough.

50. MADRID   26-27 June 1989   Felipe GONZALES
Various stages leading to EMU agreed – EC budget fraud on agenda.

51. PARIS **   18 November 1989   François MITTERRAND
Fall of the Berlin Wall and recovery of Eastern Europe discussed.

52. STRASBOURG   8-9 December 1989   François MITTERRAND
German unification – Social Charter adopted – New IGC (Maastricht).

53. DUBLIN***   28-29 April 1990   Charles HAUGHEY
German unification.

54. DUBLIN   25-26 June 1990   Charles HAUGHEY
Main issues for the IGC, Political Union and EMU agreed.

55. ROME***   27-28 October 1990   Giulio ANDREOTTI
Creation of ECB – Last meeting for 'Iron Lady' PM Thatcher.

56. ROME   14-15 December 1990   Giulio ANDREOTTI
Decision on IGCs on EMU and Political Union – Aid for Soviet Union.

57. LUXEMBOURG***   8 April 1991   Jacques SANTER
Statement on the Gulf War and protection for the Kurds.

58. LUXEMBOURG   28-29 June 1991   Jacques SANTER
Preparatory meeting for Maastricht – Yugoslavia.

59. MAASTRICHT   9-10 December 1991   R.F.M. Lubbers
Agreement on the Maastricht Treaty (TEU) with EMU and CFSP.

60. LISBON   26-27 June 1992   Anibal CAVACO SILVA
Guidelines for enlargement of EU with Eastern Europe agreed.

61. BIRMINGHAM***   16 October 1992   John MAJOR
Declaration on 'a Community close to its citizens'.

62. EDINBURGH   11-12 December 1992   John MAJOR
Delors II Package agreed – Start negotiations with Austria, Finland, Sweden.

63. COPENHAGEN   21-22 June 1993   Poul RASMUSSEN
Criteria agreed regarding enlargement with Eastern Europe.

64. BRUSSELS***   29 October 1993   Jean-Luc DEHAENE
Decision on stage 2 of EMU, Frankfurt headquarters ECB.

65. BRUSSELS   10-11 December 1993   Jean-Luc DEHAENE
White Paper 'Growth, Competitiveness and Employment' discussed.

66. CORFU   24-25 June 1994   Andreas PAPANDREOU
Cyprus and Malta accepted as candidate members.

67. BRUSSELS***   15 July 1994   Helmut KOHL
Jacques Santer designated as President of the Commission.

68. ESSEN   9-10 December 1994   Helmut KOHL
Agreement on the TENs and on a strategy for Eastern Europe.

69 PARIS **   9 June 1995   Jacques CHIRAC
Preparatory meeting for Euro-Atlantic and G7 Summits.

70 CANNES   26-27 June 1995   Jacques CHIRAC
Agreement on a Europol convention.

71 MALLORCA***   22-23 September 1995   Felipe GONZALES
Discussion on Institutional reform.

72 MADRID   15-16 December 1995   Felipe GONZALES
Common currency baptised 'euro' – Steps to EMU and IGC.

73 TURIN***   29 March 1996   Lamberto DINI
Formal opening of IGC – BSE crisis and beef embargo debate.

74 FLORENCE   21-22 June 1996   Romano PRODI
Agreement on elimination of BSE – Yugoslav wars discussed.

75 DUBLIN***   5 October 1996   John BRUTON
IGC meeting.

76 DUBLIN   13-14 December 1996   John BRUTON
Stability and Growth Pact – EMU.

77 NOORDWIJK***   23 May 1997   Wim KOK
Preparatory meeting for IGC at Amsterdam.

78 AMSTERDAM   16 -17 June 1997   Wim KOK
Treaty of Amsterdam – Adoption of Stability and Growth Pact.

79 LUXEMBOURG ***   20-21 November 1997   Jean-Claude JUNCKER
First thematic meeting with Agreement on Employment Strategy.

80 LUXEMBOURG   12-13 December 1997   Jean-Claude JUNCKER
Enlargement with ten applicant States; discussion on Turkey.

81 BRUSSELS****   2-3 MAY 1998   Tony BLAIR
Eleven States selected for euro; Duisenberg President of the ECB.

82 CARDIFF   15-16 June 1998   Tony BLAIR
March 1999 deadline set for Agenda 2000 (finances – enlargement).

83 PÖRTSCHACH***   24-25 October1998   Victor KLIMA
Variety of issues, no decisions.

84 VIENNA   11-12 December 1998   Victor KLIMA
Passage to the final stage 3 of EMU on 1 January 1999.

85 PETERSBERG***   26 February   1998   Gerhard SCHRÖDER
Preparatory meeting for the Berlin Summit.

86 BERLIN***   24-26 March 1999   Gerhard SCHRÖDER
Agenda 2000 agreed - Romano Prodi President-designate Commission.

87 BRUSSELS***   14 April 1999   Gerhard SCHRÖDER
Meeting with designated Commission President Prodi – Kosovo crisis.

88 COLOGNE   3-4 June 1999   Gerhard SCHRÖDER
Employment Pact agreed – J. Solana first HR/SG Council – IGC prepared.

89 TAMPERE***   15-16 October 1999   Paavo LIPPONEN
Measures agreed to create 'Area of Freedom, Security and Justice'.

90 HELSINKI   10-11 December 1999   Paavo LIPPONEN
CFSP 'Headline Goals' agreed – Reform of working method of the Council.

91 LISBON***   23-24 March 2000   António GUTERRES
Decision to create 'the most competitive economy' in the world.

92 FEIRA (Porto)   19-20 June 2000   António GUTERRES
Taxation of non-residents discussed – CFSP and Mediterranean issues.

93 BIARRITZ***   13-14 October 2000   Jacques CHIRAC
Clash between large and smaller Member States on institutional issues.

94 NICE   7- 11 December 2000   Jacques CHIRAC
Treaty of Nice - Removal of obstacles to enlargement with twelve States.

95 STOCKHOLM   23-24 March 2001   Göran PERSSON
Further embellishment of Lisbon Agenda - Russian President Putin guest.

96 GÖTEBORG   15-16 June 2001   Göran PERSSON
Decision to enlarge the Union in 2004 – US President Bush guest.

97 BRUSSELS***   21 September 2001   Guy VERHOFSTADT
Emergency meeting after 9/11; action plan against terrorism agreed.

98 GHENT***   19 October 2001   Guy VERHOFSTADT
Mini-Summit of 'Big Three' – Action plan against terrorism refined.

99 LAEKEN (Brussels)   14-15 December 2001   Guy VERHOFSTADT
Declaration establishing a 'Convention on the future of Europe'.

100 BARCELONA   15-16 March   2002   José-Maria AZNAR
First participation of the thirteen candidate Member States.

101 SEVILLE   21-22 June 2002   José-Maria AZNAR
Reform of European Council and Council of Ministers agreed.

102 BRUSSELS   24-25 October 2002   Anders FOGH RASMUSSEN
Agreement on financing enlargement by way of review of the CAP.

103 COPENHAGEN   12-13 December 2002   Anders FOGH RASMUSSEN
Deal for enlargement sealed with ten candidate Member States.

104 BRUSSELS***   17 February 2003   Costas SIMITIS
Conflict on Iraq splits the EU, Chirac criticising Eastern European States.

105 BRUSSELS   20-21 March 2003   Costas SIMITIS
Reactivation of the Lisbon Agenda - Outbreak of war in Iraq discussed.

106 ATHENS***   16 April 2003   Costas SIMITIS
Accession Treaty signed by 15 Member States and 10 acceding States.

107 THESSALONIKI   19-20 June 2003   Costas SIMITIS
Draft Constitutional Treaty presented - European Defence Agency.

108 ROME***   4 October 2003   Silvio BERLUSCONI
Start IGC for a 'Constitutional Treaty'.

109 BRUSSELS   16-17 October 2003   Silvio BERLUSCONI
CFSP matters (defence) discussed.

110 BRUSSELS   12-13 December 2003   Silvio BERLUSCONI
Failed attempt to agree on the Constitutional Treaty.

111 BRUSSELS   25-26 March 2004   Bertie AHERN
New, less ambitious, Lisbon Strategy adopted.

112 DUBLIN***   1 May 2004   Bertie AHERN
Accession day of Central and Eastern European States, Cyprus, Malta.

113 BRUSSELS   17-18 June 2004   Bertie AHERN
Agreement on Treaty Establishing a Constitution for Europe.

114 BRUSSELS****   29 June 2004   Bertie AHERN
José Manuel Barroso President-designate of Commission

115 ROME***   29 October 2004   Jan Peter BALKENENDE
Solemn signing of Constitutional Treaty.

116 BRUSSELS   4-5 November 2004   Jan Peter BALKENENDE
Commissioners appointed – Hague Programme for JHA adopted.

117 BRUSSELS   16-17 December 2004   Jan Peter BALKENENDE
Accession of Romania and Bulgaria agreed; date for Turkish negotiations.

118 BRUSSELS   22-23 March 2005   Jean-Claude JUNCKER
Service Directive discussed – Stability Pact (EMU) eased.

119 BRUSSELS   16-18 June 2005   Jean-Claude JUNCKER
Failure to agree Financial Perspectives 2007-2013; crisis announced.

120 HAMPTON COURT***   27 October 2005   Tony BLAIR
Start discussion on Energy Policy and a Globalisation Adjustment Fund.

121 BRUSSELS   15-17 December 2005   Tony BLAIR
Agreement on Financial Perspectives 2007-2013.

122 BRUSSELS   23-24 March 2006   Wolfgang SCHÜSSEL
Variety of (mostly economic) issues – Services Directive watered down.

123 BRUSSELS   15-16 June 2006   Wolfgang SCHÜSSEL
Extension of 'reflection period' after rejection of Constitutional Treaty.

124 LAHTI***   20 October 2006   Matti VANHANEN
Dissension on energy policy at meeting with Russian President Putin.

125 BRUSSELS   14-15 December 2006   Matti VANHANEN
Sherpas should break deadlock on Constitution - Limit on enlargement.

126 BRUSSELS   8-9 March 2007   Angela MERKEL
Agreement on ambitious energy, climate and environment policy.

127 BERLIN***   25 March 2007   Angela MERKEL
Celebration of the 50th anniversary of the Treaties of Rome.

128 BRUSSELS   21-23 June 2007   Angela MERKEL
Precise mandate agreed for Reform Treaty to replace Constitution.

129 LISBON****   18-19 October 2007   José SÓCRATES
Reform Treaty agreed as replacement for the rejected Constitution.

130 BRUSSELS   13-14 December 2007   José SÓCRATES
Reform/Lisbon Treaty signed – Reflection Group announced – Kosovo police mission decided.

*   Summit Meeting (1957-1974).
**   Meetings which took the form of a private dinner for the Heads of State or Government with a discussion
         on political problems.
***   Informal, special, thematic European Council or IGC meeting.
****   Meeting of the Council in the composition of the Heads of State or of Government.

Annex 2

List of Council Presidencies 2000 - 2020

2000	Portugal	France
2001	Sweden	Belgium
2002	Spain	Denmark
2003	Greece	Italy
2004	Ireland	Netherlands
2005	Luxembourg	United Kingdom
2006	Austria	Finland
2007	Germany	Portugal
2008	Slovenia	France
2009	Czech Republic	Sweden
2010	Spain	Belgium
2011	Hungary	Poland
2012	Denmark	Cyprus
2013	Ireland	Lithuania
2014	Greece	Italy
2015	Latvia	Luxembourg
2016	Netherlands	Slovakia
2017	Malta	United Kingdom
2018	Estonia	Bulgaria
2019	Austria	Romania
2020	Finland	To be decided later

Source: Document Council of Ministers 15865/04, 10 December 2004.

At the time of writing it was expected that shortly after the coming into force of the Reform Treaty – Treaty of Lisbon in the course of 2009 the new permanent President would take over the Presidency of the European Council. From then on the GAC and GAERC (Foreign Affairs) Councils would be presided over by the High Representative for Foreign Affairs, whereas the other Council configurations would remain presided over by Ministers from the Member States in accordance with the above half-yearly rotating schedule.

At the coming into force of Lisbon Treaty, moreover, a *team Presidency* will be introduced. It will last 18 months and comprise the current, the previous and the following Member State holding the Presidency for six months. The timetable is deliberately sequenced to include one of the larger Member States in the trio team every 18 months. At the time of writing, it is still unclear whether the introduction of a team Presidency would dramatically differ from the functioning of the current six-monthly rotation system. Practice may show that the Member State wielding the chairperson's hammer still runs the show. That certainly is the intention of the smaller Member States.

Annex 3

European Council meetings since 1991 – highlights and peculiarities

For a characterisation of the earlier Summits see Werts, 1992, p. 177-293.
For a listing of the most successful Summit meetings see under Chapter 4.

Luxembourg, 28-29 June 1991: Troïka diplomacy

This meeting took at the start the unusual decision to send the same day its Ministerial 'Troïka' – a three-member group composed of the acting, preceding and next Presidents of the Council of Ministers – plus Commissioner Abel Matutes to the belligerent parties in Yugoslavia. They brought a letter to PM Ante Markovic in which the European Council requested 'clarifications within 48 hours' in order to put an end to the gunfire. Notwithstanding the threat of an immediate suspension of all aid to Yugoslavia, the mission came within a hair's breadth of total failure since no final result was obtained.

Maastricht, 9-10 December 1991: Queen Beatrix's astonishing offer

There was a remarkable toast by Beatrix, Queen of the Netherlands. At the official dinner she offered the Heads of State and Government sympathetic towards European integration to 'gladly remove my head from our currency for the arrival of an ECU'. At the same time, however, opinion polls showed that only half the Dutch nation shared Beatrix's sentiments.

Lisbon, 26-27 June 1992: 'Coup de théâtre' by President Mitterrand

This meeting witnessed a *'coup de théâtre'* by President François Mitterrand. The French leader used the interval between the handing over of the Presidency from Portugal to the UK for an emergency diplomatic action by travelling unexpectedly from Lisbon to Sarajevo in order to try to restore peace in Bosnia-Herzegovina. The action was seen by the Heads of Government of the other Member States as an undermining of their Common Foreign and Security Policy.

Birmingham, 16 October 1992: 'Back to the people'

This was the first European Council meeting to open its eyes to the problems of lack of legitimacy and openness as important characteristics (and hence handicaps) of the Union. By promising more democracy 'we have taken steps to bring the Community back to the people for whom we are responsible' said PM John Major, after the meeting. His rhetoric failed to produce effects, since the information policy for informing the public remained unchanged.

Edinburgh, 11-12 December 1992: The Summit gossips about Charles and Diana

In Edinburgh the foreign media showed a lot of interest in the much discussed marriage of Charles and Diana. Another *'fait divers'* was that President François Mitterrand was reported to have gone for a walk wearing a rain coat suspiciously like a British Barbour. Chancellor Helmut Kohl had also been spotted incognito in a restaurant. This evoked memories of the Summit in which Kohl axed his consultation with PM Thatcher only to be caught later in a Konditorei (confectionery) behind a mountain of Mozartkugeln.

Brussels, 29 October 1993: Baptism of the European Union

This meeting saw the baptism of the term 'European Union' (instead of 'European Community') on the eve of the coming into force of the Treaty of Maastricht on 1 November, 1993. There was also agreement on the location of a series of new European Institutions with the first prize for Germany with the future European Central Bank in Frankfurt.

Brussels, 15 July 1994: The shortest meeting

This was the shortest European Council meeting ever. It took less than half an hour to appoint Luxembourg PM Jacques Santer as the successor of Jacques Delors as President of the European Commission (Chapter 3.F.5)

Turin, 29 March 1996: Meeting in 'Fiatville'

Italian FM Susanne Agnelli, the sister of Gianni Agnelli, the Fiat magnate, initiated the choice of Turin as the venue. Turin is 'Fiatville', the city of the Fabrica Italiana di Automobili Torino (FIAT) owned by the Agnellis. The meeting was held in Lingotto, an imaginative redevelopment of the original 1917 Fiat factory, by the great Italian architect Renzo Piano.

Dublin, 13-14 December 1996: A shot in the arm for drugs enforcement

Dutch PM Wim Kok here defended his policy of tolerating small-scale use of cannabis in 'coffee shops', believing this leads to a lower level of addiction to hard drugs. The other Heads of Government, and especially President Chirac, stated that such an approach would undermine their policy of zero tolerance. In the end a compromise was reached by way of a 'joint action' by all Member States to combat drug addiction and to prevent and combat illegal drug trafficking, drug tourism and money laundering (*Bull*, 12-1996, V.I.8.). To the Dutch this meant they could carry on with their liberal policy as before.

Amsterdam, 16-17 June 1997: The cry of fear of a 'journalist'

Minutes before President Mitterrand was to arrive in the media centre for his closing press conference, a cry of fear resounded from a woman in apparent mortal danger. Mitterrand's security agents immediately rammed the double doors from where the sound emanated. In the adjoining room they saw …. a television set which had transmitted the cry. The woman turned out to be an activist who was dressed as a journalist and waving a fake press card had penetrated the press conference of the Dutch Presidency elsewhere in the conference centre. She disturbed the press conference together with other anti-globalisation protesters who waved banners. Security officers removed them so heavy-handedly that for the first time at a European Council a cry was heard from someone who seemed in fear for their very life (with thanks to my collegue Frans Boogaard, of Dutch newspaper *Algemeen Dagblad*).

Cardiff, 15-16 June 1998: Costly conference table point at issue

The UK Government came under the fire of the opposition here because it had ordered a special American oak conference table costing £50,000. Foreign Secretary Robin Cook angrily rejected the charges of overspending. Cook (rightly) called the special oval shaped table with wiring for sound interpretation and messaging a necessity. The table had to seat 49 people including 15 Heads of State or Government and their Foreign and Finance Ministers. The disagreement was a foreshadowing of the problem of the growing number of participants at European Council meetings that finally in Nice in 2000 found its solution in a limitation of delegations.

Pörtschach, 24-25 October 1998: A 'Sorry Summit'

A meeting without any importance. Since the big political issues of the day were avoided, it was called 'A Sorry Summit' (*Financial Times*), the '*Gipfel des Lächelns*' ('Summit of the Smile') (*Die Welt*), or '*Un Sommet fourre-tout*' ('A lumber-room Summit') (*La Libre Belgique*). The meeting was unique in as far as it introduced Europe's 'Red October': a European Council almost exclusively composed of centre-left (Keynesian) politicians (eleven out of fifteen). At their press conferences in Pörtschach they announced that they would break with an era of commitment to budget-cutting austerity since Maastricht (1991).

Edinburgh, 11-12 December 1992; Berlin 24-26 March 1999 and Brussels 15-17 December 2005: Germany 'Zahlmeister' (paymaster) of Europe

These were three crucial meetings with the financing of the Union at stake for respectively 1993-1999, 2000-2006 and 2007-2013. There were long negotiations through the night. In all three cases it was the German Chancellor who in the final hours, when voices were raised and tempers ruffled, restored peace by once again opening his wallet (despite a massive German contribution of 22 percent of the Union's budget). In Edinburgh Chancellor Kohl had to reach into a deep pocket to finance a sharp rise in spending. In Berlin his successor Schröder had, in the final nocturnal negotiations, once again to increase the contribution by Germany. In Brussels in 2005 Chancellor Merkel, making her debut, offered €100 million of 'German money' to neighboring Poland. PM Kazimierz Marcinkiewicz, who had caused a last-minute tremor, thus received enough for Poland to agree. By her action, Merkel the *'nouvelle star européenne'* ('new European star') (*Le Figaro*) or 'Miss Europe' (tabloid *Bild am Sonntag*) saved the meeting.

Dublin, 13-14 December 1996: Toilet secrets revealed...

Sometimes even the toilet plays an important role in the course of a European Council meeting. In Dublin in December 1996 President Chirac used his mobile telephone in this closed private area to ask advice about his ultimate room for manoeuvre regarding the proposed sanctions on Member States for excessive budget deficits. But the toilet visitor next to Chirac was able to understand every word. He immediately informed Chancellor Kohl, at that moment Chirac's opponent. That way Kohl knew exactly how far he could push Chirac. It does happen more often that Heads of Government line up during a sanitary stop to discuss their 'room for manoeuvre' informally (Quatremer - Klau, p. 136-137).

Göteborg, 15-16 June 2001: A sense of disconnection with the citizens

This meeting, barricaded as it was from violent demonstrators in the streets with remarkable nasty riots, symbolised the alarming distance which had manifested itself between the EU and large parts of public opinion. Here PM Bertie Ahearn had to explain the recent 'No' vote in an Irish referendum on the Treaty of Nice. The Irish 'No' was seen as an embarrassment not only for the Irish government but for all the EU Heads of Government.

The meeting also brought the unprecedented arrival of fourteen 'new boys', the Heads of Government of thirteen future Member States (including Turkey) plus the newly elected Italian PM 'Mr Billionaire' Silvio Berlusconi, who had finally wiped the communists off the Italian political map.

Ghent, 19 October 2001: The Commission President refuses to join the press conference

In the 1960s it happened that a President of the Commission was kept out of the final press conference of a European Summit by the acting President. Ghent saw another novelty: a President of the Commission who ostentatiously stayed away from the closing press conference. Romano Prodi claimed that at the previous meeting in Brussels he had not been taken into consideration. He was tired of the monologues of PM Guy Verhofstadt. This was an extremely rare charge by the Commission against the President of the European Council.

Laeken, 14-15 December 2001: A quarrelsome, blunder-prone Summit

In a tense, late-night session France and Italy in particular blocked a proposal that would have settled the location of 13 European Agencies in nine Member States. According to the Reuters Press Agency the following exchange took place:

Berlusconi: Parma is synonymous with good cuisine. The Finns don't even know what prosciutto is. I cannot accept this.
PM Persson: This is no easy task. We had the problem during the Swedish presidency at Göteborg. But it's strange that the IT agency should go to Spain.
Verhofstadt: The gastronomic attraction of a region is no argument for the allocation of an EU agency.
Chirac: How would it be if Sweden got an agency for training models, since you have such pretty women?
Berlusconi: I already accepted the (European arrest) warrant. My final word is (shouts) 'No!'
Schröder: I love Parma, but you'll never get it if you argue like that.
Chirac: Lille is also a candidate. It lies in the heart of the (EU) political landscape.
Schüssel: The (EU) Observatory on racism (in Vienna) has only 19 civil servants. Others have thousands.
Verhofstadt: That's it. (Closes Summit.)

Berlusconi later succeeded in his attempts to win the Food Agency. The 2004 June meeting under his Presidency allocated nine agencies to as many Member States.

Barcelona, 15-16 March 2002: 'The Chancellor flexes his muscles'

According to the German media, never before in a European Council had a Chancellor played such a power game to defend his national interests. Chancellor Schröder at that moment was convinced that Brussels in various areas (for instance in its competition, environment and Internal Market policies) had for months ignored the interests of Germany's industry. Schröder threatened to stop acting as 'Zahlmeister Europa' (Europe's paymaster). He brought about a situation in which the Commission began to take greater account of German problems. The action reflects the pattern of Heads of State and Government of the larger Member States manipulating the European Council. Other examples are PM Blair in October 2003 in Brussels for the City as worldwide financial centre (Chapter 3.B), PM Aznar in Berlin in 1999 for his underdeveloped regions (Chapter 3.D.2), President Chirac in Brussels in October 2002 for 'his farmers' (Chapter 3.C.3).

Seville, 21-22 June 2002: Under pressure from nationalist right wingers

The 101st meeting of the European Council launched the 'Seville Rules of Procedure' for future Summits. In sweltering Andalusia with temperatures up in the 40s it was, moreover, the hottest European Summit ever. Agreement was reached to restrict national delegations to just 20 people with only two seats in the meeting. Until then delegations sometimes counted up to a hundred politicians, diplomats, consultants and technical assistants.

Held under pressure from the success of nationalist and populist right wingers such as Jean-Marie Le Pen (France), Pim Fortuyn (Netherlands), Jörg Haider (Austria) and Pia Kjaersgaard (Denmark), the meeting was billed as Europe's response to two growing common problems: asylum and illegal migration. Nevertheless, a British-Spanish initiative failed to tie aid for Third World countries to their willingness to take back those who are refused refugee status in the Union. France, concerned to preserve its relations with former colonies and the Middle East, and Sweden, scuttled this approach.

This was the first meeting held since 1998 without an enormous preponderance of social-democratic Heads of Government. There was also a remarkable presentation by the recently re-elected President Chirac. For many years, during an uncomfortable 'cohabitation', Chirac shared one table at the closing press conference with his Socialist archrival Lionel Jospin. In Seville the French President self-confidently addressed the media standing behind a slim chair. In Seville Chirac not only blocked the migration proposal, but also a proposal to limit the budget deficit of France. 'Chirac is now 'Europas mächtigster Mann' (Europe's most powerful man) concluded the Financial Times Deutschland; 'Chirac: the great winner' (El Pais, Spain), 'Nobody here could stand in the shade of Sun King Chirac' (ABC, Spain).

Copenhagen, 12-13 December 2002: A swell time for Europe

The Polish PM Leszek Miller turned it into a show. At the moment when the national evening television news bulletin started at home, he left the meeting to announce financial agreement in the European Council concerning the accession to the Union. Up to that moment Miller had irked many Member States by fighting a tough battle to the end for more generous terms. 'Our tough negotiation has worked', Miller said. He waxed lyrical when the deal was done. 'Poland has made a great historic step. We are shaking off the burden of Yalta', said the PM with reference to the 1945 division of Europe into Soviet and Western spheres of influence. In Copenhagen the Iron Curtain was ripped to shreds. Here it was decided that Europe's 10 new Member States and 15 'old' members with a combined total of nearly 500 million people (60% more than the US) from 2004 would be bound together by 90,000 pages of legal text and by their commitments to the four single-market freedoms allowing the free movement of people, goods, capital and services.

Brussels, 20-21 March 2003: 'An atmosphere you could cut with a knife'

This meeting convened on the day when the war in Iraq started. In an atmosphere of mutual suspicion between the 14 backers and 11 opponents of the American military action, the meeting took on a hallucinating character. The Heads of Government were hardly able to discuss the politically hypersensitive topic of Iraq. In order to prevent brawls, everyone at this meeting expressly avoided touching on the topic as if no war had just started there. During the deliberations over dinner on the first evening Chancellor Schröder suddenly stood up before dessert and disappeared to his hotel room without saying a word. President Chirac followed Schröder. *'Gipfel der Eiszeit'* (An Ice Age Summit), *Focus*; *'Gipfel der Scheinheiligkeit'* (A Summit of Hypocrisy) and *'Relativ surrealistisch'* (Somewhat surreal), *Der Spiegel*; *'Une atmosphère à couper au couteau'* (An atmosphere you could cut with a knife), *Le Figaro*; *'L'Europe déchirée'* (Europe is torn apart), *Le Monde*; and 'Embittered partners', *FT*, were apt characterisations, often based on utterings by Heads of Government. In 2003 the fear existed that the crisis around Iraq would paralyse other activities such as the current negotiations concerning the future financing of the Union. However, that did not happen.

Rome, 4 October 2003: Interference by the Vatican

Under strong Vatican pressure, Roman Catholic countries like Poland, Spain and Italy pressed here at the opening of the Intergovernmental Conference for a Constitutional Treaty for an explicit mention of Europe's Christian religious roots. During the meeting Radio Vaticana announced that 'at least eleven Member States' wanted to see the words 'in particular Christianity' added in the preamble of the Constitution where the cultural and religious heritage of Europe is mentioned. Eventually the Vatican's pressure failed to have any impact.

Brussels, 12-13 December 2003: Lady-killers in the game....

In order to break the ice, PM Silvio Berlusconi as President of the meeting asked the Germans for a few macho jokes. The candid Italian Prime Minister speculated on the marital affairs of Chancellor Gerhard Schröder who had been married four times, earning him the nickname Audi-man, after the four rings of the car maker's logo. But both Schröder, and his FM Joschka Fischer, married five times and therefore called the Olympic Man, let the invitation pass.

Dublin, 1 May 2004: Entry of ten new Member States celebrated

'From dictatorship we have created vibrant and sturdy democracies. From poverty we have created prosperity. These precious achievements were not easily won. Europe suffered terribly from the evils of tyranny and war. But destruction, division and pain inspired the search for a better way. That better way led to the creation of the European Union – the framework for the peace and prosperity we enjoy today'. These were the words of Irish PM Bertie Ahern as President of the European Council, at the Special meeting for the entry of ten new Member States.

Brussels, 17-18 June 2004: Agreement on the Union's first ever Constitution

Under a professional Irish Presidency, agreement was reached by the 25 political leaders on the Union's first ever Constitution, after two years of exhausting negotiations. The final text preserved the great majority of the draft Constitutional Treaty previously proposed by the Convention on the Future of Europe. The price of the agreement was the entrenchment of the national veto in many key areas.

Brussels, 29 June 2004: Who 'killed' PM Guy Verhofstadt?

In 2004 the European Council considered eight candidates to succeed Romano Prodi as President of the Commission. Belgian liberal PM Guy Verhofstadt enjoyed the backing of France, Germany and a number of other Member States. But a blocking minority of Member States - led by the UK and Italy – left no doubt that Verhofstadt was unacceptable. 'The Era of the Six [founder members] or of the Two [France and Germany] is definitely gone', PM Blair told President Chirac. 'Simply call me Barroso' said the eventual winner, the always sharp-witted and grinning Portuguese PM José Manuel Barroso during his first press conference after a reporter's question. (More details in 3.F.5.)

Brussels, 22-23 March 2005: A standing ovation for tinkering with the rules....

The Stability and Growth Pact, which was supposedly 'set in stone' in 1997, was recast. New 'relevant factors' were introduced to the Pact after France, Germany and Italy put strong pressure on the other Member States to let them exceed the spending limits of the discredited Pact without punishment. These factors ranged from a protracted period of low economic growth to the costs of dealing with the demographic/pensions challenges, or the costs of German unification. The new rules were hammered out during five months of negotiations between the EcoFin Ministers under the Presidency of Jean-Claude Juncker. The veteran Luxembourg Prime Minister and Finance Minister received an exceptional standing ovation as President of the European Council. The European Central Bank, however, in an unusually strong statement, reacted with alarm, expressing fears that confidence in EMU would be undermined.

Brussels, 23-24 March 2006: 'Marching to a Summit with no point'

'Marching to a Summit with no point' was the headline in *The Times*. Others put it as *'Un sommet européen à lire entre les lignes'* (A Summit where you have to read between the lines), *Le Soir*, 15 June 2006, 18; *'Der Rat der*

Ratlosen' (Council of the Perplexed), *Die Zeit*, 13 June 2006; a meeting where 'Europe's summiteers duck the big issues', FT, 17 June 2006.

The usual annual litany of promises, good intentions, new targets – as in the creation of 'at least 2 million jobs yearly until 2010' – and other commitments for economic reform in the framework of the Lisbon Strategy (Chapter 3.F). The meeting avoided the big debate of 2006 on protectionism and economic nationalism and attempts by governments to block cross-border takeovers of their largest companies. Notwithstanding Conclusions of 35 pages in length (*Bull* 3-2006, I.1-I.25), this was one of the Union's most pointless Summits.

A new feature was the participation of the Presidents of Unice (Federation of European Employers' Organisations) and ETUC (European Trade Union Confederation) in a part of the meeting.

This meeting illustrates our assessment (Chapter 4.B.3) that after a laborious meeting with important results (in this case in December 2005) some meetings follow in which no controversial issues need to be settled.

Brussels, 16-18 June 2005: Re-enacting the Battle of Waterloo (1815)

The Heads of Government failed after 15-hour-long negotiations to reach agreement on the Union's Financial Perspectives 2007-2013. In the small hours of 18 June, exactly 190 years after the Battle of Waterloo, the battlefield only a few miles away from the meeting room, PM Juncker, President of the meeting, Chancellor Schröder, President Chirac and Belgian PM Verhofstadt placed unprecedented bitter blame on PMs Blair and Balkenende (Netherlands), saying their requests for a national financial rebate had torpedoed the Summit. Juncker as President then flew off the handle when at the start of the press conference for one second the microphone failed to work. Furiously he pulled at the thing, shouting disapprovingly 'Philips!', inviting the media representatives' ridicule of the Dutch multinational electronics manufacturer. 'Downright scandalous', a British diplomat described Juncker's uttering as President (*de Volkskrant*, 6 July 2005). After the collapse of the meeting and the recent negative referenda on the Constitutional Treaty in France and the Netherlands, 'Europe finds itself in a deep crisis', Juncker concluded. Schröder told reporters that the Netherlands and the United Kingdom would have to answer to history. The media saw a new Battle of Waterloo.

Brussels, 21-23 June 2007: Angela Merkel celebrated as the 'Queen of Europe'

This was the Summit of the twins: the (actual twins) Poles Kaczynski and Kaczynski; the British Blair and Brown; Merkel and Sarkozy as problem solvers following the failure of the Constitutional Treaty. A novelty was the giving of flowers to say thank you to the President, Chancellor Angela Merkel. There was general praise for her ingenious, brilliant chairmanship of the negotiations for a precise mandate for the talks on a Reform Treaty. The newspaper *Frankfurter Allgemeine Zeitung* compared Merkel to

Chancellor Otto von Bismarck (1867-1890) for mastering the 'art of the possible'.

Brussels, 13-14 December 20007: The 'Turn the Page' Summit

The Heads of Government concluded thirty years of institutional renewal that began with the Three Wise Men in 1978. It was a strange meeting because the Heads first went to Lisbon to sign with great pomp the Reform treaty. The following day the European Council established a French-inspired panel called the 'Reflection Group Horizon 2020-2030'. Under the Presidency of the former PM of Spain Felipe Gonzáles Márquez, it has to 'identify the key issues and developments which the Union is likely to face and to analyse how these might be addressed'. With the arrival of the passionate and impulsive President Nicolas Sarkozy some observers had predicted disagreement with the more precise and methodical Angela Merkel. But according to the *Financial Times* (19 December 2007) 'this oddest of couples' cooked up the deal whereby Gonzáles was chosen.

Annex 4

Extract of the Communiqué of the Meeting of the Heads of Government of the Community,
Paris 9-10 December 1974

Reprinted from the Eighth General Report EC(1974), p. 297)

1. The Heads of Government of the nine States of the Community, the Ministers of Foreign Affairs and the President of the Commission, meeting in Paris at the invitation of the French President, examined the various problems confronting Europe. They took note of the reports drawn up by the Ministers of Foreign Affairs and recorded the agreement reached by these Ministers on various points raised in the reports.
2. Recognizing the need for an overall approach to the internal problems involved in achieving European unity and the external problems facing Europe, the Heads of Government consider it essential to ensure progress and overall consistency in the activities of the Communities and in the work on political cooperation.
3. The Heads of Government have therefore decided to meet, accompanied by the Ministers of Foreign Affairs, three times a year and, whenever necessary, in the Council of the Communities and in the context of political cooperation. The administrative secretariat will be provided for in an appropriate manner with due regard for existing practices and procedures. In order to ensure consistency in Community activities and continuity of work, the Ministers of Foreign Affairs, meeting in the Council of the Community, will act as initiators and coordinators. They may hold political cooperation meetings at the same time. These arrangements do not in any way affect the rules and procedures laid down in the Treaties or the provisions on political cooperation in the Luxembourg and Copenhagen Reports. At the various meetings referred to in the preceding paragraphs the Commission will exercise the powers vested in it and play the part assigned to it by the above texts.
4. With a view to progress towards European unity, the Heads of Government reaffirm their determination gradually to adopt common positions and coordinate their diplomatic action in all areas of international affairs which affect the interests of the European Community. The President-in-office will be the spokesman for the Nine and will set

out their views in international diplomacy. He will ensure that the necessary concertation always takes place in good time. In view of the increasing role of political cooperation in the construction of Europe, the European Assembly must be more closely associated with the work of the Presidency, for example, through replies to questions on political cooperation put to him by its Members.

5. The Heads of Government consider it necessary to increase the solidarity of the Nine both by improving Community procedures and by developing new common policies in areas to be decided on and granting the necessary powers to the institutions.

6. In order to improve the functioning of the Council of the Community, they consider that it is necessary to renounce the practice which consists of making agreement on all questions conditional on the unanimous consent of the Member States, whatever their respective position may be regarding the conclusions reached in Luxembourg on 28 January 1966.

7. Greater latitude will be given to the Permanent Representatives so that only the most important political problems need be discussed in the Council. To this end, each Member State will take the measures it considers necessary to strengthen the role of the Permanent Representatives and involve them in preparing the national positions on European affairs.

8. Moreover, they agree on the advantage of making use of the provisions of the Treaty of Rome whereby the powers of implementation and management arising out of Community rules may be conferred on the Commission.

9. Cooperation between the Nine in areas outside the scope of the Treaty will be continued where it has always begun. It should be extended to other areas by bringing together the representatives of the Governments, meeting within the Council whenever possible.

10. A working party will be set up to study the possibility of establishing a Passport Union and, in anticipation of this, the introduction of a uniform passport. If possible, this draft should be submitted to the Governments of the Member States before 31 December 1976. It will, in particular, provide for stage-by-stage harmonization of legislation affecting aliens and for the abolition of passport control within the Community.

11. Another working party will be instructed to study the conditions and the timing under which the citizens of the nine Member States could be given special rights as members of the Community.

12. The Heads of Government note that the election of the European Assembly by universal suffrage, one of the objectives laid down in the Treaty, should be achieved as soon as possible. In this connection, they await with interest the proposals of the European Assembly, on which they wish the Council to act in 1976. On this assumption, elections by direct universal suffrage could take place at any time in or after 1978. Since the European Assembly is composed of representatives of the peoples of the States united within the Community, each people must be represented in an appropriate manner. The European Assembly will be associated with the achievement of European unity. The Heads

of Government will not fail to take into consideration the points of view which, in October 1972, they asked it to express on this subject. The competence of the European Assembly will be extended, in particular by granting it certain powers in the Communities' legislative process.

13. The Heads of Government note that the process of transforming the whole complex of relations between the Member States, in accordance with the decision taken in Paris in October 1972, has already started. They are determined to make further progress in this direction. In this connection, they consider that the time has come for the Nine to agree as soon as possible on an overall concept of European Union. Consequently, in accordance with the requests made by the Paris meeting of Heads of Government in October 1972, they confirm the importance which they attach to the reports to be made by the Community institutions. They request the European Assembly, the Commission and the Court of Justice to bring the submission of their reports forward to before the end of June 1975. They agreed to invite Mr. Tindemans, Prime Minister of the Kingdom of Belgium, to submit a comprehensive report to the Heads of Government before the end of 1975, on the basis of the reports received from the institutions and of consultations which he is to have with the Governments and with a wide range of public opinion in the Community.

14. The Heads of Government having noted that internal and international difficulties have prevented in 1973 and 1974 the accomplishment of expected progress on the road to EMU affirm that in this field their will has not weakened and that their objective has not changed since the Paris Conference.

15. The Heads of Government discussed the economic situation in the world and in the Community.

16. They noted that the increase in energy prices is adding to inflationary tendencies and balance of payments deficits and intensifying the threat of general recession. The resulting alterations in the terms of trade are forcing the Member States to redirect their production structures.

22. The Heads of Government decide that the European Regional Development Fund, designed to correct the principal regional imbalances in the Community resulting notably from agricultural predominance, industrial change and structural under-employment will be put into operation by the institutions of the Community with effect from 1 January 1975.

28. The Heads of Government make it their objective to harmonize the degree of social security afforded by the various Member States, while maintaining progress but without requiring that the social systems obtaining in all Member States should be identical.

29. The Heads of Government discussed the energy problem and in this connection the related major financial problems created for the Community and for the wider world.

33. The Heads of Government, referring to the Council Resolution of 17 September 1974, have invited the Community institutions to work out and implement a common energy policy in the shortest possible time.

34. The Prime Minister of the United Kingdom indicated the basis on which Her Majesty's Government approached the negotiations regarding Britain's continued membership of the Community, and set out the particular issues to which the Government attached the highest importance.

35. The Heads of Government recall the statement made during the accession negotiations by the Community to the effect that 'if unacceptable situations were to arise, the very life of the Community would make it imperative for the institutions to find equitable solutions'.

36. They confirm that the system of 'own resources' represents one of the fundamental elements of the economic integration of the Community.

37. They invite the institutions of the Community (the Council and the Commission) to set up as soon as possible a correcting mechanism of a general application which, in the framework of the system of 'own resources' and in harmony with its normal functioning, based on objective criteria and taking into consideration in particular the suggestions made to this effect by the British Government, could prevent during the period of convergence of the economies of the Member States, the possible development of situations unacceptable for a Member State and incompatible with the smooth working of the Community.

Annex 5

Rules for organising the proceedings of the European Council, Seville 21-22 June 2002

Taken from Bulletin EU 6-2002, Annexes to the Presidency Conclusions.

In order fully to exercise its role of providing impetus and of defining the general political guidelines of the Union in accordance with Article 4 of the Treaty on European Union, the European Council has agreed on the following rules for the preparation, conduct and conclusions of its proceedings:

Preparation of the meetings

1. The European Council shall meet in principle four times a year (twice every six months). In exceptional circumstances, the European Council may convene an extraordinary meeting.
2. European Council meetings shall be prepared by the General Affairs and External Relations Council, which shall co-ordinate all the preparatory work and draw up the agenda. Contributions by other configurations of the Council to the proceedings of the European Council shall be forwarded to the General Affairs and External Relations Council not later than two weeks before the European Council meeting.
3. At a meeting held at least four weeks before the European Council, the General Affairs and External Relations Council, acting on a Presidency proposal, shall draw up an annotated draft agenda distinguishing between:

– Items to be approved or endorsed without debate;
– Items for discussion with a view to defining general political guidelines;
– Items for discussion with a view to adopting a decision as described in paragraph 9 below;
– Items for discussion but not intended to be the subject of conclusions.

4. For each of the items referred to in the second and third indents of paragraph 3 above, the Presidency shall prepare a brief outline paper setting out the issues, the questions to be debated and the main options available.
5. On the eve of the European Council meeting, the General Affairs and External Relations Council shall hold a final preparatory session and adopt the definitive agenda, to which no item may subsequently be added without the agreement of all delegations.

Except for urgent and unforeseeable reasons linked, for example, to current international events, no Council or committee may meet between the final preparatory session of the General Affairs and External Relations Council and the European Council meeting.

Conduct of the meetings

6. In principle, the proceedings of the European Council shall last for one full day, preceded the day before by a meeting restricted to Heads of State or Government and the President of the Commission, in line with current practice. The European Council meeting the next day shall continue until the end of the afternoon and shall be preceded by an exchange of views with the President of the European Parliament. Specific arrangements may be made if justified by the agenda.

7. Meetings in the margins of the European Council with representatives of third countries or organisations may be held in exceptional circumstances only. They must not disrupt the normal conduct of proceedings of the European Council meeting and they must be approved at the same time as the draft agenda drawn up by the General Affairs and External Relations Council.

8. The Presidency shall ensure that meetings proceed smoothly. To this end, it may take any measure conducive to promoting the best possible use of the time available, such as organising the order in which items are discussed, limiting speaking time and determining the order in which contributors speak.

9. In the context of enlargement and in exceptional cases, where an item is placed on the agenda of the European Council for a decision, the European Council shall discuss the item concerned. The political conclusions drawn from the positions emerging during the discussion shall be brought to the attention of the Council so that it may consider the implications for subsequent proceedings, in accordance with the applicable Treaty provisions.

10. Delegations shall receive summary briefings on the outcome and substance of the discussions on each item as proceedings continue. Such briefings shall be organised in such a way as to safeguard the confidentiality of discussions.

11. Each delegation shall have two seats in the meeting room. The total size of delegations shall be limited to 20 people per Member State and for the Commission. This number shall not include technical personnel assigned to specific security or logistic support tasks.

Conclusions of the meetings

12. The conclusions, which shall be as concise as possible, shall set out policy guidelines and decisions reached by the European Council, placing them briefly in their context and indicating the stages of the procedure to follow on from them.

13. An outline of the conclusions shall be distributed on the day of the European Council meeting in good time for the start of proceedings. The outline shall distinguish clearly between those parts of the text which have previously been approved and which are not in principle subject to discussion and those parts of the text which the European Council is to discuss with a view to reaching final conclusions at the meeting.

Annex 6

Future tasks of the European Council[1]

The following non-exhaustive analysis of the Lisbon Treaty (not yet in force) shows that it contains a series of largely new tasks for the European Council. The listing indicates that the future Office of the European Council will be heavily involved in jobs and tasks which will not, or only partly, involve the Commission and the European Parliament.

Establish by unanimity the composition of the European Parliament (Article 9a(2) TEU as amended by the Lisbon Treaty).

Establish on the basis of Article 9c(6) of the Lisbon Treaty by a qualified majority the list of other Council configurations.

Establish by a qualified majority conditions for the Presidency of Council configurations, excluding those of Foreign Affairs, on the basis of equal rotation by the Member States (Article 9c(9) TEU as amended by the Lisbon Treaty and accessory Declaration Final Act No. 9).

Establish by unanimity a system of equal rotation between the Member States represented in the European Commission (Article 9d(5) TFEU as amended by the Lisbon Treaty).

Appoint by a qualified majority, with the agreement of the President of the Commission, the High Representative for Foreign Affairs and Security Policy (Article 9e(1) TEU as amended by the Lisbon Treaty).

Adopt unanimously a decision authorising the Council of Ministers to act by qualified majority when adopting the multiannual financial framework (Article 270a(2) TFEU as amended by the Lisbon Treaty).

The European Council may adopt, on a proposal of one third of the Member States or on a proposal from the Commission, a decision, determining the existence of a serious and persistent breach by a Member State of the Union's fundamental values referred to in Article 1a TEU (Article 7 TEU as amended by the Lisbon Treaty).

Provide the guidelines for voluntary withdrawal from the Union where a Member State has applied for this (Article 35(2) TEU as amended by the Lisbon Treaty).

Try to find a solution where a Member State considers that fundamental aspects of its social security system would be affected by a draft European law or framework law in the field of social security (Article 42 TFEU as amended by the Lisbon Treaty).

Define the strategic guidelines for legislative and operational planning within the area of freedom, security and justice (Article 61a TFEU as amended by the Lisbon Treaty).

Identify the strategic interests and objectives of the Union (Article 10b TEU as amended by the Lisbon Treaty).

Try to find a solution where a Member State considers that fundamental aspects of its criminal justice system would be affected by a draft measure (Article 69a(3) and 69b(3) TFEU as amended by the Lisbon Treaty). This clause is an elaboration of the so-called 'Luxembourg Compromise'. A Member State fearing its very important interests to be threatened can appeal to the European Council, which can take the matter further only by consensus.

If desired, unanimously extend the powers of the European Public Prosecutor's Office to include serious crime having a cross-border dimension (Article 69e(4) TFEU as amended by the Lisbon Treaty).

Regularly assess the threats facing the Union regarding terrorist attacks and natural or man-made disasters in order to be able to take effective action (Article 188r(4) TFEU as amended by the Lisbon Treaty).

Be heard by the European Parliament in accordance with the rules of Procedure of the European Council (Article 197 TFEU as amended by the Lisbon Treaty).

Endnote

1   At the time of writing it was not known if and when the Lisbon Treaty that replaced the defunct Constitutional Treaty in 2007 would come into force. However it is a reasonable assumption that most of the planned changes regarding the role and the activities of the European Council will be pushed through sooner or later. The reason is simply that the six larger Member States are in favour, as became clear during the Convention of 2002-2003 and the IGCs of 2003-2004 and 2007.

Bibliography

A.   OFFICIAL SOURCES

I.   THE EUROPEAN PARLIAMENT

EP, EUROPEAN PEOPLES' PARTY, *Dossier Le Conseil Européen*, Luxembourg, 1990, 444 pp.

EP, VEDEL, 'Report of the Working Party examining the problem of the enlargement of the powers of the European Parliament', *Bull Suppl.* 4/72, 89 pp.

EUROPEAN PARLIAMENT, BATTISTA, *Towards Political Union. A selection of documents with a foreword by Mr. Emilio Battista*, Luxembourg, January 1964, (quoted as 'Parliament, 1964').

EUROPEAN PARLIAMENT, ANTONIOZZI, *Report on the role of the European Parliament in its relations with the European Council*, Doc. 1-739/81, 25 November 1981, 35 pp. (quoted as 'ANTONIOZZI Report').

EUROPEAN PARLIAMENT, *Resolution on the role of the European Parliament in its relation with the European Council*, OJ C. 11/192, 18.1.82

EUROPEAN PARLIAMENT, *Resolution on the European Parliament's position on the deliberations of the European Council on the European Union*, OJ C. 122/88, 20.5.85.

EUROPEAN PARLIAMENT, CAPOTORTI (et al.), *Working document on the draft Treaty establishing the European Union*, by professors Fr. CAPOTORTI (Rome), M.HILF (Bielefeld), Fr. JACOBS (London), and J.-P. JACQUÉ (Strasbourg), 1985.

EUROPEAN PARLIAMENT, POOS, *Report on Reform of the Council, European Parliament*, Doc. Final A5-0308/2001, 18 pp.

EUROPEAN PARLIAMENT, Corbett, Richard and Méndez de Vigo, Íñigo, *Report on the Treaty establishing a Constitution for Europe*, A6-0070/2004, 9.12.2004, 132 pp.

EUROPEAN PARLIAMENT, KUHNE, *Report on the European Security Strategy*, doc. A6-0072/2005, 23.03.2005, 32 pp.

EUROPEAN PARLIAMENT, BÖGE, *Report on the Interinstitutional Agreement on budgetary discipline and sound financial management* (2004/2099 (ACI), Final A-6-0150/2006, 141 pp.

EUROPEAN PARLIAMENT, ELLES, *Report on the 2007 budget: the Commission's Annual Policy Strategy report* (APS) (2006/2020(BUD), 23 pp.

EUROPEAN PARLIAMENT, *Selection of texts concerning institutional matters of the Community from 1950 to 1982*, Luxembourg, 561 pp.

EUROPEAN PARLIAMENT, Richard Corbett and Íñigo Méndez de Vigo, *Report on the Treaty of Lisbon*, 29.1.2008 (A6-0013/2008), 100 pp.

II.   THE COUNCIL OF THE EUROPEAN UNION

GENERALDIREKTION WISSENSCHAFT UND DOKUMENTATION, JURISTISCHER DIENST, *Aufzeichnung über die Entstehungsgeschichte, den Rechtscharakter, die Funktionsweise und die Rolle des "Europäischen Rates"* Luxemburg, 7 Februar 1979, 15 pp. (quoted as 'Council 1979')
COUNCIL OF THE EUROPEAN UNION, *Operation of the Council with an Enlarged Union in Prospect*, Report by the Working Party set up by the Secretary-General, 1999, (Known as the *Trumpf-Piris Report*), 103 pp.
COUNCIL OF THE EUROPEAN UNION, *Preparing the Council for Enlargement*, Report by Javier Solana, Secretary-General of the Council, Brussels, 11 March 2002, 5 pp.
COUNCIL OF THE EUROPEAN UNION, *Council Guide. The Presidency handbook*, 2006, Office for Official Publications of the European Communities, Luxembourg, 106 pp.
EUROPEAN COUNCIL, Organisational Rules for European Council Meetings, *Bulletin EC*, 6-1977, 2.3.1.
EUROPEAN COUNCIL, Solemn Declaration on European Union, *Bulletin EC*, 6-1983, 1.6.1.

III.   THE COMMISSION OF THE EUROPEAN UNION

ANDRIESSEN, Frans, 'In the Wake of the Brussels Summit', *European Affairs* 2/88, 14-26
COMMISSION, *Relations between the Institutions of the Community*, COM (81) 581 final, 17 pp.
EUROPEAN COMMISSION, *Economic and Monetary Union. Compilation of Community legislation*, Luxembourg, Off. Off. Publ., 1991, 258 pp.
EUROPEAN COMMISSION, White Paper 'Growth, Competitiveness, Employment. The Challenges and Ways Forward into the 21st Century', *Bull. Supplement* 6/93, 151 pp.
EUROPEAN COMMISSION, Euro 1999, *Report on the progress towards convergence and the recommendation with a view to the third stage of economic and monetary union – Part 1: Recommendation*, Luxembourg, Off. off. Publ. 25 March 1998, 56 pp.
COMMISSION, 'Agenda 2000 – For a stronger and wider Union', COM(97) 2000; *Bull. Supplement* 5/97, 138 pp.

IV.   OTHER OFFICIAL SOURCES

BRANDT, Willy, Address to Parliament, *OJ* Annex, Debates of the EP, 168/20, 13.11.73.
SCHMIDT, Helmut, farewell speech in Deutscher Bundestag, 228 Sitzung, Bonn, 10 September 1986, 17674
THREE WISE MEN, *Report on European Institutions, Presented by the Committee of Three to the European Council*, BIESHEUVEL, Barend; DELL, Edmund; MARJOLIN, Robert, Luxembourg, Off. of Publ., October 1979 (hereinafter quoted as 'THREE WISE MEN'). For a summary of the Conclusions, see *Bull* 11-1979, 1.5.1. and 1.5.2.
TINDEMANS, 'European Union', Report by PM Leo TINDEMANS to the

European Council', *Bull Suppl.* 1/76, 36 pp. (quoted as 'TINDEMANS Report').

THATCHER, Margaret, Speech Opening 39th Academic Year, College of Europe – Information, Bruges, 1988, 14 pp.

B.   BOOKS, ARTICLES and PAPERS

ALTING VON GEUSAU, 'The European Communities after The Hague Summit, Ten Characters in search for a Role', *The Year Book of World Affairs*, 1972, 24-42.

AMERICAN CHAMBER OF COMMERCE TO THE EU (Amcham EU), *Guide to the Council of the European Union*, Brussels 2007,194 pp.

ANDRIESSEN, Frans, H.J.J. see under European Commission.

ARNAUD, Jean-Louis, *European Union. The Reform of the Council of Ministers*, Notre Europe, Paris, 2001, 57 p.

ARON, Raymond, *Peace and War. A Theory of International Relations*, Malabar/Florida, Robert E. Krieger, 1981, 820 pp.

BADINTER, Robert, former president of the 'Conseil constitutionnel', 'La présidence à deux têtes', *Le Monde*, 12-02-2003.

BEACH, Derek, *The Dynamics of European Integration. Why and when EU institutions matter*, Houndmills, Palgrave Macmillan, 2005, 304 pp.

BISCOP, Sven, (ed.), 'The Development of the EU Security Architecture', *Studia Diplomatica*, 2007, 265-278.

BITSCH, Marie-Thérèse (ed)., *Le couple France-Allemagne et les institutions européennes*, Bruxelles, Bruylant, 2001, 609 pp.

BLOES, Robert, *Le 'Plan Fouchet' et le Problème de l'Europe Politique*, Bruges, De Tempel, 1970, 542 pp.

BLOME, Nikolaus, 'Der Krisengipfel' in KIRT, Romain (Hrsg), *Die Europäische Union und ihre Krisen*, Baden-Baden, Nomos Verlagsgesellschaft, 2001, 59-66.

BLUMANN, Claude, 'Le conseil européen', *RTDE* 1976, 1-20.

BO BRAMSEN, Christopher, 'Le Conseil Européen: son fonctionnement et ses résultats de 1975 á 1981', RMC 1982, 624-642.

BODENHEIMER, Susanne, J., *Political Union: A Microcosm of European Politics 160-1966*, Leyden, A.W. Sijthoff, 1967, 229 pp.

BONVICINI, Gianni and REGELSBERGER, Elfriede, 'The Decision-making Process in the EC's European Council', *The International Spectator* 1987, 152-175.

BONVICINI, Gianni and REGELSBERGER, Elfriede, 'The Organizational and Political Implications of the European Council', in HOSCHEIT and WESSELS (eds.), 155-209.

BOT, Bernard, *Liber Amicorum. Rêves européens face aux réalités quotidiennes*, Den Haag, 2003, 182 pp.

BOULOUIS, Jean, 'Quelques réflexions sur le Conseil européen', *Administration* No. 117, 1982, 25-29.

BRANDT, Willy, see under OTHER OFFICIAL SOURCES

BRANDT, Willy, *People and Politics. The Years 1960-1975*, Boston, Little, Brown and Company, 1976, 524 pp.

BUDDEN, Philip, 'Observations on the Single European Act and 'relaunch of Europe': a less 'intergovernmental' reading of the 1985

Intergovernmental Conference', *Journal of European Public Policy*, February 2002, 76-97.

BULMER, Simon, 'The European Council's First Decade: Between Interdependence and Domestic Politics', *JCMS* December 1985, 89-104.

BUNSE, Simone, MAGNETTE, Paul and NICOLAÏDIS, Kalypso, 'Shared Leadership in the EU: Theory and Reality', in CURTIN, Deirdre, KELLER-MANN, Alfred E., BLOCKMANS, Steven (eds.), *The EU Constitution: The Best Way Forward?*, The Hague, T.M.C. Asser Press, 2005, 275-296.

BUSEK, Erhard, SCHAUER, Martin (Hg.), *Eine europäische Erregung. Die 'Sanktionen' der Vierzehn gegen Österreich im Jahr 2000*, Wien, Böhlau Verlag, 580 pp.

CALLEO, David P., 'The European Coalition in a Fragmenting World', FA , October 1975, 98-112.

CALLEO, David P., *Rethinking Europe's Future*, Princeton University Press, Princeton and Oxford, 2001, 395 pp.

CAPOTORTI, F. (et al.), *Du droit international au droit de l' intégration, Liber Amicorum Pierre Pescatore*, Baden-Baden, Nomos, 1987, 869 pp.

CAPOTORTI, F., 'Le statut juridique du Conceil européen à la lumière de l'Acte unique', in CAPOTORTI, (et al.), 79-96

CLARISSE, Yves, QUATREMER, Jean, *Les Maîtres de l'Europe*, Editions Bernard Grasset, 2005, 419 pp.

CLEMENS, Clay and PATERSON, William E., *The Kohl Chancellorship*, London, Frank Cass, 1998, 166 pp.

COLE, Alistair, *François Mitterrand. A Study in political leadership*, London, Routledge, 1994, 216 pp.

COLE, Alistair, 'Political Leadership in Western Europe: Helmut Kohl in Comparative Context', *German Politics*, April 1998, 120-142.

CORBETT, Richard, see under EUROPEAN PARLIAMENT

CORBETT, Richard, JACOBS, Francis and SHACKLETON, Michael, *The European Parliament*, London, John Harper Publishing, 2007, 407 pp.

COSTA, Olivier, COUVIDAT, Anne and DALOZ, Jean-Pascal, 'The French Presidency of 2000', in ELGSTRÖM, Ole (Editor), *European Union Council Presidencies. A comparative perspective*, London, Routledge, 2003, 120-137.

CRAIG, Paul, 'Institutional Structure: A Delicate Balance', ECLR, 2005, Issue I, 52-56.

CURTIN, Deirdre, KELLERMANN, Alfred E., BLOCKMANS, Steven (eds.), *The EU Constitution: The Best Way Forward?*, The Hague, T.M.C. Asser Press, 2005, 555 pp.

CURTIN, Deirdre, *The Constitutional Structure of the Union: A Europe of Bits and Pieces*, CMLR, 1993, 17-69.

DASHWOOD, Alan, 'States in the European Union', 23 *European Law Review*, 1998, 201-216.

DASHWOOD, Alan, 'Decision-making at the Summit', *Cambridge yearbook of European legal studies*, 2000, 79-105.

DASHWOOD, Alan and JOHNSTON, Angus, 'The Institutions of the enlarged EU under the regime of the Constitutional Treaty', *CMLR*, 2004, 1481-1518.

DAUVERGNE, Alain, *L'Europe en Otage? Histoire secrète de la Convention* s.l., Éditions Saint-Simon, 367 pp.

DEBRÉ, Michel, 'Région, Europe, Nation', *Promotion*, 1966, No. 77, 13-20.

DEBRÉ, Michel, *Discours pour l'Union de la Presse Economique et Financière Européenne* , Bruxelles, 16 mai 1979, (stencil).

DE GAULLE, Charles, *Memoirs of Hope: Renewal and Endeavor*, New York, Simon and Schuster, 1971, 392 pp.

DEHAENE, Jean-Luc, *De Europese Uitdaging. Van Uitbreiding tot Integratie*, Leuven, Van Halewyck, 2004, 237 pp.

DEHOUSSE, Fernand, *Mélanges Fernand Dehousse*, Bruxelles, Labor, 1979, Volume 2, 'La Construction Européenne', 339 pp.

DELORS, Jacques, *Mémoires*, Paris, Plon, 2004, 511 pp.

DELORS, Jacques, 'The Question of A European Government', Notre Europe, *Research and European Issues* No. 20, November 2002, http://www.notre-europe.asso.fr/Etud20-fr (04.109)

DELORS, Jacques, 'Helmut Kohl et la Construction européenne', *Revue des Questions Allemandes*, Octobre-Novembre-Décembre 2001, 41-48.

DE SCHOUTHEETE, Philippe and WALLACE, Helen, *The European Council*, Paris, Notre Europe, 2002, 25 pp.

DE VREESE, Claes, *Framing Europa. Television news and European integration*, Amsterdam, Het Spinhuis Publishers, 2005, 232 pp.

DEVUYST, Youri, *The European Union Transformed. Community Method and Institutional Evolution from the Schuman Plan to the Constitution of Europe*, Bruxelles, P.I.E. Peter Lang, 2006, 213 pp.

DE ZWAAN, Jaap, *The Permanent Representatives Committee. Its Role in European Union Decision-Making*, Amsterdam, T.M.C. Asser Institute - Elsevier, 1995, 322 pp.

DINAN, Desmond, *Europe Recast. A History of European Union*, Basingstoke, 2004, Palgrave, 371 pp.

DONDELINGER, Jean, *Le Conseil Européen*, Bruxelles, 1975, 99 pp. (copygraphed manuscript).

DONDELINGER, Jean, *Les origines du Conseil Européen: Historique et Motivations*, Louvain-la-Neuve, Association des Instituts d'Etudes Européennes, 1977, 20 pp.

DONY, Marianne and BRIBOSIA, Emmanuelle (eds.), *Commentaire de la Constitution de l'Union européenne*, Bruxelles, Éditions de l'Université de Bruxelles, 2005, 451 pp.

DRAKE, Helen, 'Jacques Delors as a European Leader', in BITSCH, Marie-Thérèse (ed)., *Le couple France-Allemagne et les institutions européennes*, Bruxelles, Bruylant, 2001, 255-280.

DYSON, Kenneth, 'Chancellor Kohl as Strategic Leader: The Case of Economic and Monetary Union' in: CLEMENS, Clay and Paterson, William E., *The Kohl Chancellorship*, London, Frank Cass, 1998, 166 pp.

DYSON, Kenneth, 'Chancellor Kohl as Strategic Leader: The Case of Economic and Monetary Union', *German Politics*, April 1998, 37-63.

EDWARDS, Geoffrey and PIJPERS, Alfred, *The Politics of European Treaty Reform. The 1996 Intergovernmental Conference and Beyond*, London, Pinter, 1997, 353 pp.

ELGSTRÖM, Ole (Editor), *European Union Council Presidencies. A comparative perspective*, London, Routledge, 2003, 210 pp.

EPPINK, Derk-Jan, *Life of A European Mandarin. Inside the Commission*, Tielt (B), Lannoo Publishers, 386 pp.

EIJSBOUTS, W.T., 'De Raad van Opperhoofden. Over het regeringsstelsel van de Unie', in Koekkoek, A. (red.), *Bijdragen aan een Europese Grondwet*, Deventer, W.E.J. Tjeenk Willink, 2000, 59-87.

EIJSBOUTS, W.T. 'Europe's Single and Powerful Amphibious Model', in: KADDOUS, Christine, AUER, Andreas, (éd.), *Les principes fondamentaux de la Constitution européenne*, Bruxelles, Bruylant, 2006, 83-90.

EUROPEAN POLICY CENTER, (EPC), Brussels, Post-Summit Analyses of a series of European Council meetings.

EVERLING, Ulrich, ,'Die Europäische Gemeinschaft auf dem Wege zur Europäischen Union. Zu den Ergebnissen der Pariser Gipfelkonferenz', *Europa Archiv* , 1972, 791-800.

FERRETTI, *La Coordination de l'Action des Organisations Internationales au Niveau Européen*, Bruxelles, Bruylant, 1984, 322 pp.

FONTAINE, Pascal, 'Le Rôle de Jean Monnet dans la Genèse du Conseil Européen', *RMC* 1979, 357-365.

GALLOWAY, David, *The Treaty of Nice and Beyond. Realities and Illusions of Power in the EU*, Sheffield, Sheffield Academic Press, 2001, 232 pp

GALLOWAY, David, 'Agenda 2000: Packaging the Deal', JCMS, September 1999, 9-35.

GAZZO, Emanuele, 'Le nouveau pouvoir: Le Conseil européen', *30 Jours d' Europe*, novembre 1976, 34-36.

GAZZO, Emanuele, 'Le décevant bilan du Conseil européen de la Haye', *30 Jours d'Europe*, décembre 1976, 7-9.

GAZZO, Marina. *Towards European Union. From the European Council in Milan to the signing of the European Single Act, Part I and II, Documents selected and introduced*, Brussels, Agence Europe, 1986, 35 pp and 159 pp.

GERBET, Pierre, 'Le Président Georges Pompidou et les institutions Européennes', in BITSCH, Marie-Thérèse (ed)., *Le couple France-Allemagne et les institutions européennes*, Bruxelles, Bruylant, 2001, 355-375.

GISCARD d'ESTAING, Valéry, *Deux Français sur Trois, Flammarion*, 1984, 266 pp.

GISCARD d'ESTAING, Valéry, *Le Pouvoir et la Vie*, s.l., Compagnie 12, 1988, 401 pp.

GISCARD d'ESTAING, Valéry, 'Discours' in: MARHOLD, Hartmut (ed.), *Le nouveau débat sur l' Europe*, Nice, Presses d' Europe, 2002, 468-481.

GROS-VERHEYDE, Nicolas, 'Negotiation of the Treaty. Tales from inside a bleu submarine', *Europolitics*, (Special Edition), 7 November 2007, 38-39

HAAS, Ernst B., *The Uniting of Europe, Political, Social and Economic Forces 1950-1957*, Stanford, Stanford University Press, 1968, 552 pp.

HARRYVAN, Anjo G., *In Pursuit of Influence. Aspects of the Netherlands' European Policy during the Formative Years of the European Economic Community, 1952-1973*, Florence, European University Institute, 2007, 297 pp.

HAYES-RENSHAW, Fiona and WALLACE, Helen, *The Council of Ministers*, New York, Palgrave MacMillan, 2006, 392 pp.

HAYWOOD, Elizabeth, 'The European Policy of François Mitterrand', *JCMS*, June 1993, 269-282.

HEFEKER, Carsten, 'Between Efficiency and Stability: Germany and European Monetary Union', in: PISANY-FERRY, HEFEKER, HUGHES HALLET, 39-71.

HELLMANN, Rainer, *Weltwirtschaftsgipfel wozu?*, Baden-Baden, Nomos, 1982, 213 pp.

HOLT, Stephen and HOSCHEIT, Jean-Marc, *The European Council and Domestic Policy-Making Maastricht*, EIPA, 1984, 61 pp. (paper).

HORT, Peter, 'Der Europäische Rat', *Jahrbuch*, 1987/88, 39-59.

HOSCHEIT, Jean-Marc and WESSELS, Wolfgang (eds.), *The European Council 1974-1986: Evaluation and Prospects, Maastricht*, EIPA, 1988, 220 pp.

HOSCHEIT, Jean-Marc, 'The European Council and Domestic Policy-Making', in: HOSCHEIT and WESSELS (eds.), 61-104.

HOWE, Geoffry, *Conflict of Loyalty*, London, Macmillan, 1994.

HOWORTH, Jolyon and KEELER, John T.S. (eds), *Defending Europe. The EU, NATO and the Quest for European Autonomy*, New York, Palgrave Macmillan, 2003, 256 pp.

IKLÉ, Fred Charles, *How Nations Negotiate*, New York, Praeger, 1964, 222-223.

IPSEN, Hans Peter, 'Marginalien zum Europäischen Rat', *Europarecht*, 1981/4, 309-334.

JACQUÉ, Jean-Paul, 'Ein neuer 'Luxemburger Kompromiss'. Der Europäische Rat und die Reform der Gemeinschaft', *Integration* 1/86, 26-33.

JACQUÉ, Jean-Paul and SIMON, Denys, 'The Constitutional and Juridicial Role of the European Council', in: HOSCHEIT and WESSELS, 1988, 105-154.

JACQUÉ, Jean Paul, 'Le conseil européen au terme de son évolution?', in: DONY, Marianne and BRIBOSIA, Emmanuelle (eds.), *Commentaire de la Constitution de l'Union européenne*, Éditions de l'Université de Bruxelles, Bruxelles, 2005, 451 pp.

JACQUÉ, Jean Paul, *Droit Institutionnel de l'Union européenne*, Paris, Dalloz, 2006, 779 pp.

JANSEN, Thomas, *Europa von der Gemeinschaft zur Union. Structuren, Schritte, Schwierigkeiten*, Bonn, Europa Union Verlag, 1986, 114 pp.

JOHNSTON, Mary Troy, *The European Council. Gatekeeper of the European Community*, Boulder, Westview Press, 1994, 174 pp.

JONGEN, François, *Le Conseil européen*, Bruxelles, CRISP, 1985, 55 pp.

JOUVE, Edmond (ed.), *Le Général de Gaulle et la Construction de l'Europe (1940-1966)*, Tome I, Paris, LGDJ, 1967, 881 pp.

JOUVE, Edmond (ed.), *Le Général de Gaulle et la Construction de l'Europe (1940-1966)*, Tome II, Paris, LGDJ, 1967, 969 pp.

KADDOUS, Christine, AUER, Andreas, (éd.), *Les principes fondamentaux de la Constitution européenne*, Bruylant, Bruxelles, 2006, 372 pp.

KAMMHOLZ, Karsten and MÜLLER, Peter, 'Was in der Nacht von Brüssel wirklich geschah', *Die Welt*, (on line), 14 July 2007.

KAPTEYN, P.J.G. and VERLOREN VAN THEMAAT, P. *Introduction to the Law of the European Communities. After the coming into force of the Single European Act*, edited by GORMLEY, Laurence W., Deventer, Kluwer, 1989, 927 pp.

KAPTEYN, P.J.G. and VERLOREN VAN THEMAAT, P., Introduction to the Law of the European Communities. From Maastricht to Amsterdam, Third edition, edited by GORMLEY, Laurence W., London, Kluwer Law International, 1998, 1447 pp.

KEOHANE, Robert O. and HOFFMANN, Stanley, *The New European*

Community. Decisionmaking and Institutional Change, Boulder, Westview Press, 1991, 208 pp.

KISSINGER, Henry, 'The Industrial Democracies and the Future', Address at Pittsburgh, 11 November 1975, *Department of State Bulletin*, 1975, 757-764.

KISSINGER, Henry, *White House Years*, Boston, Little, Brown & Company, 1979, 1521 pp.

KOBBERT, Ernst, 'Auch auf dem Gipfel keine volle Fernsicht. Zur ersten Gipfelkonferenz der erweiterten Europäischen Gemeinschaften', *Europa Archiv*, 1972, 721-724.

KOHL, Helmut, *Je Voulais l'Unité de l'Allemagne*, presented by DIEK-MANN, Kai and REUTH, Ralf-Georg, Paris, Éditions de Fallois, 1996, 409 pp.

KOHL, Helmut, *Erinnerungen 1982-1990*, München, Droemer Verlag, 2005, 1134 pp.

KOK, W., *Facing the Challenge: The Lisbon Strategy for Growth and Employment*, Report from the High Level Group, Brussels, European Communities, 2004, 54 pp.

KOVAR, Robert, *Nature et Principes d' Organisation du Conseil Européen*, Louvain-la-Neuve, Association des Institutions d'Etudes Europeennes, 1977, 26 pp., (stencil).

KURPAS, Sebastien & RIECKE, Henning, *Is Europe back on track? Impetus from the German EU Presidency*, Brussels, CEPS, 2007, 47 pp.

KÜSTERS, Hanns-Jürgen, 'La controverse entre le Chancelier Helmut Kohl et le Président François Mitterrand á propos de la réforme institutionelle de la communauté européenne (1989/1990)' in: BITSCH, Marie-Thérèse (ed)., *Le couple France-Allemagne et les institutions européennes*, Bruxelles, Bruylant, 2001, 487-516.

LACOUTURE, Jean, *De Gaulle. Le Politique 1944-1959*, Paris, du Seuil, 1985, 723 pp;

LACOUTURE, Jean, *Mitterrand. Une histoire de Français. Les vertiges du sommet.* Paris, du Seuil, 1998, 630 pp.

LALOUX, Brigitte, 'En lisant le Traité de 1957: Comment son application a suscité des développements qu'il n'avait pas prevus', *RMC*, 1987, 442-449.

LAMASSOURE, Alain, *Histoire Secrète de la Convention européenne*, Paris, Fondation Robert Schuman, 2004, 526 pp.

LAMY, Pascal, *The Economic Summit and the European Community*, Toronto, University of Toronto/Centre for International Studies, 1988, 18 pp.

LANGRISH, Sally, 'The Treaty of Amsterdam: Selected Highlights', *ELR*, February 1998, 3-19.

LAUWAARS, R.H., 'The European Council', *CMLRev*, 1977/14, 25-44

LEIGH, Michael, 'Linkage Politics: The French Referendum and the Paris Summit of 1972', *JCMS*, December 1975, 157-170.

LEMAITRE, Philippe, *Les Realisations du Conseil Européen Louvain-la-Neuve*, Association des Instituts d'Etudes Europeennes, 1977, 10 pp. (stencil).

LENAERTS, Koen and VAN NUFFEL, Piet, *Constitutional Law of the European Union*, Sweet & Maxwell Limited, London, 2005, 969 pp.

LEQUILLER, Pierre, *Europe: Comment Sortir de l'Impasse. Un Traité Institutionel pour l'Europe*, Paris, Fondation Robert Schuman, 2007, 152 pp.

LEQUILLER, Pierre, *Un Président pour l'Europe*, Paris, Fondation Robert Schuman, 2003, 79 pp.

LINTHORST HOMAN, J. *Old Problems*, Brussels, 1981, 8 pp.

LODGE, Juliet, 'Toward the European Political Community: EEC Summits and European Integration', *Orbis* , 1975, 626-651.

LODGE, Juliet, 'Nation States versus Supranationalism: The Political Forum of the European Community', *Revue d' integration européenne /Journal of European Integration*, 1979, no. 2, 161-181.

LOTH, Wilfried (Ed.), *La Gouvernance Supranationale Dans la Construction Européenne*, Bruxelles, Établissement Émile Bruylant, 2005, 378 p.

LUDLOW, Peter, *The Laeken Council*, Brussels, EuroComment, 2002, 243 pp.

LUDLOW, Peter, *The Making of the New Europe. The European Councils in Brussels and Copenhagen 2002*, Brussels, EuroComment, 2004, 390 pp.

LUDLOW, Peter, *Dealing with Turkey. The European Council of 16-17 December 2004*, Brussels, EuroComment, 2005, 43 pp.

LUDLOW, Peter, *Economic Governance in the European Union. The Spring Council of 2005*, Brussels, EuroComment, 2005, 40 pp.

MAASTRICHT, Municipality of, Maastricht. *The Treaty*, Maastricht, 220 pp.

MAGNETTE, Paul and NICOLAÏDIS, Kalypso, *Large and small member states in the European Union: reinventing the balance*, Paris, Notre Europe, May 2003, 54 p.

MARHOLD, Hartmut (ed.), *Le nouveau débat sur l' Europe*, Nice, Presses d'Europe, 2002, 496 pp.

MARTENS, Wilfried, *De Memoires*, Tielt, Lannoo, 2006, 936 pp.

MARTENCZUK, 'Der Europäische Rat und die Wirtschafts- und Währungsunion', *EuR*, Heft 2,1998, 151-177.

MEERTS, Paul and CEDE, Franz, (eds.), *Negotiating European Union*, New York, Palgrave Macmillan, 2004, 261 pp.

MELISSEN, Jacob, 'Summitry over the Top?', in: VAN STADEN, Alfred, ROOD, Jan, LABOHM, Hans, *Cannons and Canons. Clingendael Views of Global and Regional Politics*, Assen, Van Gorcum, 2003, 160-183.

MÉNDEZ DE VIGO, Íñigo see under EUROPEAN PARLIAMENT

See MERLINI, Cesare (ed.), *Economic summits and western decision-making*, New York, St. Martin's Press, 1984, 212 pp.

MIARD-DELACROIX, Hélène, 'Helmut Schmidt et les Institutions européennes', in: BITSCH, Marie-Thérèse (ed.). *Le couple France-Allemagne et les institutions européennes*, Bruxelles, Bruylant, 2001, 419-434.

MICHALSKI, Anna and HEISE, Matthias, *European Convention on the Future of Europe: An Analysis of the Official Positions of EU Member States, Future Member States, Applicant and Candidate Member States*, The Hague, Clingendael, 2003, 78 pp.

MICHALSKI, Anna, *The Lisbon Process. Lack of Commitment, Hard Choices and the Search for Political Will*, The Hague, Netherlands Institute of International Relations Clingendael, 2004, 47 pp.

MICHALSKY, Anna, (ed.), *The Political Dynamics of Constitutional Reform: Reflections on the Constitutional Future of Europe*, The Hague, Clingendael Institute, 2004, 133 pp.

MILTON, Guy and KELLER-NOËLLET, Jacques, *The European*

Constitution. Its origins, negotiation and meaning, London, John Harper Publishing, 2005, 177 pp.

MILWARD, Alan S. *The European Rescue of the Nation-State*, London, Routledge, 2000, 466 pp.

MITTAG, Jürgen and WESSELS, Wolfgang, 'The 'One' and the 'Fifteen'? The Member States between procedural adaptation and structural revolution', in: WESSELS, Wolfgang, MAURER, Andreas & MITTAG, Jürgen, *Fifteen into One? The European Union and its member states*, Manchester, Manchester University Press, 2003, 472 pp.

MITTERRAND, François, *Onze Discours sur l'Europe*, Napoli, Institutio Italiano per gli Studi Filosofici, 1996, 168 pp.

MONAR, Jürg, 'Transparency in the Exercise of Power in the 'Constitutionalized' Union: the Problem of Diffused Leadership and Responsibility' in: CURTIN, Deirdre, KELLERMANN, Alfred E., BLOCK-MANS, Steven, *The EU Constitution: The Best Way Forward?*, The Hague, T.M.C. Asser Press, 2005, 209-220.

MONNET, Jean, *Mémoires, Tome 1&2*, s.l., Librairie Arthème Fayard, 1976, 830 pp. (paperback edition)

MORAVCSIK, Andrew, Negotiating the Single European Act, in: KEO-HANE, Robert O. and HOFFMANN, Stanley, *The New European Community. Decisionmaking and Institutional Change*, Boulder, Westview Press, 1991, 41-84.

MOREAU DEFARGES, Philippe, 'Twelve Years of European Council History (1974-1986): the Crystallizing Forum', in: HOSCHEIT and WESSELS (eds.), 35-60.

MORGAN, Annette, *From Summit to Council: Evolution in the EEC*, London, Royal Institute of International Affairs, 1976, 75 pp.

MORGAN, Roger, 'A new phase in European Summitry', *The World Today*, 1975, 1-3.

MORGAN, Roger and BRAY, Caroline (eds.), *Partners and Rivals in Western Europe: Britain, France and Germany*, Aldershot, Gower, 1986, 288 pp.

MORGENTHAU, Hans and THOMPSON, Kenneth, *Politics Among Nations. The Struggle for Power and Peace*, New York, Alfred A. Knopf, 1985, 688 pp.

MÜLLER-BRANDECK-BOCQUET, Gisela, *French Policy on Europe during the Mitterrand Era*, Aussenpolitik, 1995, 349-357.

NOËL, Emile, 'Quelques Réflexions sur la Préparation, le Déroulement et les Repercussions de la Réunion tenue á Paris par les Chefs de Gouvernement (9-10 December 1974)', *CDE*, 1975, No. 1-2, 3-13

NOËL, Emile, 'Reflections on the Community in the Aftermath of the Meeting of the European Council in Milan', *Government and Opposition*, 1985, 444.

NORMAN, Peter, *The Accidental Constitution. The Story of the European Convention*, Brussels, EuroComment, 2003, 406 pp.

NUGENT, Neill, 'Editorial: Building Europe – A Need for More Leadership?', *JCMS*, August 1996, 4.

OLDAG, Andreas and TILLACK, Hans-Martin, *Raumschiff Brüssel. Wie die Demokratie in Europa scheitert*, Berlin, Argon Verlag, 2003, 415 pp.

O'NUALLAIN, Colm (ed.), *The Presidency of the European Council of Ministers. Impacts and Implications for National Governments*, London, Croom Helm, 1985, 279 pp.

OPPERMANN, Thomas, 'Europäischer Rat und Europäische Politische Zusammenarbeit nach der Einheitlichen Europäischen Akte', in: CAPO-TORTI (et al.), 537-544.

PAMBOU TCHIVOUNDA, Guillaume, *La Conférence au Sommet*, Paris, LGDJ, 1980, 452 pp.

PEEL, Quentin, 'Europe's meeting of unequals', *FT*, 11 December 2000.

PESCATORE, Pierre, *The Law of Integration*, Leiden, A.W. Sijthoff, 1974, 117 pp.

PETERSON, John, 'The Santer era: the European Commission in normative, historical and theoretical perspective', *Journal of European Public Policy*, March 1999, 46-65.

PETERSON, John and SHACKLETON, Michael, *The Institutions of the European Union*, Oxford, Oxford University Press, 2002, 416 pp.

PEYREFITTE, Alain, 'L'avenir de l'Europe', *Le Monde*, 14-17 septembre 1960.

PIJPERS, Alfred, (ed.) *On Cores and Coalitions in the European Union. The Position of Some Smaller Member States*, The Hague, Netherlands Institute of International Relations Clingendael, 2000, 195 pp.

PIRIS, Jean-Claude, *The Constitution for Europe. A Legal Analysis*, Cambridge, Cambridge University Press, 2006, 267 pp.

PISANI-FERRY, Jean, HEFEKER, Carsten, HUGHES HALLET, A.J., *The Political Economy of EMU: France, Germany and the UK*, 1997, Brussels, CEPS Paper, 103 pp.

PUTNAM, Robert D., 'Summit Sense', *Foreign Policy*, Summer 1984, 73-91.

QUAGLIA, Lucia and MOXON-BROWNE, Edward, 'What Makes a Good Presidency? Italy and Ireland Compared', *JCMS*, 2006-2, 349-368.

QUATREMER, Jean, KLAU, Thomas, *Ces hommes qui ont fait l'euro. Querelles et ambitions européennes*, Paris, Plon, 1999, 376 pp.

REY, Jean, 'Les Obstacles á l'Intégration Européenne', in: DEHOUSSE, Fernand, *La Construction Européenne*, Bruxelles, Labor, 1979, 69-71.

RITTELMEYER, Yann-Sven, *Les Sommets Restreints et l'Union européenne*, Harmattan, 2006, 132 pp.

ROOD, Jan, 'A Federation in the Making? The Dynamics and Future of the European Union', in: VAN STADEN, Alfred, ROOD, Jan, LABOHM, Hans, *Cannons and Canons. Clingendael Views of Global and Regional Politics*, Assen, Van Gorcum, 2003, 107-125.

ROOD, Jan, 'The Community Method and the Institutional Balance after the European Convention', in: MICHALSKY, Anna, (ed.), *The Political Dynamics of Constitutional Reform: Reflections on the Constitutional Future of Europe*, The Hague, Clingendael Institute, 2004, 71-84.

ROSSI, Lucia Serena, 'Le Paradoxe du Mode Intergouvernemental. L'Equilibre Institutionnel dans le Projet de Traité-Constitution', in: ROSSI, Lucia Serena (ed.) *Vers une nouvelle architecture de l'Union européenne. Le projet de Traité – Constitution*, Bruxelles, Bruylant, 2004, 293 pp.

ROSSI, Lucia Serena (ed.), *Vers une nouvelle architecture de l'Union Européenne. Le Projet de Traité – Constitution*, Bruxelles, Bruylant, 2004, 117-144.

RUTTEN, Charles, *Aan de wieg van Europa. Herinneringen van een diplomaat*, Amsterdam, Boom, 183 pp.

SAP, John. W., 'The European President', *ECLR*, 2005, Issue I, 47-51.

SASSE, Christoph, POULLET, Edouard, COOMBES, David, DEPREZ,

Gérard, *Decision-Making in the European Community*, New York, Praeger Publishers, 1977, 352 pp.

SAUNIER, Georges, 'Le tandem François Mitterrand – Helmut Kohl. Une Gouvernance Franco-Allemande Symbolique?' in: LOTH, Wilfried (Ed.), *La Gouvernance Supranationale Dans la Construction Européenne*, Bruxelles, Établissement Émile Bruylant, 2005, 239-254.

SCHMIDT, Helmut, see also under OTHER OFFICIAL SOURCES

SCHMIDT, Helmut, *Die Deutschen und ihre Nachbarn. Menschen und Mächte II*, Berlin, Siedler Verlag, 571 pp.

SCHOUT, Adriaan and VANHOONACKER, Sophie, 'Evaluating Presidencies of the Council of Ministers: Revisiting Nice', *JCMS*, November 2006, 1051-1077.

SCHRÖDER, Gerhard, *Entscheidungen. Mein Leben in der Politik*, Hamburg, Hoffmann und Campe, 2006, 543 pp.

SHEARMAN, Peter and SUSSEX Matthew, (Eds.), *European Security After 9/11*, Ashgate, Aldershot, 2004, 165 pp.

SILJ, Alessandro, *Europe's Political Puzzle. A Study of the Fouchet Negotiations and the 1963 Veto*, s.l., Center for International Affairs Harvard University, 1967, 178 pp.

SOLANA, Javier, see under 'The Council of the European Union'.

SOLDATOS, Panayotis, *Le Système Institutionel et Politique des Communautés Européennes Dans un Monde en Mutation. Théorie et Pratique*, Bruxelles, Bruylant, 1989, 305 pp.

SPAAK, Paul-Henri, 'The search for consensus. A New Effort to Build Europe', *Foreign Affairs*, January 1965, 199-208.

SPAAK, Paul-Henri, *The Continuing Battle: Memoirs of A European 1936-1966*, Boston, Little, Brown and Company, 1971, 512 pp

SPENCE, David with EDWARDS, Geoffrey, (ed.), *The European Commission*, London, John Harper Publishing, 2006, 592 pp.

SPENCE, David (ed.), *The European Union and Terrorism*, London, John Harper Publishing, 2007, 268 pp.

STARK, Christine, *Evolution of the European Council: The implications of a permanent seat*, London, University of Westminster, 2002, 30 pp.

TALLBERG, Jonas, *Bargaining Power in the European Council*, Stockholm, Swedish Institute for European Policy Studies SIEPS, 2007, 59 pp. available at www.sieps.se/publ

TAULÈGNE, Béatrice, *Le Conseil européen*, Paris, Presses Universitaires de la France, 1993, 504 pp.

THATCHER, Margaret, see also under OTHER OFFICIAL SOURCES

THATCHER, Margaret, *The Downing Street Years*, London, HarperCollins Publishers, 1993, 914 pp.

TIMMERMANS, Christiaan W.A., 'Expansion of Executive, Judicial and Legislative Powers – A Contribution to the Debate', in: CURTIN, KELLERMANN, BLOCKMANS, (eds.), *The EU Constitution: The Best Way Forward?*, 345-349.

TIMMERMANS, Frans, 'Das Europa der Anderen' (English text called: 'The Europe of Others'), Speech at Humboldt University, Berlin, 21 May 2007.

TINDEMANS, Leo, 'Van Topconferentie tot Europese Raad', *Belgisch buitenlands beleid en internationale betrekkingen*, 1978, 385-400.

TINDEMANS, Leo, 'Le Conseil européen: un premier bilan, quelques réflexions', in: *Mélanges Fernand Dehousse*, Volume 2, 1979, 167-173.

TINDEMANS, Leo, 'Le Conseil Européen', in: *Annuaire Européen*, 1980, The Hague, Martinus Nijhoff, 1982, 3-15.

TINDEMANS, Leo, *De Memoires. Gedreven door een overtuiging*, Tielt, Lannoo, 2002, 608 pp.

TINDEMANS, see also under OTHER OFFICIAL SOURCES.

TORRELLI, Maurice, 'Le Conseil européen: utile ou néfaste?', *Revue Politique Parlementaire*, novembre-décembre 1986, 6-12.

TROJAN, Carlo, 'Baas en bovenbaas: de relatie tussen de Commissie en de Europese Raad', in: *Liber Amicorum Bernard Bot*, 19-28.

VAN DER HARST (coordinator), *Journal of European Integration*, special issue regarding The Hague Summit of 1969, Baden-Baden, Nomos Verlagsgesellschaft, 2003, Number 2, 155 pp.

VAN EEKELEN, Willem, *From Words to Deeds. The Continuing Debate on European Security*, Brussels, Centre for European Policy Studies, 350 pp.

VAN GRINSVEN, Peter, 'The European Council under Construction: EU Top-Level Decision Making at the Beginning of a New Century', in: MEERTS, Paul and CEDE, Franz, (eds.) *Negotiating European Union*, New York, Palgrave Macmillan, 2004, 143-169.

VANHOONACKER, Sophie, SCHOUT, Adriaan, *The Rotating Presidency of the Council of the EU: Obstinate or Obsolete*, (paper), Maastricht, University of Maastricht and European Institute of Public Administration, 2003, 19 pp.

VAN KEULEN, Mendeltje and PIJPERS, Alfred, *Chairing the Enlarged Union: The Netherlands' 2004 EU Council Presidency*, The Hague, Netherlands Institute of International Relations Clingendael, 2005, 39 pp.

VAN MIDDELAAR, Luuk, 'Verblind door de Zonnekoning. Nederland en de democratische representatie in Europa', in: STEUR, B.F., VAN DIJK, H., VAN DE NIEUWENHUIZEN (eds.), *Democratische vergezichten. Essays over de representatieve democratie in Nederland*, Den Haag, Raad voor het Openbaar Bestuur, 2004, 190 pp.

VAN MIERT, Karel, *Macht, Markt und Wettbewerb*, München, 2000, in Dutch translation *Mijn jaren in Europa*, Tielt (B), Lannoo Publishers, 2000, 342 pp.

VAN SCHENDELEN, Rinus, *Machiavelli in Brussels. The Art of Lobbying the EU*, Amsterdam, Amsterdam University Press, 2002, 344 pp.

VAN STADEN, Alfred, ROOD, Jan, LABOHM, Hans, *Cannons and Canons. Clingendael Views of Global and Regional Politics*, Assen, Van Gorcum, 2003, 366 pp.

VAN THIEL, S., DE GUCHT, K & LEWIS, R (ed), *Understanding the new European Constitutional Treaty*, Brussels, Institute for European Studies - VUB Press, 2005, 316 pp.

VERHOFSTADT, Guy, *The United States of Europe*, The Federal Trust for Education & Research, London, 2006, 75 pp.

VIGNES Daniel, CHALTIEL, Florence and THOUVENIN, Jean-Marc, 'Les Occasions Manquées pour l' Intégration Européenne du Fait de la Non-Entrée en Vigueur du Traité Établissant une Constitution pour l'Europe, *RMC* June 2006, 371-390.

VON BRENTANO, Heinrich, 'Die Bonner Erklärung vom 18 Juli 1961. Rückblick und Vorausschau', *Europa Archiv*, 1961, 463-466.

WALLACE, Helen and HAYES-RENSHAW, Fiona, *Reforming the Council:*

A Work in Progress, Stockholm, Swedish Institute for European Policy Studies (SIEPS), 2003, 41 pp.

WEILER, Joseph, 'The Community System : the Dual Character of Supranationalism', *Yearbook of European Law*, 1981, 267-306.

WEINACHTER, Michèle, 'Valérie Giscard d'Estaing et les institutions européennes', in: BITSCH (ed.), *Le couple France-Allemagne et les institutions européennes*, Bruxelles, Bruylant, 2001, 435-460.

WEINACHTER, Michèle, 'Le Tandem Valéry Giscard d' Estaing - Helmut Schmidt et la Gouvernance européenne', in: LOTH, Wilfried (Ed.), *La Gouvernance Supranationale Dans la Construction Européenne*, Bruxelles, Bruylant, 2005, 205-238.

WELLENSTEIN, E.P., 'Toppop of floptop? De Europese Raad van 25/26 juni 1984 te Fontainebleau', *Internationale Spectator*, 1984, 538-543.

WERTS, Jan, *The European Council*, The Hague, T.M.C. Asser Instituut – Elsevier Science, 1992, 377 pp.

WERTS, Jan, 'Agenda 2000: Hoe Nederland stilletjes in Berlijn de Zilvervloot haalde', (How the Netherlands quietly gathered in the 'Silver Fleet' in Berlin). *Internationale Spectator*, 1999, 463-470.

WERTS, Jan, 'Waarom de kleine landen de strijd om de Europese Raad gaan verliezen' (Why the smaller Member States will be losing the fight for the European Council) , *Internationale Spectator*, 2003, 420-424.

WERTS, Jan, 'The Unstoppable Advance of the European Council', in: CURTIN, KELLERMAN, BLOCKMANS, *The EU Constitution: The Best Way Forward?*, The Hague, 2005, 297-307.

WESSELS, Wolfgang, MAURER, Andreas & MITTAG, Jürgen, *Fifteen into One? The European Union and its member states*, Manchester, Manchester University Press, 2003, 472 pp.

WESTLAKE, Martin and GALLOWAY, David, *The Council of the European Union*, London, (3rd edition), John Harper Publishing, 2004, 456 pp.

WIEGEL, Michaela, 'Versprechen gehalten, Vertrauen gebrochen. Deutschland und Frankreich haben sich in Nizza weiter entfremdet', *FAZ*, 13 Dezember 2000, 3.

WYNIA, Syp, 'The Constitutional Treaty as an Emergency Brake: the Dutch get off the Train of Integration', in: SAMUELSEN, Anders (ed.) *One Union, Many Voices*, Brussels, EuroComment, 2005.

INDEX

Page references for notes are followed by n